Korean Families Yesterday and Today

CONTEMPORARY
KOREA

SERIES EDITORS: NOJIN KWAK AND YOUNGJU RYU

Perspectives on Contemporary Korea is devoted to scholarship that advances the understanding of critical issues in contemporary Korean society, culture, politics, and economy. The series is sponsored by The Nam Center for Korean Studies at the University of Michigan.

Hallyu 2.0: The Korean Wave in the Age of Social Media
 Sangjoon Lee and Abé Mark Nornes, editors

Smartland Korea: Mobile Communication, Culture, and Society
 Dal Yong Jin

Transgression in Korea: Beyond Resistance and Control
 Juhn Y. Ahn, editor

Cultures of Yusin: South Korea in the 1970s
 Youngju Ryu, editor

Entrepreneurial Seoulite: Culture and Subjectivity in Hongdae, Seoul
 Mihye Cho

Revisiting Minjung: New Perspectives on the Cultural History of 1980s South Korea
 Sunyoung Park, editor

Rediscovering Korean Cinema
 Sangjoon Lee, editor

Korean Families Yesterday and Today
 Hyunjoon Park and Hyeyoung Woo, editors

Korean Families Yesterday and Today

Hyunjoon Park and Hyeyoung Woo, Editors

UNIVERSITY OF MICHIGAN PRESS

Ann Arbor

Copyright © 2020 by Hyunjoon Park and Hyeyoung Woo
All rights reserved

For questions or permissions, please contact um.press.perms@umich.edu

Published in the United States of America by the
University of Michigan Press
Manufactured in the United States of America
Printed on acid-free paper
First published February 2020

A CIP catalog record for this book is available from the British Library.

Library of Congress Cataloging-in-Publication Data

Names: Park, Hyunjoon, editor. | Woo, Hyeyoung, editor.
Title: Korean families yesterday and today / Hyunjoon Park, Hyeyoung Woo, editors.
Description: Ann Arbor : University of Michigan Press, [2020] | Series: Perspectives on contemporary Korea | Includes bibliographical references and index. |
Identifiers: LCCN 2019050066 (print) | LCCN 2019050067 (ebook) | ISBN 9780472074389 (hardcover) | ISBN 9780472054381 (paperback) | ISBN 9780472126361 (ebook)
Subjects: LCSH: Families—Korea. | Marriage—Korea. | Parenting—Korea. | Korea—Social conditions.
Classification: LCC HQ682.5 .K68 2020 (print) | LCC HQ682.5 (ebook) | DDC 306.8509519—dc23
LC record available at https://lccn.loc.gov/2019050066
LC ebook record available at https://lccn.loc.gov/2019050067

This work was supported by the Core University Program for Korean Studies through the Ministry of Education of the Republic of Korea and Korean Studies Promotion Service of the Academy of Korean Studies (AKS-2016-OLU-2240001).

Acknowledgments

We thank the Nam Center for Korean Studies at the University of Michigan and its Director, Nojin Kwak, PhD, for their support in hosting the *Korean Families in Economic and Demographic Transitions: Parenting, Children's Education, and Social Mobility* conference in November 2016. All but two of the chapters in this edited volume were initially presented at this conference. We are thankful for Allison Alexy, PhD, who was a discussant at the conference. We benefited greatly from useful comments and suggestions made by anonymous reviewers, and we appreciate all of the support from Christopher Dreyer, our editor with the University of Michigan Press, throughout the publication process.

Contents

Introduction: Change and Persistence in Korean Families: Parenting, Children's Outcomes, Gender Roles, and Family Formation   1
   Hyunjoon Park and Hyeyoung Woo

Historical Contexts

1. The Evolution of the Korean Family: Historical Foundations and Present Realities   19
   Paul Y. Chang

Diversity in Parenting and Children's Education

2. The Strength of Information: Maternal Education and Child-Rearing in Urban Korea   43
   Eunsil Oh

3. Reshaping Educational Strategies: Habitus Transformation of Immigrant Mothers in South Korea   71
   Hyejeong Jo

Family and Children's Education and Well-Being

4. Consequences of Educational Assortative Mating for Children's Academic Achievement in South Korea   95
   Soo-yong Byun, Yifan Bai, and Hee Jin Chung

5. Does Marriage Matter for Children? Parental Marital Status and Children's Health in South Korea   119
   Hyeyoung Woo, Sojung Lim, Sun Young Jeon, and Wonjeong Jeong

6. Does Grandparents' Education Matter for Grandchildren's
   Education in South Korea?   144
   Hyunjoon Park and Heewon Jang

7. Living Arrangements and Obesity among Korean College
   Students: Living Away from One's Family Home as a Factor
   Affecting Weight Gain   163
   Haram Jeon

Gender and Family

8. Educational Background, Gender-Role Attitudes,
   and Parenting Time for Young Children   185
   Yean-Ju Lee, Kitae Park, and Ivan Sanidad

9. Gender Roles of Married Women in Korean Immigrant
   Families in the United States   210
   Byung Soo Lee

Family Formation and Alternative Family Life

10. Who Gets Married? Parent's Household Income, Individual's
    Education, and Entry into Marriage in South Korea   243
    Jihye Oh, Jae Kyung Lee, and Hyeyoung Woo

11. Integrating Men's Gender Roles and Fertility Attitudes
    into the Study of Low Fertility in South Korea   271
    Soo-Yeon Yoon

12. *Kwinong kwich'on kwihyang* (Back to the Land) Discourse
    of Young South Korean Families: Exchanging "Hell Chosŏn"
    for Breathing Room (*Yŏyu*)   296
    Bonnie Tilland

Contributors   323

Index   329

Digital materials related to this title can be found on
the Fulcrum platform via the following citable URL:
https://doi.org/10.3998/mpub.10195705

Introduction

Change and Persistence in Korean Families: Parenting, Children's Outcomes, Gender Roles, and Family Formation

Hyunjoon Park and Hyeyoung Woo

South Korean families have changed significantly during the last few decades in their composition, structure, attitudes, and function. Major changes, including delay in marriage, the rise of divorce, and an increase of international marriages, have diversified Korean families. As various studies have documented, the mean ages at first marriage have continuously increased, reaching 33 and 30 in 2015 among Korean men and women, respectively (Raymo et al. 2015; Statistics Korea 2017; also see Park, Lee, and Jo 2013; Park and Lee 2017). Thirty years earlier, in 1985, the corresponding ages were only 27 and 24. While marriage has declined, divorce has increased. During the same period between 1985 and 2015, the number of divorces per 1,000 population (i.e., the crude divorce rate) increased from 0.9 in 1985 to 3.4 in 2003 and then declined to 2.1 in 2015 (Statistics Korea 2017; also see Raymo et al. 2015). According to a study that examined changes in divorce in Korea, 21 percent of marriages would be dissolved within 10 years of marriage, assuming duration-specific divorce probabilities from 2003 (Park and Raymo 2013). The share of marriages between a native Korean and a foreigner among total marriages registered in a given year was minimal even until the early 2000s. However, it sharply increased to about 14 percent in 2005 and then declined to 7 percent in 2015 (T. Kim 2017; K. Kim 2017). Notably, compared to marriages between a Korean woman and a foreign-born man, marriages between a Korean man and a foreign-born woman have made up the majority of international marriages in recent decades. Foreign-born women who marry Korean men usually come from China, Vietnam, and other Asian countries.

The increases in divorce and international marriage have also affected children's living arrangements, increasing the shares of children living with a single parent and also children having a native parent (typically the father) and a foreign-born parent (typically the mother) (Lee 2014; Park, Choi, and Jo 2016; Park and Raymo 2013). Although the share of children in Korea living with a single parent or born from parents of an international marriage is not comparable yet with the shares in Western countries, the implications of such family changes should not be underestimated, considering the substantial impacts of traditional family and gender norms on Koreans' family behaviors over a long time.

However, as Raymo and his colleagues (2015) emphasize in their review of family changes in East Asia, persistence and change simultaneously characterize Korean and other East Asian families: Still, these families are influenced by the stabilizing forces of "the powerful linkages between marriage and childbearing . . . highly asymmetric gender relations within marriage, [and] strong norms of intensive maternal investment in children" (473). Similar to Raymo et al.'s diagnosis, we see that traditional norms and attitudes toward gender and family still shape to some extent current Korean men's and women's family behaviors, which is evident in several chapters of the present edited volume. This influence of traditional gender norms and attitudes, although weakening over time, is particularly surprising given the dramatic expansion of higher education among Korean men and women (Park 2007a). Both young men and young women in Korea today exceed their peers of young adults in most other countries with respect to educational attainment.

Korean families are at a turning point. Although some shifting attitudes open up new forms of family structure and arrangements, some other persistent traditional attitudes, such as those toward the division of labor within households and toward working mothers, still linger (see chapters 9 and 11). As in most contemporary societies, family socioeconomic and demographic conditions significantly shape children's education and well-being (see chapters 4, 5, 6, and 7). However, recent changes in socioeconomic circumstances in Korea may even strengthen, rather than weaken, the traditional roles of family for its members. We see that, under rising economic inequality and declining job opportunities, family background, independent of young adults' own characteristics, influences Korean men's and women's likelihood of marriage (see chapter 10). We

Introduction—Change and Persistence in Korean Families | 3

also notice continued intensive or even more intensified parenting for children's cognitive and social development among Korean parents, both native and immigrant (see chapters 2, 3, and 8). Although an emerging group of Korean families is challenging the dominant mode of family life and searching for an alternative style in rural areas (see chapter 12), it is not clear yet whether such a route can be a main road for the majority of Korean families.

Consisting of 12 independent chapters, this edited volume portrays diverse aspects of contemporary Korean families. By explicitly or implicitly situating contemporary families within a comparative (historical) perspective, some chapters also examine Korean families from previous periods and show how Korean families have evolved to the current shape. While the study of families can be approached from many different angles (e.g., exchanges between old parents and adult children), our lens through which to look into contemporary Korean families focuses on families with children or on young adults who are about to forge family through marriage and other means (note that marriage is a still dominant form of family formation in Korea, which is another indication of persistent family norms). There are several reasons why we pay attention to families with children. Delayed marriage and declined fertility are two sweeping demographic trends in Korea affecting family formation (Raymo et al. 2015). Once young adults marry and become parents, they are involved in their children's education in various ways. Although parenting is universally practiced, the pattern, degree, and meaning of parenting vary across societies (Park 2008a, 2008b). "Intensive" parenting has characterized Korean young parents. Therefore, by examining change and persistence in parenting, we can get a clue for family change in Korea. Moreover, parenting is a litmus with which to test the force of existing gender ideology and attitudes toward division of labor and gender roles. Interest in parenting is closely related to the larger question of how family matters for children's education and well-being. How do Korean families shape the destiny of their children? Our investigation into the specific ways through which families influence their children's education and well-being will help understand the roles of family for reproducing and transforming social inequality.

Specifically, this edited volume consists of five sections: (1) historical contexts; (2) diversity in parenting and children's education; (3) family and children's outcomes; (4) gender and family; and (5) family formation and alternative family life. Here, we briefly preview chapters included in each section, with the goal of highlighting key findings of each study in a short paragraph and identifying some issues across chapters in the same section. We also attempt to connect sections by discussing how each section of the volume is naturally related to another section. All the chapters, except for chapters 1 and 2 (which were added later), were originally presented at the Korean Families in Economic and Demographic Transitions: Parenting, Children's Education, and Social Mobility conference held at the University of Michigan in Ann Arbor on November 11–12, 2016, which was organized with support from the Nam Center for Korean Studies at the university. Since most of the chapters included in this volume were selected to be presented at the conference, they are well connected under the theme centered on *change and persistence in Korean families*.

As a whole, this edited volume is a collection of both quantitative and qualitative approaches to Korean families (seven chapters of quantitative approach and five chapters of qualitative), encompassing a wide range of methodological approaches and data sources. Most authors in the volume are sociologists by training. However, three contributing chapters are written by scholars in education and anthropology. Together these authors cover important topics of Korean families from diverse perspectives, further appealing to a broader audience in social science. Korean families, along with other East Asian families, offer an interesting case study with which to test existing theories of family changes that are primarily based on Western experiences and furthermore to formulate new or alternative perspectives on family changes (see Raymo et al. 2015). In this regard, our edited volume should be of value to those who are interested not only in Korea but also in East Asia or even in families globally.

Historical Contexts

It is well known that Korea has undergone dramatic changes in families and family behaviors in recent years. However, it is less known what has been driving such shifts in the historical contexts. Existing studies tend to focus on specific demographic indicators at the individual level, including higher levels of educational attainment and increased rates of labor force participation (especially for women), to explain such changes (e.g., Kim and Sŏn 2011; Kim, Yi, and Kim 2006; Yu and Pak 2009). As a result, a discussion on how industrial changes and urbanization in the past might have led to family changes remains sparse. With no doubt, individual behaviors are consistently influenced by sociopolitical structures at the macro level as well as by economic gains and costs presented by society at a given time. How, then, can we explain family changes observed in Korea in the context of societal changes over the past decades?

In chapter 1, Chang first notes that while Korea has seen a rise in the share of those unmarried, has reached a total fertility rate below the replacement level, and has achieved prolonged longevity, other "new" ways of forming a family observed in Western countries, such as cohabitation and nonmarital birth, are still relatively rare. Chang traces back to the 1960s and 1970s, when government-driven industrialization as well as urbanization took place in Korea, in searching for an answer to how economic-political shifts have shaped family change in Korea. First, he draws attention to changes in gender composition and dynamics in the labor force after the rise of workforce participation among (mostly young and low-educated) females. The increase in women's labor force participation was driven by the government's five-year economic plans in the 1960s and 1970s rather than by improved women's social status. Chang discusses how the unique alteration in traditional gender ideology and emerging individualism stemmed from the expansion of access to higher education and growing purchasing power over the 1980s and 1990s. Combined with emerging (and now dominating) "precarity" at work and vulnerability of family life after the economic recession in the late 1990s, these economic-political changes laid out the basis for more recent generations to take different paths for living their lives that had not been much observed in the past. While the following chapters in the volume shed light on specific aspects of families in Korea, Chang's work provides important historical perspectives that allow us to situate the current changes in Korean families in a broader social context.

Diversity in Parenting and Children's Education

Parenting is a core interest both to the public and to family scholars, given that socioeconomic and cultural differentials in parenting logics and styles may account for how children from different family backgrounds vary in their participation in extracurricular activities during childhood, which can have long-term consequences for educational and socioeconomic outcomes in adulthood (Lareau 2003; Miller 2015). Parenting is particularly relevant for Korean families, as parents' involvement and investment in their children's education have been essential aspects of Korean families (Seth 2002). Its centrality in Korean family life makes parenting a key component to be closely investigated in order to understand how contemporary Korean families with children function. It is important, however, to note that the overall high level of parental involvement and investment in Korea does not negate socioeconomic and cultural differences in parenting among Korean families. Previous studies have still found that Korean parents differ by their socioeconomic circumstances in the degree of and approach to parental involvement in children's education (Park and Abelmann 2004).

In chapter 2, Oh delves into heterogeneity in parenting by social class, which she defines primarily by maternal education. Beyond existing literature that focuses on the cultural or economic basis for parenting, Oh emphasizes relevance and the importance of understanding how mothers with different levels of education vary in the ways they obtain and use information for their children's education and well-being (such as schools, books, private tutors, and diseases). Based on in-depth interviews with 98 mothers, Oh finds that more educated mothers have more diverse information, obtained from multiple methods and informants, than their less-educated counterparts. The difference in information diversity leads to different parenting strategies between more and less educated mothers, which Oh summarizes as horizontal diversification and vertical cultivation, respectively, as well as different emotional statuses of mothers who rely on the two different strategies.

In chapter 3, Jo further pushes the issue of diverse parenting by exploring educational strategies of foreign-born, immigrant mothers (who are married to Korean men) for their children. Along with the rapid rise of international marriages, numerous studies have also examined the social, emotional, and cognitive development of children from multicultural families (typically consisting of a Korean father and a foreign-born mother), highlighting various challenges these children face at both home and school (Cho 2010). As Jo summarizes in her literature review, studies often point out limited Korean language use and other cultural disadvantages of immigrant mothers as a factor associated with their children's educational disadvantages, tending to overlook immigrant mothers' active roles in educating their children. Similar to native mothers, immigrant mothers also want their children's educational success and want to be involved in their children's education in various ways within their limited cultural and economic resources. On the basis of interview data with 29 immigrant mothers, Jo illustrates the process of "habitus transformation" through which immigrant mothers come to understand the educational contexts of Korea, which are often quite different from those of their origin countries, and to develop various educational strategies along with interactions with natives.

Family and Children's Education and Well-Being

In addition to (or through) parenting, a family's socioeconomic and demographic circumstances matter for children's educational and socioeconomic outcomes. The next four chapters in the section "Family and Children's Education and Well-Being" explore how children from different socioeconomic and demographic backgrounds fare in education and health. Specifically, Byun, Bai, and Chung (chapter 4) examine the extent to which both mothers' and fathers' educational levels and their combinations are related to children's English test scores by comparing children whose mothers and fathers both have a four-year college degree with their counterparts in 11 different combinations of a mother's and father's educational levels. It is notable that Korea has shown a comparably high degree of educational homogamy, where spouses have the same level of education (Smits and Park 2009). In this context of educational assortative mating, the question of how children of educationally homogamous couples fare in education and well-being compared to children of educationally heterogamous couples is interesting. Using individual-level data from a nationally representative sample of middle school students, Byun, Bai, and Chung show that children whose mothers and fathers both have a four-year college degree were advantaged in socioeconomic circumstances and did better on the English test than children from other types of families with respect to parents' education. However, after taking into account socioeconomic backgrounds, parental involvement, and children's characteristics, the difference in English test scores between children of both parents with a four-year college degree and children of only one parent with a four-year college degree disappears, suggesting that having one parent with a four-year college degree is a critical factor differentiating children's educational outcomes.

In chapter 5, Woo, Lim, Jeon, and Jeong shift interest to another aspect of the family structure that family scholars have found to be significantly related to children's outcomes in the United States and Europe: single parenthood (McLanahan and Sandefur 1994; Pong, Dronkers, and Hampden-Thompson 2003). The rising divorce rate in Korea makes the issue of single parenthood and its consequences for children timely and relevant. Although the authors could not distinguish causes of single parenthood in their analysis due to the data limitation, single parenthood among children is more likely due to divorce than to widowhood or nonmarital birth. Although unmarried parents constitute another form of single parenthood, the share of children living with an unmarried parent is still minimal in Korea (Raymo et al. 2015). The trend of the rising divorce rate can have important implications when children growing up with a divorced single parent are systematically disadvantaged in educational, social, emotional, and health outcomes compared to their peers from two-parent families. Analyzing longitudinal data of children, the authors compare four health outcomes (self-rated health, depression, aggression, and self-esteem) between children who live with both parents and those who live with a single parent. A key finding is that once baseline health measures and family socioeconomic backgrounds are taken into account, there is no significant difference in any of the four outcomes between the two groups of children. This finding contradicts some studies in the United States where single parenthood, particularly due to divorce, tends to be negatively associated with children's outcomes (Amato 2001; McLanahan and Sandefur 1994). However, it is consistent with previous studies that found negligible, or weak at most, relationships between single parenthood and children's educational outcomes in Asia, including Korea (Park 2007b).

Most studies of families deal with two-generation relations between parents and children. The first four chapters we have previewed so far (chapters 2 through 5) also deal with the relationship between parents and children. However, "family" does not have to be limited to parents and children but can include extended family members such as grandparents and other relatives. As Park and Jang claim in their study (chapter 6), the changing economy and demography of Korea, represented by rising economic inequality and rapid aging, likely make extended family members, particularly grandparents, increasingly relevant for children's education and well-being. In other words, in determining children's outcomes, not only parents but also grandparents may matter. Of course, grandparents have always mattered for children indirectly through their influences on parents. But a growing literature on multigenerational relations beyond two generations is interested in identifying a direct relationship between grandparents and children beyond the indirect relationship (Mare 2011; Park and Kim 2019; Pfeffer 2014). A critical challenge to multigenerational relations is the lack of data that include information across three generations. Effectively utilizing data from a social survey that asked respondents about their parents' and their first child's education as well as their own education, Park and Jang empirically assess the extent to which grandparents' schooling is related to (adult) children's schooling in Korea. Contradicting the expectation that grandparents should matter directly for children in the Korean context, where strong family ties have long been a key element of family life, the authors find that the relationship between grandparents' and children's schooling disappears once parents' schooling is taken into account. In other words, in contemporary Korea, grandparents influence children only indirectly through parents.

It is notable that the three chapters by Byun, Bai, and Chung, Woo et al., and Park and Jang show comparably weak relationships between family environments and children's education and health in Korea. Once a family's socioeconomic conditions are taken into account, children whose two parents hold a four-year-college degree do not differ much from children who have only one parent with a four-year college degree (chapter 4). Children who grow up with a single parent do not necessarily show worse health outcomes than their peers with two parents (chapter 5). There is no evidence of direct influences of grandparents' schooling on their grandchildren's schooling (chapter 6). The findings reported in the three chapters are consistent with some previous studies showing relatively narrow disparities in test scores among Korean secondary school students in international comparisons of student achievement (Chmielewski and Reardon 2016; OECD 2001).

However, caution is needed in drawing any conclusion about family influences in Korea from these three chapters. There is some evidence showing increased inequality in students' test scores in relation to a family's socioeconomic status in Korea (Byun and Kim 2010; Park 2013). In chapter 7, Jeon adds evidence to confirm the significant influences of family on children's health outcomes by showing the worse health status, indicated by more weight gain, among college students who live away from home compared to their counterparts who live with their parents and commute to campus. According to Jeon, due to the lack of campus housing in Korean higher education institutions, many Korean college students who have to live away from home tend to live in off-campus housing, where affordability and cost concerns often compromise their quality of living. In addition, the lack of immediate family support and supervision may aggravate unhealthy eating and nutrition problems, potentially leading to more weight gain among college students living independently than among their peers who live with family members. Although Jeon did not directly measure the amount of support that college students receive from their families in eating and nutrition, a more substantial weight gain among the former than the latter is consistent with his hypothesis, indirectly confirming the influence of family on children's health status.

Gender and Family

In discussing the topic of parenting in the book's first two sections, we allude to potential gender issues, as parental involvement in children's education has been primarily a mother's responsibility in Korean families. Where are the fathers? How much are Korean fathers involved in parenting and child-rearing? Gender inequality, particularly in labor market outcomes, is a distinctive feature of Korean society. Korea shows the largest gender wage gap among OECD countries and a comparably high gender gap in the employment rate due to the relatively low level of Korean women's labor force participation (OECD 2017). Korea still displays the M-shaped curve of women's labor force participation by age: a considerable share of women withdraw from the labor force upon marriage and childbearing and then return to the labor force once their children get older (OECD 2012). These indicators of substantial gender inequality in labor market outcomes reveal serious challenges that Korean women face in balancing family and work. Therefore, it is natural for the next three chapters to examine how equally men and women or mothers and fathers spend time on work and family, as well as their gender attitudes toward work and family.

In chapter 8, Lee, Park, and Sanidad use data from time-use surveys to compare how much time mothers and fathers spend on childcare as well as other activities and how the gender difference in time use for childcare has changed between 1999 and 2014, the earliest and latest time points of available data. The authors show that both Korean mothers and fathers spent more time on childcare in 2014 than in 1999, but the relative increase in childcare time was greater among fathers, leading to the reduced gender ratio of childcare time between the two time points. According to the authors, the trend of increased time for childcare in Korea is similar to the trend in the United States, reflecting the increased tendency for middle-class parents to be involved in their children's education from early ages. The authors also show some variation in time spent on childcare in the most recent data (i.e., 2014) by educational attainment of mothers and fathers, while the specific patterns of educational difference depend on the age of children and type of activities. Another important finding from the authors' analysis of time-use data is that parents' gender attitudes are related to time use for childcare: parents with more liberal gender attitudes tend to spend more time on childcare activities, which contradicts an alternative hypothesis that mothers with more liberal gender attitudes spend less time on childcare.

How have traditional gender norms strongly shaped Korean men's and women's behaviors and attitudes regarding family life? How can the gender division of labor and gender attitudes among Korean families change toward more equality? A useful case with which to examine traditional gender norms among Korean families, and in which context such gender norms can change, is immigration. When Korean families migrate to another country that is substantially different in gender and family contexts from those in Korea, do traditional gender relations between husbands and wives change or persist? Based on data from group interviews with 56 married women who migrated from Korea to the United States, Lee in chapter 9 explores change and persistence in traditional gender ideology and gender attitudes after immigration among Korean immigrant husbands and wives. Korean immigrant women in group interviews generally pointed out changes in their husbands' gender roles and attitudes toward more equality after migration, facilitated by the geographic separation from parents-in-law and also by social environments in the United States that are more gender equal than those in Korea. However, Lee also finds some persistent, internalized gender role attitudes among Korean immigrant women who still consider household work as primarily their responsibility. Korean immigrant women also reduce substantially their involvement in filial piety and kin network (usually their husbands' family side) after immigration. However, considering the potentially harmful influences on their children, Korean immigrant women do not entirely cut the connection with extended family members, which is an interesting twist of gender ideology for the sake of children's well-being. As a whole, Lee's analysis reveals the complicated impacts of immigration experiences on Korean immigrants' traditional gender roles and attitudes.

Family Formation and Alternative Family Life

Change and persistence in gender ideology and attitudes among Korean families ultimately lead to our final question: Where are Korean families headed? To answer this question, it is useful to examine how Korean young men and women view marriage and parenthood. The changing ways in which young men and women deal with marriage and parenthood can be informative to reveal an emerging type of Korean families. The three chapters in the last section, therefore, look into the issues of how (relatively young) men and women in Korea get married, how many children they want to have, and what kind of lifestyle they want to pursue, offering a glimpse into Korean families of tomorrow.

In chapter 10, Oh, Lee, and Woo assess who gets married in Korea, focusing on the impact of Korean men's and women's own education and their family background on the likelihood of marriage. Considering the function of marriage in Korea, which is "not only between two individuals but also between two families," it is reasonable to ask how one's family background as well as one's own characteristics are related to marriage. Moreover, as the authors emphasize, family background may have become even more important in recent years in determining the likelihood of marriage within the context of rising economic inequality in Korea. Following a longitudinal sample of young men and women over time, the authors find that both one's own education and his parents' household income are positively associated with marriage among Korean men. Educational differentials in marriage tend to be greater among men whose parents are poorer. However, neither educational attainment nor parents' household income is related to women's marriage. The authors speculate that men's economic burden to buy or rent a house upon marriage is a reason why parents' household income facilitates men's marriage. This economic perspective also accounts for why men's own education matters more when parents are poorer. If the authors' economic explanation is valid, we expect that the marriage gap between Korean men with more economic resources (indicated by either their own education or parents' household income) and their counterparts with fewer resources may increase further in the near future, given the trend of delayed marriage and rising economic inequality (see Park and Lee 2017).

Delayed marriage has important consequences for declining fertility. In chapter 11, Yoon turns her focus to fertility by assessing the ideal number of children that Korean men and women ages 18–49 report. According to Yoon, despite total fertility rates far below two children (Raymo et al. 2015), both Korean men and women report two or three as an ideal number of children, suggesting a gap between realized and ideal fertility levels. Yoon links the variation in the ideal number of children to men's and women's gender attitudes. Based on data from a social survey, Yoon finds that both Korean men and women show relatively egalitarian attitudes toward division of labor, while they show somewhat traditional attitudes toward the potential impact of working mothers on children and toward the value of being a housewife as compared to working for pay. Similar to what Lee shows in chapter 9 for the case of Korean immigrant women, gender attitudes are multifaceted depending on the dimensions of gender relations. It is important to note that Korean men and women show a similar pattern with respect to differences between their attitudes toward division of labor and their attitudes toward the impact of working mothers on children and the value of being a housewife as compared to working for pay. However, Yoon's analysis shows that gender attitudes, except for those toward division of labor, are related to the ideal number of children only among Korean men, not among Korean women. Men with more egalitarian attitudes toward the impact of working mothers on children and the value of being a housewife as compared to working for pay report a lower ideal number of children.

Although changes in marriage and fertility are important elements of the family structure for the near future, the specific types of future families will depend on the family lifestyle that current Korean young families want to pursue. When young couples and their children seek a new family experience, rejecting the current mode of family life conditioned by competitive educational systems and unequal gender division of labor, emerging families may take a different shape. Utilizing memoirs, manuals, various online writings, and some interviews, Tilland (chapter 12) reveals motivations and causes underlying recent movements of young Korean families to migrate to the countryside and give up their city life. Although the individualistic concern for the health and well-being of families is an important motivation for migrating to the countryside, Tilland identifies a related, but different, motivation for families to search for an alternative lifestyle, one that goes beyond the narrow focus on individual well-being to a greater desire to connect with the local, rural community, with its increasingly diversified and global character due to the rising number of multicultural families in rural Korea. It is an open question whether the rising tide of "back to the land" will gain momentum strong enough to fundamentally challenge the current, dominant life mode of Korean families and can offer a substantial alternative to attract many young Korean families. However, we can certainly discern a clue about the possible direction in which Korean families are headed.

REFERENCES

Amato, Paul. R. 2001. "Children and Divorce in the 1990s: An Update of the Amato and Keith (1991) Meta-analysis." *Journal of Family Psychology* 15: 355–70.
Byun, Soo-yong, and Kyung-keun Kim. 2010. "Educational Inequality in South Korea: The Widening Socioeconomic Gap in Student Achievement." *Research in the Sociology of Education* 17: 155–82.
Chmielewski, Anna K., and Sean F. Reardon. 2016. "Patterns of Cross-National Variation in the Association between Income and Academic Achievement." *AERA Open* 2: 1–27.
Cho, Youngdal. 2010. "Policy Note: Diversification of the Student Population and Multicultural Educational Policies in Korea." *Research in the Sociology of Education* 17: 183–198.
Kim Hye-yŏng and Sŏn Po-yŏng. 2011. "Yŏsŏng ŭi manhonhwa wa kyŏrhon ŭihyang: kyŏlchŏng yoin ŭl chungsim ŭro" (Delayed Marriage and Marriage Intension among Women). *Han'guk sahoe (Korean Society)* 12 (2): 3–25 (in Korean).
Kim, Keuntae. 2017. "Cross-Border Marriages in South Korea and the Challenges of Rising Multiculturalism." *International Migration* 55 (3): 74–88.
Kim T'ae-hŏn, Yi Sam-sik, Kim Tong-hŭi. 2006. "In'gu mit sahoe kyŏngjejŏk ch'abyŏl ch'ulsallyŏk: in'gu sensŏsŭ charyo punsŏk ŭl chungsim ŭro (Fertility Differentials by Demographic and Socioeconomic Characteristics: Analysis of Korean Population Census Data). *Han'guk in'guhak (Korean Journal of Population Studies)* 29 (1): 1–23 (in Korean).
Kim Tong-gyŏm. 2017. "Tamunhwa honin ŭi pyŏnhwa ch'ui t'ŭkching" (Trends and Features of Changing Multicultural Marriages). *Koryŏnghwa ribyu (Aging Review)* (Korea Insurance Research Institute) 5: 29–31 (in Korean).
Lareau, Annette. 2003. *Unequal Childhoods: Class, Race, and Family Life*. Berkeley: University of California Press.
Lee, Min-Kyung. 2014. "Multicultural Education in Republic of Korea: Social Change and School Education." In H. Park and K-k. Kim, eds., *Korean Education in Changing Economic and Demographic Contexts*, 173–89. Singapore: Springer.
Mare, Robert D. 2011. "A Multigenerational View of Inequality." *Demography* 48: 1–23.
McLanahan, Sara, and Gary Sandefur. 1994. *Growing Up with a Single Parent: What Hurts, What Helps*. Cambridge, MA: Harvard University Press.
Miller, Claire C. 2015. "Class Differences in Child-Rearing Are on the Rise." *New York Times*, December 17. https://www.nytimes.com/2015/12/18/upshot/rich-children-and-poor-ones-are-raised-very-differently.html
OECD 2001. *Knowledge and Skills for Life*. Paris: OECD.
OECD 2012. *Closing the Gender Gap: Act Now—Korea*. http://www.oecd.org/gender/Closing%20the%20Gender%20Gap%20-%20Korea%20FINAL.pdf
OECD 2017. OECD Family Database. Accessed August 27, 2017. http://www.oecd.org/els/family/database.htm
Park, Hyunjoon. 2007a. "South Korea: Educational Expansion and Inequality of Opportunity for Higher Education." In Y. Shavit, R. Arum, and A. Gamoran, eds., *Stratification in Higher Education: A Comparative Study*, 87–112. Stanford, CA: Stanford University Press.

Park, Hyunjoon. 2007b. "Single-Parenthood and Children's Reading Performance in Asia." *Journal of Marriage and Family* 69: 863–77.

Park, Hyunjoon. 2008a. "Home Literacy Environments and Children's Reading Performance: A Comparative Study of 25 Countries." *Educational Research and Evaluation* 14: 489–505.

Park, Hyunjoon. 2008b. "The Varied Educational Effects of Parent-Child Communication: A Comparative Study of Fourteen Countries." *Comparative Education Review* 52: 219–43.

Park, Hyunjoon. 2013. *Re-Evaluating Education in Japan and Korea*. London: Routledge.

Park, Hyunjoon, Jaesung Choi, and Hyejeong Jo. 2016. "Living Arrangements of Single Parents and Their Children in South Korea." *Marriage and Family Review* 52: 89–109.

Park, Hyunjoon, and Kuentae Kim. 2019. "The Legacy of Disadvantaged Origins: Blocked Social Mobility of Descendants of Nobi Great-Grandfathers in Korea (1765–1894)." *Social Forces*. https://doi.org/10.1093/sf/soz011

Park, Hyunjoon, and Jae Kyung Lee. 2017. "Growing Educational Differentials in the Retreat from Marriage among Korean Men." *Social Science Research* 66: 187–200.

Park, Hyunjoon, Jae Kyung Lee, and Inkyung Jo. 2013. "Changing Relationships between Education and Marriage among Korean Women." *Korean Journal of Sociology* 47 (3): 51–76.

Park, Hyunjoon, and James M. Raymo. 2013. "Divorce in Korea: Trends and Educational Differentials." *Journal of Marriage and Family* 75: 110–26.

Park, So Jin, and Nancy Abelmann. 2004. "Class and Cosmopolitan Striving: Mothers' Management of English Education in South Korea." *Anthropological Quarterly* 77: 645–72.

Pfeffer, Fabian T. 2014. "Multigenerational Approaches to Social Mobility: A Multifaceted Research Agenda." *Research in Social Stratification and Mobility* 35: 1–12.

Pong, Suet-ling, Jaap Dronkers, and Gillian Hampden-Thompson. 2003. "Family Policies and Children's School Achievement in Single- Versus Two-Parent Families." *Journal of Marriage and Family* 65: 681–99.

Raymo, James R., Hyunjoon Park, Yu Xie, and Wei-jun Jean Yeung. 2015. "Marriage and Family in East Asia: Continuity and Change." *Annual Review of Sociology* 41: 471–92.

Seth, Michael J. 2002. *Education Fever: Society, Politics, and the Pursuit of Schooling in South Korea*. Honolulu: University of Hawaii Press.

Smits, Jeroen, and Hyunjoon Park. 2009. "Five Decades of Educational Assortative Mating in Ten East Asian Societies." *Social Forces* 88: 227–56.

Statistics Korea. 2017. "2016-yŏn honin, ihon t'onggye" (Marriage and Divorce Statistics 2016). Media Briefing, Statistics Korea (in Korean).

Yu Kichŏl and Pak Yŏng-hwa. 2009. "Han'guk yŏsŏng ŭi ch'ulsanyul pyŏnhwa wa ch'ulsan kan'gyŏk yŏnghyang yoin" (The Change in the Fertility Rates and the Determinants of Birth Interval of Korean Women). *Han'guk in'guhak* (*Korean Journal of Population Studies*) 32 (1): 1–23 (in Korean).

Historical Contexts

1

The Evolution of the Korean Family

Historical Foundations and Present Realities

Paul Y. Chang

To note that South Korean society, since the nation's inception in 1948, transformed at an unprecedented speed has become a cliché in both academic and popular writing. Whether referring to economic modernization, democratization, globalization, or some other aspect of social life, the chasm separating the lived experiences of younger and older generations is as wide in South Korea (hereafter Korea) as in any nation that made the transition from developing to developed status. Indeed, scholars have popularized novel concepts, such as "compressed modernity," to describe the rapid pace of social change in Korea (Chang 1999, 2010).

This volume attests to the dramatic transformation of Korean society as manifest in the realm of family. Expectations for family life that were taken for granted even one generation ago—necessity to marry, bear children, support elderly parents, among others—have faltered with the emergence of new family forms. Because intimate family experiences are universal, whether positive or negative, it is easy for scholars and laypersons alike to assume normatively charged a priori definitions of what constitutes family. However, as George Peter Murdock noted many decades ago, "Used alone, the term 'family' is ambiguous. The layman and even the social scientist often apply it undiscriminatingly to several social groups which, despite functional similarities, exhibit important points of difference" (1949: 1).

Diversity is the story today. It is not a story unique to the Korean case. Demographers and family scholars have long pointed to fundamental changes in family life in European societies. Several trends that were initially deemed part of that "European exceptionalism"—later age of marriage; lower fertility rates; and rising rates of divorce, cohabitation, interracial marriages, same-sex partnerships, and single-person households—have emerged in other contexts as well, including in the United States (Rosenfeld 2009; Klinenberg 2012). Taken together, these trends are characterized in the literature as the "second demographic transition." If the first demographic transition in Europe marked "historical declines in mortality and fertility" from the 18th century on, the second transition starts roughly in the 1970s and refers to a new era dominated by "sustained subreplacement fertility, a multitude of living arrangements other than marriage, a disconnection between marriage and procreation," and "much older" populations due to the combination of extended longevity and low fertility (Lesthaeghe 2014: 18112).

It is important to note that although some attributes of the second demographic transition have spread to societies outside of Europe, both the pace and coverage of transitions are not uniform across regions and nations. Japan, for example, has since the 1960s experienced starker subreplacement fertility rates even compared to European nations, earning them the reputation of a "lowest-low fertility" society (Brinton et al. 2018; Muramatsu and Akiyama 2011). Other attributes of the second demographic transition, however, have not been replicated in Asian societies. Cohabitation and out-of-wedlock births stand out as conspicuous manifestations of the European trend that are missing in Asia, suggesting that the underlying mechanisms motivating family behaviors may vary across regions. Consequently, there is much empirical work left to be done to better understand the diverse range of processes governing the "modernization" of the family in different national, social, and cultural contexts.

Given the significant discrepancies in demographic transitions that are allegedly "stretching outward beyond the European cultural realm" (Lesthaeghe 2014: 18114), a better understanding of the unique trajectories of family formation in Asia and other non-European societies is clearly in order. The original research that constitutes the chapters of this volume goes a long way in providing both a descriptive overview of how families are changing in Korea and theoretically informed explanations to account for these changes. In the spirit of taking stock of the past to better understand present realities and future possibilities, I reflect in this chapter on Korea's particular path to modernity to provide a larger contextual understanding of how the economic and social policies of past governments facilitated the dramatic transformation of the Korean family.

Historical Foundations

State Family Planning

The story of Korea's modernization involves two central subplots. The first is the economic story, what has been dubbed the "miracle on the Han," with the central protagonist being the developmental state. The second is the political story with Korea transitioning to democracy in 1987 after decades of authoritarian rule. These economic and political forces are related as the developmental state, or the "developmental dictatorship" as some have labeled it (Lee 2005), proffered two justifications for the suppression of democratic reforms: national security vis-à-vis North Korea and the necessity to efficiently execute its economic program designed to pull the country out of poverty. As discussed below, both industrialization and democratization facilitated profound shifts in the macro sociopolitical structures of society that would fundamentally affect family formation patterns in Korea.

The state has always been in the business of influencing family formation. Upon liberation from Japanese colonial rule in 1945, the newly formed Republic of Korea (founded in 1948) inherited a family registration system that had gone through several renditions from its origins in the premodern Chosŏn dynasty (1392–1910). The premodern "family registration system" (*hogu tanja chedo*) documented the population based on clearly defined members of a household: head of household, spouse, children, and other "members," including slaves (Chŏng 2006: 7). The promulgation of the Revised Family Registration Law (*kaejŏng hojŏkpŏp*) by the Japanese colonial government in 1914 further solidified the privileges of the head of the household (*hoju*) relative to all other members of the family, a legal structure that was not reformed until 2005 (Yang 2010b: 292). The primary goal of these registration systems was to enumerate the population for the purpose of effective rule, which, invariably, meant accounting for the size of families.

Family size was a significant concern for successive Korean governments after liberation in 1945. Starting in the 1950s, under the leadership of President Syngman Rhee (Yi Sŭng-man), the government launched several national programs intended to influence the fertility behavior of Korean citizens. In hindsight, it is remarkable that the central purpose of these "family planning campaigns" (*kajok kyehoek undong*) was to lower the fertility rate. As the nation stabilized after the devastation of the Korean War (1950–53), the expansion and rationalization of agrarian production led to larger families (Chang K.S. 2018: 170). In the mid-1950s the average number of children born to women in childbearing years peaked at nearly 6.5. To curtail this spike in fertility, the government launched the first of many propaganda campaigns to pressure families to have fewer children. As shown in table 1.1, beginning with the modest goal of limiting families to 5 children, successive governments revised their ideal number of children several times before eventually arriving at 1 child in the 1980s. It was only in the mid-1990s, after the total fertility rate had dropped to around 1.5, that the government reversed its course and began to encourage Koreans to have more children.

In addition to poster campaign slogans used to disseminate ideal fertility rates, the government institutionalized and executed family planning policies through various government organs and local community centers. Beginning in 1958, Family Planning Counseling Centers (Kajok Kyehoek Sangdamso) were installed throughout the country to provide families with the information and resources they needed to conform to government objectives. These counseling centers would fall under the aegis of the newly

TABLE 1.1. Government Slogans Related to Fertility Campaigns

Years	Fertility goals	Slogans
1953–60	Five children	"3 sons, 2 daughters, have to have 5 children." (*3 nam, 2 yŏ ro 5 myŏng ŭn naayajyo.*)
Early 1960s	Four children	"It's good for parents and good for children, to have fewer children who are raised well." (*Chŏkke naa chal kirŭmyŏn pumo chok'o chasik chot'a.*)
Mid-1960s	Three children	"3335–3 year age gap, 3 children, give birth before 35 years old." (*3 sal t'ŏul, 3 chanyŏ, 35 sal ijŏnch'ulsan.*)
1970s	Two children	"Let's not discriminate between daughters and sons, let's only have two and raise them well." (*Ttal adŭl kubyŏl malgo tul man naa chal kirŭja.*)
1980s	One child	"Even two is too many. Let's have one and live frugally." (*Tul to mant'a. Hana nak'o alttŭl salttŭl.*)
1990s	More than one child	"The greatest gift to one's child is a younger sibling." (*Chanyŏ ege kajang k'ŭn sŏnmul ŭn tongsaeng imnida.*)

established Korea Family Planning Association (Taehan Kajok Kyehoek Hyŏphoe), founded in 1961, which was tasked with implementing the government's long-term population control policy as articulated in the "10-Year Plan for Family Planning Program" (Korea Family Planning Association 1975: 54). In addition to relying on less intrusive methods, such as "counseling" Koreans about fertility behaviors and disseminating contraceptives, the Korea Family Planning Association coordinated the availability of medical services, including subsidized vasectomy and IUD insertion procedures on their "family planning buses" (Korea Institute for Health and Social Affairs 2016: 78, 80).

It is important to situate the family planning programs pursued by the Korean government in the context of the all-encompassing industrialization drive of the 1960s and 1970s. After Park Chung Hee (Pak Chŏng-hŭi) assumed political charge of the country in 1961, the government embarked on a systematic effort to modernize the nation. It was through a series of "five-year economic plans," orchestrated by the Economic Planning Board and the Ministry of Finance, that Korea developed from an impoverished agrarian-based society to the industrial power it is today. It is not a coincidence that the initial 10-Year Plan for Family Planning Program (1962–71) was folded into the first and second Five-Year Economic Development Plans (1962–66, 1967–71). Slowing the rate of population growth was a central concern of the developmental state as the babyboom in the years immediately following the resolution of the Korean War was seen as a major factor delaying economic development (National Archives of Korea 2018). In addition to these concerted efforts to curb fertility rates through various family planning programs, the state-led economic drive fundamentally transformed the macrostructures of Korean society, which, in turn, would have a profound impact on family formation.

Urbanization and the Expansion of Higher Education

Urbanization accompanied industrialization as populations historically entrenched in rural Korea flocked to newly emerging cities to take advantage of the economic opportunities afforded by the rapid expansion of industry. The government encouraged the transition to factory work, as cheap labor was one of Korea's only resources (Koo 2001). The program that brought young people from the countryside to cities to work in textile and manufacturing factories was part of a larger strategy to transition Korea from agrarianism to manufacturing as the basis of the national economy. The most visible aspect of social transformation during the 1960s

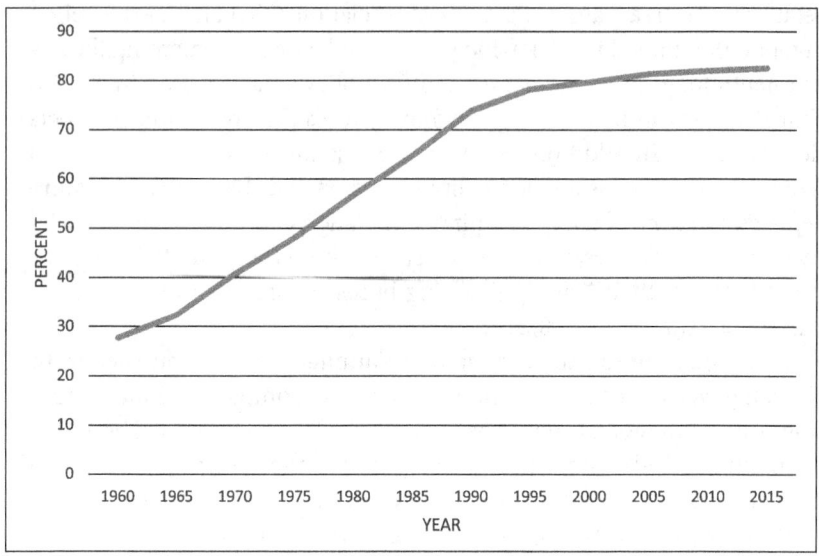

Fig. 1.1. Percent urban population. (Data from World Bank 2018.)

through the 1980s was arguably the rapid growth of cities and urban populations. As seen in figure 1.1, in 1960, 28 percent of the population lived in cities. That figure grew to a whopping 79 percent by 1997, when Korea faced an unprecedented financial crisis (World Bank 2018).

Through the five-year economic plans, President Park Chung Hee's government (1961–79) not only fundamentally altered Korea's economic trajectory but inadvertently disrupted traditional forms of family that were dominant in the preindustrial period. In 1963, Park Chung Hee's government chose to pursue export-led industrialization focused on the light industries. Specific sections of cities, the Dongdaemun (Tongdaemun) District in Seoul, for example, were designated as garment districts with dense concentrations of textile companies. Thousands of young women were mobilized from the countryside to sit at the sewing machines in factories located in new industrial centers (Ogle 1990; Koo 2001). This constituted the first significant wave of focused domestic migration after the Korean War and the first time that large numbers of unmarried young people were separated from their parents, who, for the most part, remained in the heartland.

The government-directed transition to heavy and chemical industries in the 1970s reduced the proportional scale of the textile industry in Korea's economy, but still the reliance on female labor continued (Moon and Jun

2011). Overall, as Park notes, "women's participation was crucial in the success of the manufacturing industry, the 'engine' of South Korea's economic development" (1993: 132). The spark plugs for this economic engine were working-age girls and women (14 years and older), many of whom migrated from the countryside to enter the industrial labor force. A large number lived in dormitories connected to their place of work, and these "factory girls" (*kongsuni*) contributed to the growing "economically active female population . . . from two million in 1960 to six million by 1985" (Cho and Chang 2017: 65). Overall, female labor participation increased from 37 percent in 1963 to 45 percent in 1988, just after Korea made the transition to democracy (KOSIS 2015). In the 1960s and 1970s, the majority of workers in many key manufacturing industries—such as textile and clothing, rubber and plastics, and electronic goods—were women, who contributed to the national economy in significant ways. Indeed, these "female manufacturing industries" produced "70 percent of the total national export earnings in 1975" (Park 1993: 132, quoted in Cho and Chang 2017: 65).

It is difficult to overstate the significance of this first large wave of female entry into the workforce for not only economic development but also for new patterns of family formation. Although the kinds of work women pursue have changed with greater educational attainment and the growth of the professional service economy, it is clear that the government's push for rapid industrialization fundamentally altered the gender dynamics of the public sphere. As in many developing societies, the entry of women into the workforce is associated with several characteristics of the second demographic transition: rising age in marriage, rising rates of divorce, and decreasing fertility rates.

Urbanization also coincided with smaller family sizes. In figure 1.2, we can see that family size steadily decreased throughout the industrialization period from the 1960s through the 1980s. That trend was more acute after the transition to a neoliberal economy following the Asian financial crisis in 1997, when family size continued to dwindle with the plummeting fertility rate and the striking growth of "one-person households." A complicated combination of factors accounts for the shrinking size of families in Korea, including the aforementioned government family planning policies that encouraged fewer children (Kendall 1996). In regard to urbanization specifically, it is telling that early urban planning in the 1960s and the launch of the "mass housing policy" in the 1970s already envisioned smaller families, as reflected in the architectural blueprints for apartment construction. The impressive widespread construction of high-rise apartments during this time, leading Valérie Gelézeau (2007) to characterize

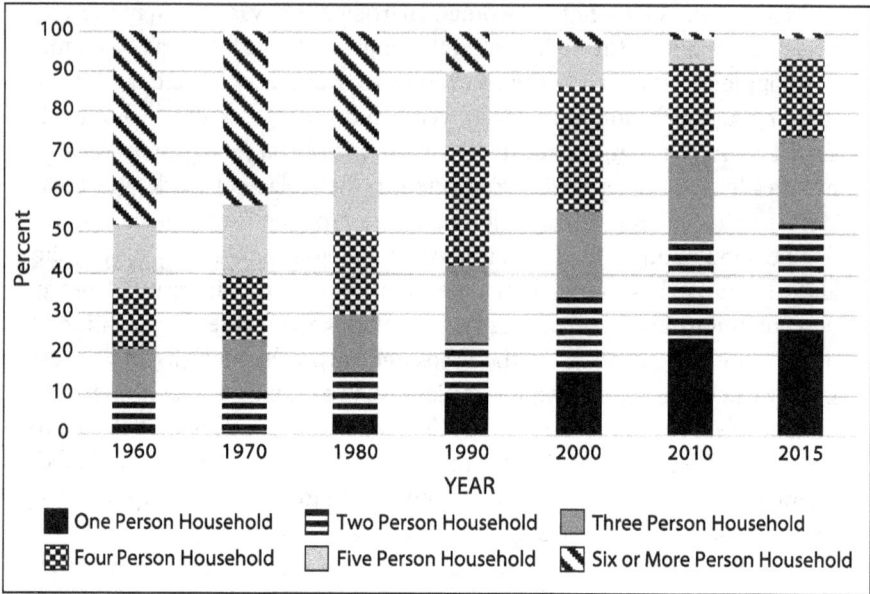

Fig. 1.2. Household size. (Data from KOSIS 2017.)

Korea as an "Apartment Republic" (*ap'at'ŭ konghwaguk*), not only housed the large number of domestic migrants flocking to the cities but also recast living arrangements to reflect the transition from the extended family to the nuclear family as the dominant household model for modern Korea.

In addition to urbanization, the government greatly expanded opportunities for higher education as part of its effort to grow a skilled labor force. From 1963 to 1980, "the number of post-secondary institutions increased by 160 percent from 86 to 222" (Korean Economic Planning Board, 1963–80, quoted in Cho and Chang 2017: 66). The increasing number of public schools was augmented by the dramatic growth in private institutions, which constituted the majority of the higher education sector from 1962 to 1973. Commenting on the expansion of education, a UNESCO mission notes, "The remarkable and rapid economic growth that has occurred in Korea . . . has been based to a large degree on human resources, and education has assisted in the production of a literate and industrial people" (Mason et al. 1980: 342).

The supply side of educational expansion coincided with prodigious growth in the number of Korean university students. In 1945, there were only 7,819 college students, a population that grew steadily to 296,640 by 1975 (Mason et al. 1980: 348). But by the 1980s, there were more than three million students enrolled in colleges and universities (Cho and Chang 2017: 66). And although the matriculation rates at tertiary education institutions were relatively low in 1980—30.3 percent for men and 22.9 percent for women—the first wave of college students in the 1970s and 1980s set an important precedent: today, roughly 70 percent of all high school graduates go on to attend college in some form (Park H. 2007). Predictably, access to higher education opened up new opportunities, and college-educated women today primarily seek professional white-collar employment in contrast to the first wave of factory workers. This trend is the product of an intentional strategy as Korea supplemented its manufacturing industry with a rapidly growing corporate service sector.

Political Freedoms and the "New Generation Culture"

Both urbanization and the expansion of tertiary education were at the same time byproducts and drivers of an economic strategy orchestrated by authoritarian governments. The state logic prioritized development over democracy because of the desperate need to pull the country out of poverty in the wake of the Korean War. Over time, however, as Korea made remarkable economic gains, it was increasingly difficult to justify authoritarian rule. Although social movements for democracy were active in the 1960s and 1970s (Kim C. 2017; Chang 2015), it was not until the summer of 1987, when the middle class joined "radical" students, that pressures from civil society led to the government's decision to reinstitute direct presidential elections (Kim S.-C. 2017). Partly because of the role that professional office workers played in the June protests of 1987, Korea has been hailed as a model case proving the merits of modernization theory. Of course the growth of a stable middle class in the 1980s and their short-lived politicization in 1987 are not the only reasons Korea transitioned to democracy, but suffice to say for the current discussion that democratic reforms presented to Koreans new political and cultural opportunities that facilitated the evolution of the Korean family.

By the mid-1980s, the Korean economy grew large enough to support a thriving middle class (Lett 1998). The summer Olympics held in Seoul in 1988 confirmed to the Korean people, and signaled to the world, that Korea had finally "made it." Already in the 1980s the middle class had begun to show their stripes as consumerism reached new heights—a rather significant indicator of progress, given that the government's decision to pursue export-led development in 1963 over import substitution was largely based on the lack of confidence in domestic spending to fuel the growth of emerging conglomerates. As Laura C. Nelson notes, by 1990 "South Korea's domestic market was no longer a trivial part of the economy" (2000: 21).

In the 1980s, middle-class consumption revolved around the usual sorts of spending indicative of a burgeoning modern society. Comparing where things stood in 1970 versus 1985, Laura C. Nelson (2000: 87) reports that there was a stark increase in the proportion of homes with televisions (6.4 percent vs. 99.1 percent), telephones (4.8 percent vs. 48.7 percent), and other household appliances such as refrigerators (2.2 percent vs. 71.1 percent) and washing machines (1.0 percent vs. 26 percent). Perhaps the most brazen signpost of the newfound wealth was the dramatic rise in the number of private passenger cars. In 1981 there were 267,605 private cars, but in a short seven years, that number jumped to 844,350 in 1987 (Nelson 2000: 96).

In the 1980s, even with greatly expanded spending power, the ability of Koreans to consume diverse products, especially international goods and culture, was limited, given the political restrictions imposed by President Chun Doo Hwan's (Chŏn Tu-hwan) authoritarian government (1980–87). With democratization, however, several reform policies granted Koreans greater exposure to the world. Lifting the severely limiting travel ban and rescinding censorship laws, for example, allowed Koreans to experience other societies and cultures, most significantly Western Europe and the United States, by either visiting foreign countries directly or importing international cultural goods. For 10 years, from democratic transition in 1987 to when the economy collapsed in spectacular fashion in 1997, Korean society underwent a fundamental ideational shift characterized by new cultural possibilities. Along with transformations in macro social structures—urban living and expanded higher education—this decade-long process of cultural opening in the 1990s had profound effects on ideas of family formation in Korea.

Although it is difficult to measure cultural change, especially when applied to large swaths of society, there are several indirect signs that Koreans were exploring new lifestyles in the 1990s. As noted, the wealth accumulated throughout the industrialization period materialized in a new consumption culture that emerged in the 1980s. The political breakthrough in 1987 allowed Koreans to enjoy their lives in increasingly diverse ways as access to international experiences was made possible by the lifting of travel bans that were in place throughout the authoritarian period. In the 1960s and 1970s, Korean passports were granted to government officials, business actors, and select groups of students who pursued education abroad. Applicants in the latter two categories had to receive permission from the government and were primarily traveling for purposes that coincided with nation-building goals: many of the students who pursued graduate work in the United States and other countries were financially supported by the government with the explicit expectation that they would study fields relevant to industrialization (e.g., engineering, science, and technology) and bring back that knowledge to help modernize Korea.

It was not until 1983 that the government first allowed travel for purely tourism purposes. That allowance, however, was restricted to those who were over 50 years old and who could pay the steep price of two million Korean won for the travel visa (Son and Ch'oe 2014). Interest in global cultures grew after the 1988 summer Olympics in Seoul, and as part of the process of political liberalization, the government lifted all bans on overseas travel in 1989. The abrupt opening of travel opportunities, coupled with the command of resources available to the middle and upper classes, prompted a rush of tourists to international destinations. As figure 1.3 shows, the numbers of outbound tourists increased significantly until 1997, when the economy crashed. In addition to the unprecedented opportunity for large numbers of Koreans to witness and experience foreign cultures, travel fueled and diversified consumption, as goods brought back from overseas (from liquor to handbags) became status symbols for the families who could afford them (Nelson 2000).

In the 1990s, exposure to international cultures was not limited to the time tourists spent in a foreign country and the necessarily small number of goods they could bring back to Korea. Through constitutional amendments in 1987 and 1992, the government relaxed censorship laws that were used throughout the authoritarian period to limit access to outside influences (Constitutional Court 2013). The influx of predominately Western and Japanese television programming, movies, music, literature, and other cultural products galvanized the transformation of Korea's own popular culture. In 1992, for example, the advent of the music group Seo Taiji and Boys (Sŏ T'ae-ji wa aidŭl) was a watershed moment in Korean popular consciousness, as they introduced contemporary Western musical genres and accompanying dance forms, including hip-hop, to a wide audience. Clearly, a new cultural spirit was in the air.

Coinciding with the government's own emphasis on globalization (*segyehwa*), starting with President Kim Young Sam's (Kim Yŏng-sam) tenure in 1993, the 1990s cultural shift has been dubbed the "new generation culture" (*sinsedae munhwa*; Chu 2003). One stereotype about participants in

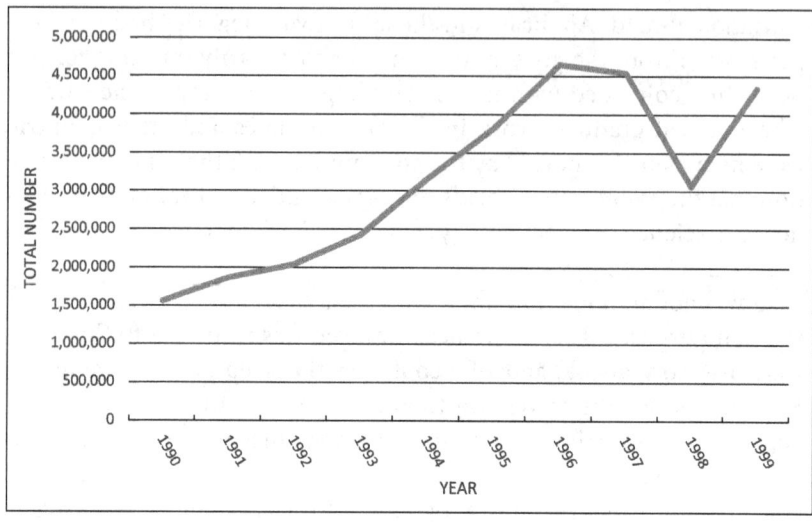

Fig. 1.3. Outbound tourists. (Data from Korean Tourism Corporation 2017.)

this new culture is their refusal to make the same sacrifices previous generations were expected to make for the nation, either in the factories working for economic development or in the streets fighting for democracy. Members of this new post-authoritarian generation grew up in a more affluent Korea and turned away from national concerns toward individualistic interests. Indeed, as both pundits and scholars have noted, the 1990s mark the beginning of "Korean individualism" (see, e.g., Yi 2006). An insightful reflection of this new culture emphasizing the pursuit of individual enjoyment is the rapid growth of the leisure industry in the 1990s. In figure 1.4, we can see that per capita spending on leisure steadily climbs in the 1980s but really starts to take off between democratic transition in 1987 and financial crisis in 1997.

The rise in the pursuit of individual leisure, in the larger context of growing consumption of international products and cultures, occurred at the same time that the government moved to reform laws regulating family practices. A series of family laws were revised in 1991 around the issues of equal inheritance rights for male and female progeny, greater equality in marriage between husbands' and wives' families, and a clearer articulation of responsibilities and rights for parents who have and do not have custody of children upon divorce (Yang 2007, 2010a). These sets of laws,

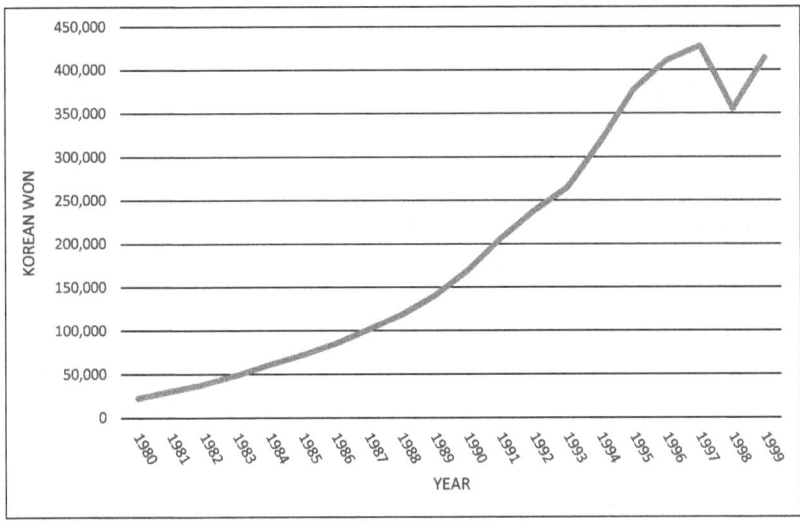

Fig. 1.4. Per capita expenditure on leisure. (Data from Park S.-H. 2007.)

tangibly and in spirit, represented a move away from traditional family practices in Korea, including most notably a revised household system diminishing, but not removing, male privilege (later fundamentally revised in 2005).

It is notable that the idea of "love marriage" (*yŏnae kyŏrhon*) also becomes popular in this period, even as romantic love was, of course, not a new concept. The advent of love marriages, surprisingly a recent invention in larger human history (Coontz 2005), and its popularity in Korea mirror trends in other nations, such as Japan, where the proportion of marriages based on emotionally grounded individual preferences surpassed traditional arranged marriages in 1967, continuing to grow to 85 percent of all marriages by 1993 (Takahashi et al. 1997). Although arranged marriages (*chungmae kyŏrhon*) are admittedly still relevant in Korea today, relative to past generations love marriages are taken for granted as a legitimate form of marital union. In the 1990s there was, in short, much optimism surrounding the pursuit of individual happiness and new possibilities for family life, as the economy was booming and Koreans enjoyed political freedoms denied to them during the previous 40 years of autocratic rule.

Present Realities

The Neoliberal Economy

By 1997, on the eve of national financial ruin, Korea had already witnessed dramatic economic and political transformations. The mobilization of the population for industrialization, and the ensuing urbanization and expansion of higher education, fundamentally altered the possibilities for work and family. In the 1980s Koreans were able to enjoy the fruits of their labor, reflected in the conspicuous consumption practices of a growing middle class. After democratic transition in 1987, for a full decade until 1997, new cultural possibilities arose as resources were combined with political freedoms to facilitate the emergence of a generation identified by the "new individualism." As Korea headed into the worst economic crisis in the modern period, the great majority of the population were living in smaller families in cities, women played an integral role in the labor market, and individualism had become part of the cultural milieu.

If we imagine the onset of the 1997 financial crisis as the entrance to a tunnel, it is clear Korea as a whole emerged on the other side fundamentally altered. The transformation is most evident in the economy, but reforms instituted in the aftermath of the crisis continue today to have significant consequences for diverse aspects of life. As the dust settled after the economic, political, and social upheaval, Korea found ways to quickly pay back the International Monetary Fund's (IMF) 57-billion-dollar bailout loan. The Korean strategy to recover, as opposed to Japan's, involved recapitalizing its financial institutions by lifting restrictions on foreign direct investment, which, in turn, fundamentally compromised the government's ability to influence lending and to direct the course of economic development (Kang 2009). This marked the end of the developmental state system, as the government no longer controlled banking practices and conglomerates gained independence by diversifying capital sources, primarily by accessing international money markets.

The independence of the banks and conglomerates after 1997 would have a profound impact on Korean households. The reforms mandated by the IMF included liberalizing labor laws to give greater competitive edge to businesses, which put an end to de facto lifetime employment schemes prevalent in the industrialization period. In addition, foreign investment in, and in some cases foreign control of, Korean banks coincided with the rise in retail banking, where the proportion of individual loans (e.g., mortgage loans and credit cards) grew to surpass commercial loans by 2001 (see Kang and Ma 2007). This inadvertently led to a dramatic increase in the household debt-to-income ratio, where spending is higher than disposable income. As early as 2003, the stability of the Korean economy was again threatened when the country went through a "credit card crisis" (Kang and Ma 2007).

Overall, precarity characterizes Korea's new neoliberal economy. Koreans are facing uncertainties in both public and private life as non-regular work commands a greater proportion of employment and household debt is at record highs ("Korea's Household Debt" 2016). Growing inequality after the financial crisis, as reflected in a shrinking middle class, is driving what is commonly referred to in public discourse as a "hypercompetitive" culture. Appreciating the precarity in contemporary Korean society also helps us to better understand several trends in family behavior, as the chapters in this volume clearly demonstrate.

Inequality and the Family

The subsequent chapters show how the family, as a social institution, is both a cause and a consequence of growing inequality in Korean society. Several chapters point to educational outcomes where family practices are consequential. In chapter 2, Eunsil Oh explains how variations in mothers' education impact the potential human capital they bestow on their children. Her analysis of 98 in-depth interviews shows that highly educated mothers are more likely to pursue a broad strategy of exposing their children to a variety of afterschool opportunities, whether in academics, music, or sports. In contrast to this "horizontal diversification," mothers with less education attempt to more efficiently expend their limited resources on a smaller set of educational outlets for their children—what she calls "vertical cultivation"—in the hopes that depth of engagement will make up for breadth of exposure.

Expanding the scope of parental advantage to both mothers and fathers, Soo-yong Byun, Yifan Bai, and Hee Jin Chung show in chapter 4 that highly educated individuals are more likely to marry each other, what is known in the literature as educational homogamy, and that the resultant pooled human capital significantly affects children's outcomes on English tests—further proof that education is a potent mechanism for exacerbating inequalities across generations. Contributing to our understanding of how this mechanism works, Yean-Ju Lee, Kitae Park, and Ivan Sanidad argue in chapter 8 that although time spent with children has universally risen in recent years, one reason why highly educated parents are effective is their ability to adapt their parenting strategies to the particular developmental stage of their children. By differentially tailoring their focus on physical care versus reading and playing versus teaching, depending on their child's age, highly educated parents are better able to meet the stage-specific needs of their children compared to less educated parents.

The focused intensity of child-rearing practices, what has been labeled as "concerted cultivation" in some contexts (Lareau 2011) and "tiger parenting" in others (Chua 2011), is so prevalent in Korean society that these pressures can sometimes force parents to subscribe to them even if they consciously resist. In the fascinating case of marriage migrants—non-ethnic Korean women married to Korean men—Hyejeong Jo reports in chapter 3 that these mothers who are initially "shocked" upon learning the "rules of the game" quickly acquiesce as they struggle to help their children compete in Korea's hypercompetitive academic environment. This "habitus transformation" is a testament to the powerful influence of social norms on parenting specifically and family practices generally. In a related vein, the stakes in educating children are so high that even extended family members are called upon to contribute to the cause. In chapter 6, Hyunjoon Park and Heewon Jang argue for the importance of adopting a multigenerational lens to understand the wider range of resources available to Korean children. And although their data did not show a direct effect of grandparents' education on levels of schooling among grandchildren, their indirect influence should not be ignored: grandparents matter for the education of parents, who then confer greater human capital to their children.

The role of the family in exacerbating inequality is not limited to children's educational outcomes. As two chapters in this volume show, health is a significant area of interest when contemplating the diverse ways family structures matter. In chapter 5, Hyeyoung Woo, Sojung Lim, Sun Young Jeon, and Wonjeong Jeong argue that marital stability can fundamentally affect children's overall health. Their analysis of longitudinal survey data shows that children reared in two-parent households are more likely to report good health compared to children in single-parent families. Worrisome is their additional finding that children of single parents score higher on depression and aggression measures. These physical and mental health discrepancies, they suggest, are largely driven by the relatively limited socioeconomic resources of single-parent households. The health of individuals can also be significantly influenced by the physical absence of family. Haram Jeon shows in chapter 7 that Korean college students who live away from parents are more likely to be obese compared to their counterparts who live with their families. To the degree that college students in dormitories and other temporary residential arrangements transition to living alone upon graduation, this finding has broader implications for the rapidly growing proportion of single-person households.

The discussion thus far has construed the family as a mechanism facilitating greater inequality in educational and health outcomes. Family values and practices are, however, also consequences of the unequal distribution of resources in Korea's stratified society. In their chapter with the compelling title "Who Gets Married?" Jihye Oh, Jae Kyung Lee, and Hyeyoung Woo argue that both financial and educational resources are important considerations that influence the possibility of marriage. Drawing on impressive panel data following nearly 4,000 respondents over 18 years, they show that highly educated men are more likely to marry than men with less education. But also, in line with the emphasis on multigenerational effects, their results indicate that men with high-income parents are more likely to marry than men whose families are less affluent. One fascinating finding when considering the interaction between family income and education is that a man's education becomes even more important when his family is not well off, suggesting that some form of resource is necessary in the absence of others. Interestingly, individual or family resources seem to matter less for women's marriage prospects.

Although it is difficult to empirically verify the direct connections between the processes related to industrialization—urbanization, expansion of education, female employment—and large-scale shifts in cultural understandings, it is clear that attitudes about gender roles in Korean society are in flux. It is perhaps not surprising that female labor participation has led to more egalitarian attitudes about who may fill the role of breadwinner in Korean households. But as Soo-Yeon Yoon points out in chapter 11, this move toward greater equality may be less about the recognition of women's work and more about the precarious economy where dual incomes are increasingly necessary to sustain families. The debate regarding what drives gender "egalitarian" attitudes may be moot, however, as the intensity of child-rearing practices leads Koreans to fall back on restrictive notions of mothering. Her chapter shows that, even with greater acceptance of female work, both men and women subscribe to the traditional belief that mothers are primarily responsible for the education of children. If working women continue to take on the largest burden of child-rearing, it is no wonder that this "second shift" (Hochschild 1989) compromises both their professional careers and their private lives. This fundamental conflict between work and family, a product of the persistence of traditional motherhood values, is also consequential for fertility, as women in the labor force report wanting fewer children.

Given the incredible pressures surrounding family and public life, we might wonder if there is respite somewhere. Two chapters address this possibility. In chapter 9, Byung Soo Lee highlights changes in family values among Koreans who have immigrated to the United States. Living in a potentially more "progressive society," the Korean-American family is indeed an interesting case. But as Lee's interviewees convey, when it comes to the education of children, Korean-American women still adhere to the same traditional norms governing mothering practices in Korea. Although these immigrant women report that some things did change after moving to America (e.g., husbands are more helpful around the house), ultimately, Korean-American families are bound by the same norms that discourage significant participation of fathers in child-rearing.

Overall, what has been dramatized as the "tyranny of children's education" is a central hurdle that fortifies traditional family values and practices. The chapters in this volume show that in addition to obstructing the progress of gender equality, families, through varying education strategies, act as the mechanism through which intergenerational inequality is reproduced. The pressures to compete and succeed are so great that some Korean families are beginning to pursue quite radical solutions to resist them. In chapter 12, Bonnie Tilland discusses the new trend of Korean families moving back to the countryside in an effort to opt out of a society filled with unbearable pressures. Perhaps driven by romantic notions of a more idyllic "rural life," some Koreans are carving out an alternative lifestyle in the hopes that their children will be spared the crushing stresses of urban living. But still, it is sobering that even these families fall back on some narrative of competition when they insist that their move to the heartland gives them access to greater "global capital" in the form of increased exposure to the multicultural families prevalent in rural Korea. Evidently, as the saying goes, it is possible to take someone out of a competitive environment, but it is not as easy to take the competition out of the person.

Conclusion

That macro-level structures shape both opportunities and constraints for micro-level action is a sociological axiom. Because of the universality of the family experience, at least some version of it, we tend to explain family matters in regard to individual considerations. This chapter and this volume as a whole, however, testify to the importance of considering larger historical contexts facilitating the evolution of family formation in Korea. I have attempted in this chapter to relate contemporary family patterns to specific policies set by authoritarian governments. The government mobilized the population for the sake of development, leading to the prevalence of urban living today. The expansion of tertiary education, intended to create a literate labor force, continued the pattern of encouraging female labor participation that initially accompanied the rise of manufacturing in the 1960s and 1970s. And political freedoms, afforded by the transition to democracy in 1987, unleashed new cultural opportunities as individualism and personal life satisfaction became salient values.

The structural transformation of Korean society from the 1960s through the 1980s, and the ensuing decade-long opening to Western cultures in the 1990s, provided the foundations for the diversification of family formation, values, and practices. These new possibilities for family life were imbued with a darker urgency in the wake of the financial meltdown in 1997 and the neoliberal economy that emerged from its ashes. As Koreans manage the precarity of social life today, fueled by labor flexibility, a hypercompetitive education culture, and prohibitive housing costs, it is possible that traditional family forms will continue to diminish. In many ways, it seems quite rational that Koreans are marrying later or not at all, having fewer children and at older ages, less willing to take on the responsibilities of caring for aging parents, choosing to live alone, and in some cases opting out of urban life completely by moving to the countryside. Without dramatic intervention of some sort, possibly in the form of an effective welfare state, it is unlikely that these trends will be restrained.

NOTE

Research for this chapter was supported by the Ministry of Education of the Republic of Korea and the National Research Foundation of Korea (NRF-2016S1A3A2925085).

REFERENCES

Brinton, Mary C., Xiana Bueno, Livia Oláh, and Merete Hellum. 2018. "Postindustrial Fertility Ideals, Intentions, and Gender Inequality: A Comparative Qualitative Analysis." *Population and Development Review* 44 (2): 281–309.

Chang, Kyung-Sup. 1999. "Compressed Modernity and Its Discontents: South Korea Society in Transition." *Economy and Society* 28 (1): 30–55.

Chang, Kyung-Sup. 2010. *South Korea under Compressed Modernity: Familial Political Economy in Transition*. New York: Routledge.
Chang, Kyung-Sup. 2018. "The Logics of Compressed Modernity: The Transformative Structure of Korean Society." Unpublished manuscript.
Chang, Paul Y. 2015. *Protest Dialectics: State Repression and South Korea's Democracy Movement, 1970–1979*. Stanford: Stanford University Press.
Cho, Joan E., and Paul Y. Chang. 2016. "The Socioeconomic Foundations of South Korea's Democracy Movement." In Youna Kim, ed., *The Routledge Handbook of Korean Culture and Society: A Global Approach*, 63–75. London: Routledge.
Chŏng Hyŏn-su. 2006. "Hojŏk chedo ŭi pyŏnchŏn kwa saeroun sinbun tŭngnok chedo e kwanhan koch'al" (A Study on the Change of the Family Registry System and the New Identity Registry System). *Kajokpŏp yŏn'gu (Korean Journal of Family Law)* 20 (2): 1–36 (in Korean).
Chu Ch'ang-yun. 2003. "Sinsedae munhwa ŭi ijungsŏng: p'yŏnip kwa chŏhang" (Two Sides of the New Generation Culture: Prejudice and Resistance). *Munhak kwa kyŏnggye (Literature and Boundary)* 3 (2): 53–62 (in Korean).
Chua, Amy. 2011. *Battle Hymn of the Tiger Mother*. London: Bloomsbury.
Constitutional Court. 2013. Constitutional Court Cyber Museum. http://history.ccourt.go.kr/cckhome/history/open/constitution.do#tab6 (retrieved October 2017).
Coontz, Stephanie. 2005. *Marriage, a History: How Love Conquered Marriage*. New York: Penguin Books.
Gelézeau, Valerie (Palleri Chullejo). 2007. *Ap'at'ŭ konghwaguk (The Apartment Republic)*. Seoul: Humanit'asŭ (in Korean).
Hochschild, Arlie Russell, with Anne Machung. 1989. *The Second Shift: Working Families and the Revolution at Home*. New York: Penguin Books.
Kang, Myung-koo. 2009. "Too Fast to Adjust: The Sequence and Consequences of Bank Restructuring in South Korea, 1998–2006." *Asian Survey* 49 (2): 243–67.
Kang, Tae Soo, and Guonan Ma. 2007. "Recent Episodes of Credit Card Distress in Asia." *BIS Quarterly Review*, June, 55–68.
Kendall, Laurel. 1996. *Getting Married in Korea: Of Gender, Morality, and Modernity*. Berkeley: University of California Press.
Kim, Charles. 2017. *Youth for Nation: Culture and Protest in Cold War South Korea*. Honolulu: University of Hawaii Press.
Kim, Sun-Chul. 2017. *Democratization and Social Movements in South Korea: Defiant Institutionalization*. London: Routledge.
Klinenberg, Eric. 2012. *Going Solo: The Extraordinary Rise and Surprising Appeal of Living Alone*. New York: Penguin Books.
Koo, Hagen. 2001. *Korean Workers: The Culture and Politics of Class Formation*. Ithaca: Cornell University Press.
Korea Family Planning Association. 1975. *10-Year History of Korean Family Planning*. Republic of Korea: Korea Family Planning Association (in Korean).
Korea Institute for Health and Social Affairs. 2016. *50 Years of Korean Population Policy: From Antinatalist to Pronatalist*. Republic of Korea: Fifty Year History of Population Policies Compilation Committee (in Korean).
Korean Statistical Information Service (KOSIS). 2015. "Female Labor Participation, 1963–2014." Republic of Korea: Ministry of Strategy and Finance (in Korean).

Korean Statistical Information Service (KOSIS). "Population Census Household Structure." http://kosis.kr/eng/ (retrieved October 2017).
Korean Tourism Corporation. "Tourism Statistics." https://kto.visitkorea.or.kr/kor/notice/data/statis.kto (retrieved October 2017).
"Korea's Household Debt Hits All-Time High." 2016. *Korea Herald*, November 24. http://www.koreaherald.com/view.php?ud=20161124000761 (retrieved October 2017).
Lareau, Annette. 2011. *Unequal Childhoods: Race, Class, and Family Life*. Berkeley: University of California Press.
Lee, Byeong-Cheon, ed. 2005. *Developmental Dictatorship and the Park Chung-Hee Era: The Shaping of Modernity in the Republic of Korea*. Paramus, NJ: Homa and Sekey Books.
Lesthaeghe, Ron. 2014. "The Second Demographic Transition: A Concise Overview of Its Development." *Proceedings of the National Academy of Sciences of the United States of America* 11 (51): 18112–15.
Lett, Denise Potrzeba. 1998. *In Pursuit of Status: The Making of South Korea's "New" Urban Middle Class*. Cambridge, MA: Harvard University Asia Center.
Mason, Edward S., Mahn Je Kim, Dwight H. Perkins, Kwang Suk Kim, and David C. Cole, with Leroy Jones, Il Sakong, Donald R. Snodgrass, and Noel F. McGinn. 1980. *The Economic and Social Modernization of the Republic of Korea*. Cambridge, MA: Harvard University Asia Center.
Moon, Chung-in, and Byung-joon Jun. 2011. "Modernization Strategy: Ideas and Influences." In Byung-Kook Kim and Ezra F. Vogel, eds., *The Park Chung Hee Era: The Transformation of South Korea*, 115–39. Cambridge, MA: Harvard University Press.
Muramatsu, Naoko, and Hiroko Akiyama. 2011. "Japan: Super-Aging Society Preparing for the Future." *Gerontologist* 51 (4): 425–32.
Murdock, George Peter. 1949. *Social Structure*. New York: The Free Press.
National Archives of Korea. "Kajok kyehoek saŏp" (Family Planning Activities). http://theme.archives.go.kr/next/populationPolicy/issue02.do (retrieved October 2018).
Nelson, Laura C. 2000. *Measured Excess: Status, Gender and Consumer Nationalism in South Korea*. New York: Columbia University Press.
Ogle, George. 1990. *South Korea: Dissent within the Economic Miracle*. London: Zed Books.
Park, Hyunjoon. 2007. "South Korea: Educational Expansion and Inequality of Opportunity for Higher Education." In Yossi Shavit, Richard Arum, and Adam Gamoran, eds., *Stratification in Higher Education: A Comparative Study*, 87–112. Stanford, CA: Stanford University Press.
Park, Kyung Ae. 1993. "Women and Development: The Case of South Korea," *Comparative Politics* 25: 127–45.
Park, Se-Hyuk. 2007. "The Current Status and Future Directions of Leisure Industry in Korea." *Journal of Leisure and Recreation Studies* 8 (1): 28–59 (in Korean).
Rosenfeld, Michael J. 2009. *The Age of Independence: Interracial Unions, Same-Sex Unions, and the Changing American Family*. Cambridge, MA: Harvard University Press.
Son Minho and Ch'oe Sŭng-p'yo. 2014. "Chayuhwa 25-yŏn . . . haeoe yŏhaeng ŏje wa onŭl" (Liberalization 25 Years . . . Overseas Travel, Yesterday and Today). *Chungang ilbo*, January 3. http://news.joins.com/article/13548604 (retrieved October 2017).

Takahashi, Shigesato, Ryuichi Kaneko, Ryuzaburo Sato, Masako Ikenoue, Fusami Mita, Tsukasa Sasai, Miho Iwasawa, and Yuriko Shintani. 1997. "Marriage Fertility in Present-Day Japan." *Journal of Population and Social Security* 1(1): 1–32.

World Bank. 2018. "Urban Population (% Total)," Republic of Korea. https://data.world bank.org/indicator/SP.URB.TOTL.IN.ZS?locations=KR (retrieved November 2018).

Yang, Hyunah (Yang Hyŏn-a). 2007. "1987-yŏn ihu kajokpŏp ŭi pyŏnhwa e kwanhan pŏpsahoehakchŏk koch'al" (Legal and Sociological Evaluations on the 20 Years after June Democratization Struggle: A Sociological Review of Family Law in Korea after 'Democratization' in 1987). *Pŏp kwa sahoe (Korean Journal of Law & Society)* 32:103–38.

Yang, Hyunah (Yang Hyŏn-a). 2010a. "A Journey of Family Law Reform in Korea: Tradition, Equality, and Social Change." *Journal of Korean Law* 8: 77–94.

Yang, Hyunah (Yang Hyŏn-a). 2010b. "Minji sigi Han'guk kajokpŏp ŭl t'onghae pon kabu changje ŭi kukka chedohwa wa 'kwansŭp' munje" (National Institutionalization of the Patriarchal System and the Issue of 'Custom' through Korean Family Law during the Colonial Period). *Minji sigi Han'guk kajokpŏp ŭl t'onghae pon kabu changje ŭi kukka chedohwa wa 'kwansŭp' munje (2nd Korea-Japan History Co-Research Report)* 5: 289–317.

Yi Chu-chŏn. 2006. "Han'guk taejung munhwa ŭi t'ŭksŏng kwa munjejŏm - 1990-yŏndae minjuhwa ihu rŭl chungsim ŭro" (Characteristics and Problems of the Korean Mass Culture in 1990s). *Yŏksa wa sahoe (History and Society)* 36: 39–60 (in Korean).

Diversity in Parenting and Children's Education

2

The Strength of Information

Maternal Education and Child-Rearing in Urban Korea

Eunsil Oh

How parents assess what their young children need and what they as parents need to provide to successfully raise their children has attracted considerable attention from sociologists, child development experts, and the public. This issue continues to be important because in all postindustrial societies, despite policy efforts to provide equal opportunities for children, disparities persist in the amount and kinds of education that young children receive from their parents (Becker 2011; Bornstein and Bradley 2014; Lareau 2011; Lee and Burkam 2002).

Sociological studies have shown that family resources, including financial, social, and cultural capital, play a salient role in reproducing an educational achievement gap and labor market inequalities (Bourdieu 1973; Grusky 1994; Hart and Risley 2003; Lareau and Weininger 2003; Lareau 2011). Among various measures of social class, maternal education especially is found to play a significant role in the educational outcomes of children and adolescents, in addition to paternal education, family income, and neighborhood (Augustine et al. 2015; Lareau and Weininger 2008; Weininger, Lareau, and Conley 2015). This finding provoked researchers to focus on the underlying mechanisms utilized by mothers that are likely to produce the disparities in education that young children receive. This chapter aims to contribute to this line of research by leveraging qualitative data from South Korea (hereafter Korea) to explore how urban mothers with different educational backgrounds construct aspirations and strategies toward child-rearing. In mapping the connections between mothers' resources, skills, and perceptions, I focus on the similarities shared by mothers as well as dissimilarities that arise based on maternal education.

Korea is known to have the largest "shadow" (or private) education system in the world (Baker and LeTendre 2005). Korean parents are known for having extremely high desires in educating their children (Seth 2002) and for spending a high proportion of household income on children's education (Anderson and Kohler 2013). However, empirical studies of the micro-level processes that explain how parents provide education and approach child-rearing are scant in the literature. More importantly, recent studies have shown that disparities in the amount and kinds of private education that Korean students receive have been widening based on parents' resources (Byun, Schofer, and Kim 2012; Park 2006; Park, Byun, and Kim 2011). Yet variation in beliefs and practices related to child-rearing has been less explored due to the uniform image that all Korean parents, especially mothers, are obsessive toward educating their children. Therefore, in this chapter, I ask: How do theories on parents' influence on early childhood education explain child-rearing approaches utilized by mothers, and how does an empirical analysis of Korean mothers' aspirations and practices for child-rearing extend our knowledge about this linkage between the resources that parents have and the education that children receive? Because of the gender-unequal division of labor for childcare and the high expectation toward mothers to ensure the well-being and educational success of young children, this chapter focuses on urban Korean mothers and investigates how they define what their children need and how they utilize resources in child-rearing.

In this chapter, I first give an overview of the literature on social class and child-rearing, paying attention to the role maternal education and resources play in making and remaking divergent parenting practices. Then, the Korean context is addressed, focusing on early childhood education and exploring why it is important to examine mothers in order to understand the source of disparities in early childhood education. Following the context section, I introduce the data and methodology used in this chapter and explain how the research is designed to answer questions about whether—and, if so, how and why—less-educated mothers' child-rearing approaches and practices diverge from those of highly educated mothers. Last, based on the findings from the analysis, I show the interplay between aspirations, information gap, and economic constraints to explain how child-rearing approaches diverge based on maternal education. In the end, I propose that accounting for the process of mobilizing and sorting information related to education for preschool children may yield a more accurate explanation of how mothers' educational background becomes the source for divergent child-rearing approaches.

Background

Socioeconomic Disparities in Early Childhood Education

In all postindustrial societies, the socioeconomic background of parents plays a significant role in the educational outcomes of children (Bornstein and Bradley 2014). Although public interventions and changes in family structure over the life course influence the academic lives of children, there is a growing consensus that disparities in education based on family background begin in early childhood (Hart and Risley 2003). Scholars trace socioeconomic disparities in early childhood education in part to financial, social, cultural, and cognitive resources available in families (Bourdieu 1973; Grusky 1994). In *Unequal Childhoods* (2011), Lareau provides rich ethnographic data that demonstrate how divergent child-rearing approaches emerge based on family background. According to Lareau, compared to lower-class parents, middle- and upper-class parents treat their children as adults and as developmental projects. Middle- and upper-class parents engage in concerted cultivation, a set of structured activities that promote skills, behaviors, and attitudes that in the long term lead to greater academic success for their children. In contrast, lower-class parents emphasize discipline or strict rules, and their child-rearing strategies are based on the notion of accomplishment of natural growth, which requires much less parental involvement in children's daily lives.

After *Unequal Childhoods* was published, researchers investigating the transmission of educational advantage increasingly focused on the active role of parents and their parenting styles. However, such attention provoked a debate about the underlying mechanisms that produce the class gradient in extracurricular activities, in particular, in nonacademic activities such as sports, arts, and music. On the one hand, scholars of the line of the literature consistent with Lareau (2011) argue that the relationship between parents' class background and the particular strategy of enrolling children in organized nonacademic activities is shaped by distinctive cultural understandings. Some argue that middle-class parenting focuses more on nonacademic areas, approaching their own children as educational and developmental projects (Vincent and Ball 2007). On the other hand, other scholars argue that family differences in material resources and objective circumstances (i.e., access to institutions) produce distinctive child-rearing patterns (Bennett, Lutz, and Jayaram 2012; Chin and Phillips 2004), suggesting that how parents think about child-rearing is only minimally important.

This ongoing debate over whether soft resources (i.e., cultural beliefs and approaches) have more explanatory power than hard resources (i.e., material and institutional resources) for divergent child-rearing practices, however, misses two important points. First, within existing literature, it is not clear how parents' resources, such as human capital, information, knowledge, and personal and social ties that help to accumulate knowledge and information, fit in child-rearing. When knowledge and information are acquired through cultural upbringing, what you know represents a form of cultural understanding. However, when specific information about a way to educate children (e.g., a well-respected tutor for private education) is shared through social or personal ties, it is not clear whether such information is the result of parents' cultural understandings or financial resources. Also, information obtained from teachers or peer parents is highly contingent on neighborhood or school (Small 2009) and thus is a product of both the parents' social ties and organizations. Therefore, we can further extend our understanding of how families shape disparities in children's private education by going beyond the dichotomy of cultural understanding versus material resources and by mapping various resources including cultural beliefs, material resources, social resources, and information.

The second key point is that existing studies have not fully acknowledged how maternal—relatively more so than paternal—background is an important indicator of social position, one that is particularly relevant for early childhood education. This is worth noting because in most postindustrial societies, mothers are expected to engage in "intensive mothering"—defined by Hays (1998) as a logically cohesive combination of beliefs dictating that a mother must be the central caregiver who devotes copious amounts of time, energy, and material resources to the child—a claim supported by the fact that mothers spend relatively more time in childcare compared to fathers (OECD 2016). Negative views toward employment of mothers with young children persist even in countries where a majority of women participate in the workforce (Jacobs and Gerson 2016). Furthermore, in countries where women tend to leave the workforce during childbearing or child-rearing years (such as Japan and

Korea, where fewer than 60 percent of women ages 30 to 39 are in the workforce), household income is not an accurate measurement of parental resources. For these reasons, I consider maternal education as a potential key driver for different types of education that children receive.

Maternal Education, Child-Rearing Approaches, and Early Childhood Education

Those studies in the sociology of education that rely primarily on data from American families have demonstrated that maternal education plays an especially significant role in the educational outcomes of children and adolescents (Lareau and Weininger 2008; Weininger, Lareau, and Conley 2015). However, the underlying logic of how and why maternal education has such a strong influence on the kinds of education that children receive has not been adequately explored. Several explanations have been offered to explain how maternal education can shape different child-rearing styles and cause disparities in early childhood education. They are not mutually exclusive but are instead related. First, when mothers have more education, they likely have larger vocabularies; as a result, their children are likely to be exposed to larger lexical choices, and the children are likely to develop greater lexical range (Hart and Risley 2003). Second, connecting the parenting approach with early childhood education, Lareau (2011) argues that mothers' different approaches and perceptions about what the child needs lead highly educated mothers to invest more time and money in children's participation in various nonacademic activities outside of a formal curriculum. Third, Ramey and Ramey (2009) demonstrate how mothers with higher education anticipate their children will attain higher education, so they are more likely to invest in activities in early childhood that can have long-term payoffs in the academic world. Last, scholars argue that there might be variations in the personal networks of families with highly educated mothers. This explanation (Weininger, Lareau, and Conley 2015) assumes that personal ties relate to unobservable resources such as information or cultural ideas; however, this assumption remains untested and does not clarify how information is different from cultural ideas.

Despite the salient nature of the topic and persistent interest in exploring the mechanisms by which families, particularly mothers, influence unequal childhood education, empirical evidence testing these hypotheses and exploring other underlying mechanisms is still thin. In particular, there exists a big gap in the literature about how maternal education shapes acquired knowledge and information about early childhood education. Information acquisition is a product of various resources, such as mothers' human, social, and cultural resources and those provided by formal organizations such as daycare centers (Small 2009). Such assessment of information and knowledge is found to be salient in providing education for young children, but how maternal education shapes such process is underexplored in the existing literature.

Maternal Education and Child-Rearing in the Korean Context

There are two main reasons why Korea is a compelling case in which to explore the interplay between maternal education, information acquisition, and disparities in the education that young children receive. First, despite having a good reputation for high achievement and having the highest educational attainment level in the world, for both men and women (OECD 2015), the education that Korean children receive from their parents persists to be unequal (Byun, Schofer, and Kim 2012; Park and Abelmann 2004; Park 2006; Park, Byun, and Kim 2011). The standardized educational system plays a structural role in widening the overall academic achievement gap of students (Park 2013), and currently, the Korean educational system focuses heavily on test preparation. In this context, forms of cultural capital, especially children's attendance in activities of classical culture such as opera, ballet, or classical symphony orchestra have a relatively small effect on academic achievement (Byun, Schofer, and Kim 2012). Rather, children have experienced increasing disparity in the supplemental education they receive to prepare for academic subjects and standardized tests. Park, Byun, and Kim (2011) found that parents' active selection and monitoring of private tutoring for middle school students increased math and English scores. Additionally, Park and Abelmann (2004) showed that English acquisition is often identified as the marker of unequal education because both the desire and the opportunity to learn English diverge as a result of the family's socioeconomic status.

Second, Korea is an especially good case through which to explore how maternal education shapes mothers' child-rearing perceptions and practices. The division of labor in contemporary Korean society is highly unequal and gender based. Korea is a postindustrial society, often described as a compressed modern country because of the rapid pace of economic, political, and social transformation that occurred from the 1960s to the 1980s (Chang 2010). One of the most rapid structural changes that occurred was educational expansion, a growth that included women. In

2012, 8 percent of the female population between the ages of 55 and 64 had a college education or more, compared to 69 percent of the female population between the ages of 25 and 34 (OECD 2012). Despite the increase in educational attainment level and in female labor force participation, Korean mothers are still expected to engage in intensive motherhood (Park 2006; Park and Abelmann 2004). Embedded in the culturally rewarding system of educating children from an early age (Seth 2002), Korean women become managers of their children's lives to sustain their own and their children's status (Lett 1998; Park 2006). Survey and interview data show that mothers identify with their children and fulfill their own dreams and life goals vicariously through them (Park and Abelmann 2004; Lett 1998). However, a uniform image of Korean mothers as strong, obsessive about their children's education, and willing to sacrifice their own needs for their children produces an empirical gap in understanding the variation. Few studies in the literature examine *how* Korean mothers engage in child-rearing and *how* their educational background shapes their child-rearing approaches. Therefore, by moving beyond a uniform image of Korean mothers as education-obsessed parents and by exploring commonalities and differences among different types of mothers, I aim to map the interplay between mothers' resources, perceptions, and actual practices.

Data and Methods

This study mainly uses qualitative interview data and relies on an interactive process of inductive insights and deductive analysis (Glaser, Strauss, and Strutzel 1967). Although a limited sample size and case-based approaches make it hard to draw general inferences about large populations, qualitative data using a ground approach can uncover and interpret constellations of forces that change or reproduce social processes (Ragin 1987). To conduct structured interviews by preparing a questionnaire that can grasp respondents' rationale and ideas, I used an online survey. Thus, there are in total two sources of data: One is an online survey with 1,100 mothers who are married with at least one preschool child, and the other is a data set of 98 in-depth interviews.

Online Survey

Using Ovey, a top online and smartphone app-based survey company that has access to over 350,000 respondents as their survey panel, I requested a survey be conducted with a group from their panel. The sample, therefore, was a nonrandom convenient sample. I asked 17 questions related to perceptions and behaviors of child-rearing to mothers who are married, have at least one preschool child, and live in Seoul or surrounding areas. To find a coherent commonality within a diverse group with a limited number of respondents, I restricted my sample for both the online survey and the in-depth interviews to Seoul and surrounding areas. Because the goal of this study is to explore whether mothers with different educational backgrounds engage in distinctive child-rearing, I incorporated mothers with diverse household incomes, employment statuses, and educational attainment levels.

The online survey was conducted in the spring of 2015.[1] A majority of participants in the online survey were in their 30s (78 percent), and the rest were divided into those in their 20s (10 percent) and in their 40s (12 percent). They were divided into four different categories based on educational background. Based on the highest educational attainment level completed, 25 percent graduated from high school, 35 percent graduated from two-year college, 34 percent graduated from four-year college, and 6 percent had a graduate degree. In terms of employment status, 40 percent were currently not employed, whereas 60 percent were currently participating in the workforce with varying employment statuses (i.e., full-time, part-time, or self-employed).

The online survey asked how they defined a good parent, what they saw as the most important resources when raising a child in Korea, by what means they obtained such resources, where mothers accessed knowledge about children's education, and what kind of information they trusted. As table 2.1 shows, responses to the survey clearly showed that mothers considered money and information as the most important resources when raising a child in the Korean context. More specifically, there were several sources evenly mentioned as important when gathering information, including internet search engines, the internet community, books or articles written by professionals, friends or colleagues, and other mothers. Also, mothers' own accumulated experiences of trial and error were considered to be the most important skill in sorting and searching for information for almost all mothers except for those with graduate degrees, who said that their skills obtained through education and workplaces were utilized the most. Last, when asked, "Who do you think is a better mother than yourself?" many mentioned mothers who have a lot of money. Interestingly, employed mothers pointed to stay-at-home mothers and stay-at-home mothers pointed to employed mothers as mothers who are better than themselves.

TABLE 2.1. Summary of Responses from Online Survey

		Highest level of education			
	Total	High school	2-yr college	4-yr college	Graduate school
Total (N)	1,100	275	385	377	63

Q. What is the most important thing when raising children in Korea?

(answers in percentage)	Total	HS	2-yr	4-yr	Graduate
Money	45	47	50	41	35
Information	12	12	11	11	17
Neighborhood (school district)	3	4	3	3	2
Physical ability	8	7	7	10	8
My own standards and opinion	13	11	11	16	14
Patience	19	18	18	19	24
Other	0	1	0	0	0
Total (%)	100	100	100	100	100

Q. When raising your child(ren), which information source do you trust the most?

(answers in percentage)	Total	HS	2-yr	4-yr	Graduate
Internet (Google, Daum, Naver)	17	18	20	14	13
Internet café (community) or blog	16	12	17	16	19
Books or articles by professionals	20	15	18	25	24
My parents or parents-in-law	9	10	11	8	6
Friends or colleagues	23	29	21	22	21
Other mothers	14	13	13	14	17
Other	1	3	0	1	0
Total (%)	100	100	100	100	100

Q. In your opinion, how do you think you have obtained your ability to sort through the abundant information about childcare?

(answers in percentage)	Total	HS	2-yr	4-yr	Graduate
From schools that I attended	4	3	2	5	17
From working experience (outside home)	20	21	18	18	30
From my own trial and error	65	63	70	66	37
From natal family members	10	12	8	10	14
Other	1	2	1	1	2
Total (%)	100	100	100	100	100

Q. Who do you think are better moms than yourself? (Multiple answers possible)

(answers in absolute number)	Total	HS	2-yr	4-yr	Graduate
I cannot think of better mothers than myself	201	39	65	83	14
Working mothers	217	58	81	68	11
Stay-at-home mothers	345	80	131	109	25
Mothers with high educational level	180	63	62	45	10
Mothers who have a lot of money	377	88	135	132	22
Other	162	41	54	57	10
Total (N)	1,482	369	528	494	92

The online survey reveals three patterns that helped me construct my in-depth interview questions and choose sample groups to compare. First, the responses of high school graduates and two-year-college graduates were largely similar. The responses of four-year university graduates and those with graduate degrees differed from the responses of those with less education on a few important questions, such as the use of skills obtained from the public sphere (school and workplace) and a greater emphasis on information than on money as the salient resource for child-rearing in Korea. This led to a focus on recruiting three groups of mothers for the in-depth interviews: high school and two-year college graduates, four-year university graduates, and graduate degree holders. Second, money and information were both considered important resources for child-rearing. To build on this descriptive finding, some of the questions in the in-depth interviews were aimed at understanding the contexts in which money and information became important. Last, it was not clear from the online survey whether mothers' approaches to child-rearing and their use of information and money were influenced by their employment status. Based on such preliminary observation, I diversified the employment status of mothers in my sample.

In-Depth Interview Design

For in-depth interviews, I used two sampling strategies to recruit 98 interviewees, who are the main source of analysis for the results section. First, with an aim to interview 50 mothers from different neighborhoods and with varied ages, work histories, and educational attainment levels, I randomly selected 80 interviewees from the sample of 1,100 mothers who answered the online survey. After contacting them, the response rate was 62 percent, and thus I met with 50 mothers in total. To minimize the unobservable bias of the online survey panel, including the possibility that those who respond to online surveys might share similar personal characteristics of being active in searching online or in sharing their views, I recruited another 48 interviewees through my personal ties using a restricted snowball sampling strategy where one respondent could be a referral for only up to two interviewees. Two interviewees were going through a divorce, so I removed them from my sample because I did not have enough individuals to represent single mothers.

I interviewed all 98 mothers face-to-face in 2015, and the interviews lasted from 60 minutes to more than two hours, with the majority taking about 90 minutes. Interviews were semi-structured; I prepared 40 questions based on five large themes: (1) experiences of professional achievements and work pathways; (2) definitions of ideal motherhood and childhood; (3) aspirations related to children's achievement and perceptions about what is needed for children at the preschool stage; (4) personal ties, informants, and mothers with whom respondents interact and those whom they ask for information and opinions; and (5) children's daily schedules. I began each interview by administering a structured questionnaire. Questions were organized to ask events in a chronological order to avoid potential rationalization of the past based on present decisions.

Study Participants

The 98 respondents were from urban areas (in and around Seoul), and their ages ranged from 25 to 45, a range in which mothers make key decisions about work and family. The mean age was about 31, and the average ages at first marriage and first childbirth were almost identical to the national averages: the average age at first marriage for women in 2013 was 29, and the average age at first childbirth was 30 (retrieved from Statistics Korea 2015). Twenty-eight mothers held a graduate degree, 38 held a bachelor's degree, and 32 were high school or two-year college graduates. Throughout this chapter, I use the phrase *less-educated mothers* to refer to the 32 mothers who are high school or two-year college graduates and *highly educated mothers* to refer to the 66 mothers with at least a bachelor's degree. At the time of the interview, 32 percent were nonemployed, 49 percent worked full-time, and 19 percent were freelancers, part-time employees, or self-employed. Last, the median monthly household income was US$5,850 for all respondents, US$4,285 for the less-educated group, and US$7,120 for the highly educated group.[2]

Analysis

The main source of data for this study is transcriptions of the 98 in-depth interviews. After coding basic background information on the respondents using Excel, I carefully reviewed all the transcripts multiple times to inductively identify themes. Based on qualitative methodologies proposed by Emerson (2001) and Lofland and Lofland (2006), which suggested several steps of coding to construct an elaborate conceptual framing of what is happening on the ground (Emerson 2001: 282), I used three steps for coding. For the first step, I organized the data under five primary themes: (a) definition of ideal motherhood (including descriptions of other mothers whom the respondent respects and overall perceptions of good and successful mothers); (b) views about what they expect from their children; (c) their children's daily schedules; (d) descriptions of their core information network and how they acquire information about how best to educate their children; and (e) explanations of how their own education and employment relate to how they approach child-rearing.

In the second step I used a focused coding strategy. I selectively coded line by line (Lofland and Lofland 2006: 202) to understand respondents' views, rationales, and behaviors and also to find core ideas. For the theme of deciding how to educate a child, I wrote a separate memo for each respondent to examine how she constructed her opinions and how she came to trust particular information and institutions.[3]

For the third step, I wrote a list of conceptual framings to capture processes that respondents went through and to pinpoint the core mechanism that differentiated their strategies. Based on the third step, I organized the section of findings below.

Findings

The analysis reveals three important patterns that extend our understanding of the relationship between maternal education and child-rearing for mothers in my sample. First, although Korean mothers across different educational attainment levels share similar beliefs toward ideal childhood and agree with the kind of education a child needs before entering school, a difference in the realization of their aspirations emerges. The second pattern demonstrates how human capital and social ties shape how mothers mobilize and utilize information differently. In the end, two different child-rearing approaches, which I call *horizontal diversification* and *vertical cultivation*, emerge as strategies that mothers used when providing education for their children. The third pattern is another consequence of different levels of resources: the emotional fluctuations that mothers experience that reinforce the diverging approaches toward child-rearing.

Korean Mothers Engaging in Collective Concerted Cultivation: Motivation and Rationale

Notably, all mothers in my sample, regardless of education or employment status, express that they generally feel extreme pressure to engage in intensive child-rearing. Min (employed, high school graduate) represents this perspective: "As a mother, you are always expected to take full, 100-percent care of your child, including developmental issues, education that needs to be provided, and overall well-being." In particular, although almost all mothers wish their children to simply have a happy childhood, mothers emphasize the importance of providing education in order for their children to survive in Korea. Jin (non-employed, BA) explains this aspect: "This country is a jungle when it comes to educating your children. You would expect you could just feed your [very young] child and that is the end, but no, you have to start early on. You have to know at what stage it is best to start teaching your child how to speak and write. There is so much to do to make your child survive in this jungle."

Under strong pressure to focus on child-rearing, mothers spend a substantial amount of physical, mental, and emotional energy on it, in particular, on finding appropriate programs for both academic and nonacademic subjects. Because all mothers in this study have children who had not yet entered school, one of the main issues they talk about is the future choice of a school or schools. Mothers draw on various sources of information about the quality of potential elementary schools, of which there was a wide—and sometimes confusing—variety. Hŭiju (employed part-time, BA) explains her preparation process: "Nowadays, whenever there is a family gathering, we talk about my daughter's [future] elementary school. My husband and I are not really satisfied with the public schools in our neighborhood, so we searched for innovative public schools." Hŭiju and her husband do not trust the public schools because of the schools' lack of creative teaching and diverse curricula. Their daughter is an active girl who learned through playing and interacting, so Hŭiju searched for schools that were innovative in teaching style and curriculum. At the top of her list was a school that focused on a debate style of teaching: "This school gets funding from the government but has full control over its organization of time and content. Usually, one class is two hours long, but the break is 30 minutes long. They do a lot of experimentation and play when they teach science and math concepts." Asked how she had learned about this school, she echoes what many of the mothers emphasize, which is the hard work mothers put into searching: "It is all about searching for information and asking around."

Employed mothers also spend copious time and energy in searching for good information. As a working mother, Saerom (employed, graduate degree) was looking for a private elementary school where her son could stay until 3:00 p.m.; public schools—in particular, for first graders—typically end around noon. She explains that talking with her colleagues who are parents, with her sister-in-law, and with her best friend from high school has made her aware that private schools vary a lot. When we met, she had narrowed her options down to three private schools, each with its own philosophy, and one public school that had diverse after-school programs. Represented by Saerom, the process of searching and listing continues until mothers finally find the right fit for their children: "There are so many unknown factors, such as friends, teachers, and learning programs. I will see how it goes, but just in case my son has a hard time adjusting, I am compiling information about which schools are good." For each subject or activity that mothers wanted their children to learn—math, reading, sports, and so on—they mobilize as large and diverse a body of information as they can.

Both employed and non-employed mothers, regardless of their educational attainment background, almost always use the phrase "the power of information" as they describe the motivation for their intensive daily searching. Table 2.2 shows the average hours spent per week on caretaking, according to mothers' employment status and level of education. Taking care of children included not only feeding them, playing with them, and driving them around, but also spending time searching for information on educational programs and specific institutions that provide education. Although overall time spent with children is lower for full-time employed mothers than for part-time employed and non-employed mothers, the time spent searching for information about what education to provide for children is similar for all the mothers. Most mothers, on average, spend one hour per day on searching, and this was only slightly higher for mothers with more education.

TABLE 2.2. Average Time Spent on Childcare by Mother's Employment and Educational Attainment Level

	Employment	
	Employed (full-time and part-time)	Non-employed
Number of hours spent daily with children (feeding, playing, and providing rides)		
Highly educated	1–2 hours	3–7 hours
Less educated	1–3 hours	2–8 hours
Average time spent daily on one's own searching for information about what to provide one's children		
Highly educated	60 minutes	70 minutes
Less educated	50 minutes	60 minutes

Notably, mothers are frustrated that their own standards for what kinds of academic and nonacademic skills their children should acquire before entering school did not matter as much as the presumed skills and knowledge of the other children with whom their own children would be interacting—and competing—once they were in school. Mothers feel enormous pressure to find out what other kids were doing and to prepare their children academically and nonacademically (mainly through sports, music, and art) to match the other kids. As Yena (employed, graduate degree) explains, mothers' rationale behind collectively engaging in intensive mothering is that they did not want to risk their children's self-esteem:

> YENA: I really did not want my child to start memorizing English words from the age of four. I just wanted him to play and do nothing [academically]. However, all the elementary schools will be full of kids who already know how to speak English. I heard that only 10 percent of first graders are unable to speak English. Within the current system, it is impossible to follow your own philosophy, because then you are risking your child's life.
>
> INTERVIEWER: What do you mean when you say you are risking the child's life?
>
> YENA: Well, the cost of maintaining my ideal image of what my children's childhood should be, which is just freely playing and not studying, is my child's self-esteem. As soon as he becomes one of the 10 percent who cannot say a word [in English] when he enters elementary school, he will feel like a loser. I am not worried about his English-speaking skills. I am worried about him feeling like he is far behind on the first day of school. I mean, the [social] pressure is real.

However, despite the commonly held ideas regarding a list of skill sets expected among children and the role of mothers in helping their children attain them, the *means* for acquiring these skills differ greatly. The mother's agency is mainly dedicated to specific ways to provide the necessary opportunities. As Ari (non-employed, high school graduate) explains, the key question was not "What do I need to provide for my children?" but "How do I provide all the skills that my child needs before entering school?" This was the point at which the strategies of mothers with different levels of education diverge.

Diverging Child-Rearing Approaches

Different Ways of Mobilizing and Sorting Information

In realizing the desire to fulfill what children need, one valuable, and often priceless, resource plays a salient role for mothers in this study: information. What is distinguishable among mothers is how—with whom and how frequently—they interact with each other and how mothers with different experiences and embodied skills (i.e., searching, sorting, or coding skills) utilize their skills in gathering information. Table 2.3 summarizes the coherent difference in how mothers searched for and mobilized information based on their educational background.

First, experiences and skills that mothers accumulate in the public sphere shape the process of searching for and sorting information. All mothers describe their frequent usage of a portal website (e.g., Google) and those online communities with abundant information about local institutions. As Sina, a high school graduate with two children (the older one turned four in the year of the interview), explains, the easiest option for mothers to search for information and to validate existing information is to use a computer or phone. However, on top of the default option of using popular portal sites, highly educated mothers utilize their searching and analyzing skills learned from college and workplaces. Ch'orong, who had a three-year-old daughter, often got into fights with her husband about what kinds of books to read to their daughter at a certain age. Tired of fighting every day and of reading all different sorts of opinions on the internet, she and her husband decided to get a second opinion from one of the top-cited child development journals. They now do their research using JSTOR, a digital library, and KISS, a search site for journals published in Korea, to find expert opinions. Almost always, highly educated mothers apply more diverse means to obtain and validate information compared to less-educated mothers. As a result, highly educated mothers emphasize that they end up with different opinions and diverse information, whereas less-educated mothers stress the fact that other mothers to whom they are close usually share similar ideas and information.

Also, how mothers acquire information and knowledge through social and personal ties differs. Ties that are mentioned include grandparents, spouses, friends, relatives, colleagues, neighbors, and other mothers in the neighborhood or from daycare centers to whom they become very close. Although all mothers mobilize information from as many informants as they could find, the ways in which mothers use accumulated social and personal ties are different based on the mothers' educational background. Less-educated mothers dominantly focus on using fewer ties and new ties that they formed after becoming mothers. In contrast, highly educated mothers mix their accumulated ties (ties that they had until motherhood) and new ties (ties that they formed after becoming mothers).

Among the existing ties that highly educated mothers utilize to obtain information, familial ties are also included. Kyuri, who has a bachelor's degree, said her mother (a public school teacher) interacts often with other mothers from the kindergarten to exchange information about her granddaughter's education. Grandmothers would go to parents' meetings when employed mothers could not attend and would interact with other mothers, asking for information about the best ways to learn particular subjects such as math and what strategies other mothers used.

Notably, the different composition of the informants and mobilized information is not divided categorically (into few versus abundant) but

TABLE 2.3. Summary of the Information Searching and Mobilizing Process

Dimension observed	Pattern 1	Pattern 2
Key elements	Mother mobilizes new and previously accumulated knowledge and information	Mother mobilizes new knowledge and information
Searching process	Through Naver or Google, online communities, best-seller books written by experts, JSTOR or KISS (websites for scholarly articles), and reports written by doctors	Through Naver or Google, online communities, and best-seller books written by experts
Informal and formal ties	Siblings, relatives, spouses, grandparents (both sides), friends from school, colleagues, and other mothers whom they become friends with after becoming mothers.	Siblings, relatives, and other mothers whom they become friends with after becoming mothers.
Information redundancy	Low	High
Consequences	Diverse options, opinions, and information	Relatively less diverse options, opinions, and information
Composition	Mainly highly educated mothers	Mainly less-educated mothers

continuously (fewer versus more) based on the educational background of mothers. For instance, even among the highly educated group, mothers with a graduate degree have more diverse ties to utilize as their informants than do mothers with a bachelor's degree.

One example highlighting the different patterns in the ways mothers used their ties was when they gathered information about the medical and developmental issues of their children: Less-educated mothers ask other mothers whose children share a similar issue, or they visit doctors for consultation. On the other hand, highly educated mothers dominantly use their ties to find experts with whom they had mutual friends or social ties (e.g., colleagues and husbands' colleagues). As Inyŏng, a mother enrolled in an MBA program, says, "I felt like my daughter was slow to speak. She seems to understand things quickly, but she was really slow in expressing her feelings and thoughts through speech. I was getting worried, so I talked with a pediatrician, who said nothing was wrong. For a second opinion, I called another pediatrician, who was the husband of my sister's best friend." It is not uncommon for highly educated mothers to utilize multiple informants to gather more and diverse opinions about their children's well-being.

These variations in the process of mobilizing information and in the composition of informants result in different levels of diversity of and amounts of information. For example, for each subject or activity (e.g., math, reading, or sports), highly educated mothers go through a process of mobilizing as much diverse and abundant information as they can. They dominantly focus on gathering a variety of options to ensure their children's education is appropriate. The following section addresses how this difference interacted with mothers' economic situations to produce diverging child-rearing approaches.

Information, Financial Resources, and Diverging Approaches

How mothers utilize existing information in arranging their children's everyday schedules is closely related to the economic constraints they face. Such interaction—between the information and the financial resources—causes child-rearing approaches of mothers with different educational backgrounds to diverge into two categories, which I label *horizontal diversification* and *vertical cultivation*. Horizontal diversification refers to an approach where mothers try their best to prepare various options for each activity or subject area to find a means of education that fits best with the child, while vertical cultivation refers to an approach where mothers focus on investing in only a few activities to efficiently use limited information and financial resources.

Table 2.4 illustrates the main patterns of the two approaches. The horizontal diversification approach primarily is found from highly educated mothers who have access to diverse options and resources (information, money, and social ties). They have multiple options for each criterion that they defined as being necessary for their children, and most of them have financial resources to try multiple options until they could find the right fit for their child. Criteria include finding the right neighborhoods, specific schools, channels to information about schools, and private education to support academic and nonacademic subjects. The mothers aim to embrace their children's tastes, temperaments, and talents to raise self-

TABLE 2.4. Summary of Differences in Child-Rearing Approaches

Dimension observed	Horizontal diversification	Vertical cultivation
Key elements	Mother has diverse options and interprets that the child needs to be above average with diverse skills.	Mother chooses one or two subjects early on to invest in and tries her best to ensure her children obtain appropriate skills.
Focus of investment	Spends a lot of money and time trying different institutions.	Large *proportion* of income is invested in children's education, but it is hard to invest in various institutes for one subject, and it is hard to invest in multiple subjects.
Choosing institutions	Intensive information gathering; choosing from a wide range of options for every subject; choosing several.	Intensive information gathering; choosing a few institutions to provide learning opportunities.
Communication with the child	Tries many things and engages in interactive and responsive processes to find what kind of educational style best fits the child.	Compares a few options, finalizes the choice based on the child's behaviors, then tries to make the child get the most out of the institute.
Composition	91 percent of highly educated mothers	94 percent of less-educated mothers
Median number of institute (child aged 4–6)	5	3
Median number of programs (child aged 1–3)	4	1

motivated children who would be above average across diverse subjects and activities. Their rationale behind such a goal is that children must be self-motivated and have basic skills in both academic and nonacademic activities in order to have options as they grow up and to have a happy life in the long run.

The vertical cultivation strategy, in contrast, is utilized mostly by mothers with less education and more economic constraints. Less-educated mothers also invest a large proportion of their household income as well as physical, mental, and emotional labor in educating their children. These mothers give top priority to educating their children and maximizing support for their children's well-being and achievement. While these mothers also engage in similarly intense child-rearing in terms of time, energy, and emotional investment, compared to mothers with more education and higher income, they have a narrower range of information and fewer options in terms of schools and neighborhoods. The strategy for them is to choose one or two activities or skills that a child could focus on and succeed at. These women see investing in multiple activities or skills as a useless tactic; rather, they feel it is more efficient to find subjects that a child liked and was good at and focus on them.

Revisiting the issue of school choice, many less-educated mothers stress that for elementary school, their role was to support their children within the given situation. Aram, a 31-year-old high school graduate with a 4-year-old daughter, argues,

> Of course, I am stressed out about the fact that our neighborhood is not the best place for my daughter's education. But, I think it is better to be the head of a snake than the tail of a dragon. I can't afford to live in *Gangnam* [in the southern part of Seoul, known for its affluent residents] or *Mokdong* [in the northwest part of Seoul, known as the mecca for education in the northern region], but even if I moved to those places, borrowing money from the bank, my daughter won't be getting as much private education as other kids. Then, she will fall behind, a lot. My child will just try to follow what rich kids are doing but will never be able to be in the top of that group. I would rather raise a child who can be happy as a big fish in a smaller pond.

Several mothers echo her point, but this does not mean that they would give up on searching for a good school or that they would just send their children anywhere.

In relation to the aspiration to raise a big fish in a smaller pond rather than a small fish in a bigger pond, less-educated mothers concentrate on finding a public school that could augment the talent and skills that their children already excelled in compared to other kids. Pureum, a 38-year-old mother of a 5-year-old daughter, exemplifies this process:

> You do not have to invest in three or four things and send your children to four different institutions and a private elementary school. One thing a mother needs to remember is to discover her child's talent. Every child is good at one or two things and they shine when they are doing certain things. It is unlikely that there will be four or five areas that my daughter will excel in.

Pureum dislikes the idea of sending her daughter to multiple institutions and to schools that focused on many subjects with various methods. She strongly believes that if a child is good at sports or drawing, parents should guide them to grow in that field instead of investing in all subjects. Mirroring her perspective, T'aein, a 32-year-old mother with two sons, explains that when her first son turned 10, she could tell that he was good at sports and therefore needed to focus on more nonacademic activities. Her second son, who would enter school the next year, already had been showing some talent in math and science. She explains, "You can make a rough estimation about your child's temperament, skills, and interests from an early age. My two sons are very different, so I paid careful attention to find what I needed to provide for them." Providing a customized education for each child was most important when choosing schools, so T'aein decided to send her second child to a different public school with fewer hours spent on sports, art, and music and more hours spent on the academic curriculum.

In the case of English education, highly educated mothers approach the issue of English education with one goal in mind—motivating the child to like learning a new language so that the child could study with self-will—whereas less-educated mothers often try their best to monitor their children's homework after finding an institution with a good reputation. There is a long and ongoing process of searching, listing, and comparing many options among highly educated mothers, and this process fulfilled their desire to encourage children to be self-motivated and excited to study English. Mothers with less education, economic constraints, and the lack of information end up sending their children to a nearby institution and focusing on observing whether their children performed well there.

Notably, issues of providing education in reading, math, and nonacademic activities also follow a similarly coherent pathway based on mothers' backgrounds. Mothers are always trying their best to provide the most appropriate style of curriculum for their children. However, the interplay between the goal of raising a self-motivated child and having diverse options to ensure the right fit is frequently utilized by highly educated mothers. Less-educated mothers are as considerate and concentrate on providing the maximum support for their children's education and spend roughly one-third of their household income on educating their children. A majority of mothers try hard to sit down with their children and help them perform well (such as finishing homework on time). At the center of their diligent monitoring is their belief that if their children invested their time and energy in studying, they would excel in each subject.

In sum, the horizontal diversification approach is used mostly among highly educated mothers to find the perfect fit for the child. In this approach, their children would be exposed to diverse subjects and activities and could excel at many of them. In contrast, vertical cultivation is used among less-educated mothers to raise happy and satisfied children who could find their talent and skill for a smaller number of subjects and activities that the children are interested in and could excel at.

Emotional Consequences of the Different Pools of Information and Informants

Besides the two different approaches toward child-rearing, there are emotional aspects. The magnitude of fear and anxiety is not equivalent across mothers with different educational attainment levels. Prior experiences, feelings, and assessments of the Korean educational system as well as the number of sources are never uniform across mothers. Mothers had divergent educational trajectories, and levels of confidence toward the Korean educational system vary.

In general, highly educated mothers express more confidence than other mothers and felt that their children would do fine. Although highly educated mothers also say that they are stressed about providing education and raising a child in the Korean context, they are not as anxious about their children's future as were less-educated mothers. Min argues, "We prepare as much as we can, including for problems that might happen, and then when unexpected issues come up, we again try our best to find the most appropriate way to solve the issue." Highly educated mothers seem to always have various options to choose from, which are the result of having a combination of more money and more information.

Contrary to how highly educated mothers lessen their anxiety by listing multiple options as part of their method for reacting immediately to problems and preparing solutions, less-educated mothers express that they are passionate about educating their children but simultaneously very anxious when they thought about their children's future. Their consistent anxiety is about whether they are doing the right thing for their children and whether their efforts would pay off. Often, they feel that they depend too much on their children's opinion or on what their children's friends are doing. They express the desire to provide better opportunities for their children compared to what they received from their natal parents, but they are not sure if they are doing a great job because other mothers always seem to be more knowledgeable about education than they were. If they did not have a chance to learn a subject such as English as a young child, and if they interpreted this as one of the reasons they did not do well in the Korean educational system, they try to make sure that their children would not experience the same. However, throughout the process of investigating and choosing which book or institution to utilize, they express how they often feel unsure whether the education they are providing through private institutions was beneficial to their children. They describe that this is mainly because there are so many ways to educate their children, but because they were never the smartest kids in school, they often feel lost while trying to identify the best options for their own children. Overall, less-educated mothers explain that although they are trying not to be depressed about it every day, they are indeed concerned about their children's success in acquiring necessary skills.

Mothers' emotional state is related to their relationship with their children because they provide educational resources and interact with their children daily. Highly educated mothers set their main goal for early childhood education to ensure that their children became self-motivated when studying and engaging in activities. Mothers emphasize that if children were not engaging in activities according to their own will, all the extra educational effort is useless. Their overall confidence about their ability to find the right kind of education style that would suit their children's traits ironically leads them to be patient and engaging with what their children want.

Distinctive patterns emerge among mothers with less education. Mothers are anxious about their children's future despite their efforts and huge investments in children's education. Whenever their children miss classes or fail to finish their homework, they become emotionally and mentally stressed out because they feel like their endeavors to provide a good education have failed. Mothers describe how, while monitoring their children, they would yell at their children or threaten them with not sending them to the institution in the future. Mothers express their mixed feelings about the need to scold their children. In describing children's attitudes toward homework and academic activities, less-educated mothers address how their children were not yet motivated. Therefore, they try to check every day whether their children had finished their daily requirements. In comparison to highly educated mothers, who describe how their interactions with their children are centered on checking their children's motivation in each activity, less-educated mothers' interactions with their children are more focused on making sure that their children finish their assignments and successfully follow the curriculum.

In sum, the two divergent child-rearing styles lead to different emotional states on the mothers' side. Highly educated mothers are relatively more confident that their children would do fine regardless of the exact combination of out-of-school activities, whereas less-educated mothers express significant anxiety. These emotional states are related to how mothers interact with their children emotionally and behaviorally on a daily basis. One style—for highly educated mothers—focuses more on prioritizing the relationship between the mother and the child while encouraging self-motivation, and the other style—for less-educated mothers—focuses more on helping the child get the most out of the education that the mothers have provided. In the end, the two different child-rearing approaches appear to lead to two types of children: one type self-motivated but less pressured and the other less motivated but more pressured.

Discussion

Using qualitative methodology, this study shows how divergent child-rearing strategies based on maternal education derive from different processes for mobilizing and utilizing information. Findings show that when mothers have higher educational attainment, they are more likely to use their own experience of surviving in the competitive educational system and are more likely to have diverse social and personal ties to mobilize information. In comparison, less-educated mothers try their best to provide maximum support by searching for new information and purposefully forming new ties with other mothers and experts to gather information. The different levels of human and social capital that mothers accumulated and mobilized resulted in the diversity, amount, and redundancy of information that mothers acquired. These different kinds and amounts of information are utilized in practicing child-rearing, and mothers' economic situations play an important role in this process.

A majority of less-educated mothers engage in vertical cultivation, in which they selectively invest in a few subjects and nonacademic activities and spend most of their time monitoring their children to avoid the economic risk of investing in diverse areas that children might fail to excel in. In contrast, highly educated respondents with greater economic resources and a greater amount and higher diversity of information are more likely to let children experience as many diverse options for academic and nonacademic activities as possible. Furthermore, the interaction of economic constraints and different diversity and amounts of information utilized in providing education shapes the emotional states of mothers. Highly educated mothers are relatively more confident than less-educated mothers that their children would do fine regardless of the exact combination of out-of-school activities. Less-educated mothers search with significant anxiety for the right combination of educational opportunities for their children.

The implications of the two divergent approaches are that the risk aversion of constrained families with access to fewer resources and less information may shape children's early childhood education in ways that contribute to socioeconomic disparities in both quantity and diversity of education. Also, the emotional state of mothers implies that economic and informational constraints shape not only divergent child-rearing approaches but also the emotional well-being of mothers in Korea.

The key contribution of this chapter is extending our understanding about the underlying mechanisms of the link between maternal education and children's achievement. Literature on familial influence on early childhood education dominantly emphasizes either cultural orientation or objective resources when exploring how parents influence early childhood education. Thus, other forms of resources, or resources that are in the gray area of cultural understanding and financial and institutional resources, were underexplored. This study pinpoints the salient role that information plays as one of the key underlying mechanisms between maternal education and divergent child-rearing approaches. Neither cultural understanding nor economic constraints fully explain the different types of education mothers provide for their children. The process of mobilizing and utilizing information enables us to explain the interplay between the cultural understandings shared by a group of mothers, accumulated human and knowledge resources owned by mothers themselves, social and personal ties used in sharing ideas and mobilizing diverse information, and the economic conditions.

Another contribution is unpacking the simplistic "education fever" narrative (Seth 2002) so often applied to Korea and looking instead at the specific parenting styles and strategies employed from different class positions. One image has dominated both public media and academic studies regarding how Korean mothers educate their children: mothers who are obsessed with ensuring that their children get the maximum support when growing up (especially in terms of education), mothers who are managers of their children, and mothers who identify their own self-actualization through their children's success. Compared to other mothers in different societal contexts, Korean mothers have been portrayed as engaging in intense child-rearing. However, mothers are not homogeneous in their background and upbringing, and as a result they have different ideas and strategies for ensuring successful lives for their children. Thus, this chapter extends our understanding about how mothers with young children utilize resources, in particular, information, in providing early childhood education for their children.

NOTES

I am grateful to Bonnie Tilland, Caitlin Daniel, Hyeyoung Woo, Hyunjoon Park, Mary Brinton, Paul Chang, Alexandra Killewald, and the participants at the 2016 Perspectives Conference, "Korean Families in Economic and Demographic Transitions," at the University of Michigan Nam Center for Korean Studies.

1. I asked the online survey company to collect responses from approximately 300 to 400 mothers from each of three education levels: high school graduate, two-year vocational college graduate, and four-year university graduate. Because Ovey uses both downloadable apps for smartphones and their online website to send out surveys to their targeted panel who meet the criteria for interviews and because they have a relatively high response rate (over 50 percent) on average, the company first randomly picked respondents among the panel who met the criteria for my study. For instance, the company had in total approximately 1,000 high school graduate mothers who met the criteria, so within this sample, they randomly picked 400 potential respondents and sent out the survey request. There were in total more mothers (approximately 3,000 for each group) with higher education in the company's panel, so they randomly picked 500 respondents for the two-year and four-year college degree holders. After the company closed the survey, the response rate was 69 percent for high school graduates, 77 percent for two-year college degree holders, and 88 percent for bachelor's degree holders. Among the bachelor's degree holders, 14 percent also had a graduate degree, so I later separated them from the bachelor's degree holders.

2. The median household income of this study's participants is higher than that of households in Korea. This indicates that the sample for this study is composed of not only people who are living in Seoul and its surrounding area (urban setting) but also people who have relatively higher household income than the overall population in Korea.

3. In this chapter, I use the term "institution" instead of *hagwŏn* to broadly indicate both for-profit private and public institutes or academies. This reflects expressions that mothers use.

REFERENCES

Anderson, Thomas, and Hans-Peter Kohler. 2013. "Education Fever and the East Asian Fertility Puzzle: A Case Study of Low Fertility in South Korea." *Asian Population Studies* 9 (2): 196–215.

Augustine, Jennifer March, Kate C. Prickett, Sarah M. Kendig, and Robert Crosnoe. 2015. "Maternal Education and the Link Between Birth Timing and Children's School Readiness." *Social Science Quarterly* 96 (4): 970–84.

Baker, David, and Gerald K. LeTendre. 2005. *National Differences, Global Similarities: World Culture and the Future of Schooling*. Stanford, CA: Stanford University Press.

Becker, Birgit. 2011. "Social Disparities in Children's Vocabulary in Early Childhood. Does Pre-school Education Help to Close the Gap?" *British Journal of Sociology* 62 (1): 69–88.

Bennett, Pamela R., Amy C. Lutz, and Lakshmi Jayaram. 2012. "Beyond the Schoolyard: The Role of Parenting Logics, Financial Resources, and Social Institutions in the Social Class Gap in Structured Activity Participation." *Sociology of Education* 85 (2): 131–57.

Bornstein, Marc H., and Robert H. Bradley, eds. 2014. *Socioeconomic Status, Parenting, and Child Development*. New York: Routledge.

Bourdieu, Pierre. 1973. "Cultural Reproduction and Social Reproduction." In J. Karabel and A. H. Halsey, eds., *Power and Ideology in Education*, 487–511. New York: Oxford University Press.

Byun, Soo-yong, Evan Schofer, and Kyung-keun Kim. 2012. "Revisiting the Role of Cultural Capital in East Asian Educational Systems: The Case of South Korea." *Sociology of Education* 85 (3): 219–39.

Chang, Kyung-Sup. 2010. *South Korea under Compressed Modernity: Familial Political Economy in Transition*. New York: Routledge.

Chin, Tiffani, and Meredith Phillips. 2004. "Social Reproduction and Child-Rearing Practices: Social Class, Children's Agency, and the Summer Activity Gap." *Sociology of Education* 77 (3):185–210.

Emerson, Robert M., ed. 2001. *Contemporary Field Research: Perspectives and Formulations*. Long Grove, IL: Waveland Press.

Glaser, Barney G., Anselm L. Strauss, and Elizabeth Strutzel. 1967. *The Discovery of Grounded Theory: Strategies for Qualitative Research*. New Brunswick, NJ: Aldine Transaction.

Grusky, David B. 1994. *Social Stratification: Class, Race, and Gender in Sociological Perspective*. Boulder: Westview.

Hart, Betty, and Todd R. Risley. 2003. "The Early Catastrophe: The 30 Million Word Gap by Age 3." *American Educator* 27 (1): 4–9.

Hays, Sharon. 1998. *The Cultural Contradictions of Motherhood*. New Haven: Yale University Press.

Jacobs, Jerry A., and Kathleen Gerson. 2016. "Unpacking Americans' Views of the Em-

ployment of Mothers and Fathers Using National Vignette Survey Data: SWS Presidential Address." *Gender & Society* 30 (3): 413–41.
Lareau, Annette. 2011. *Unequal Childhoods: Class, Race, and Family Life.* 2nd ed. Oakland: University of California Press.
Lareau, Annette, and Elliot B. Weininger. 2003. "Cultural Capital in Educational Research: A Critical Assessment." *Theory and Society* 32 (5–6): 567–606.
Lareau, Annette, and Elliot B. Weininger. 2008. "The Context of School Readiness: Social Class Differences in Time Use in Family Life." In Alan Booth and A. Crouter, eds., *Disparities in School Readiness: How Families Contribute to Transitions to School*, 155–88. New York: Psychology Press.
Lee, Valerie E., and David T. Burkam. 2002. *Inequality at the Starting Gate: Social Background Differences in Achievement as Children Begin School.* Washington, DC: Economic Policy Institute.
Lett, Denise Potrzeba. 1998. *In Pursuit of Status: The Making of South Korea's "New" Urban Middle Class.* Cambridge, MA: Harvard University Asia Center.
Lofland, John, and Lyn H. Lofland. 2006. *Analyzing Social Settings.* Belmont, CA: Wadsworth Publishing.
OECD. 2012. *Education at a Glance.* Paris: OECD.
OECD. 2015. *Education at a Glance.* Paris: OECD.
OECD. 2016. "Balancing Paid Work, Unpaid Work, and Leisure." http://www.oecd.org/gender/data/balancingpaidworkunpaidworkandleisure.htm
Park, Hyunjoon. 2013. *Re-evaluating Education in Japan and Korea.* New York: Routledge.
Park, Hyunjoon, Soo-yong Byun, and Kyung-keun Kim. 2011. "Parental Involvement and Students' Cognitive Outcomes in Korea: Focusing on Private Tutoring." *Sociology of Education* 84 (1): 3–22.
Park, So Jin. 2006. "The Retreat from Formal Schooling: 'Educational Manager Mothers' in the Private After-School Market of South Korea." PhD diss., University of Illinois, Urbana-Champaign.
Park, So Jin, and Nancy Abelmann. 2004. "Class and Cosmopolitan Striving: Mothers' Management of English Education in South Korea." *Anthropological Quarterly* 77 (4): 645–72.
Ragin, Charles. 1987. *The Comparative Method: Moving Beyond Qualitative and Quantitative Methods.* Berkeley: University of California Press.
Ramey, Garey, and Valerie A. Ramey. 2009. "The Rug Rat Race." NBER Working Paper No. 15284. Cambridge, MA: National Bureau of Economic Research.
Seth, Michael J. 2002. *Education Fever: Society, Politics, and the Pursuit of Schooling in South Korea.* Honolulu: University of Hawaii Press.
Small, Mario Luis. 2009. *Unanticipated Gains: Origins of Network Inequality in Everyday Life.* New York: Oxford University Press.
Statistics Korea. "Vital Statistics." http://kostat.go.kr/portal/korea/index.action
Vincent, Carol, and Stephen J. Ball. 2007. "Making Up the Middle-Class Child: Families, Activities and Class Dispositions." *Sociology* 41 (6): 1061–77.
Weininger, Elliot B., Annette Lareau, and Dalton Conley. 2015. "What Money Doesn't Buy: Class Resources and Children's Participation in Organized Extracurricular Activities." *Social Forces* 94 (2): 479–503.

3
Reshaping Educational Strategies

Habitus Transformation of Immigrant Mothers in South Korea

Hyejeong Jo

Korean families have become diverse in last few decades. One of the most noticeable changes in the landscape of Korean families is the increasing number of "multicultural families,"[1] a term that broadly refers to both the multiethnic families that are formed through international marriages and the families of labor immigrants or North Korean defectors in South Korea (hereafter Korea). The rapid increase of international marriages between native Korean men and foreign women has been leading the growth of the multicultural family since the 1990s (Bélanger, Lee, and Wang 2010; Kim 2007; M. Kim 2013). In fact, about 7 percent of new marriages in 2016 were between Korean natives and foreign-born spouses; and among these marriages, more than 65 percent were between Korean men and non-Korean women (KOSIS 2017). When it comes to children born to multicultural families, approximately 2 percent of elementary school students in 2016 have at least one parent who is not a Korean. The clear majority of the multicultural children are those born to native Korean fathers and marriage migrant mothers (KESS 2016). Among various types of multicultural families, this chapter focuses on those with immigrant mothers, native Korean fathers, and their children.

There are documented educational disadvantages for multicultural children with immigrant mothers (Han 2012; Song et al. 2008). Multicultural children are reported to experience various difficulties in early education, such as the school adaptation issue and the language acquisition problem (Ŭn 2010; Kim 2008). Moreover, research shows that multicultural children have lower educational achievement compared with their peers with native parents (Y. Kim 2013; Yi 2013). Researchers posit that the educational struggles of multicultural children are derived from their mothers' lack of cultural competencies coupled with their fathers' lower socioeconomic status (Ŭn 2010; Pak et al. 2012). This diagnosis often leads to a policy suggestion that immigrant mothers should have more social support so they can develop better cultural skills, such as Korean language competency, parenting techniques, and self-efficacy as mothers (Han 2012; Song et al. 2008; Yang et al. 2011).

However, researchers have given less attention to how immigrant mothers play an active role in children's education. The ways in which they cultivate their educational strategies to transmit educational advantages to their children have not been studied sufficiently. According to a recent research report, immigrant mothers get involved in children's education more actively than the social stereotype about immigrant mothers describes and they believe in the importance of children's educational achievement (i.e., college attendance) similarly to native mothers (Yang et al. 2011). In other words, despite their cultural vulnerabilities, immigrant mothers can be active players who seek to facilitate their children's educational development. Nevertheless, the scholarship on multicultural families in Korea has overlooked the social process through which these mothers form their educational strategies.

Drawing on the data from in-depth interviews with 29 immigrant mothers, in this chapter I fill this gap in the literature by illustrating the process whereby they change their perceptions of Korean education and forge the educational strategies for their children. I conceptualize this transformative process as the "habitus transformation"—the shift in their understanding of and responses to the cultural rules in Korean education. Particularly, I describe two aspects of this process. First, in their early years of motherhood, immigrant mothers experience confusion and struggle to educate their children based on their own experience in their homelands. Second, when their children struggle at school, they actively shift their strategies with the help of "cultural mentors"—institutional gatekeepers and native mothers who better understand the unwritten rules of Korean education and offer advice on how to support children's educational development. Through these findings, this chapter argues that immigrant mothers should be understood as active actors; they can understand the institutional rules, adopt dominant strategies to comply with them, and strategize for their children's education.

Conceptual Framework: Habitus Transformation

Habitus transformation is a useful conceptual tool to understand how immigrant mothers build their educational strategies for children. In most research, habitus is used to describe one's unchanging "second nature" (Bourdieu 1990: 53). Early socialization experiences in the family and school are believed to shape one's habitus differently for his or her social locations. Once established, habitus guides one's cultural tastes, attitudes, and practices for a long time. Since social institutions (e.g., schools) recognize and reward a certain type of habitus better than others (see Bodovski 2014; Dumais 2002; Gaddis 2013), habitus is the key mechanism of social reproduction. Highlighting the role of habitus in social reproduction, Bourdieu (1990: 53) defines habitus as "structured structures predisposed to function as structuring structures." Overall, the theory of habitus implies that the different cultural traits of individuals for their social class, gender, or other social categories shape their interactions with institutions distinctively and yield different outcomes accordingly.

While the concept of habitus describes an invariable disposition and practice that individuals possess, some researchers posit that habitus can change (Jenkins 1994; King 2000; Reay 2004). For example, Atkinson (2011) conceptualizes as "institutional habitus" a new form of habitus that individuals acquire through their experiences in new institutional settings. Lee and Kramer's (2013) study empirically supports Atkinson's conceptualization by showing that working-class college students at a US elite university learn new habitus from their interactions with middle-class actors at the school. Similarly, Horvat and Davis's (2011) study on school dropouts in the United States elucidates how educational programs can reshape their understanding of the importance of educational achievement and facilitate their mobility aspirations. Overall, previous studies illustrate how habitus transformation can occur as an important mechanism of social mobility.

Despite the recent theoretical development, I suggest that the literature on habitus transformation is limited in two ways. First, the previous studies do not discuss how the concept of habitus is linked to the concept of "field." Theoretically, a field defines which form of habitus is more advantageous than others. Bourdieu (1990) explains that the field is a social universe where individuals compete with one another to achieve desired social rewards (e.g., occupation or prestige). However, the field is not neutral for all participants (Lareau 2015). Each field has its own sets of rules, and it rewards individuals whose habitus complies with the rules better than others whose habitus is not aligned with them. Therefore, those individuals who have opportunities to develop dominant forms of habitus in the field are more likely to achieve social rewards compared with others who do not have those opportunities. Moreover, since the workings of habitus are subject to the field, individuals can experience difficulties when they enter a new field with their old habitus. Bourdieu (1996) calls this discrepancy between one's habitus and the rules of the game as the "habitus hysteresis." Individuals can feel "out of water" since their old habitus does not fit the new environment and can feel confused about how to behave properly (Lee and Kramer 2013).[2] While habitus hysteresis can cause individuals to experience struggles and failures in a new social setting, these people can argumentatively come up with a new strategy by learning and emulating a dominant form of habitus in the new field. In the new field, they can observe the ways in which others play the game of the competition for social rewards and determine how they can develop their play to win the game. Nevertheless, this dynamic process whereby individuals forge a strategy by adopting a new form of habitus has not been empirically explored.

Second, the literature on habitus transformation has not sufficiently addressed how the change occurs outside educational settings. While most research focuses on school as a site of transformation, there are signs that individuals can experience habitus transformation outside institutional settings. For instance, Yoon, Kim, and Eom's (2011) study demonstrates that media consumption in the host country can help immigrants develop a hybrid form of habitus. Moreover, while they do not focus on the concept of habitus, Lareau and Calarco (2011: 65) argue that working-class parents can "acquire a limited set of middle-class cultural resources" (e.g., knowledge, skills, and competences) by learning directly from middle-class parents. According to their study, these acquired cultural skills can help the working-class parents to engage and negotiate efficiently with their children's schoolteachers. Nevertheless, except for these few studies, researchers have yet to investigate thoroughly the transformation of habitus in various social settings. Particularly, less known are the ways in which individuals go through habitus transformation through their social interactions with other individuals from different social backgrounds and how this transformative process shapes their actual practices.

Therefore, in the following sections, I will show the process of habitus transformation by analyzing how immigrant mothers forge the educational strategies for their children through their interactions with various individuals. As for the process of their habitus transformation, I present two aspects. First, I illustrate the habitus hysteresis—the cultural gaps between immigrant mothers' initial perception of how to raise children (old habitus) and the dominant educational practices of Korean parents (dominant habitus). Second, I demonstrate how they cope with these gaps by adjusting their strategies based on their interactions with various types of cultural mentors.

"The Field": The Rules of the Game in Korean Education

To understand habitus transformation, which drives the shift in the ways immigrant mothers strategize their children's education, it is important to first understand the field that they are participating in as mothers. As immigrants, mothers encounter a set of new rules of the game as they start their motherhood in a new social setting. Whereas some scholars suppose that there is considerable convergence in the education system and culture between Asian countries—especially among East Asian countries (Jeynes 2008; Marginson 2011), there are two distinctive cultural features in Korean education that immigrant mothers might find to be challenging to accept.

The first rule states that children and parents (often mothers) participate in intense competition to secure a seat in a selective college because of the high stakes of an elite education in children's life opportunities. A salient feature of the Korean education system is horizontal stratification across colleges and universities. Horizontal stratification refers to various aspects within postsecondary education that differentiate life opportunities of individuals and hence reproduce social inequalities systematically (Gerber and Cheung 2008). For example, the type and reputation of the institution that one attends or one's particular postsecondary experiences (e.g., extracurricular activities) can shape one's labor market outcome (Rivera 2016). In Korea, life opportunities are distributed disproportionately across individuals by their alma mater (Hwang 2005; Yi 2007). It matters not only from what type of college (i.e., junior college vs. four-year university) one has graduated but also how prestigious the school is for the graduate's postcollege experiences. For example, research shows the premiums in the labor market of attending a four-year university located in Seoul, which are generally considered to be better institutions compared with those outside of Seoul: job seekers with degrees from universities in Seoul experience a smoother transition to full-time employment after college graduation (Ch'ae and Kim 2009; Cho and Kim 2014) and have better incomes when they are employed (O 2007). In addition, researchers argue that alumni from elite universities can expect social benefits from their "academic cliques" (*hakpŏl*) (Hwang 2005; Lee and Brinton 1996): graduates from these elite schools dominate economic, social, and political opportunities by excluding other individuals from non-elite institutions. These unequal outcomes of college education make children's college placement a family project. Parents actively seek to help children's educational achievement as a crucial way of transmitting social advantages to their children (Lee and Larson 2000; Seth 2002). Especially in this project of social reproduction, mothers often take a leading role, while fathers are expected to take a secondary role as breadwinners (Nelson 2000; Park 2010).

The second rule is that participation in shadow education is a dominant practice for Korean parents to facilitate children's academic advancement. Shadow education often means various forms of supplementary education in the private educational market to help students improve their academic performance or to enrich students' academic development (Buchmann, Condron, and Roscigno 2010; Byun and Park 2012). Korea has the largest shadow education system in the world (Byun, Schofer, and Kim 2012). A recent national survey showed that 74.6 percent of primary and secondary students in Korea were enrolled in at least one kind of shadow education program (KOSIS 2017). Moreover, according to the same survey, Korean families spent approximately US$19 billion on shadow education in 2008. It was almost one-tenth of the national annual budget and slightly more than the total education budget in Korea.

Researchers of shadow education in Korea consider it as a form of parental involvement (Byun, Schofer, and Kim 2012; Park, Byun, and Kim 2011). To use shadow education efficiently requires parental cultural knowledge (Park, Byun, and Kim 2011). Unlike public education, which is highly standardized in Korea, shadow education is diversified and stratified.[3] Parents have a wide variety of options to choose from for their children. As a result, they should know whether their children need shadow education and, if so, which program would serve their educational needs the best. In addition, parents should have nuanced knowledge about shadow education programs in the local context. To find an educational service suitable for their children, it is necessary for parents to know the differences between cram schools or tutors in terms of the strengths, characteristics, or reputations of the service providers.

For immigrant mothers, these rules can be challenging to follow. They can experience habitus hysteresis because of the cultural gap between their old understanding of their roles in children's education and the new rules for parents they face as newcomers in Korean society. When they deal with the challenge, two types of cultural mentors can help them to learn about these new rules and to develop educational strategies for their children accordingly. First, in the Korean context, institutional gatekeepers, including social workers and educators, can be cultural mentors for immigrant mothers. To help marriage migrant women settle down in Korea and assist their children's education, the Korean government and local governments provide support programs for multicultural families. Marriage migrant women can use Multicultural Family Support Centers, where the national government offers various services for their family lives and children's education (e.g., language classes for marriage migrant women and educational services for multicultural children). In addition, local governments often provide multicultural children with educational support such as private tutoring services for children or educational vouchers for shadow education. In fact, in 2015, 54.9 percent of marriage migrants in Korea reported that they had an experience of using government-provided services; 20.7 percent reported that their children had participated in educational support programs for multicultural families (KWDI 2016). Since some of these programs aim to orient immigrant mothers to Korean education, the interactions with individuals who work to support multicultural families can help orient immigrant mothers to Korean education. Furthermore, the compulsory education that mandates all children to attend six years of elementary school and three years of middle school can give immigrant mothers opportunities to interact with educators of their children. While communicating with children's schoolteachers, immigrant mothers can acquire information about the ways that they educate children in Korea.

Second, native Koreans (e.g., friends, coworkers, neighbors, and church members) can be cultural mentors for immigrant mothers. While ethnic communities serve as a social resource for immigrant mothers (Kim 2014), these mothers also interact with native Koreans outside their ethnic communities. They can work, participate in religious communities, and become members in their local communities, through which they can develop relationships with native Koreans. Indeed, according to a representative survey, 59.5 percent of marriage migrants had paid jobs in 2015. Also, in the same year, 21.2 percent of marriage migrants had religious affiliations and 13.2 percent participated in local community gatherings (KWDI 2016). These social interactions that immigrant mothers have with native Koreans in their daily lives can be information sources from which they can obtain knowledge about Korean education. Native Koreans who know the educational field in Korea better than immigrant mothers can walk them through the cultural rules in the field of Korean education and give them advice on how to educate their children. Their cultural advice can help immigrant mothers deal with habitus hysteresis derived from the gap between their old habitus about education and the cultural rules in Korean education.

Data and Methods

For the study, I conducted in-depth interviews with 29 immigrant mothers in a southern industrial city in Korea in 2011. Through the snowballing sampling method, I recruited 29 interviewees from seven different countries of origin. For the recruitment, I first contacted two local organizations helping marriage migrant women. These two organizations connected me with one immigrant mother from each of seven different countries whose children attended elementary school. I interviewed these seven immigrant mothers and asked them to introduce me to their friends who moved to Korea from the same countries. Through their personal networks, I was able to recruit eight interviewees who migrated from the Philippines, six from China, five from Japan, three from Mongolia, three from Vietnam, two from Thailand, and two from Uzbekistan. By investigating the diverse narratives of interviewees from various ethnic groups, I sought to find the common, rather than diverging, experiences as immigrant mothers in Korea.

As described in table 3.1, except for one informant who was raising her son alone after a divorce, all interviewees in this chapter were married to their first husbands at the time of the interviews. Their average age was 37 years old; the average age of their spouses was 44 years old. The average duration of marriage was 13 years. On average, they had two children. Their children's average age was 10 years old. The occupations of the interviewees varied, though they generally had low-income jobs. Moreover, whereas three interviewees were married to husbands who were working as operators in the industrial district, most interviewees' spouses had low-paying manual occupations: three husbands worked as drivers, another three were construction workers, and eight worked in small factories as part-time workers. In terms of education, most interviewees had high school or higher education in their homelands. Specifically, eleven interviewees graduated from four-year colleges. Five had at least some two-year-college education. Ten mothers had high school diplomas. One was a high school dropout, and two completed elementary school.

I conducted interviews at the interviewees' houses or workplaces. The interviews lasted from one hour to two hours. During the interviews, I asked questions mainly about their own educational experiences in childhood and their parenting practices in Korea. Particularly, I probed questions about how they learned about the Korean education system and culture and who helped them to learn about and find various options to educate their children. All interviews were audiotaped with the consent of the interviewees. I analyzed the interview transcriptions by using open coding techniques (Saldaña 2015). While reading the transcripts repeatedly, I manually applied conceptual labels to those narratives that were relevant to the research questions to identify themes both inductively and deductively. I captured the themes commonly emerging from the narratives of the interviewees and organized them by paying attention to their theoretical relevance to habitus transformation. Next, I sought to find meta-themes by comparing and categorizing the themes across interviews. Through this process, I tried to capture the common experiences across the interviewees as well as the differences to understand how they understood Korean education and how they formed their educational strategies for children with the interactions of others.

TABLE 3.1. Summary of Socioeconomic Characteristics of Interviewees

Variable	
Average age	
Interviewees	36.7
Spouses	43.6
Children	10.2
Median income	
Interviewees	US$300
Spouses	US$2,100
Household	US$2,140
Average duration of marriage	12.6 years
Occupations	
Homemaker	48.3%
Language instructors	27.6%
Factory workers	10.3%
Service workers	13.8%
Total number of interviewees	29

TABLE 3.2. The Respondents of the Study

Name[a]	Origin country	Age	Occupation	Monthly family income (USD)	Education	Age of the first child
Elvie Santos	Philippines	38	Instructor	1,180.00	BA	13
Abril Reyes	Philippines	36	Instructor	1,820.00	BA	12
Joy Navarro	Philippines	36	Instructor	1,180.00	High school	10
Stella Salazar	Philippines	35	Instructor	2,730.00	BA	12
Rem Ocampo	Philippines	33	Housewife	1,820.00	High school	11
Maika Torres	Philippines	40	Instructor	2,450.00	BA	12
Verlly Santos	Philippines	32	Factory worker	2,140.00	2-year college dropout	11
Jenny Aquino	Philippines	30	Housewife	2,730.00	High school	6
Ch'oe Kŭn-ok	Chinese	34	Housewife	2,730.00	BA	9
Han Mi-ja	Chinese	36	Instructor	4,100.00	BA	4
Cho Chun-nae	Chinese	29	Office worker	1,910.00	High school	6
Kim Kyŏng-ja	Chinese	37	Baker	2,000.00	High school	9
Kim Sŏng-nye	Chinese	35	Housewife	2,270.00	BA	8
Yi Myŏng-ja	Chinese	42	Housewife	2,270.00	2-year college	12
Moe Saka	Japanese	45	Housewife	1,590.00	2-year college	11
Midori Watanabe	Japanese	32	Housewife	1,820.00	High school	8
Naoko Ishikawa	Japanese	44	Housewife	2,270.00	High school	13
Sachi Shibata	Japanese	47	Sales Clerk	1,270.00	2-year college	12
Yuri Ichiro	Japanese	40	Housewife	1,820.00	High school	13
Solongo	Mongolia	44	Sales clerk	1,540.00	2-year college	10
Ariunbold	Mongolia	36	Housewife	1,820.00	BA	12
Baichu	Mongolia	42	Housewife	1,360.00	BA	13
Dung Trang	Vietnam	27	Waitress	2,180.00	High school dropout	7
Phoung Chu	Vietnam	30	Waitress	3,520.00	High school	7
Chi Ha	Vietnam	33	Baker	5,730.00	High school	9
Thai Shuttikul	Thailand	36	Massager	3,640.00	Elementary school	12
Wipa Montri	Thailand	38	Housewife	4,620.00	Elementary school	16
Nila Ashrafi	Uzbekistan	37	Housewife	1,360.00	BA	8
Miram Babaev	Uzbekistan	33	Housewife	2,730.00	BA	8

[a] The names here are fictitious to protect the interviewees' privacy.

Findings

"It's Unacceptable in Japan!": The Gaps between Old Habitus and the Rules of the Game

The interviewees reported their experiences that illustrate habitus hysteresis in the form of the gap between their old habitus derived from their experiences in their homelands and the prevalent educational culture and practices in Korea. Moe, a Japanese mother with an 11-year-old son, vividly remembered her "shock" when she saw a group of students leaving a big shuttle bus while she was taking a walk with her husband around midnight. It was her second month in Korea after she had moved to marry her husband. She recalled that she first thought those students must have been returning from a school field trip. However, her husband corrected her by explaining that the students were coming back from cram school classes. She said that she was both shocked and furious at seeing students roaming around at midnight. While describing her emotion at that moment, Moe raised her voice. "What kinds of parents on earth can let children walk alone at night? It's unacceptable in Japan! I was shocked and angry. Children should be under protection of their parents all the time. Study may be important, but that is not all [for children's development]." She added that the incident taught her that Korea is different from Japan. She said she learned that Korean parents prioritized children's educational development, which was not always the case in Japan.

Thai from Thailand agreed with Moe. While she was socializing with friends of her husband when her first daughter, Tayŏng, was two and a half years old, Thai realized the drastic differences between Korean educational culture and her own experience in Thailand. She reported that the conversation with her husband's friends felt overwhelming because they only talked about children's education. It surprised her that they could spend several hours talking about it; however, what surprised her more was the educational obsession they shared:

> There was a wife of my husband's best friend, and she was so obsessed with education. She knew all famous cram schools in the town and even the names of instructors. I thought to myself, "Wow, she must do nothing but research cram schools!" I was also shocked by how much money they spent on cram schools. Their kids were enrolled in four or five cram school programs. The family was not even wealthy.

However, realizing the difference between the educational environment in Korea and their home countries did not immediately change the interviewees' habitus toward education. All interviewees said that they first tried to raise their children as they "would do in their homelands." When their children were younger, the interviewees focused on the behavioral and moral development of their children instead of emphasizing their educational achievement. They worried that children would be spoiled and disrespectful if parents put greater emphasis on the importance of academic success. Therefore, the interviewees reported that they initially did not get involved intensively in their children's education.

Yumiko described this less intervening approach as "laissez-faire" parenting. She recalled that her eldest son, Chŏnghun, "had too much fun" until he became a fifth grader. She explained that this was because she did not actively intervene in his studies. She said, "I didn't tell him to study. I only emphasized respecting others and following the rules because that was what I used to be taught [in Japan]." Though her son suffered low academic performance, she did not encourage him academically. She believed that he would catch up when "he realizes he should [study hard]."

However, Yumiko became skeptical about her approach toward his education when she saw that Chŏnghun was stressed out about his low grades, which were "below the average of the class." He felt especially hurt because his homeroom teacher scolded him for not working hard enough. Yumiko was upset that the teacher was blaming Chŏnghun without fully considering his responsibility as a teacher to help students learn better. However, at the same time, she blamed herself for Chŏnghun's struggle. She started to feel that her son was doing poorly at school because she "did not do as Korean mothers would do." Yumiko confessed that she was now worried about her son because she might have raised him to be less suitable for the Korean social environment, where educational competition is the norm and academic achievement is critical for children's future life opportunities. Letting out a long sigh, she added, "I was thinking too naively. I feel sorry for my son because he is suffering because of his ignorant mom."

Thai similarly felt that she failed to nurture the academic potential of her daughter, Tayŏng, and that this caused struggles at school for her. Like Yumiko, Thai had taken a less intervening approach toward her daughter's education based on her own educational experience as an elementary school graduate from Thailand. She used to think that "children will grow up fine if they are physically healthy and they will be eventually able to find a way to feed themselves." Thai herself helped to support her family by working a full-time job at the age of 15, which "was not uncommon at all" when she was young. Furthermore, Thai had believed that "having good life skills is equally good as or sometimes better than having a college degree." She had been optimistic about Tayŏng's future because she thought that her daughter could be successful if she developed a job-specific skill such as hairdressing or cooking.

However, Thai told me that she was now dubious about her own approach as she watched Tayŏng struggle at school. Thai had become more anxious about Tayŏng as she realized that it could be crucial for her daughter's future to have good academic credentials:

> I didn't know that studying well is so important in this country. I thought that skill mattered the most. However, it is not the case in Korea. Study just matters the most. You won't be treated well unless you have a college degree. I wish someone else had told me this. I am now worried about Tayŏng. She is going to middle school soon, but her teacher said that she was very concerned with Tayŏng's academic ability. She said that Tayŏng might not be able to catch up with other students. I told Tayŏng, "You may have met a wrong mother."

The interviewees felt confused about how to raise their children in Korea, where academic performance was overly emphasized for children's future life chances. Whereas they first adopted the less intervening parenting style based on their own educational experience, they gradually questioned their own way of educating children as they realized what other Korean mothers usually do to facilitate children's educational development and, more importantly, when they saw their own children struggling academically. They felt uneasy about their parenting style and worried that it might hurt their children's educational development.

"You Must Do Something as a Mother": Cultural Mentors and Habitus Transformation

Habitus Transformation through Interactions with Institutional Gatekeepers

Witnessing children's academic struggles, the interviewees reported that they actively sought a way to help their children. In their endeavors, various types of "cultural mentors" played a crucial role. Cultural mentors are those individuals who know the cultural rules of a field and guide others who are not familiar with the rules in their understanding of them. The interviewees reported that they had cultural mentors who helped them to strategize their parenting schemes in Korea. They commonly described two types of mentors: institutional gatekeepers and native mothers.

For the interviewees, the key institutional gatekeepers were educators who helped them learn about the unwritten rules in Korean education. For example, schoolteachers helped immigrant mothers, as narrated by Solongo, a Mongolian immigrant. When her son, Chihun, was struggling, his homeroom teacher suggested Solongo "do something as his mother":

> One day Chihun's teacher called me. He asked me if I knew that he gets distracted easily during class. The teacher also worried that his grades were not good. He said, "You must do something as his mother." He explained to me that it's important to study well in Korea. I was shocked [by his remarks]. I thought that my son was lively and active. I didn't imagine that it could cause him trouble.

The teacher specifically advised Solongo to enroll her son in a cram school (*hagwŏn*) to help him to catch up with his classmates. Following the teacher's instruction, Solongo searched for shadow education programs for Chihun and his sister. It was not easy for her to find a program that could be helpful for her children, not only because she had a limited budget[4] but also because there were "countless *hagwŏn* in the neighborhood." To find the best service for her children, Solongo had Chihun get the phone number of his best friend's mother, a native Korean. Solongo knew that the friend was doing better at school than her son. Solongo called the mother, whom she barely knew, and asked her to share the information about cram school programs in her neighborhood. The friend's mother explained to Solongo "which one is 'the good one' and which one is 'the bad one.'"

In addition to schoolteachers, educational service providers from the local government were also important cultural mentors. The local government in Harbortown provided diverse educational services for low-income multicultural families, such as private tutors for children. The interviewees found the advice from these tutors to be helpful. Rem, a Filipina mother of a 10-year-old girl named Aram, explained that her interactions with her daughter's tutor, sent by the local government, helped her to understand Korean education and to change her educational strategies. Before she met the tutor, whom Rem called Teacher Chang, she had thought that the "school should take care of her [daughter's] education, while it was her husband's and her responsibility to take care of her moral and physical development."

Therefore, though Aram's school grades were not good, Rem had not taken it seriously. Rem used to believe that "she is too young to study, and she would get better when she felt the necessity of studying."

However, she changed her point of view after she met Aram's government-sponsored private tutor. When Aram began her second year at elementary school, Teacher Chang visited her twice a week and helped her with schoolwork. She advised Rem to get involved more actively in Aram's education. Rem explained, "She told me that Aram would never be able to catch up with other kids once she began being left behind. She said that elementary school is a critical period of life for Aram because it will affect her later achievement." Also, Teacher Chang told her that "immigrant mothers are less enthusiastic about children's education [compared with Korean mothers]," which made her worried that Aram would be left behind at school because of her mother.

Based on Teacher Chang's advice, Rem began getting involved in Aram's education more extensively. She contacted Aram's schoolteachers to make sure that she was doing well at school. Moreover, she became more proactive in helping Aram's education through shadow education. Rem subscribed Aram to multiple worksheet services. At the time of the interview, she was planning to send Aram to a cram school three days a week once Teacher Chang stopped visiting her daughter. Rem was appreciative of Teacher Chang's advice. She said, "I am lucky to meet the teacher. Aram likes her, and so do I. She helps us a lot."

As the experiences of Rem and Solongo illustrate, the interactions with institutional gatekeepers helped the interviewees reconsider their understanding of the rules of the game in Korean education. Institutional gatekeepers as cultural mentors advised the immigrant mothers on how to get involved in children's education as well as on the importance of educational achievement.

Habitus Transformation through Interactions with Korean Mothers

Another channel of habitus transformation for the interviewees was the interactions with native mothers. Elvie, a Filipina with three children, received advice from one of her colleagues at work. Elvie had worked as an elementary teacher in the Philippines before moving to Korea. After she moved, she taught English at cram schools and community centers in her neighborhood. Elvie met Kyŏnghŭi at her first job in Korea. Kyŏnghŭi was the key individual who helped her to develop her understanding of Korean education:

I was afraid that something would go wrong with my daughters and son because of me. I didn't know about Korean society and Korean culture. She taught me about many things and helped me understand the education system, which is different from the one in the Philippines. How could I learn it by myself? [When I had a hard time navigating it,] she was helpful.

Specifically, Kyŏnghŭi explained that mothers should help their children with their studies through cram schools because cram school instructors know how to facilitate children's educational development better than mothers. Moreover, Kyŏnghŭi taught Elvie "how important education is in Korea" and that "Korean people invest lots of money and time for children's education because they believe that education enables children to have a better life." Elvie said that Kyŏnghŭi helped her to realize why Korean mothers were obsessed with shadow education and eager to enroll their children in private educational services.

Similarly, for Naoko, a Japanese immigrant, her church friend played a role as a cultural mentor. Whereas the other interviewees said that their children were academically struggling, Naoko's son was a high performer at his school. Sŏngju was particularly interested in science. Yet, Naoko "did not care much about his school life" because he did not show any signs of behavioral problems and was satisfied with his school. Furthermore, she did not pay attention to his scientific talent that was demonstrated by several awards he received from science competitions. She felt that "he was just playing with robots." At the same time, she did not know how to help him. She just assumed that the "school would take care of him well" because the teachers know his best interests. At home, she tried to teach Sŏngju to get along with friends and to enjoy his childhood. Naoko said, "It was not like I never understood why Korean mothers were so into children's education, but I worried that children would be self-centered if they are taught to study all the time and are not given any chance to play with peers."

However, when Sŏngju was a second grader, Naoko's church friend taught her that her son might need "early education" to further develop his special talent in science. The friend persuaded Naoko to "invest now" for Sŏngju's future. She insisted that parents help children with learning to develop their academic aptitudes and talent early. Also, she advised Naoko that it would be too late if they try to help children when they become middle school or high school students. She gave Naoko the advice to send him to a science cram school that was widely known among mothers in the town:

She told me to enroll Sŏngju in this science cram school. [She said that] the school specialized in science education. It is expensive. Honestly, we can't afford it. My friend told me that schoolteachers do not know much about science [because they are not science majors] but that the instructors at the cram school studied science at college. Also, she said that other Korean kids would be eventually better than Sŏngju though Sŏngju is doing better than them now. [She said that] since they are working hard now, they will be able to run ahead of Sŏngju.

As the cases of Elive and Naoko show, the interviewees' interactions with native Korean mothers caused them to rethink their initial educational strategies for their children. When their children were young, the interviewees rejected the rules of the game in Korean education, believing that the intensive educational competition or shadow education might not be helpful. However, after being coached by their native friends or colleagues, they changed their habitus and reshaped their educational strategies.

Conclusions

Research on immigrant mothers and their children's education in Korea describes various challenges that these mothers experience when they educate their children, who have educational disadvantages as multicultural children (Kim 2008; Han 2012; Song et al. 2008). However, previous studies have not investigated the ways in which immigrant mothers sufficiently manage these challenges. Moreover, there is a gap in our knowledge about how their interactions with various actors in Korean society can shape and reshape their educational strategies. This chapter fills this important gap in the literature by illustrating the process by which immigrant mothers develop and revise their educational strategies through their interactions with Koreans. The most salient way this chapter extends the scholarship on immigrant mothers in Korea is through its study of immigrant mothers as active players in their children's education. The findings of this chapter demonstrate that they do not remain as passive recipients of social support and instead seek to facilitate children's educational development based on their understanding of the cultural rules in Korean education. The current study suggests that we should pay attention to immigrant mothers beyond capturing the unique challenges that they experience as immigrants in Korea. We need to pay closer attention to the dynamic processes whereby they solve the challenges they face in a new social environment.

Particularly, two interesting questions can be further pursued in future research on immigrant mothers. First, it can be an important approach to incorporate immigrant mothers' ethnicity and socioeconomic status into the analysis to further understand variations in experiences of mothers. Researchers argue that the term "multiculturalism" treats diverse immigrant groups in Korea as homogeneous, failing to recognize the heterogeneities between immigrant groups (Kim 2007; Yang et al. 2011). To develop our understandings of the ways in which immigrant mothers shape children's education, it should be examined how their different social locations and cultural backgrounds interweave with their strategies for educating their children.

Second, it should be investigated when and why their strategies succeed or fail. With the data limitation, it is hard to discuss the consequences of the mothers' habitus change for children's educational outcomes in a systematic way. Yet, we can discuss two possible ways that the habitus transformation of the immigrant mothers can affect children's education. The first scenario is that children can benefit from mothers' active involvement in education through shadow education. Whereas the effect sizes of parental involvement in children's education vary among studies, many researchers have shown a positive impact of parental involvement on children's academic achievement (Castro et al. 2015). Moreover, some of the immigrant mothers cited in this chapter reported improvement in their children's learning, such as doing homework efficiently or doing better at school examinations after they started shadow education. However, it is also reasonable to expect that children of immigrant mothers remain disadvantaged in education even when their mothers adopt new strategies. Many studies about multicultural children in Korea show that they are more likely to struggle academically compared to children of Korean native parents (Y. Kim 2013; Yi 2013). The lower academic achievement and the higher school dropout rates among multicultural children, compared with their peers of Korean native parents, imply their marginality in education. Since their disadvantages can be derived by multiple factors, not only by the limited cultural resources of their mothers, the positive impact of the educational strategies that their mothers deploy can be limited. These two conflicting scenarios call for a systematic investigation into how the cultural transformation that immigrant mothers experience affects children's educational outcomes. This future research will be able to enhance our understanding of the dynamic process of educational strategies that immigrant mothers adopt for their children and its consequences on children's education.

NOTES

The research presented here was supported by a Gertrude and Otto Pollak Fellowship. An earlier version of this chapter was presented at the 2012 American Sociological Association Annual Meeting and the 2013 Korea Inequality Symposium. I am deeply grateful to Hyunjoon Park, Annette Lareau, Emily Hannum, Aliya Rao, Rachel Ellis, Valerio Bacak, Sarah Spell, and Sarah Zelner for their comments on earlier drafts of this research as well as to the editors and the reviewers for their input on this chapter.

1. Feminist scholars have criticized the term "multicultural families," which the Korean government has used (Kim 2013). For example, Hyun Mee Kim (2007: 102) argues that the term ignores "the diversity of desires, differences, and unpredictability on the part of the participants," while "the kinds of social relations that migrant women establish with their Korean families and every single process of multicultural family formation are diverse, fragmented, and individualistic." While I believe that this criticism is valid, I choose to use the term "multicultural families" in this chapter to refer to those families with Korean native husbands and immigrant wives.

2. For example, Lehmann's (2007) study illustrates that first-generation students with solid academic performance choose to drop out of universities due to the discrepancies between their old habitus and the college culture.

3. One of the shadow education programs is a weekly workbook delivery service called *haksŭpchi*. Students receive a set of worksheets once a week based on their academic development. An instructor visits a student once a week and keeps track of the student's progress. Another form of shadow education is cram school, or *hagwŏn*, which students attend after school. *Hagwŏn* usually has a very similar curriculum to school curriculum and uses a similar teaching technique. In the classroom, the teacher uses a textbook to preview or review what the students learn at school. Finally, some students hire an instructor to come into their home once or twice a week. Students usually spend one or two hours with the instructor, who customizes the learning based on the student's educational needs and learning progress. This form of shadow education is called *kwaoe*.

4. The tuition she was paying for *hagwŏn* accounts for the largest part of her family's total budget. At the time of the interview, Solongo was paying around US$200 every month, which accounts for 11 percent of the family's total income. Outside of rent, savings, and educational expenses, she was spending US$250 on living expenses.

REFERENCES

Atkinson, Will. 2011. "From Sociological Fictions to Social Fictions: Some Bourdieusian Reflections on the Concepts of 'Institutional Habitus' and 'Family Habitus.'" *British Journal of Sociology of Education* 32 (3): 331–47.

Bélanger, Danièle, Hye-Kyung Lee, and Hong-Zen Wang. 2010. "Ethnic Diversity and Statistics in East Asia: 'Foreign Brides' Surveys in Taiwan and South Korea." *Ethnic and Racial Studies* 33 (6): 1108–30.

Bodovski, Katerina. 2014. "Adolescents' Emerging Habitus: The Role of Early Parental Expectations and Practices." *British Journal of Sociology of Education* 35 (3): 389–412.
Bourdieu, Pierre. 1990. *The Logic of Practice*. San Francisco: Stanford University Press.
Bourdieu, Pierre. 1996. *The State Nobility: Elite Schools in the Field of Power*. Palo Alto: Stanford University Press.
Buchmann, Claudia, Dennis J. Condron, and Vincent J. Roscigno. 2010. "Shadow Education, American Style: Test Preparation, the SAT and College Enrollment." *Social Forces* 89 (2): 435–61.
Byun, Soo-Yong, and Hyunjoon Park. 2012. "The Academic Success of East Asian American Youth: The Role of Shadow Education." *Sociology of Education* 85 (1): 40–60.
Byun, Soo-yong, Evan Schofer, and Kyung-keun Kim. 2012. "Revisiting the Role of Cultural Capital in East Asian Educational Systems: The Case of South Korea." *Sociology of Education* 85 (3): 219–39.
Castro, Maria, Eva Exposite-Casas, Esther Lopez-Martin, Luis Lizasoanic, Enrique Navarro-Asencio, and Jose Luis GaViria. 2015. "Parental Involvement on Student Academic Achievement: A Meta-analysis." *Educational Research Review* 14: 33–46.
Ch'ae Ch'ang-gyun, Kim T'ae-gi. 2009. "Taejul chŏngnyŏnch'ŭng ŭi ch'wiŏp sŏnggwa kyŏlchŏng yoin punsŏk" (Determinants of Employment Status of University (College) Graduates Youth). *Chigŏp kyoyuk yŏn'gu* (*Journal of Vocational Education Research*) 28 (2): 89–107 (in Korean).
Cho Hŭi-suk, and Kim Anna. 2014. "Taejulcha ŭi chŏt chikchang imgŭm e yŏnghyang ŭl mich'inŭn kaein kwa taehak t'ŭksŏng yoin" (Individual and Institutional Factors Affecting College Graduates' Wages at the First Job). *Kyoyuk chonghap yŏn'gu* (*Journal of Educational Research*) 12 (4): 263–80 (in Korean).
Dumais, Susan A. 2002. "Cultural Capital, Gender, and School Success: The Role of Habitus." *Sociology of Education* 75 (1): 44–68.
Gaddis, Michael S. 2013. "The Influence of Habitus in the Relationship between Cultural Capital and Academic Achievement." *Social Science Research* 42 (1): 1–13.
Gerber, Theodore P., and Sin Yi Cheung. 2008. "Horizontal Stratification in Postsecondary Education: Forms, Explanations, and Implications." *Annual Review of Sociology* 34: 299–318.
Han Kyŏng-nim. 2012. "Tamunhwa kajŏng ŏmŏnidŭl ŭi chanyŏ yangyuk ŭl wihan pumo kyoyuk e taehan yogu" (Mothers' Parental Education Demand for Child-Rearing in Multicultural Families). *Han'guk yŏngyua poyukhak* (*Korea Journal of Child Care and Education*) 73: 171–90 (in Korean).
Horvat, Erin M., and James E. Davis. 2011. "Schools as Sites for Transformation: Exploring the Contribution of Habitus." *Youth & Society* 43 (1): 142–70.
Hwang, Kap Jin. 2005. "An Analysis on the Studies of University Ranking." *Research in Social Studies Education* 12 (2): 335–54.
Jenkins, Richard. 1994. *Pierre Bourdieu*. New York: Routledge.
Jeynes, William. 2008. "What We Should and Should Not Learn from the Japanese and Other East Asian Education Systems." *Educational Policy* 22 (6): 900–927.
KESS. 2016. *Multicultural Student Statistics*. Jincheon: Korean Educational Development Institute (in Korean).
Kim, Hyun Mee. 2007. "The State and Migrant Women: Diverging Hopes in the Making of 'Multicultural Families' in Contemporary Korea." *Korea Journal* 47 (4): 100–122.
Kim Kap-sŏng. 2008. "Han'guk nae tamunhwa kajŏng ŭi chanyŏ kyoyuk silt'ae chosa

yŏn'gu" (A Study on the Realities of Child Education in a Multi-Cultural Family in Korea). *Ch'ŏngsonyŏn munhwa p'orŏm* (*Forum for Youth Culture*) 18: 58–95 (in Korean).

Kim, Minjeong. 2013. "Citizenship Projects for Marriage Migrants in South Korea: Intersecting Motherhood with Ethnicity and Class." *Social Politics* 20 (4): 455–81.

Kim Tu-sŏp. 2014. "Kŏju chiyŏk ŭi minjok kusŏng i honin iju yŏsŏng ŭi sahoe hwaltong kwa chŏgŭng yuhyang e mich'inŭn yŏnghyang: Chubyŏn hyogwa ŭi kŏmjŭng" (Effects of Ethnic Composition of Residential Area on Social Activities and Adaptation Type of Foreign Wives in Korea: An Analysis of Neighborhood Effects). *Han'guk in'guhak* (*Korean Journal of Population Studies*) 37 (1): 1–29 (in Korean).

Kim Yŏng-nan. 2013. "Kukka sujun hagŏp sŏngch'wido p'yŏngga kyŏlgwa e nat'anan ch'o-6 tamunhwa kajŏng haksaeng ŭi kugŏgwa hagŏp sŏngch'wido: kuknae ch'ulsaeng, chungdo ipkuk, oegugin kajŏng haksaeng ŭl chungsim ŭro" (Educational Achievement of 6th Graders with Multicultural Background in the Subject Korean: Using Data from the 2011 NAEA Korean Tests). *Kugŏ kyoyukhak yŏn'gu* (*Korean Language Education Research*) 48: 125–51 (in Korean).

King, Anthony. 2000. "Thinking with Bourdieu against Bourdieu: A 'Practical' Critique of the Habitus." *Sociological Theory* 18 (3): 417–33.

KOSIS. 2017. *Marriage and Divorce Statics in 2017*. Daejeon: Statistics Korea (in Korean).

KWDI (Korea Women's Development Institute). 2016. "2015-yŏn chŏn'guk tamunhwa kajok silt'ae chosa punsŏk" (National Multicultural Family Survey Analysis). Seoul, Korea (in Korean).

Lareau, Annette. 2015. "Cultural Knowledge and Social Inequality." *American Sociological Review* 80 (1): 1–27.

Lareau, Annette, and Jessica McCrory Calarco. 2011. "Class, Cultural Capital, and Institutions: The Case of Families and Schools." In S. T. Fiske and H. R. Markus, eds., *Facing Social Class: How Societal Rank Influences Interaction*, 61–86. New York: Russell Sage Foundation.

Lee, Elizabeth, and Roy Kramer. 2013. "Out with the Old, In with the New? Habitus and Social Mobility at Selective Colleges." *Sociology of Education* 86 (1): 18–35.

Lee, Meery, and Reed Larson. 2000. "The Korean 'Examination Hell': Long Hours of Studying, Distress, and Depression." *Journal of Youth and Adolescence* 29 (2): 249–71.

Lee, Sunhwa, and Mary C. Brinton. 1996. "Elite Education and Social Capital: The Case of South Korea." *Sociology of Education* 69 (3): 177–92.

Lehmann, Wolfgang. 2007. "'I Just Didn't Feel Like I Fit In': The Role of Habitus in University Dropout Decisions." *Canadian Journal of Higher Education* 37 (2): 89–110.

Marginson, Simon. 2011. "Higher Education in East Asia and Singapore: Rise of the Confucian Model." *Higher Education* 61 (5): 587–611.

Nelson, Laura C. 2000. *Measured Excess: Status, Gender, and Consumer Nationalism in South Korea*. New York: Columbia University Press.

O Ho-yŏng. 2007. "Taehak sŏyŏl kwa nodong sijang sŏnggwa: chibang daesang imgŭm ch'abyŏl ŭl chungsim ŭro" (University Hierarchy and Labor Market Outcome: Wage Differentials between Provincial and Seoul Metropolitan Area University Graduates). *Nodong kyŏngje nonjip* (*Korean Journal of Labor Economics*) 30 (2): 87–118 (in Korean).

Pak Hyŏn-sŏn, Yi Ch'ae-wŏn, No Yŏn-hŭi, and Yi Sang-gyun. 2012. "Tamunhwa kajŏng ŭi ijung ŏnŏ, ijung munhwajŏk yangyuk hwan'gyŏng i chanyŏ paltal e mich'inŭn yŏnghyang: ŏmŏni yangyuk ch'amyŏ ŭi maegae hyogwa rŭl chungshim ŭro" (Impact of Bilingual, Bicultural Home Environment on Mother's Parenting and Children's Outcomes). *Sahoe pokchi yon'gu* (*Korean Journal of Social Welfare Studies*) 43 (1): 365–88 (in Korean).

Park, Hyunjoon, Soo-yong Byun, and Kyung-keun Kim. 2011. "Parental Involvement and Students' Cognitive Outcomes in Korea: Focusing on Private Tutoring." *Sociology of Education* 84 (1): 3–22.

Park, So Jin. 2010. "Educational Manager Mothers as Neoliberal Maternal Subjects." In Jesook Song, ed., *New Millennium South Korea: Neoliberal Capitalism and Transnational Movements*, 101–14. New York: Routledge.

Reay, D. 2004. "Gendering Bourdieu's Concepts of Capitals? Emotional Capital, Women and Social Class." *Sociological Review* 52: 57–74.

Rivera, Lauren. 2016. *Pedigree: How Elite Students Get Elite Jobs*. Princeton, NJ: Princeton University Press.

Saldaña, Johnny. 2015. *The Coding Manual for Qualitative Researchers*. London: Sage.

Seth, Michael J. 2002. *Education Fever: Society, Politics, and the Pursuit of Schooling in South Korea*. Honolulu: University of Hawaii Press.

Song Mi-gyŏng, Chi Sŭng-hŭi, Cho Ŭn-gyŏng, and Im Yŏng-sŏn. 2008. "Tamunhwa kajŏng oegugin mo ŭi pumo kyŏnghŏm e kwanhan yŏn'gu" (A Study on the Parental Experience of a Foreign Mother in a Multicultural Family). *Han'guk simnihak hoeji: sangdam mit simni ch'iryo* (*Korean Journal of Counseling and Psychotherapy*) 20 (2): 497–517 (in Korean).

Ŭn Sŏn-gyŏng. 2010. "Tamunhwa kajok chanyŏ ŭi hakkyo chŏgŭng e yŏnghyang ŭl mich'inŭn yoin e kwanhan yŏn'gu" (A Study on the Factors Influencing School Adjustment of Bicultural Children: Focused on Family Functioning). *Han'guk adong pokchihak* (*Journal of the Korean Society of Child Welfare*) 33: 37–74.

Yang Kye-min, Kim Sŭng-gyŏng, Pak Chu-hŭi, and Chŏng So-hŭi. 2011. *Tamunhwa kajok adong, ch'ŏngsonyŏn ŭi paltal kwajŏng ch'ujŏk ŭl wihan chongdan yŏn'gu II* (*A Longitudinal Study of Children and Adolescents from Multi-cultural Families II*). Research Report 11-R07. Seoul, Korea: National Youth Policy Institute (in Korean).

Yi Kŏn-man. 2007. "Han'guk sahoe ŭi hakpŏlchuŭi wa kyegŭp kaltŭng hakpŏl chabon ŭi ironhwa rŭl hyanghae" (A Study on "Hakbeolism" and Class Conflict in Korea Society: Toward a Theorization of "Hakbeol" Capital). *Kyoyuk sahoehak yŏn'gu* (*Korean Journal of Sociology of Education*) 17 (4): 63–85 (in Korean).

Yi Yŏng-ju. 2013. "Chung, kodŭng hakkyo tamunhwa kajŏng haksaeng ŭi yŏngŏ hagŏp sŏngch'wi t'ŭksŏng punsŏk" (An Analysis of the English Performance Characteristics of Middle and High School Students from Multicultural Backgrounds). *Oegugŏ kyoyuk* (*Foreign Language Education*) 20 (2): 57–78 (in Korean).

Yoon, Tae-Il, Kyung-Hee Kim, and Han-Jin Eom. 2011. "The Border-Crossing of Habitus: Media Consumption, Motives, and Reading Strategies among Asian Immigrant Women in South Korea." *Media, Culture & Society* 33 (3): 415–31.

Family and Children's Education and Well-Being

4

Consequences of Educational Assortative Mating for Children's Academic Achievement in South Korea

Soo-yong Byun, Yifan Bai, and Hee Jin Chung

While social stratification researchers have long been interested in studying "the degree of openness of the system of social inequality" (Blossfeld 2009: 514), most social stratification literature focuses on the mobility mechanisms that link individuals to jobs (Grusky 2014). Yet, examining the link between social class and job mobility is only one way to measure the openness of societies (Blossfeld 2009). Another important way to measure the openness of societies is to study the patterns of who marries whom (Blossfeld 2009; Mare 1991). This is because marriage creates intimate ties between partners as well as among families and social groups (Blossfeld 2009; Mare 1991). Thus, assortative mating may contribute to social reproduction, as it weaves people into certain textures of family culture, shapes the quality of parents, and affects the distribution of resources across families (Blossfeld 2009; Oppenheimer 1988; Schwartz 2013).

Among other factors, education has been suggested as a key determinant of marriage in many contemporary industrialized societies not only because it is closely related to occupational status and financial resources but also because it reflects cultural resources that shape "individuals' preferences for specific partners" (Blossfeld 2009: 514). Therefore, educational assortative mating suggests that the degree of social inequality can be further enhanced through marriage, as advantageous (or disadvantageous) economic and sociocultural resources of two individuals are pooled and accumulated into one household (Blossfeld 2009; Oppenheimer 1988). Accordingly, most prior research focuses on mechanisms and processes of educational assortative mating as well as its trends over time (e.g., Smits and Park 2009; Smits, Ultee, and Lammers 1998). To better understand how educational assortative mating contributes to social reproduction, however, one should address how educational assortative mating affects children's educational and occupational attainment. Yet, few studies empirically examine intergenerational effects of educational assortative marriage.

In this study, we address this lack of research by investigating the intergenerational effect of educational assortative mating on children's academic achievement in South Korea (hereafter Korea). Korea presents a fascinating setting for studying educational assortative mating because it is one of the countries that show high prevalence of homogamy (Smits and Park 2009). In addition, while there is a growing concern about increasing educational inequality in Korea (Byun and Kim 2010), educational assortative mating has been suggested as one of the mechanisms through which educational inequality intensifies (Park and Kim 2011). Therefore, our study will offer important insights into the role of educational assortative mating in social stratification in Korea as well as elsewhere.

Background

Literature on Educational Assortative Mating

Most literature on educational assortative mating focused on studying the patterns and processes of educational homogamy. This line of research documents an increase in educational homogamy in many advanced industrial countries (Blossfeld and Timm 2003; Schwartz and Mare 2005). Among other reasons, educational expansion especially for women and women's participation in the labor market have been suggested to explain the increase in educational homogamy in the modern world (Schwartz 2013). For example, educational expansion increases the chance of people meeting their potential partners with the same level of education at similar ages (Blossfeld and Timm 2003). In addition, as more women work outside the home through increasing access to schooling and the labor market, people can also meet someone at work who has not only a similar level of education but also common interests and lifestyles (McClendon, Kuo, and Raley 2014).

Much literature studying the Korean case also focused on documenting the patterns and trends of educational homogamy, generally suggesting that the prevalence of educational homogamy is much higher in Korea than in other countries (Smits and Park 2009; Smits, Ultee, and Lammers 1998) and that the degree of educational homogamy has increased over time in the country (Park and Smits 2005). Park and Smits (2005) suggested that Korea's high prevalence of education homogamy may reflect a high degree of educational competition led by the rapid expansion of education. To be specific, while more than 80 percent of high school graduates go to college in Korea, competition to enter selective colleges is extremely intense (Byun, Schofer, and Kim 2012). As a result, individuals, especially those who are highly educated, aspire to marry someone with at least a college degree so that they can pool their resources together to invest in their children's education (Park and Kim 2011; Park and Smits 2005).

However, recent research indicates that the degree of educational homogamy has somewhat decreased in Korea since the 1990s, especially among young generations (Park and Kim 2011, 2012; Smits and Park 2009). Park and Kim (2011, 2012) suggested that since the economic crisis in 1997, the middle class might have come to value economic capital (or wealth) more than human capital (or educational credentials) when choosing their spouse due to increased economic insecurity. Meanwhile, previous research documented yet another interesting pattern of educational homogamy in Korea. In general, educational homogamy is most prevalent among highly educated people in many countries (Blossfeld and Timm 2003; Schwartz and Mare 2005). This is also the case for Korea, yet educational homogamy is also prevalent among the least educated in this country (Park and Smits 2005), suggesting the polarization of educational homogamy by the level of education.

Implications of Educational Assortative Mating for Children's Educational Outcomes

Several scholars discussed the potential intergenerational impact of educational assortative mating. For example, Mare (1991) noted that the increase in educational homogamy might exacerbate social inequality among families because educational homogamy affects the socioeconomic achievement of their offspring. An underlying assumption is that each parent brings economic, social, and cultural resources to a family, and thus the total level of resources available within a family can be doubled. In addition, when both parents have attained the same level of schooling, they may have fewer conflicts in parenting standards and practices (Beck and Gonzalez-Sancho 2009).

Little research has empirically tested this assumption. One notable exception is a study by Beck and Gonzalez-Sancho (2009). Using data from the Fragile Families and Children Wellbeing Study in the United States, which collected both mothers' and fathers' reports on children, they examined the impact of parental educational homogamy on children's school readiness at age five. The authors found that, compared to children from educationally heterogamous families, children from educationally homogenous families showed a higher level of school readiness even after controlling for other variables. Yet, they focused mainly on estimating the average effect of educational homogamy, paying little attention to potential heterogeneity in the effect of educational homogamy across the different levels of education.

In fact, the assumption underlying the positive effect of educational homogamy described above makes sense for highly educated couples (e.g., both having bachelor's degrees). However, it is questionable whether it is also the case for the least educated couples. In other words, poorly educated parents would bring few economic, social, and cultural resources with them, and their children may still suffer from disadvantages even if these parents may have fewer disagreements on parenting. In this regard, it is important to examine the heterogeneous effects of educational homogamy on children's educational outcomes by the level of parental education. In this study, we address this issue by additionally examining how the effect of educational homogamy on children's academic achievement differs by the level of parental education, in addition to estimating the average effect of educational homogamy.

The Current Study

The current study aims to investigate the effect of educational assortative mating on children's academic achievement in Korea. Our primary research question is (1) whether there is a significant effect of educational assortative mating on children's academic achievement and (2) how the effect, if any, differs by the level of parental education. In addition, we address the following secondary research questions:

(3) Are there significant differences in household and child characteristics across different types of educational assortative mating (i.e., homogamy, hypergamy, and hypogamy) and different levels of parental education (i.e., middle school, high school, two-year college, and four-year college)?

(4) To what extent do differences in household and child characteristics across different types of educational assortative mating and different levels of parental education, if any, help to explain the effect of educational assortative mating on children's academic achievement?

Answering these secondary research questions will help us understand the way by which educational assortative mating affects children's academic achievement.

Data and Methods

Data and Sample

We used data from the Korean Education Longitudinal Study of 2005–2007 (hereafter KELS 2005–2007), which was conducted among a nationally representative sample of seventh graders by the Korean Educational Development Institute (KEDI), a government-funded educational research agency. KELS is one of the most recent, comprehensive longitudinal surveys to trace changes in student achievement, educational resources, and support. Although the most recent wave of KELS currently available is the 2016 survey, KELS 2005–2007 is particularly useful for the current study. This is because, unlike other large-scale surveys available in Korea that only include students' self-reported academic performance, it administered achievement tests in Korean language, English, and mathematics, scaled by Item Response Theory (IRT) scores, for the first three (i.e., 2005, 2006, and 2007) waves of data collection in addition to the student questionnaire. Therefore, KELS allows us to examine the effect of educational assortative mating on children's academic achievement, net of prior achievement.

KELS employed a two-stage stratified sampling design in which (1) middle schools were randomly sampled within each of four types of regions proportionally to the population size; and then (2) approximately 50 students (all if less than 50) in seventh grade were randomly sampled within each selected school. In 2005, the base year, a total of 6,908 seventh graders from 150 schools across the nation were sampled. Respondents in the base year were followed every year (i.e., 2006 and 2007). In the third year (2007), 6,568 (95 percent) of the original 6,908 respondents were resurveyed. In addition to the students, separate surveys were administrated each year to families, teachers, and school principals of the students to collect a wide range of family, class, and school information. For the current study, we focused on those students who participated in the base year survey as well as the two follow-up surveys and whose information about parental education, which is the key variable in this study, was available. This process results in the analytic sample of 6,310 students.

Measures

Parental Education and Educational Assortative Marriage

The primary independent variable was constructed from information about parental education. Parental education was based on parents' reports on their education, and the education level of each parent was measured respectively by four indicators: 1 = middle school graduates (or less); 2 = high school graduates; 3 = two-year college graduates; and 4 = four-year college graduates (or higher). Table 4.1 shows the distribution of pa-

TABLE 4.1. Distribution of Paternal and Maternal Education

			Paternal education				
			Middle school graduate	High school graduate	Associate's degree	Bachelor's degree or higher	Total
Maternal education	Middle school graduate	N	351	225	7	6	589
		% row	59.6	38.2	1.2	1.0	100.0
		% column	65.6	7.5	0.9	0.3	9.3
	High school graduate	N	174	2,636	532	660	4,002
		% row	4.4	65.9	13.3	16.5	100.0
		% column	32.5	87.7	70.6	32.8	63.4
	Associate's degree	N	5	94	182	341	622
		% row	0.8	15.1	29.3	54.8	100.0
		% column	0.9	3.1	24.1	16.9	9.9
	Bachelor's degree or higher	N	5	51	33	1,008	1,097
		% row	0.5	4.7	3.0	91.9	100.0
		% column	0.9	1.7	4.4	50.0	17.4
	Total	N	535	3,006	754	2,015	6,310
		% row	8.5	47.6	12.0	31.9	100.0
		% column	100.0	100.0	100.0	100.0	100.0

Source: Data from Korean Education Longitudinal Study of 2005–2007.

ternal and maternal education among 6,310 students. Results clearly show that the majority of students (4,177 out of 6,310; 66.2 percent) came from educationally homogamous families, where the father and mother have the same level of education. Educationally homogamous families were particularly prevalent among those children with highly educated mothers. For example, among 1,097 children who had mothers with a four-year college degree, approximately 92 percent of them also had fathers with a four-year college degree. By contrast, among 2,015 children who had fathers with a four-year college degree, 50 percent of them had mothers with a four-year college degree. On the other hand, results of table 4.1 show that a small percentage of children (362 out of 6,310; 5.7 percent) came from hypogamous families, where the education level of the mother was higher than that of the father. In particular, only about 2 percent (10 out of 535) came from hypogamous families where the father was a middle school graduate while the mother was either a two-year or a four-year college graduate. Meanwhile, approximately 28 percent (177 out of 6,310) came from hypergamous families where the education level of the father was higher than that of the mother.

Based on this information in table 4.1, we measured parental education/educational assortative mating status jointly with a categorical variable indicating whether the father and the mother were one of 12 categories: (1) both father and mother were middle school graduates; (2) both father and mother were high school graduates; (3) both father and mother were two-year college graduates; (4) both father and mother were four-year college graduates (reference group); (5) the father was a high school or two-year college or four-year college graduate and the mother was a middle school graduate; (6) the father was a two-year college graduate and the mother was a high school graduate; (7) the father was a four-year college graduate and the mother was a high school graduate; (8) the father was a four-year college graduate and the mother was a two-year college graduate; (9) the father was a middle school graduate and the mother was a high school or two-year college or four-year college graduate; (10) the father was a high school graduate and the mother was a two-year college graduate; (11) the father was a high school graduate and the mother was a four-year college graduate; and (12) the father was a two-year college graduate and the mother was a four-year college graduate. Note that we collapsed the categories for the lowest level (i.e., middle school graduates) of paternal and maternal education for hypogamy and hypergamy due to small sample sizes.

Academic Achievement

As noted above, KELS 2005–2007 provides IRT scores in the subject areas of Korean, English, and mathematics for participating children in grades seven through nine. In this study, we only present the findings in relation to English due to space limitation. However, our supplemental analyses show that the results for other subject areas (i.e., Korean and mathematics) are comparable to that of English (results not shown, but available upon request). English achievement was measured by IRT scores in the ninth grade and scaled to have a mean of 500 and a standard deviation of 50.

Household Characteristics

To better understand the way by which parents' educational assortative mating affects children's English achievement, we included a number of household characteristics, including (1) monthly household income, (2) marital status, (3) paternal and maternal age, (4) mother's working status, and (5) number of siblings. Monthly household income was measured by parents' report on their monthly household income and was transformed with the natural logarithm to resemble the normal distribution. The marital status was measured as a dichotomous variable indicating whether or not parents were continuously married. Parental and maternal age was measured by parents' self-reported age. Mother's working status was measured as a dichotomous variable indicating whether or not the mother was currently working. The number of siblings was measured by the number of brothers and sisters. All aforementioned measures were from the base year survey (i.e., 2005). One exception was the number of siblings, which was from the second follow-up survey (i.e., 2007).[1]

We also included various forms of parental involvement, which are found to be important to predict English achievement in the Korean context (Park, Byun, and Kim 2011), as potential mechanisms by which educational assortative mating influences children's English achievement. Parental involvement variables included (6) parental educational expectation for the child, (7) school contact, (8) parent-child discussion, (9) monitoring, and (10) private tutoring-related activities. Parental educational expectation was measured by a categorical variable indicating whether parents wanted their child to earn (a) an associate's degree, (b) a bachelor's degree, or (c) an advanced degree. School contact was derived from parents' reports on how many times (1 = none, 2 = once or twice, 3 = three or four times, 4 = five or more times) they or their spouse had contacted the school about (a) their seventh grader's school program, (b) their seventh grader' plans after leaving middle school, (c) doing volunteer work such as supervising lunch or chaperoning a field trip, and (d) providing information for school records such as their address or work telephone number (alpha = .59). Parent-child discussion was derived from parents' reports on (a) how strongly (1 = strongly disagree, 2 = disagree, 3 = neither disagree nor agree, 4 = agree, 5 = strongly agree) they agree or disagree with the statement "I or my spouse talk(s) to my seventh grader about grades"? (b) how often (1 = never, 2 = sometimes, 3 = often) they had talked to their seventh grader this year to provide advice or information about maintaining good grades, and (c) how often (1 = never, 2 = sometimes, 3 = often) they had talked to their seventh grader this year to provide advice or information about homework (alpha = .58). Monitoring was derived from parents' reports on how strongly they agreed or disagreed with the following statements: (a) "I or my spouse check(s) whether my seventh grader has completed all homework," (b) "I or my spouse know(s) where my seventh grader is when he/she is not at home or in school," and (c) "I or my spouse establish(es) and enforce(s) curfews for my seventh grader on school nights" (alpha = .61). Private tutoring-related activities were derived from parents' reports on (a) how strongly (1 = strongly disagree, 2 = disagree, 3 = neither disagree nor agree, 4 = agree, 5 = strongly agree) they agreed or disagreed with the following statement: "I or my spouse collect(s) information on private tutoring for my child" and (b) how much (1 = not at all, 2 = not so much, 3 = somewhat, 4 = much, 5 = very much) information they gathered about their child's academic career from a private tutor or *hagwon* instructor (alpha = .49). Note that each of the measures of parental involvement was scaled to have a mean of zero and a standard deviation of one to facilitate easy interpretations. Meanwhile, all measures of parental involvement were from the base year survey. One exception was private tutoring-related activities, which was from the first follow-up survey (i.e., 2006).

Child Characteristics

We also controlled for a number of child characteristics, including (1) gender, (2) prior achievement, (3) educational expectations, (4) weekly hours spent on homework or/and self-study, and (5) weekly hours spent on private tutoring. Gender was based on children's report on their sex. Prior achievement was measured by IRT test scores on English in the seventh grade and scaled to have a mean of 300 and a standard deviation of 50. Educational expectations were measured by a categorical variable indicating whether children wanted to have (a) an associate's degree, (b) a bachelor's degree, or (c) an advanced degree, or (d) whether children did not know how far they wanted to go. Both weekly hours spent on homework or/and self-study and weekly hours spent on private tutoring were based on children's reports on how much they spent on homework or/and self-study and on private tutoring per week, respectively. All measures of student characteristics were from the base year survey.

Analytic Strategies

We first performed descriptive statistics by the combination of the type of educational assortative mating (i.e., homogamy, hypergamy, and hypogamy) and the level of parental education (i.e., middle school, high school, two-year college, and four-year college) as well as for the pooled sample.[2] The aim was to examine whether there were significant differences in household and child characteristics across different types of educational assortative mating combined with the different levels of parental education. Next, we conducted ordinary least squares (OLS) regression to estimate the average effect of educational assortative mating on children's English achievement as well as its heterogenous effects by the level of parental education. For missing data (see table 4.2 for the percentage of missing data), we used multiple imputations to avoid potential bias resulting from the sample attrition.[3]

Results

Differences in Household and Child Characteristics

We first examine differences in key household and child characteristics by the type of educational assortative mating and the level of parental education. Table 4.2 presents descriptive statistics for the variables included in analyses by the combination of the type of educational assortative mating and the level of parental education. With respect to household characteristics, results showed that the average monthly household income for children from homogamous families where both the father and the mother were four-year college graduates was about 4,660,000 Korean won (approximately US$4,160), and this was significantly different from that for

TABLE 4.2. Descriptive Statistics for Variables Included in Analyses by the Type of Educational Assortative Mating

A. Homogamy

Variable	Both father and mother are middle school graduates		Both father and mother are high school graduates		Both father and mother are 2-year college graduates		Both father and mother are 4-year college graduates	
	M	SD	M	SD	M	SD	M	SD
Outcomes (ninth grade)								
English achievement	494.69	53.53	514.09	58.22	526.17	54.75	568.10	68.88
Household characteristics								
Monthly household income (logged)	5.15	0.56	5.62	0.60	5.84	0.47	6.14	0.49
Continuously married	0.90	—	0.95	—	0.95	—	0.97	—
Paternal age	47.02	5.89	43.50	4.33	43.25	3.46	43.90	3.25
Maternal age	43.33	6.11	40.31	4.19	40.29	3.20	41.34	3.01
Mother worked	0.61	—	0.57	—	0.60	—	0.55	—
Number of siblings	2.62	1.03	2.22	0.70	2.09	0.58	2.08	0.59
Educational expectation of parents								
Associate's degree or less	0.13	—	0.04	—	0.02	—	0.01	—
Bachelor's degree	0.71	—	0.71	—	0.54	—	0.39	—
Advanced degree	0.16	—	0.25	—	0.44	—	0.61	—
School contact	0.05	1.27	−0.06	0.94	0.08	1.07	0.14	1.05
Parent-child discussion	−0.46	1.00	−0.05	0.96	0.22	0.96	0.28	0.98
Monitoring	−0.59	1.13	−0.07	0.98	0.35	0.79	0.31	0.88
Private tutoring-related activities	−0.61	0.98	−0.05	0.99	0.24	0.89	0.35	0.94
Child controls								
Gender, child female	0.48	—	0.50	—	0.46	—	0.48	—
Prior achievement (seventh grade)	259.06	51.88	286.69	51.25	302.87	52.13	341.94	59.48
Educational expectation of the child								
Associate's degree or less	0.11	—	0.08	—	0.04	—	0.03	—
Bachelor's degree	0.53	—	0.59	—	0.62	—	0.50	—
Advanced degree	0.06	—	0.10	—	0.17	—	0.30	—
Don't know	0.30	—	0.23	—	0.17	—	0.16	—

TABLE 4.2.—Continued

A. Homogamy (cont.)

Variable	Both father and mother are middle school graduates		Both father and mother are high school graduates		Both father and mother are 2-year college graduates		Both father and mother are 4-year college graduates	
	M	SD	M	SD	M	SD	M	SD
Weekly hours spent on homework or/and self-study	2.11	1.35	2.63	1.76	3.16	2.14	3.97	2.38
Weekly hours spent on private tutoring	2.33	2.04	3.34	2.39	3.88	2.63	4.42	2.63
N	351		2,636		182		1,008	

B. Hypergamy

Variable	Father is a high school or 2-year college or 4-year college graduate and mother is a middle school graduate		Father is a 2-year college graduate and mother is a high school graduate		Father is a 4-year college graduate and mother is a high school graduate		Father is a 4-year college graduate and mother is a 2-year college graduate	
	M	SD	M	SD	M	SD	M	SD
Outcomes (ninth grade)								
English achievement	504.10	55.41	526.40	59.94	539.47	61.40	551.96	65.52
Household characteristics								
Monthly household income (logged)	5.40	0.54	5.78	0.52	5.87	0.54	5.98	0.46
Continuously married	0.93	—	0.96	—	0.95	—	0.97	—
Bachelor's degree	0.76	—	0.63	—	0.52	—	0.41	—
Advanced degree	0.17	—	0.34	—	0.47	—	0.59	—
School contact	−0.04	0.90	−0.06	0.90	0.05	1.12	0.02	1.01
Parent-child discussion	−0.19	1.02	0.02	0.96	0.10	0.98	0.20	0.96
Monitoring	−0.23	1.05	0.10	0.91	0.12	0.96	0.30	0.84
Private tutoring-related activities	−0.35	1.01	0.13	0.90	0.09	0.92	0.33	0.94
Child controls								
Gender, child female	0.51	—	0.45	—	0.47	—	0.48	—

TABLE 4.2.—Continued

B. Hypergamy (cont.)

Variable	Father is a high school or 2-year college or 4-year college graduate and mother is a middle school graduate		Father is a 2-year college graduate and mother is a high school graduate		Father is a 4-year college graduate and mother is a high school graduate		Father is a 4-year college graduate and mother is a 2-year college graduate	
	M	SD	M	SD	M	SD	M	SD
Prior achievement (seventh grade)	273.09	53.67	303.16	47.65	310.09	51.41	321.63	55.47
Educational expectation of the child								
Associate's degree or less	0.10	—	0.07	—	0.05	—	0.04	—
Bachelor's degree	0.57	—	0.58	—	0.58	—	0.55	—
Advanced degree	0.05	—	0.16	—	0.19	—	0.23	—
Don't know	0.28	—	0.19	—	0.19	—	0.18	—
Weekly hours spent on homework or/and self-study	2.38	1.55	2.92	1.95	3.19	2.11	3.31	2.06
Weekly hours spent on private tutoring	2.74	2.23	3.80	2.46	3.97	2.50	4.26	2.64
N	238		532		660		341	

C. Hypogamy

Variable	Father is a middle school graduate and mother is a high school or 2-year college or 4-year college graduate		Father is a high school graduate and mother is a 2-year college graduate		Father is a high school graduate and mother is a 4-year college graduate		Father is a 2-year college graduate and mother is a 4-year college graduate	
	M	SD	M	SD	M	SD	M	SD
Outcomes (ninth grade)								
English achievement	501.33	58.30	522.45	61.41	531.31	59.22	534.45	46.39
Household characteristics								
Monthly household income (logged)	5.29	0.72	5.82	0.53	5.84	0.42	5.96	0.56
Continuously married	0.88	—	0.91	—	0.92	—	0.97	—
Paternal age	44.97	4.26	43.56	3.76	44.21	3.75	43.48	2.36
Maternal age	40.78	4.69	41.09	4.90	40.51	3.66	40.85	2.43
Mother worked	0.56	—	—	—	0.50	—	0.48	—	0.61	—
Number of siblings	2.37	0.97	2.10	0.65	2.18	0.76	2.12	0.70

TABLE 4.2.—Continued

C. Hypogamy (cont.)

Variable	Father is a middle school graduate and mother is a high school or 2-year college or 4-year college graduate		Father is a high school graduate and mother is a 2-year college graduate		Father is a high school graduate and mother is a 4-year college graduate		Father is a 2-year college graduate and mother is a 4-year college graduate	
	M	SD	M	SD	M	SD	M	SD
Educational expectation of parents								
Associate's degree or less	0.12	—	0.01	—	0.00	—	0.00	—
Bachelor's degree	0.72	—	0.59	—	0.48	—	0.33	—
Advanced degree	0.17	—	0.40	—	0.52	—	0.67	—
School contact	−0.07	0.83	0.07	1.15	−0.06	0.71	0.10	0.84
Parent-child discussion	−0.31	1.05	0.16	0.99	0.31	0.97	0.00	1.00
Monitoring	−0.35	1.11	0.19	0.95	0.16	0.93	−0.14	1.00
Private tutoring-related activities	−0.29	1.09	0.10	1.10	0.01	0.90	0.32	0.99
Child controls								
Gender, child female	0.43	—	0.43	—	0.47	—	0.55	—
Prior achievement (seventh grade)	271.89	47.70	296.77	52.56	311.69	56.29	309.33	38.72
Educational expectation of the child								
Associate's degree or less	0.13	—	0.03	—	0.02	—	0.12	—
Bachelor's degree	0.52	—	0.65	—	0.61	—	0.61	—
Advanced degree	0.08	—	0.09	—	0.20	—	0.12	—
Don't know	0.27	—	0.23	—	0.18	—	0.15	—
Weekly hours spent on homework or/and self-study	2.51	1.70	2.73	1.90	3.59	2.16	4.16	2.86
Weekly hours spent on private tutoring	2.69	2.21	3.31	2.36	3.38	2.46	3.97	2.54
N	184		94		51		33	

TABLE 4.2.—Continued

D. Total

Variable	M	SD	missing cases (%)
Outcomes (ninth grade)			
English achievement	527.35	64.35	8.2
Household characteristics			
Monthly household income (logged)	5.73	0.62	7.2
Continuously married	0.95	—	2.5
Paternal age	43.96	4.20	14.1
Maternal age	40.86	4.09	3.9
Mother worked	0.55	—	2.1
Number of siblings	2.22	0.71	6.8
Educational expectation of parents			2.5
Associate's degree or less	0.04	—	
Bachelor's degree	0.61	—	
Advanced degree	0.36	—	
School contact	0.00	1.00	5.3
Parent-child discussion	0.02	0.99	2.3
Monitoring	0.02	0.99	3.5
Private tutoring-related activities	0.03	0.99	11.3
Child controls			
Gender, child female	0.48	—	0.0
Prior achievement (seventh grade)	299.70	57.50	0.6
Educational expectation of the child			1.2
Associate's degree or less	0.07	—	
Bachelor's degree	0.57	—	
Advanced degree	0.15	—	
Don't know	0.21	—	
Weekly hours spent on homework or/and self-study	2.96	2.01	5.7
Weekly hours spent on private tutoring	3.59	2.50	5.8
N		6,310	

Note: The estimates are an average of the results across 25 complete data sets by using Rubin's rules.

children from other types of families except for those from hypogamous families where the father was a two-year college graduate and the mother was a four-year college graduate.[4] Results also showed that when both parents were four-year college graduates, they were more likely to be continuously married compared to the other groups.

By contrast, when either the father or the mother was a middle school graduate, parents were less likely to be continuously married. For example, the proportion of parents who were continuously married was the lowest (.88) among hypogamous families where the father was a middle school graduate while the mother had a higher level of education. Regarding the family size, children in the families where the father and the mother were both four-year college graduates had the smallest number of siblings (2.08), and this was statistically different from that of many other types of families. As for parental involvement, results showed that parents who were both four-year college graduates were engaged in many forms of parental involvement to a greater extent, especially regarding parent-child discussion and private tutoring–related activities, compared to other groups of parents.

With respect to child characteristics, results showed that children from homogamous families where parents were both four-year college graduates far outperformed children from other types of families on the English test in the seventh grade. Children from homogamous families where parents were both four-year college graduates also had a higher level of educational expectations and spent more time on studying or private tutoring compared to children from other types of families. In the following, we examine whether there is a significant effect of educational assortative mating on children's English achievement and the extent to which differences in household and child characteristics across different types of educational assortative mating involved in different levels of parental education help to explain the effect of educational assortative marriage.

Effects of Educational Assortative Mating

We first examine the average effect of educational assortative mating on children's English achievement. Figure 4.1 presents a summary of results for the average effect of educational homogamy on children's English achievement (full regression results and tables are available from the authors upon request). Note that the reference group was children who were from educationally heterogamous families. Accordingly, the negative values in figure 4.1 indicate a lower average score of children from education-

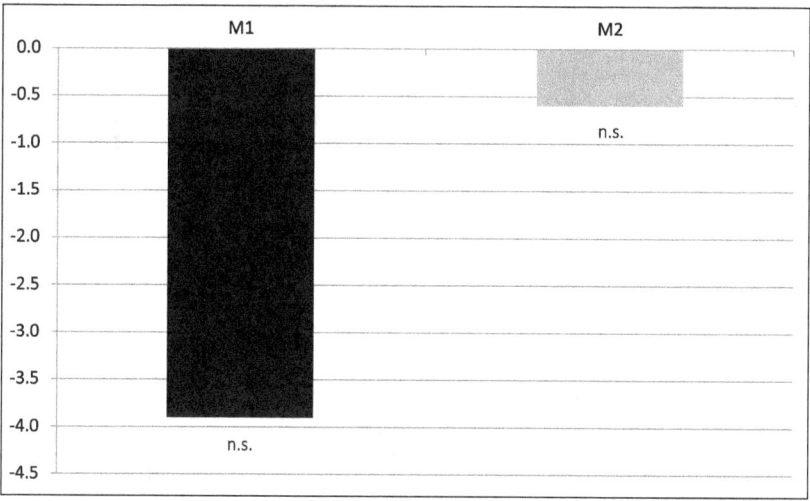

Fig. 4.1. Unadjusted and adjusted differences in English achievement between children from educationally homogamous families and children from educationally heterogamous families

Note: n.s. = (statistically) nonsignificant. M1 included only the dummy variable for educational assortative mating, and M2 included all other variables. The reference group was those children from educationally heterogamous families where the level of parental education differed from each other.

ally homogamous families compared to children who were from educationally heterogamous families. In Model 1, we included only the dummy variable denoting whether children were from educationally homogamous families. We found that although children from educationally homogamous families on average underperformed their counterparts from educationally heterogamous families on English tests by approximately four points, this difference was not statistically significant.

Because there were no significant differences in English achievement between children from educationally heterogamous families and those from educationally homogamous families even before taking into account other variables, it might be less useful to further examine what factors would explain differences in English achievement between these two groups of children. However, it might be still useful to take into account other variables when estimating the average effect of educational homogamy on children's English achievement because of potential suppressor relationships. Accordingly, in Model 2, we additionally included all other variables, including the level of parental education. We found that on aver-

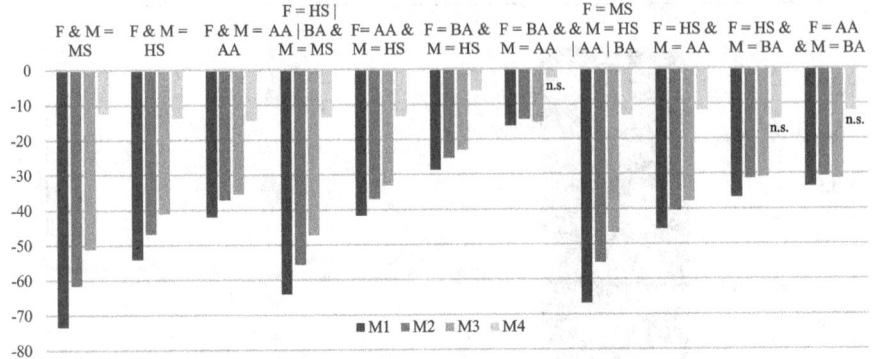

Fig. 4.2. Unadjusted and adjusted differences in English achievement by the type of educational assortative mating and the level of parental education

Note: F = father's education, M = mother's education, MS = middle school, HS = high school, AA = associate's degree, BA = bachelor's degree. n.s. = (statistically) nonsignificant. M1 included a series of dummy variables for the different types of educational assortative mating combined with the different levels of parental education, M2 = M1 + household characteristic variables except for parental involvement, M3 = M2 + parental involvement variables, and M4 = M3 + all child characteristic variables. The reference group was those children from educationally homogamous families where both parents were four-year college graduates (i.e., F & M = BA). Differences are all statistically significant at $p < .05$, unless noted.

age, children from educationally homogamous families slightly underperformed their counterparts from educationally heterogamous families, but again this difference was not statistically significant. In short, there was no significant average effect of educational homogamy on children's English achievement with or without taking into account other variables.

Next, we examine the heterogenous effect of educational assortative mating on children's English achievement depending on the level of parental education. Figure 4.2 presents a summary of results for the heterogenous effect of educational homogamy on children's English achievement by the level of parental education (full regression results and tables are available from the authors upon request). Recall that the reference group was those children from educationally homogamous families where both parents were four-year college graduates. Accordingly, the negative values in figure 4.2 indicate lower scores of children in each type of family compared to the reference group (i.e., children whose fathers and mothers were both four-year college graduates).

In Model 1, we included only a series of dummy variables for the different types of educational assortative mating combined with the different levels of parental education. We found considerable advantages for growing up in homogamous families where both parents were four-year college graduates in terms of higher English achievement. In other words, children from homogamous families where both parents were four-year college graduates showed much higher levels of English achievement than their counterparts from other types of families. The largest gap was observed between children from homogamous families where both parents were four-year college graduates and their counterparts from homogamous families where both parents were middle school graduates.

What might explain such differences? To answer this question, we added the household characteristic variables except for parental involvement to Model 2 and found that these achievement gaps remained significant even though their degrees were somewhat reduced. These results suggested that household characteristics, especially income, marriage status, and the mother's working status, account for the effect of educational assortative mating on children's English achievement to some extent. In Model 3, we additionally added parental involvement variables. We found that while significant gaps in English achievement between children from homogamous families, where both parents were four-year college graduates, and those from other types of families remained, the degree of the observed achievement gaps was further reduced. These results suggested that parental involvement further accounts for some of the heterogenous effects of educational assortative mating.

Finally, in Model 4, we further added child characteristics variables, including prior achievement. Note that since we included prior achievement measured in the seventh grade, results of Model 4 indicated whether factors were associated with achievement gains between seventh and ninth grades. Results showed that there were significant differences in English achievement between children from homogamous families where both parents were four-year college graduates and children from many other types of families. Yet some significant differences observed in Model 4 became nonsignificant for children from some other types of families. For example, there were no significant differences in English achievement between children from homogamous families, where both parents were four-year college graduates, and children from hypergamous families, where the father was a four-year college graduate and the mother was a two-year college graduate, when controlling for child characteristic variables. Likewise, there were no significant differences in English achievement between children from homogamous families where both parents were four-year college graduates and children from hypogamous families where the father was a high school graduate or a two-year college graduate and the mother was a four-year college graduate.

Discussion

In this study, we examined educational assortative mating in Korea from an intergenerational perspective by examining the impact of educational assortative mating on children's academic achievement using longitudinal data for a representative sample of seventh graders in Korea. We found that while the majority of children were from homogamous families, a very few children came from hypogamous families, which is consistent with previous literature. In addition, although we did not find the significant average effect of educational homogamy on children's English achievement, we did find its significant heterogenous effect depending on the level of parental education. Specifically, we found that children from educationally homogamous families, where both parents were four-year college graduates, on average outperformed their counterparts from many other types of families on English tests. Furthermore, we found that differentiated family environments and educational strategies partially explained the positive effect of educational homogamy on children's English achievement. Together, findings suggest that educational homogamy, especially among highly educated parents, may exacerbate educational inequality among children potentially through differentiated family arrangements and investment strategies.

Meanwhile, it is an interesting and unexpected finding that the differences in English test scores became insignificant between children whose parents were both four-year college graduates and those whose father was a four-year college graduate and the mother was a two-year college graduate once children's characteristics were taken into account. This was also the case between children whose parents were both four-year college graduates and those whose father was a high school graduate or a two-year college graduate and whose mother was a four-year college graduate. One possible explanation is that the parent who had a four-year tertiary education assumed a leading role in their child's education, maximizing the benefits of parental education.

Indeed, there were few differences in many aspects of parental involvement between children from families where both parents were four-year college graduates and children from families where at least one parent was a four-year college graduate. In fact, when it came to parental educational expectations, parents tended to have higher educational expectations for their children when at least one of them was a four-year college graduate than when both parents were four-year college graduates. This finding suggests that the parents of these families might be engaged in some sort of strategy to overcome deficiencies that may have come from less education compared to families where both parents are four-year college graduates. Yet, to truly understand the strategies utilized by these families, it is pivotal to investigate the bargaining and decision-making process between the parents in relation to the education of their child.

Another area for future research pertains to the potential differences in the way by which fathers and mothers are involved in children's academic success. A critical assumption underlying the effect of educational homogamy on children's educational outcomes is that fathers and mothers make equal contributions to promoting children's academic success. However, this presumption may not be true in every culture. As a matter of fact, some scholars point out the different roles and responsibilities that each parent takes on for their children's education. In the Korean context, for example, it has been said that mothers play a much more important role in children's education than do fathers because they are the persons who usually gather a wide range of vital information regarding private tutoring as well as mainstream education (Park, Byun, and Kim 2011). Such disparities in the roles that fathers and mothers assume may lead to different effects on their children's educational outcomes even though they have the same level of education.

There are some other limitations that need to be addressed in future research. First, KELS collected either mother or father reports[5] rather than both mother and father reports and thus did not allow us to examine consensus in the way that parents invest in children's education. As Beck and Gonzalez-Sancho (2009) discussed, it is essential to collect information separately from parents to study the homogeneity in parental involvement and educational strategies that can serve as mechanisms linked to educational homogamy. In this vein, future research should use data collected from both mother and father reports when available. Second, the current study focused on children's English achievement. However, future studies should examine a variety of educational and occupational outcomes of children to better understand the intergenerational effects of educational assortative marriage.

NOTES

This study was inspired by and dedicated to Suet-ling Pong, who passed away in 2015. An earlier version of this chapter was presented at the spring meeting of the International Sociology Association Research Committee on Social Stratification and Mobility (RC 28), May 26–28, 2016, at the National University of Singapore, in Singapore. The authors thank Lingxin Hao, Yu Xie, Paul Chang, Hyunjoon Park, and Hyeyoung Woo for their helpful comments on earlier drafts. The authors acknowledge assistance provided by the Population Research Institute at Penn State University, which is supported by an infrastructure grant by the Eunice Kennedy Shriver National Institute of Child Health and Human Development (P2CHD041025). Direct all correspondence to Soo-yong Byun.

1. The base year survey asked students about the number of brothers and sisters, but the deprived variable of the number of siblings provided by KEDI was included in the second follow-up data.

2. χ^2 or t-tests are usually used to examine the bivariate relationship among variables, but there is no consensus on how to combine χ^2 or t-test results across imputed data sets. Therefore, we used regression approaches to test differences. When it came to monthly household income, for example, we conducted OLS regression analysis, where monthly household income was used as the dependent variable and a set of dummy variables for the combination of the type of educational assortative mating and the level of parental education as the independent variables (children from educationally homogamous families, where both parents were four-year college graduates, were the reference group). Meanwhile, in addition to household and child characteristics, we also examined whether there were regional differences (indicated by the location of the school that children attended) across different types of educational assortative marriage combined with the different levels of parental education. We found that the proportion of homogamous families where both father and mother were middle school graduates was much higher in rural areas than in other regions. In addition, we found that differences in English achievement across different types of educational assortative marriage combined with the different levels of parental education became greater after taking region into account.

3. Following recommendations set forth by Johnson and Young (2011), we included all of the dependent and independent variables in the imputed model to predict missing values and generated 25 imputed data sets to improve the stability of estimates using the chained equations approach with the Stata ICE module (Royston and White 2011). Then, using Rubin's rules (1987), we pooled estimates from the 25 data sets with the MIM prefix in Stata. To address the nested nature of the data (i.e., students nested within schools), we employed cluster robust standard errors, which downwardly adjust inflated standard errors resulted from violations of the independent errors assumption due to clustering, thereby reducing the likelihood of making a Type I error (Rogers 1993).

4. Yet, this statistically nonsignificant difference in the average monthly household income between these two groups would be likely attributable to the small sample size ($N = 33$) for this group of children where the father was a two-year college graduate and the mother was a four-year college graduate. Accordingly, results should be interpreted with caution.

5. A supplementary analysis suggested that more mothers (approximately 73 percent) than fathers (approximately 21 percent) responded to KELS.

REFERENCES

Beck, Audrey, and Carlos Gonzalez-Sancho. 2009. "Educational Assortative Mating and Children's School Readiness." Center for Research on Child Wellbeing Working Paper #2009-05-FF. Princeton, NJ: Center for Research on Child Wellbeing, Princeton University.

Blossfeld, Hans-Peter. 2009. "Educational Assortative Marriage in Comparative Perspective." *Annual Review of Sociology* 35: 513–30.

Blossfeld, Hans-Peter, and Andreas Timm, eds. 2003. *Who Marries Whom? Educational Systems as Marriage Markets in Modern Societies*. Dordretch: European Association for Population Studies and Kluwer Academic Publishers.

Byun, Soo-yong, and Kyung-keun Kim. 2010. "Educational Inequality in South Korea: The Widening Socioeconomic Gap in Student Achievement." *Research in the Sociology of Education* 17: 155–82.

Byun, Soo-yong, Evan Schofer, and Kyung-keun Kim. 2012. "Revisiting the Role of Cultural Capital in East Asian Educational Systems: The Case of South Korea." *Sociology of Education* 85 (3): 219–39.

Coleman, James S. 1988. "Social Capital in the Creation of Human Capital." *American Journal of Sociology* 94: S95–S120.

Grusky, David B. 2014. *Social Stratification. Class, Race, and Gender in Sociological Perspective*. 4th ed. Philadelphia: Westview.

Johnson, David R., and Rebekah Young. 2011. "Toward Best Practices in Analyzing Datasets with Missing Data: Comparisons and Recommendations." *Journal of Marriage and Family* 73: 926–45.

Lareau, Annette. 2003. *Unequal Childhoods: Class, Race and Family Life*. Berkeley: University of California Press.

Mare, Robert D. 1991. "Five Decades of Educational Assortative Mating." *American Sociological Review* 56 (1): 15–32.

McClendon, David, Janet Chen-Lan Kuo, and R. Kelly Raley. 2014. "Opportunities to Meet: Occupational Education and Marriage Formation in Young Adulthood." *Demography* 51 (4): 1319–44.

OECD. 2014. *PISA 2012 Results: What Students Know and Can Do—Student Performance in Mathematics, Reading and Science*. Vol. 1, Rev. ed., February, PISA, OECD Publishing. https://www.oecd.org/pisa/keyfindings/pisa-2012-results-volume-I.pdf

Oppenheimer, Valerie K. 1988. "A Theory of Marriage Timing." *American Journal of Sociology* 94 (3): 563–91.

Park, Hyunjoon, and Kyung-keun Kim. 2011. "Han'guk sahoe ŭi kyoyukchŏk tongjirhon punsŏk: sigyeyŏl ch'use mit kŭ hamŭi" (Educational Homogamy in Korea: Recent Trends and Their Implications). *Kyoyuk sahoehak yŏn'gu* (*Korean Journal of Sociology of Education*) 21 (3): 51–76 (in Korean).

Park, Hyunjoon, and Kyung-keun Kim. 2012. "Han'guk sahoe ŭi kyoyukchŏk tongjirhon punsŏk: 1966–2010" (Educational Homogamy in Korea: 1966–2010). *Kyoyuk sahoehak yŏn'gu* (*Korean Journal of Sociology of Education*) 22 (4): 113–39 (in Korean).

Park, Hyunjoon, Soo-yong Byun, and Kyung-keun Kim. 2011. "Parental Involvement and Students' Cognitive Outcomes in Korea: Focusing on Private Tutoring." *Sociology of Education* 84 (1): 3–22.

Park, Hyunjoon, and Jeroen Smits. 2005. "Educational Assortative Mating in South Korea: Trends 1930–1998." *Research in Social Stratification and Mobility* 23: 103–27.

Rogers, William. 1993. "Regression Standard Errors in Clustered Samples." *Stata Technical Bulletin* 13: 19–23.
Royston, Patrick, and Ian R. White. 2011. "Multiple Imputation by Chained Equations (MICE): Implementation in Stata." *Journal of Statistical Software* 45 (4): 1–20.
Rubin, Donald. B. 1987. *Multiple Imputation for Nonresponse in Surveys*. New York: John Wiley.
Schwartz, Christine R. 2013. "Trends and Variation in Assortative Mating: Causes and Consequences." *Annual Review of Sociology* 39: 451–70.
Schwartz, Christine R., and Robert D. Mare. 2005. "Trends in Educational Assortative Mating from 1940 to 2003." *Demography* 42 (4): 621–46.
Smits, Jeroen, and Hyunjoon Park. 2009. "Five Decades of Educational Assortative Mating in 10 East Asian Societies." *Social Forces* 88 (1): 227–55.
Smits, Jeroen, Wout Ultee, and Jan Lammers. 1998. "Educational Homogamy in 65 Countries: An Explanation of Differences in Openness Using Country-Level Explanatory Variables." *American Sociological Review* 63 (2): 264–85.

5
Does Marriage Matter for Children?
Parental Marital Status and Children's Health in South Korea

Hyeyoung Woo, Sojung Lim, Sun Young Jeon, and Wonjeong Jeong

An increasing body of literature has attempted to examine health disparities among adults in South Korea (hereafter Korea) in recent years (An and Kim 2013; Kim 2010; Kim 2011; Kim, Song, and Paek 2013; Kim, Kim, and Yi 2013; Pak 2013; Yi 2005). Yet, health of children has received less attention. Children suffer relatively less from serious chronic health conditions compared to adults in general. However, childhood is a critical period for physical, cognitive, and emotional development. Health issues during this period may interfere with physical growth, proper schooling and learning progress, and emotional development, which may result in substantial implications for health and other life outcomes over the life course. Individuals who experienced these effects, especially those who suffered from physical or psychological health issues while growing up, are less likely to achieve high levels of educational attainment, and, in turn, they have fewer employment opportunities, higher levels of economic hardship, and less stable romantic relationships in adulthood compared to those who did not (Palloni 2006).

Among a number of social factors associated with health outcomes of children, the importance of family cannot be overstated in Korea. As a primary social institution for children, family often plays fundamental roles in children's physical, emotional, and social development (Repetti, Taylor, and Seeman 2002; Woo, Jung, and Kim 2013). While family remains as a strong social institution and is still highly valued in contemporary Korea, the proportion of single-parent households has increased, partly attributed to higher divorce rates in recent years (Statistics Korea 2016). Divorce rates substantially increased during the economic recession in the late 1990s and have stayed high even after economic recovery (Park and Raymo 2013; Statistics Korea 2016). As a result, the proportion of children ages 18 and younger who live with a divorced parent more than doubled (from 3.0 percent to 6.2 percent) in the last 10 years (Park, Choi, and Jo 2016). Based on a recent report showing a high ratio of divorce filings to marriage registrations (38 percent) (Office of Court Administration 2015), the proportion of children living with a single parent may continue to grow.

Despite rising divorce rates, the proportion of children living with a single parent in Korea (over 6 percent) may be considered small in comparison to proportions observed in Western countries (e.g., about 25 percent in the United States) (Payne 2013). However, since the proportion of children of single parents only captures those who *currently* live with a single parent at the time of interview, parental divorce would influence far more children who *have ever lived* with a single parent at some point during their childhood. Additionally, because Korea is a strong familial society with traditional family norms, divorce is still highly stigmatized, often imposing additional psychological burden and stress on divorced parents and possibly on their children (Kim and Woo 2017; Yi 2010). Moreover, as pointed out in a study by Park, Choi, and Jo (2016), despite recent increases in national public spending on family benefits, such as financial support for childcare and early education, the percentage of gross domestic product spent on family benefits in Korea is far lower than the average among the 36 countries in the Organization for Economic Co-operation and Development (OECD 2016a). Female labor force participation is relatively lower in Korea, especially for women in their 30s and 40s (OECD 2016b)—partly due to non-family-friendly work environments (e.g., common overtime work, social gatherings after work, and inflexible work hours). Combined with a rigid Korean labor market, where it is difficult to exit and reenter the workforce, increases in single parents raise important health concerns for children of single parents in Korea.

To our surprise, however, little research has examined how parental marital status is associated with children's well-being. A few previous studies reported higher levels of aggression as well as lower levels of self-esteem, psychological well-being, reading performance, and educational aspiration among children with single parents compared to those with two parents (Chŏng 1993; Hong 2004; Park 2007, 2008). However, the studies looking at health outcomes are based on small community samples (Chŏng 1993; Hong 2004). Considering a limited generalizability of these findings, an examination of data based on a nationally representative sample is still required to understand overall health patterns among children by family structure. Using data from the Korean Children and Youth Panel Survey (KCYPS), we aim to fill this gap by evaluating the extent to which parental marital status is associated with children's health outcomes in Korea. As a longitudinal data set based on a large national sample of children in Korea, the KCYPS is ideal for this study since it provides a wide range of information on children's health, family, and other sociodemographic characteristics. Given the persistently high divorce rate and the potentially negative implications of parental divorce for health of children, findings of this study will advance our knowledge of the impact of parental marital status on the well-being of children (e.g., McLanahan and Percheski 2008). In doing so, our study will also offer valuable insights for determinants of early childhood health disparities that may have enduring influence over the life course. These insights may further help design effective policies and programs to address such health disparities among children in Korea.

Background

Parental Marital Status and Health of Children

Previous literature suggests that health of children from single-parent households is likely to be worse than that of their counterparts in two-parent families (with an exception of Kim and Woo 2011). The main mechanism for this association is through socioeconomic resources, which are often indicated by education, income, and employment status (e.g., Elo 2009; Mirowsky, Ross, and Reynolds 2000; Phelan, Link, and Tehranifar 2010). Undoubtedly, socioeconomic resources of parents are also direct and indirect sources for children's physical growth and their cognitive and emotional development through proper nutrition and a safe living environment. In addition, when children have issues requiring medical attention, financial resources of parents are often the primary means to pay for treatment as needed. In general, married couples are financially better off than their unmarried counterparts due to increased household income, the benefit from economies of scale, better access to health care, and higher savings and wealth (Waite 1995). It is therefore reasonable to expect that children of single-parent households (mostly due to either divorce or bereavement of a spouse in Korea) may have worse health outcomes than their counterparts and that financial resources of parents may be at least partially responsible for the health disadvantages.

There are also other mechanisms to explain the health disadvantages of children with a single parent, including elevated levels of stress from experiencing a parental marital dissolution, a lack of social support resulting from the absence of one of the parents in the household, and a higher tendency of engaging in unhealthy behaviors with a lack of supervision from a parent. First, parental divorce and the death of a parent are stressful events for children, which may require a substantial amount of time to overcome or to adjust to at least. Especially, children of divorced parents may have witnessed their parents' conflicts, which often precede the divorce and may continue for years even after the divorce. Also, parental divorce more often requires adjusting for substantial changes in children's living arrangements and the amount of time that children can spend with parents (Cooper et al. 2009). Not surprisingly, research has confirmed that children who experience parental divorce are more likely than children in intact families to exhibit disruptive behaviors or to have higher levels of psychological distress (Amato and Sobolewski 2001; Hodges and Bloom 1984; Jekielek 1997; McLanahan and Sandefur 1994; Ross and Mirowsky 1999), which may also lead to other health issues later on.

Second, children of single-parent households are likely to experience reduced support from parents in general, and because of the absence (or less availability) of one parent, social circles for children may also be limited (Jang et al. 2001). Children go through a socialization process by interacting with various social agents, and direct interaction with their significant role models, such as parents, is crucial (Haveman and Wolfe 1995; Hetherington 1972). However, children in a single-parent household may not have stable role models and therefore might not have enough social resources to develop social skills, which are found to be important for children's emotional development (Sigle-Rushton and McLanahan 2004).

Last, growing up with a single parent during childhood may also influence children's health behaviors, which may last through adulthood. Single parents tend to experience greater levels of time constraints compared to their married counterparts, and thus, the amount and quality of time that they spend with their children are likely to be limited (e.g., McLanahan and Percheski 2008). Greater levels of time constraints among single parents may result in more difficulties closely engaging in and supervising their children's activities and social lives (McLanahan and Sandefur 1994). Children with a lack of supervision are less likely to discipline themselves in general, maintain a healthy diet, and excise regularly. Indeed, there is evidence that children in single-parent families are subject to a higher risk of committing delinquent behaviors, such as underage smoking and drinking (Kim 2007). These unhealthy behavioral habits that were formed during childhood are found to remain even later in the life course. For example, research found that those who started smoking at earlier ages tend to continue smoking as an adult (Chen and Millar 1998; Khuder, Dayal, and Mutgi 1999). Similarly, children who experienced drinking at earlier ages (especially binge drinking) are at a higher risk of developing alcoholism later (DeWit et al. 2000; Hingson, Heeren, and Winter 2006).

The Korean Context

The above mechanisms for the association between parental marital status and health of children (i.e., socioeconomic resources, social support, and health behaviors) suggest that similar to their peers in other countries, children with a single parent in Korea may also experience health disadvantages compared to children of two-parent families. However, the influence of parents' socioeconomic resources, especially educational attainment, on children's health may be even more critical in Korea. Previous research documented that individuals of lower socioeconomic positions are at greater risk of experiencing a divorce in the United States (Amato and Previti 2003; White 1991). While previous research on divorce in Korea is relatively sparse, a few existing studies confirmed that those with lower education are more likely to divorce in Korea (Chun and Sohn 2009; Park and Raymo 2013; Yi and Kim 2011) and that this negative association between education and divorce is more salient among younger cohorts (Park and Raymo 2013). In another study examining levels of family values using data from the International Social Survey Programme, Ŭn and Yi (2005) found that people in Korea had the highest level of traditional and conservative attitudes about divorce among developed countries. Because the rapid increase of divorce is only recent in Korea, social approval for divorce may still be low in Korea.

Putting them together, we expect that among the factors described earlier, the socioeconomic status of a parent is the most fundamental factor to explain potential health disparities among children with a single parent in Korea. In addition, because of the low levels of social approval for divorce (often accompanied by stereotypes against divorced parents and their children) in Korea, children with a single parent are particularly vulnerable to psychological distress and aggression (rather than self-rated health) compared to children with two parents. To test the hypotheses, the current study examines the associations between parental marital status and children's health using various health outcomes such as self-rated health, depressive symptoms, aggression, and self-esteem. Given the significant differences in parents' socioeconomic resources between two-parent families and single-parent families in Korea, we also evaluate the extent to which this association is explained by the socioeconomic status of parents, with other controls adjusted.

Data and Methods

Data

We use data from the Korean Children and Youth Panel Survey, an annual longitudinal survey that has been conducted by the National Youth Policy Institute since 2010. The KCYPS is designed to collect information about physical growth and cognitive development of school-age children in the context of family, school, and community. In this study, we utilize data from five waves, conducted from 2010 to 2014. As a nationally representative sample of children, the KCYPS consists of three cohort surveys: Cohort 1 for children in the first grade of elementary school; Cohort 2 for those in the fourth grade; and Cohort 3 for the seventh graders (i.e., the first grade of middle school). The sample of the first wave of the KCYPS includes 7,071 children in total (2,342 for Cohort 1; 2,378 for Cohort 2; and 2,351 for Cohort 3). For analytic sample, we select two waves for each health outcome per cohort with two years apart (e.g., waves 2 and 4 are used for self-rated health) for two reasons: (1) survey years when questions about specific health conditions are included differ across cohorts; and (2) we estimate models with lagged health outcomes (i.e., health outcomes are measured in year $t + 2$, and independent and control variables are measured in year t). This analytic approach allows us to estimate models in a way that parents' marital status precedes health outcomes of children with the same follow-up period for all of our health outcomes. The waves used for the analysis are presented by cohort in table 5.1.

As for our analytic sample, we select children who live with either two biological parents or a single biological parent at both waves (i.e., stable two-parent or stable single-parent families). In other words, we exclude those whose biological parent is remarried (after divorce or death of a spouse) at the baseline to avoid potential confounding effects of experiencing parents' multiple marital transitions on children's well-being. Because the proportion of children whose parents experienced more than one marital transition is very small (2.2 percent), the exclusion of those children is not likely to bias our results in meaningful ways. Then, we also exclude the cases where at least one of two selected waves is missing for the lagged health outcome from our analytic sample. The percentages of missing cases range from 4 percent (for the self-rated health variable) to 6.8 percent (for parent's educational attainment). After applying "listwise" deletion, the final sample consists of 5,748 to 5,789 observations depending on the (lagged) health outcome examined.

Measures

We look at four health outcomes, including self-rated health (SRH), depression, aggression, and self-esteem, to examine various dimensions of children's health in this study. First, SRH measures respondents' overall health status. As a measure of respondents' subjective assessment of their own health, SRH is a widely used indicator of health due to its simplicity and high validity, which is often higher than validities of more "objective" health measures assessed by clinical exams (Idler and Kasl 1991; Mirowsky and Ross 2003). While SRH has been widely used among adults, the prevalence of SRH in research of children and adolescents is increasing (e.g., Boardman 2006; Breidablik, Meland, and Lydersen 2008; Eder 1990; Mechanic and Hansell 1987). In the KCYPS, children are asked to rate their

TABLE 5.1. KCYPS Waves Used in the Analysis by Cohort (2010–14)

	Cohort 1	Cohort 2	Cohort 3
Self-rated Health			
Dependent variable (Self-rated health at year $t + 2$)	4	4	4
other variables	2	2	2
Depression			
Dependent variable (Depression at year $t + 2$)	4	5	4
other variables	2	3	2
Aggression			
Dependent variable (Aggression at year $t + 2$)	4	5	4
other variables	2	3	2
Self-Esteem			
Dependent variable (Self-esteem at year $t + 2$)	5	4	5
other variables	3	2	3

health conditions (i.e., "How would you rate your health in general?") with four response options ("very good," "good," "poor," and "very poor"). We collapse those who rated their health to be "very good" or "good" into one category (coded as 1) and those with "poor" or "very poor" health into another category (i.e., reference group, coded as 0), because the proportion of children reporting they have "very poor" health is too small to produce reliable estimates.

Second, we use 10 items from the Center for Epidemiologic Studies Depression Scale (CES-D) to capture depressive symptoms and their frequencies. The CES-D has been proved as a reliable and valid measure of psychological distress for children (Fendrich, Weissman, and Warner 1990). In the KCYPS, respondents are asked to report to what extent they usually experience the following 10 depressive symptoms: (1) I don't have energy; (2) I feel unhappy; (3) I worry a lot; (4) I talk about committing suicide; (5) I cry often; (6) I often blame myself when something goes wrong; (7) I feel lonely; (8) I have interests in nothing; (9) I talk negatively about my future; and (10) I feel everything I do is an effort. The response categories are (1) "strongly agree," (2) "agree," (3) "disagree," and (4) "strongly disagree." All the responses are reverse coded, and then an average value of the 10 responses is computed, with higher values indicating more frequent levels of depressive symptoms. The alpha reliability scores are 0.89 for Cohort 1 (wave 4), 0.90 for Cohort 2 (wave 5), and 0.89 for Cohort 3 (wave 4).

Our third health measure, aggression, provides a unique aspect of psychological well-being of children resulting from either chronic or acute stressors. Derived from the Behavior Problems Index (Peterson and Zill 1986), which assesses children's behavioral development, aggression commonly serves as a reliable measure of psychological well-being of children, capturing children's emotional status and levels of stress in a form of more observable behavior problems (Zill 1990). Aggression is based on six items about respondents' usual experience of aggressive symptoms: (1) I pick on small things; (2) I often interfere with other people's work; (3) I fight when I am told "no" to what I want to do; (4) I fight for a trivial thing; (5) I am angry all day; and (6) I often cry without any reason. Response options for these questions include (1) "strongly agree," (2) "agree," (3) "disagree," and (4) "strongly disagree." We also reverse code the responses to all the six questions and average them so that a higher score indicates a greater level of aggression. The alpha reliability scores are 0.81 for Cohort 1 (wave 4), 0.82 for Cohort 2 (wave 5), and 0.79 for Cohort 3 (wave 4).

Last, we use five items from the Rosenberg Self-Esteem Scale to measure self-esteem. As another commonly used mental health indicator (e.g., Mann et al. 2004), self-esteem among children is also closely linked to various health outcomes as well as behavioral issues (e.g., French, Story, and Perry 1995; Trzesniewski et al. 2006). The KCYPS employs the original self-esteem scale (10 items) for Cohorts 2 and 3, but only 5 items are asked for Cohort 1. To achieve consistency and to avoid potential measurement errors, we use the 5 items that are asked for all three cohorts. The 5 items used in this study are (1) I am satisfied with myself; (2) I am useless; (3) I have many strengths; (4) I feel I am as good as other people; and (5) I have nothing to be proud of. The same response options are (1) "strongly agree," (2) "agree," (3) "disagree," and (4) "strongly disagree." Two negatively worded items ("I am useless" and "I have nothing to be proud of") are reverse coded, and average values of the responses are calculated, with higher scores indicating higher levels of self-esteem. The alpha reliability scores range from 0.83 for Cohort 1 (wave 5) and 0.84 for Cohort 2 (wave 3) to 0.86 for Cohort 3 (wave 5).

Parental marital status, our independent variable, is a dummy variable: 1 is assigned to children of stable single parents between two waves; and 0 is assigned to children of stable two-parent married parents between two waves (reference group). We construct this variable from a survey question on the parental marital/family composition of a respondent at both waves (see table 5.1 for waves used for each cohort), distinguishing children living with "two biological parents," from those living with "a single biological mother or father." When two biological parents live together, the parental marital status is considered married. Single-parent families combine the parents who are divorced, separated, or widowed, given the small sample sizes for each group.

The current analysis considers various demographic and socioeconomic characteristics of parents and children that may affect both parental marital status and children's health outcomes. Specifically, we include the gender of children and cohort (i.e., a proxy of age), parents' educational attainment ("high school or less," "junior college," and "college or more") and employment status ("employed" and "unemployed"), annual household income (logged), region ("Seoul," "metropolitan cities," "small cities," and "rural area"), and whether grandparents co-reside. For parents' education and work status, we use information of the parent who is the respondent's primary guardian. That is, for the respondents living with both parents, we considered the father's education and work status. For the respondents with a single mother or father, we use the education and work status of the single parent who resides with the respondent. Last, health measures obtained at the baseline (year t) are included to estimate changes in the well-being of children associated with parental marital status during the time interval observed in this study.

Analytic Strategy

We estimate ordinary least squares (OLS) regression models for depressive symptoms, aggression, and self-esteem, and logistic regression models for self-rated health considering the nature of these dependent variables. For each health outcome, we estimate three models. The first model (baseline model) evaluates the association between parental marital status and children's health while controlling for cohort (as a proxy for children's age) and gender. As noted, each cohort consists of respondents in the same grade, and we thus treat the cohort variable as a proxy of children's age. In the second model (Model 2), we add children's baseline health, measured in year t, to examine the extent to which the association between parental marital status and children's health outcome is attributed to children's preexisting health conditions. Then, the final model (Model 3), which includes all control variables (e.g., household income, parents' education and work status, region, and co-residence with grandparents), evaluates the extent to which sociodemographic conditions of parents account for the association of parental marital status with children's health outcomes observed in Model 2.

Results

Sample Characteristics

Table 5.2 presents sample characteristics (proportions/means and standard deviations) for all variables considered in our analyses for the entire sample and separately by parental marital status. As mentioned above, we utilize data from different waves across three cohort surveys depending on the availabilities of health measures (see table 5.1 for detailed information). For the purpose of a simple presentation, we provide descriptive statistics based on data from wave 2 in table 5.2, except for a few (lagged) health outcomes (see notes in table 5.2 for more information). Our supplement analysis indicates that the characteristics presented here in table 5.2 are largely consistent with the statistics based on the total sample of the KCYPS (results not shown).

Table 5.2 shows that our analytic sample consists of 52 percent of boys and 48 percent of girls and almost 94 percent of children who live with both biological parents and 6 percent who live with one parent—more likely the mother (results not shown). The proportion of those in two-parent households is lower among older cohorts, reflecting a higher risk of parental divorce with a longer exposure to marriage duration. More importantly, table 5.2 reveals stark differences in compositional characteristics of children and their families by parental marital status. First, children of single-parent families fare worse than their counterparts in two-parent families in all of the health measures, including those measured at the baseline (year t). For example, only 6 percent of children living with both parents rate their health as "poor" or "very poor," but the proportion of children in poor or very poor health is more than twice (about 13 percent) in single-parent families. In addition, single-parent families are much more socioeconomically disadvantaged than two-parent families: They have lower household income (logged) and a lower percentage of parents with college degrees and jobs ($p < 0.001$). Last, children of single parents are more likely than those living with both parents to live with grandparents. In fact, living with grandparents is a common living arrangement among single parents in East Asia (Raymo et al. 2014).

Given the substantial differences in demographic and socioeconomic characteristics between two-parent families and single-parent families shown in table 5.2, it is plausible that worse health outcomes of children of single-parent families observed in both time periods (i.e., year t and year $t + 2$) may be due to compositional characteristics of single-parent families (e.g., low SES) rather than to parental marital status per se. For this reason, we next estimate multiple regression models, which examine the association between parental marital status and children's health outcomes while taking into account such compositional characteristics.

Results from Multiple Regression Models

Table 5.3 presents results from logistic regression models to predict the logged odds of children having good health as a function of parental marital status. As noted, the baseline model included parental marital status and children's demographic characteristics (i.e., age and gender). Results from the baseline model (Model 1) show that children living with a single parent are 44 percent less likely to rate their health good compared to those living with both biological parents (i.e., OR = 0.56, $p < 0.01$). The next model (Model 2) includes children's baseline health (i.e., self-rated

TABLE 5.2. Sample Characteristics of Children (KCYPS, N = 5,629)

	Total		Both parents		Single parent		
	mean/%	S.D.	mean/%	S.D.	mean/%	S.D.	
Gender							
Male	51.57		51.52		52.37		
Female	48.43		48.48		47.63		
Cohort (grade)							
Cohort 1 (1st grade)	34.30		35.28		20.06		**
Cohort 2 (4th grade)	32.78		32.73		33.43		
Cohort 3 (7th grade)	32.92		31.99		46.52		**
Self-rated health at year t							
Poor/Very poor	6.02		5.58		12.53		*
Good/Very good	93.98		94.42		87.47		***
Self-rated health at year $t + 2$[a]							
Fair/Poor	4.89		4.61		8.91		
Good/Very good	95.11		95.39		91.09		**
Depression at year t[b]	1.77	0.76	1.75	0.75	1.92	0.85	***
Depression at year $t + 2$[c]	1.72	0.75	1.71	0.74	1.86	0.75	**
Aggression at year t[b]	1.99	0.57	1.98	0.57	2.08	0.57	**
Aggression at year $t + 2$[c]	1.86	0.56	1.85	0.55	1.96	0.61	***
Self-esteem at year t[d]	3.11	0.55	3.12	0.55	2.98	0.55	***
Self-esteem at year $t + 2$[e]	3.14	0.52	3.14	0.52	3.03	0.51	***
Parent's marital status							
Both parents	93.62		100.00		NA		
Single parent	6.38		NA		100.00		
Household income (logged)	8.35	0.73	8.40	0.66	7.61	1.14	***
Parent's education							
High school or less	42.25		40.09		73.82		***
Junior college	13.52		13.72		10.58		
University or more	44.24		46.19		15.6		***
Parental employment status							
Employed	98.10		98.73		88.86		***
Unemployed	1.90		1.27		11.14		**
Region							
Seoul	9.81		10.06		6.13		
Metropolitan cities	32.35		32.2		34.54		
Other small cities	43.08		43.02		44.01		
Rural area	14.76		14.72		15.32		
Live with grandparent							
No	91.06		92.35		72.14		***
Yes	8.94		7.65		27.86		***
N	5,629		5,270		359		

Note: All statistics without notes are estimated using wave 2.
[a] Wave 4 is used for all three cohorts.
[b] Wave 2 is used for cohort 1 and 3. Wave 3 is used for cohort 2.
[c] Wave 4 is used for cohort 1 and 3. Wave 5 is used for cohort 2.
[d] Wave 3 is used for cohort 1 and 3. Wave 2 is used for cohort 2.
[e] Wave 5 is used for cohort 1 and 3. Wave 4 is used for cohort 2.
* $p < 0.05$; ** $p < 0.01$; *** $p < 0.001$ (two-tailed)

health measured in year *t*) to examine the extent to which poorer self-rated health of children in single-parent families observed in Model 1 is due to health selection (i.e., children's existing health conditions). When children's baseline health is included in Model 2, the association of parental marital status with children's self-rated health is no longer statistically significant at a conventional level ($p < 0.05$). This change implies that the negative association between single-parent families and children's self-rated health observed in Model 1 is due largely to poorer baseline health conditions of children in single-parent families relative to children in two-parent families (see table 5.3).

Results from the full model (Model 3) show that, with the inclusion of compositional characteristics, children in single-parent families do not appear disadvantaged compared to those living with both parents in terms of self-rated health. According to our supplemental analysis, co-residing with a grandparent, along with parents' educational attainment, explains away some of the negative association (results not shown). This result implies that children in single-parent families are more likely to live with grandparents (Raymo et al. 2014; Yi and Kim 2011), as grandparents can help with various tasks around the house (e.g., preparing meals for children and supervising them after school). However, we also find that living with grandparents is negatively associated with self-rated health of children. This negative association is somewhat consistent with other studies documenting that co-residence with grandparents does not necessarily benefit children's well-being (e.g., Raymo et al. 2014). Grandparents are often less strict about eating a unhealthy diet and monitoring improper food intake (Jingxiong et al. 2007), and as a result, children may see themselves as less healthy than those who do not live with grandparents.

Next, table 5.4 presents results for depressive symptoms estimated from OLS regression models. Results from Model 1 show that older children (Cohorts 2 and 3) are more likely to experience depressive symptoms compared to younger children (Cohort 1). However, no gender difference is observed in terms of depressive symptoms. In addition, similar to findings for self-rated health in table 5.3 (Model 1), children of single parents report higher levels of depressive symptoms (the reference group is children living with both parents). The significantly higher levels of depressive symptoms among children living with single parents do not change when the baseline health (depressive symptoms measured in year *t*) is included (Model 2). In other words, previous levels of depressive symptoms do not explain higher levels of depressive symptoms reported by children in single-parent families.

TABLE 5.3. Regression Coefficients for "Good/Very Good" Health, based on Self-Rated Health ($N = 5,629$)

Variables	Model 1			Model 2			Model 3		
Cohort									
Cohort 1 (1st grade, omitted)									
Cohort 2 (4th grade)	−0.749	***	(0.18)	−0.671	***	(0.18)	−0.664	***	(0.18)
Cohort 3 (7th grade)	−0.964	***	(0.17)	−0.759	***	(0.18)	−0.756	***	(0.18)
Gender									
Male (omitted)									
Female	−0.095		(0.12)	−0.123		(0.13)	−0.108		(0.13)
Parent's marital status									
Both parents (omitted)									
Single parent	−0.587	**	(0.20)	−0.395	†	(0.21)	−0.374		(0.23)
Health at year *t*									
Poor/Very poor									
Good/Very good				2.053	***	(0.15)	2.071	***	(0.15)
Household income (logged)							0.003		(0.09)
Parent's education									
High school or less (omitted)									
Junior college							0.111		(0.23)
University or more							−0.262	†	(0.15)
Parental employment status									
Employed (omitted)									
Unemployed							−0.129		(0.43)
Region									
Seoul (omitted)									
Metropolitan city							0.109		(0.23)
Other small city							0.194		(0.22)
Rural area							−0.090		(0.25)
Live with grandparent									
No (omitted)									
Yes							−0.437	*	(0.19)
Constant	3.704	***	(0.16)	1.836	***	(0.20)	1.838	*	(0.79)
−2LL	2,148.692			1,995.474			1,982.604		

Note: Statistics in parentheses are standard errors.
† $p < .10$; * $p < 0.05$; ** $p < 0.01$; *** $p < 0.001$ (two-tailed)

TABLE 5.4. Regression Coefficients for Depression Score ($N = 5{,}649$)

Variables	Model 1			Model 2			Model 3		
Cohort									
Cohort 1 (1st grade, omitted)									
Cohort 2 (4th grade)	0.275	***	(0.02)	0.205	***	(0.02)	0.206	***	(0.02)
Cohort 3 (7th grade)	0.339	***	(0.02)	0.233	***	(0.02)	0.234	***	(0.02)
Gender									
Male (omitted)									
Female	0.013		(0.02)	0.003		(0.02)	0.003		(0.02)
Parent's marital status									
Both parents (omitted)									
Single parent	0.109	**	(0.04)	0.086	*	(0.04)	0.052		(0.04)
Depression at year t				0.225	***	(0.01)	0.223	***	(0.01)
Household income (logged)							−0.043	**	(0.02)
Parent's education									
High school or less (omitted)									
Junior college							−0.018		(0.03)
University or more							−0.002		(0.02)
Parental employment status									
Employed (omitted)									
Unemployed							0.005		(0.07)
Region									
Seoul (omitted)									
Metropolitan city							0.003		(0.04)
Other small city							−0.002		(0.03)
Rural area							0.009		(0.04)
Live with grandparent									
No (omitted)									
Yes							−0.014		(0.03)
Constant	1.507	***	(0.02)	1.175	***	(0.03)	1.539	***	(0.13)
R-squared	0.0419			0.0905			0.0922		

Note: Statistics in parentheses are standard errors.
* $p < 0.05$; ** $p < 0.01$; *** $p < 0.001$ (two-tailed)

In Model 3, we introduce various demographic and socioeconomic characteristics of parents and household to examine whether these characteristics account for significant association between a single-parent family structure and pronounced depressive symptoms observed in the previous models. Results show that living with a single parent is no longer significantly associated with greater risk of experiencing depressive symptoms. This finding suggests that the detrimental association of living with a single parent with depression is likely due to parents' socioeconomic conditions, and our supplemental analysis confirms that this shift was driven especially by income (results not shown).

Table 5.5 presents results from OLS regression models for aggression. Results from Model 1 show that, consistent with other health outcomes (see Model 1, tables 5.3 and 5.4), children living with a single parent tend to exhibit higher levels of aggression relative to those in two-parent fami-

TABLE 5.5. Regression Coefficients for Aggression ($N = 5,649$)

Variables	Model 1		Model 2		Model 3	
Cohort						
Cohort 1 (1st grade, omitted)						
Cohort 2 (4th grade)	0.266 ***	(0.02)	0.207 ***	(0.02)	0.21 ***	(0.02)
Cohort 3 (7th grade)	0.291 ***	(0.02)	0.205 ***	(0.02)	0.205 ***	(0.02)
Gender						
Male (omitted)						
Female	−0.003	(0.01)	−0.001	(0.01)	−0.002	(0.01)
Parent's marital status						
Both parents (omitted)						
Single parent	0.081 **	(0.03)	0.065 *	(0.03)	0.036	(0.03)
Aggression at year t			0.275 ***	(0.01)	0.274 ***	(0.01)
Household income (logged)					−0.035 **	(0.01)
Parent's education						
High school or less (omitted)						
Junior college					−0.023	(0.02)
University or more					0.008	(0.02)
Parental employment status						
Employed (omitted)						
Unemployed					0.011	(0.05)
Region						
Seoul (omitted)						
Metropolitan city					0.037	(0.03)
Other small city					0.043 †	(0.03)
Rural area					0.122 ***	(0.03)
Live with grandparent						
No (omitted)						
Yes					−0.004	(0.03)
Constant	1.673 ***	(0.01)	1.174 ***	(0.03)	1.419 ***	(0.10)
R-squared	0.0591		0.134		0.1395	

Note: Statistics in parentheses are standard errors.
† $p < .10$; * $p < 0.05$; ** $p < 0.01$; *** $p < 0.001$ (two-tailed)

lies. Also, older cohorts are more likely to report aggressive behaviors (the reference is Cohort 1). In Model 2, we find that the levels of aggression among children with a single parent are still higher after adjusting for the level of aggression observed at year t. However, this significant association between living with a single parent and children's aggression disappears in Model 3, which includes controls such as socioeconomic conditions of the parent and demographic characteristics (e.g., co-residence with grandparents and region of residence). Similar to depression, the higher levels of aggression in children of single parents are explained mainly by income (results not shown). In addition, the older cohorts reveal higher levels of aggression on average even after adjusting for the previous levels of aggression at the baseline.

Last, table 5.6 presents results for self-esteem. According to the results from Model 1, children of single parents report lower levels of self-esteem on average compared to those living with two parents. When the level of self-esteem at the baseline (i.e., year t) is controlled for (Model 2), however, the disparity by the parental marital status in terms of children's self-esteem becomes only marginally significant ($p < 0.10$). This change indicates that significantly lower self-esteem of children of single parents observed in the previous model (Model 1) may be explained by disparity in children's self-esteem already observed at the baseline (table 5.2). Again, the association between family structure and children's self-esteem turns not statistically significant in the full model (Model 3) when all of the covariates are included. In our supplemental analysis, the lower levels of self-esteem among children with a single parent are largely explained by parents' education, income and employment status (results not shown).

Conclusions and Discussion

In the context of increases in the divorce rates and in the share of children growing up in single-parent households in Korea, we evaluate the association between parental marital status and multiple health outcomes of children. To fully understand various health aspects linked to parental marital status, we consider both physical and mental health outcomes as available in the data set, which include self-rated health, depressive symptoms, aggression, and self-esteem. Our results show that children living with a single parent fare worse than those living with both parents for all of the health outcomes examined. Previous health conditions (i.e., health measured at the baseline) explain some of the health disadvantages among children in single-parent families (e.g., self-rated health and self-esteem), but statistically significant health differences among children by parental marital status still remain even after controlling for the baseline health (Model 2 in tables 5.3–5.6).

We also find that worse health outcomes of children with single parents (relative to their counterparts with two parents) are largely due to low

TABLE 5.6. Regression Coefficients for Self-Esteem ($N = 5,630$)

Variables	Model 1		Model 2		Model 3	
Cohort						
Cohort 1 (1st grade, omitted)						
Cohort 2 (4th grade)	−0.149 ***	(0.02)	−0.075 ***	(0.02)	−0.080 ***	(0.02)
Cohort 3 (7th grade)	−0.315 ***	(0.02)	−0.153 ***	(0.02)	−0.158 ***	(0.02)
Gender						
Male (omitted)						
Female	−0.085 ***	(0.01)	−0.091 ***	(0.01)	−0.090 ***	(0.01)
Parent's marital status						
Both parents (omitted)						
Single parent	−0.077 **	(0.03)	−0.043 †	(0.03)	−0.023	(0.03)
Self-esteem at year t			0.393 ***	(0.01)	0.389 ***	(0.01)
Household income (logged)					0.000	(0.01)
Parent's education						
High school or less (omitted)						
Junior college					−0.011	(0.02)
University or more					0.032 *	(0.01)
Parental employment status						
Employed (omitted)						
Unemployed					−0.081 †	(0.04)
Region						
Seoul (omitted)						
Metropolitan city					0.039 †	(0.02)
Other small city					−0.014	(0.02)
Rural area					−0.032	(0.03)
Live with grandparent						
No (omitted)						
Yes					−0.035	(0.02)
Constant	3.336 ***	(0.01)	2.034 ***	(0.04)	2.038	(0.09)
R-squared	0.0697		0.2234		0.2281	

Note: Statistics in parentheses are standard errors.
† $p < .10$; * $p < 0.05$; ** $p < 0.01$; *** $p < 0.001$ (two-tailed)

socioeconomic status of their parents, with an exception of the role of co-residing grandparents for self-rated health. For example, income substantially accounts for higher levels of depressive symptoms and aggression among children with a single parent. In addition, for lower levels of self-esteem among those of single-parent families, parental socioeconomic status (i.e., education, income, and employment status) largely explains the disparities. These findings imply that health disadvantages of children in single-parent families may be prevented by implementing relevant social policies and programs to offset resource deficits in these families. To further tease out the roles that parental marital status plays in children's health outcomes, it is important to examine specific pathways through which socioeconomic conditions of single parents lead to poor health outcomes of children in single-parent families (e.g., availability and quality of afterschool programs, and health-care access and its utilization).

We acknowledge a few limitations of the present study and offer several suggestions for future research. First, we are unable to compare children's health before and after changes in parental marital status (e.g., parental divorce or the death of a parent) due to a lack of information on the timing of the parental dissolution for children living with single parents. Instead, we employ a lagged model approach, where the baseline health status is taken into account. This approach allows us to estimate the association of parental marital status with health of children in a proper time order. In other words, we examine whether and to what extent *changes* in the health outcomes of children during the two-year survey interval are associated with stable marital status of parents. While not intending to estimate the effect of change of parental marital status, this approach captures the influence of family structure on children's health over time, taking advantage of the longitudinal information of the KCYPS.

Additionally, we recognize that support from family members (e.g., grandparents and siblings of the parents) and friends of parents is important, especially for the well-being of children with a single parent whose socioeconomic resources are limited. As noted, in Korea, social approval for divorce is low, and childcare arrangements for a working single parent are costly and challenging ("Best and Worst Places" 2017). In this study, we do find that living with grandparents is beneficial for children in single-parent families in terms of self-rated health. Unfortunately, our data do not allow us to explore the roles of support from other family members or friends. We suggest that future research look into this mechanism when data become available.

We would also like to note that, because not all the health measures are collected every year, our analysis examining the health consequences of living with a single parent is based on only a two-year follow-up. While there might still be potential enduring impacts of parental marital dissolution and the resultant living arrangements (i.e., growing up with a single parent) on health of children over time, the extent that changes in parental marital status influence health of children may diminish, as parents and children adjust to their new living arrangements and given family structure. If so, it would be useful for a future study to evaluate what social conditions and factors may make it easier for children and their parents to cope with the potentially negative consequences of parental divorce over a longer-term period.

In spite of these limitations, this study, as the first attempt to look at children's health associated with parental marital status using a nationally representative sample of children in Korea, demonstrates that children living with single parents have much worse health outcomes than those in two-parent families. These health disadvantages are largely explained by lower socioeconomic conditions of single parents, and family structure (i.e., single-parent family versus two-parent family) does not seem to have significant effects on children's health when parents' socioeconomic conditions are taken into account. This result implies that still only socioeconomically "selected" married individuals are likely to divorce in Korea and that detrimental health outcomes of children with single parents seem attributed to their family resources rather than to the direct result of living in single-parent families (e.g., stress from social stigma against children of single parents). Nonetheless, despite some positive aspects of parental divorce for children's social skills and sense of control (e.g., Kim and Woo 2011), in Korea, children living with a single parent are likely to face more health disadvantages compared to those living with two parents.

The trend of the divorce rate is likely to continue to increase (or to continue to stay high, at least) in Korea. However, more childcare support and after-school programs for working parents, which can reduce adversary health consequences of children living with single parents, have yet to be provided. Our findings raise the importance of designing and implementing policies and programs for the healthy development of children of single parents. Future research should further investigate specific explanatory mechanisms (i.e., relationships with parents, other family members/relatives, and friends, and health behaviors) for each health outcome of children linked to family structure across children's age groups in order to help design more effective policies and programs.

NOTE

This chapter was presented at Korean Families in Economic and Demographic Transitions: Parenting, Children's Education, and Social Mobility, a conference held at the University of Michigan, Ann Arbor, on November 11–12, 2016. We thank Paul Y. Chang, Hyunjoon Park, and the two anonymous reviewers for helpful comments on earlier versions of the chapter. Direct correspondence to Hyeyoung Woo.

REFERENCES

Amato, Paul R., and Denise Previti. 2003. "People's Reasons for Divorcing: Gender, Social Class, the Life Course, and Adjustment." *Journal of Family Issues* 24 (5): 602–26.
Amato, Paul R., and Juliana M. Sobolewski. 2001. "The Effects of Divorce and Marital Discord on Adult Children's Psychological Well-being." *American Sociological Review* 66: 900–921.
An Chin-sang and Kim Hŭi-jŏng. 2013. "Adong, chŏngsonyŏn ŭi kŏn'gang pulp'yŏngdŭng kyŏlchŏng yoin punsŏk" (A Study on the Determinants of Children and Adolescents' Health Inequality in Korea). *Han'guk chŏngsonyŏn yŏn'gu* (*Studies on Korean Youth*) 24 (2): 205–31 (in Korean).
"The Best and Worst Places to Be a Working Woman." 2017. *Economist*, March 8. http://www.economist.com/blogs/graphicdetail/2017/03/daily-chart-0 (retrieved July 2017).
Boardman, Jason D. 2006. "Self-Rated Health among U.S. Adolescents." *Journal of Adolescent Health* 38 (4): 401–8.
Breidablik, Hans-Johan, Eivind Meland, and Stian Lydersen. 2008. "Self-Rated Health in Adolescence: A Multifactorial Composite." *Scandinavian Journal of Public Health* 36 (1): 12–20.
Chen, Jiajian, and Wayne J. Millar. 1998. "Age of Smoking Initiation: Implications for Quitting." *Health Reports-Statistics Canada* 9: 39–48.
Chŏng Chin-yŏng. 1993. "Han'guk ŭi ihon silt'ae wa ihon kajŏng chanyŏdŭl ŭi munje e kwanhan yŏn'gu" (Problems of Children in Divorced Families of Korea). *Han'guk adong pokchihak* (*Journal of the Korean Society of Child Welfare*) 1: 81–108 (in Korean).
Chun, Young-Ju, and Tae-Hong Sohn. 2009. "Determinants of Consensual Divorce in Korea: Gender, Socio-economic Status, and Life Course." *Journal of Comparative Family Studies* 40 (5): 775–89.
Cooper, Carey E., Sara S. McLanahan, Sarah O. Meadows, and Jeanne Brooks-Gunn. 2009. "Family Structure Transitions and Maternal Parenting Stress." *Journal of Marriage and Family* 71: 558–74.
DeWit, David J., Edward M. Adlaf, David R. Offord, and Alan C. Ogborne. 2000. "Age at First Alcohol Use: A Risk Factor for the Development of Alcohol Disorders." *American Journal of Psychiatry* 157: 745–50.
Eder, Anselm. 1990. "Risk Factor Loneliness: On the Interrelations between Social Integration, Happiness and Health in 11-, 13- and 15-Year Old Schoolchildren in 9 European Countries." *Health Promotion International* 5 (1): 19–33.

Elo, Irma T. 2009. "Social Class Differentials in Health and Mortality: Patterns and Explanations in Comparative Perspective." *Annual Review of Sociology* 35: 553-72.

Fendrich, Michael, Myrna M. Weissman, and Virginia Warner. 1990. "Screening for Depressive Disorder in Children and Adolescents: Validating the Center for Epidemiologic Studies Depression Scale for Children." *American Journal of Epidemiology* 131 (3): 538-51.

French, Simone A., Mary Story, and Cheryl L. Perry. 1995. "Self-Esteem and Obesity in Children and Adolescents: A Literature Review." *Obesity Research* 3 (5): 479-90.

Haveman, Robert, and Barbara Wolfe. 1995. "The Determinants of Children's Attainments: A Review of Methods and Findings." *Journal of Economic Literature* 33: 1829-78.

Hetherington, E. Mavis. 1972. "Effects of Father Absence on Personality Development in Adolescent Daughters." *Developmental Psychology* 7: 313-26.

Hingson, Ralph W., Timothy Heeren, and Michael R. Winter. 2006. "Age at Drinking Onset and Alcohol Dependence: Age at Onset, Duration, and Severity." *Archives of Pediatrics & Adolescent Medicine* 160: 739-46.

Hodges, William F., and Bernard L. Bloom. 1984. "Parent's Report of Children's Adjustment to Marital Separation: A Longitudinal Study." *Journal of Divorce* 8: 33-50.

Hong Sun-hye. 2004. "Pumo ŭi ihon i chŏngsonyŏn chanyŏ ŭi simni sahoejŏk chŏgŭng e mich'inŭn yŏnghyang: yangyok pumo ŭi kyŏngje sujun mit yangyuk haengdong ŭi maegae hyogwa rŭl chungsim ŭro" (The Effect of Parental Divorce on Psycho-Social Adjustment of Adolescent Children: The Mediating Effects of Family Income and Parenting). *Han'guk adong pokchihak (Journal of the Korean Society of Child Welfare)* 17: 151-77.

Idler, Ellen L., and Stanislav V. Kasl. 1991. "Health Perceptions and Survival: Do Global Evaluations of Health Status Really Predict Mortality?" *Journal of Gerontology* 46: S55-S65.

Jang, Hye Kyung, Dayoung Song, Young Ran Kim, and Jung Hoon Kim. 2001. *Social Support Measures for Female Single-Parent Families*. Seoul: Korean Women's Development Institute (in Korean).

Jekielek, Susan M. 1997. "Parental Conflict, Marital Disruption and Children's Emotional Well-being." *Social Forces* 76: 905-36.

Jingxiong, Jiang, Wang Huishan, Ted Greiner, Lian Guangli, and Anna Sarkadi. 2007. "Influence of Grandparents on Eating Behaviors of Young Children in Chinese Three-Generation Families." *Appetite* 48 (3): 377-83.

Khuder, Sadik A., Hari H. Dayal, and Anand B. Mutgi. 1999. "Age at Smoking Onset and Its Effect on Smoking Cessation." *Addictive Behaviors* 24: 673-77.

Kim Chin-yŏng. 2011. "Kyoyuk chiptanbyŏl kŏn'gang ch'use e taehan punsŏk" (Trends in Health across Educational Groups). *Han'guk in'guhak (Korea Journal of Population Studies)* 34 (1): 99-127 (in Korean).

Kim Chin-yŏng, Song Yeria, and Paek Ŭn-jŏng. 2013. "Hangnyŏk kwa chugwanjŏk kŏn'gang ŭi kwan'gye: nodong sijang chiwi wa kyŏngjejŏk chiwi rŭl t'onghan yŏn'gyŏl" (Education and Self-Rated health: The Links through Labor-Market Status and Economic Status). *Han'guk sahoehak (Korean Journal of Sociology)* 47 (2): 211-39 (in Korean).

Kim Hyŏng-yong. 2010. "Chiyŏk sahoe kŏn'gang pulp'yŏngdŭng e taehan koch'al: sahoe chabon maengnak hyogwa e taehan haesŏk" (Community Inequalities in Health:

The Contextual Effect of Social Capital)" *Han'guk sahoehak* (*Korean Journal of Sociology*) 44 (2): 59–92 (in Korean).
Kim, Jinyoung, and Hyeyoung Woo. 2017. "A Longitudinal Study on Marital Status and Depression—Variations by Gender and Age Cohorts." *Korea Journal of Population Studies* 40 (2): 79–105.
Kim, Joongbaeck, and Hyeyoung Woo. 2011. "The Complex Relationship between Parental Divorce and the Sense of Control." *Journal of Family Issues* 32: 1050–72.
Kim Sŭng-yŏn, Kim Se-rin, and Yi Chin-sŏk. 2013. "Chugŏ hwan'gyŏng i kŏn'gang sujun e mich'inŭn yŏnhyang" (The Effect of Housing on Health). *Pogŏn kwa sahoe kwahak* (*Health and Social Science*) 34: 109–33 (in Korean).
Kim Tong-sik. 2007. "Pumo kwallyŏn pujŏngjŏk saenghwal sagŏn ŭi kyŏnghŏm kwa chŏngsonyŏn ŭi chŏngsin kŏn'gang mit pihaeng haengwi" (Experience of Parent-Related Negative Life Events, Mental Health, and Delinquent Behavior among Korean Adolescents). *Yebang ŭihak hoeji* (*Journal of Preventive Medicine and Public Health*) 40: 218–26.
Mann, Michal Michelle, Clemens M. H. Hosman, Herman P. Schaalma, and Nanne K. De Vries. 2004. "Self-Esteem in a Broad-Spectrum Approach for Mental Health Promotion." *Health Education Research* 19 (4): 357–72.
McLanahan, Sara, and Christine Percheski. 2008. "Family Structure and the Reproduction of Inequalities." *Annual Review of Sociology* 34: 257–76.
McLanahan, Sara, and Gary Sandefur. 1994. *Growing Up with a Single Parent: What Hurts? What Helps?* Cambridge, MA: Harvard University Press.
Mechanic, David, and Stephen Hansell. 1987. "Adolescent Competence, Psychological Well-Being, and Self-Assessed Physical Health." *Journal of Health and Social Behavior* 28 (4): 364–74.
Metbulut, Azize Pinar, Elif N. Ozmert, Ozlem Teksam, and Kadriye Yurdakok. 2018. "A Comparison between the Feeding Practices of Parents and Grandparents." *European Journal of Pediatrics* 177: 1785–94.
Mirowsky, John, and Catherine E. Ross. 2003. *Social Causes of Psychological Distress*. New York: Aldine de Gruyter.
Mirowsky, John, Catherine E. Ross, and John Reynolds. 2000. "Links between Social Status and Health Status." In *Handbook of Medical Sociology*, edited by Chloe E. Bird, Peter Conrad, and Allen M. Fremont, 47–67. Upper Saddle River, NJ: Prentice Hall.
OECD. 2016a. "Society at a Glance 2016: OECD Social Indicators." Paris: OECD Publishing. http://dx.doi.org/10.1787/9789264261488-en (retrieved July 2017).
OECD. 2016b. "OECD Employment Outlook 2016." Paris: OECD Publishing. http://dx.doi.org/10.1787/empl_outlook-2016-en (retrieved July 2017).
Office of Court Administration. 2015. *Jurisdiction Yearbook*. Seoul, Korea: Supreme Court (in Korean).
Palloni, Alberto. 2006. "Reproducing Inequalities: Luck, Wallets, and the Enduring Effects of Childhood Health." *Demography* 43: 587–615.
Pak Ŭn-ok. 2013. "Si, kon, ku tanwi chiyŏk sahoe simnoe hyŏlgwan chirhwan p'yojunhwa samangnyul kwa kwallyŏn yoin punsŏk" (Cardiovascular Disease-Specific Standardized Mortality and the Related Factor in South Korea). *Pogŏn kwa sahoe kwahak* (*Health and Social Science*) 34: 257–71 (in Korean).
Park, Hyunjoon. 2007. "Single Parenthood and Children's Reading Performance in Asia." *Journal of Marriage and Family* 69 (3): 63–77.

Park, Hyunjoon. 2008. "Effects of Single Parenthood on Educational Aspiration and Student Disengagement in Korea." *Demographic Research* 18: 377–408.

Park, Hyunjoon, Jaesung Choi, and Hyejeong Jo. 2016. "Living Arrangements of Single Parents and Their Children in South Korea." *Marriage & Family Review* 52: 89–105.

Park, Hyunjoon, and James M. Raymo. 2013. "Divorce in Korea: Trends and Educational Differentials." *Journal of Marriage and Family* 75: 110–26.

Payne, Krista K. 2013. "Children's Family Structure, 2013." (FP-13-19). National Center for Family & Marriage Research. https://www.bgsu.edu/content/dam/BGSU/college-of-arts-and-sciences/NCFMR/documents/FP/FP-13-19.pdf (retrieved December 2018).

Peterson, James L., and Nicholas Zill. 1986. "Marital Disruption, Parent-Child Relationships, and Behavior Problems in Children." *Journal of Marriage and Family* 48 (2): 295–307.

Phelan, Jo C., Bruce G. Link, and Parisa Tehranifar. 2010. "Social Conditions as Fundamental Causes of Health Inequalities: Theory, Evidence, and Policy Implications." *Journal of Health of Social Behavior* 51 (1): S28–S40.

Raymo, James M., Hyunjoon Park, Miho Iwasawa, and Yanfei Zhou. 2014. "Single Motherhood, Living Arrangements, and Time with Children in Japan." *Journal of Marriage and Family* 76 (4): 843–61.

Repetti, Rena. L., Shelley E. Taylor, and Teresa E. Seeman. 2002. "Risky Families: Family Social Environments and the Mental and Physical Health of Offspring." *Psychological Bulletin* 128: 330–66.

Ross, Catherine E., and John Mirowsky. 1999. "Parental Divorce, Life-Course Disruption, and Adult Depression." *Journal of Marriage and the Family* 61: 1034–45.

Sigle-Rushton, Wendy, and Sara McLanahan. 2004. "Father Absence and Child Wellbeing: A Critical Review." In *The Future of the Family*, edited by D. P. Moynihan, T. M. Smeeding, and L. Rainwater, 116–55. New York: Russell Sage Foundation.

Statistics Korea. 2016. *2015 Marriage Divorce Statistics*. Daejeon, Korea: Statistics Korea (in Korean).

Trzesniewski, Kali H., M. Brent Donnellan, Terrie E. Moffitt, Richard W. Robins, Richie Poulton, and Avshalom Caspi. 2006. "Low Self-Esteem during Adolescence Predicts Poor Health, Criminal Behavior, and Limited Economic Prospects during Adulthood." *Developmental Psychology* 42 (2): 381–90.

Ŭn Ki-su and Yi Yun-sŏk. 2005. "Han'guk ŭi kajok kach'i e taehan kukche pigyo yŏn'gu" (Family Values in Korea from a Comparative Perspective). *Han'guk in'guhak* (*Korea Journal of Population Studies*) 28 (1): 107–32 (in Korean).

Waite, Linda J. 1995. "Does Marriage Matter?" *Demography* 32: 483–507.

White, Lynn. 1991. "Determinants of Divorce: A Review of Research in the Eighties." *Journal of Marriage and Family* 52: 904–12.

Woo, Hyeyoung, Youn Jung, and Jingyoung Kim. 2013. "Parental Death and Offspring Psychological Well-Being in Korea." *Korean Journal of Sociology* 47 (3): 91–114.

Yi Min-a. 2010. "Kyŏrhon sangt'ae e ttarŭn noin ŭi uul to wa sŏngch'a" (Marital Status and Depression among Korean Older Adults: Gender Differences). *Han'guk sahoehak* (*Korean Journal of Sociology*) 44 (4): 32–62 (in Korean).

Yi Mi-suk. 2005. "Han'guk sŏngin ŭi kŏn'gang pulp'yŏngdŭng: sahoe kyech'ŭng kwa chiyŏk ch'ai rŭl chungsim ŭro" (Health Inequalities among Korean Adults: Socioeconomic Status and Residential Area Differences). *Han'guk sahoehak* (*Korean Journal of Sociology*) 39 (6): 183–209 (in Korean).

Yi Yŏn-ju, Kim Sŭng-gwŏn. 2011. "12 se iha adong i innŭn p'yŏnbu, p'yŏnmo kagu ŭi sahoe kyŏngjejŏk t'ŭksŏng pigyo" (Socioeconomic Characteristics of Single-Mother versus Single-Father Households of Children 12 or Younger: Focusing on Divorced Parents). *Han'guk in'guhak* (*Korea Journal of Population Studies*) 34 (2): 17–43 (in Korean).

Zill, Nicholas. 1990. *Behavior Problems Index Based on Parent Report*. Child Trends. https://www.childtrends.org/wp-content/uploads/2013/01/Behavior-Problems-Index.pdf (retrieved December 2018).

6

Does Grandparents' Education Matter for Grandchildren's Education in South Korea?

Hyunjoon Park and Heewon Jang

A growing body of research in social stratification explores the extent to which grandparents (and even great-grandparents) directly affect grandchildren's education and socioeconomic outcomes, net of the influences of parents, across a wide range of contexts (Chan and Boliver 2013; Chiang and Park 2015; Hällsten 2014; Knigge 2016; Pfeffer 2014; Zeng and Xie 2013). The literature on multigenerational effects challenges the dominant approach in social stratification that has long focused on the two-generation relationship between parents and children (Mare 2011). A significant association of grandparents' characteristics with grandchildren's educational and occupational outcomes, even after parents' characteristics are taken into account, suggests that inequality may persist longer than what the two-generation model would indicate (Lindahl et al. 2015). Of course, some existing studies show that no significant relationship between grandparents' socioeconomic characteristics and grandchildren's socioeconomic outcomes remains after controlling for parents' socioeconomic characteristics, suggesting that the Markovian process may be still valid, at least in some contexts, to describe the process of intergenerational transmission of advantages (Erola and Moisio 2007; Warren and Hauser 1997).

On the one hand, the rising interest in grandparents' roles in grandchildren's educational and occupational success reflects the increased life expectancy of the elderly in many societies, who can now spend a fair amount of time interacting with their grandchildren. Population aging increases opportunities for grandparents to directly influence grandchildren throughout the periods of childhood and youth. On the other hand, rapidly growing economic inequality in many contemporary societies has led scholars to explore sources and consequences of economic inequality (Piketty and Saez 2014). The endeavors to find various sources of economic inequality likely have spurred interest in resources that can be drawn from grandparents and other extended family members beyond parents.

Interestingly, the growing importance of grandparents for grandchildren's educational success is being recognized in Korean society. A joke widely heard in contemporary Korea points out three important conditions to be met for children's educational success: (1) the mother's ability to gather information (on private supplementary education); (2) the father's indifference to children's education; and (3) the grandfather's wealth. The first two conditions reflect the educational context in Korea, where mothers are heavily involved in children's education but fathers primarily play the role of breadwinner without much direct involvement in children's education (Park and Abelmann 2004). The third condition of the grandfather's wealth highlights how costly it is to educate a child in Korea, where children from very early ages take a variety of private supplementary education besides formal schooling, which requires substantial financial investment (Park, Byun, and Kim 2011; Park et al. 2016). Moreover, the need for additional economic support from grandparents for children's educational success has likely increased, given a sharp rise of economic inequality in Korea during the last two decades (Kim and Kim 2015; Jain-Chandra et al. 2015).

In this chapter, we examine whether grandparents' educational levels are directly related to grandchildren's educational levels after taking into account parents' educational levels. Specifically, we assess the relationship between adult grandchildren's completed years of schooling and their grandparents' completed years of schooling, net of parents' completed years of schooling, to see if there is any direct relationship between grandparents' and grandchildren's years of schooling. As far as we are aware, ours is the first study to investigate three-generation relationships in educational attainment in contemporary Korea. Data for more than two generations are hardly available in Korea. Using data from a social survey that asked those born between 1943 to 1965 (mostly between 1943 to 1955) about their parents' (and spouse's parents') and first child's educational attainment as well as their own education, we were able to construct a data set that includes information on educational attainment across three generations.

Korean Contexts

Korea provides an interesting case in which to examine multigenerational relationships in educational attainment. In particular, the significance of family lineage and extended family members for individuals' behaviors and well-being may suggest a substantial role of grandparents for grandchildren's education and other socioeconomic outcomes in Korea (see Raymo et al. 2015). Traditionally, Korean families, along with other East Asian families, have been known for strong family ties, and extended family members often provide economic and social support for—and receive it from—these strong familial bonds (Park, Choi, and Jo 2016; Reher 1998). Studying the grandparent effects on grandchildren's education in rural China, Zeng and Xie (2014) found that grandparents matter for grandchildren's education only if they live together so that grandparents can influence grandchildren daily. If the idea can be extended to include interactions between grandparents and grandchildren, even if they do not live together, strong family ties in Korea may facilitate influences of grandparents on grandchildren's education through frequent interactions between grandparents and grandchildren.

The extensive competition for children's educational success among Korean families, often known as "education fever," may also provide a context under which grandparents' support can be important resources for children's educational success (Seth 2002). Educational success of an individual and her or his upward social mobility through educational attainment in Korea have been perceived not only as the individual's achievement but also as fame for the whole family (often including extended family lineages) (Sorensen 1994). Therefore, a whole family is often involved in children's education. Under this context, grandparents likely help parents educate children by providing social and economic support as well as being consistent with parents toward the goal of educational success for their grandchildren.

In contrast to these contexts of education and family in Korea that may imply a substantial effect of grandparents on grandchildren's education, other developments over the last decades suggest otherwise. Most of all, the degree of educational expansion in Korea has been extraordinary, showing a comparably large difference in the proportion of the population with tertiary education between the older cohort aged 55 to 64 and the younger cohort aged 25 to 34 (OECD 2012; Park 2007a, 2007b). In other words, average levels of educational attainment have dramatically increased from grandparents' and parents' to the children's generation. The rapid expansion of education means that the generation of parents in Korea had a comparatively low level of education, with the generation of grandparents having even less education. Such a rapid increase in access to higher education among children's generation compared to a fairly small share of grandparents with secondary and tertiary education may suggest a relatively weak association between grandparents' and grandchildren's education. A recent study of multigenerational relationships in educational attainment in Taiwan, which has experienced a similarly rapid expansion of education, shows that the direct relationship between grandparents' and grandchildren's education is negligible (Chiang and Park 2015).

Moreover, although recent educational reforms in the 2000s have changed its features, the Korean educational system, particularly before the 2000s, was recognized for its relatively equal nature (Park 2013). To prevent between-school differences in student outcomes and school resources, the Korean government implemented a high school equalization policy in 1974 to randomly assign middle school graduates to high schools within school districts. In other words, school choice was fairly limited. Moreover, standardized curricula and instruction across classrooms reduced the likelihood that students were exposed to unequal learning opportunities within schools. Some evidence, indeed, suggests a comparatively narrow academic gap among Korean students, reflecting these institutional characteristics of Korean educational system before recent educational reforms (Park 2013). These policy efforts may have weakened family influences on educational outcomes, including both parent and grandparent effects.

Considering these different factors that may facilitate or prevent multigenerational effects in Korea, we assess the extent to which grandparents' education is directly related to grandchildren's education beyond grandparents' indirect influence on grandchildren through parents. Finding a significant grandparental influence, net of parental influence, in the Korean context, can extend our understanding of how family contexts can shape the way grandparents influence grandchildren's education (see Mare 2011). As described earlier, studies across different societies have shown inconsistent results for the significance of multigenerational effects, making it critical to assess multigenerational effects across a wide range of societal contexts.

We acknowledge that grandparents' education represents only one aspect of the socioeconomic and cultural resources with which grandparents can influence grandchildren's education. Grandparents' occupational status and particularly their economic resources such as income and wealth are certainly important resources from which grandchildren can benefit for their improved educational outcomes (Hällsten and Pfeffer 2017; Warren and Hauser 1997). However, our data include information only on grandparents' education, which prevents any further analysis of grandparents' characteristics other than education. It is notable, however, that existing studies of grandparent effects across a wide range of societies have indeed focused on grandparents' education (Celhay and Gallegos 2015; Chiang and Park 2015; Kroeger and Thompson 2016; Zeng and Xie 2014).

Data and Methods

Data and Variables

We use data from the Education and Social Mobility Survey conducted by the Korean Educational Development Institute. In 2008, a nationally representative sample of 1,526 men and women born between 1943 and 1955 was asked to provide a variety of information on their own education and occupational histories (Pak et al. 2008). They were also asked about the educational and occupational attainment of their parents and their spouses' parents, as well as the educational history of the first child (for those who have at least one child). In 2009, another round of the survey collected corresponding information for those born between 1956 and 1965 ($N = 2{,}038$).[1] Note that the survey asked questions about only the first child. Among a total of 3,564 respondents surveyed either in 2008 or 2009, only 108 cases had no child. The respondents, who were surveyed in 2008 or 2009 and had at least one child, consist of the parent generation in our study. Parents and parents-in-law of the respondents consist of the grandparent generation, while (first) adult children of the respondents refer to the grandchildren generation. To examine the completed years of schooling, we include only grandchildren who were 25 years old or over.[2] In the end, our final sample consists of 1,794 men and women who were born between 1943 and 1965 and also had at least one child who was 25 years old or over as of 2008 or 2009.

The respondents reported the highest levels of educational attainment of their mothers and fathers and (in cases where they were married) their mothers-in-law and fathers-in-law. Therefore, from grandchildren's perspective, both maternal and paternal grandparents' educational levels are available. Information on the highest levels of education of all grandparents, parents, and grandchildren is based on a detailed classification of educational levels that separates dropouts from graduates in each level of primary schools, lower secondary schools (middle school), higher secondary schools (high school), junior colleges, four-college colleges, and graduate schools. We transformed the highest level of education to the completed years of schooling by assigning typical years of schooling required to complete a given level of education. For instance, 12 years of schooling were assigned to those whose highest level of education was a high school diploma and who did not pursue any postsecondary education.

We define grandparents' years of schooling as the average years of schooling among all four (maternal and paternal) grandparents. If information on any of grandparents' years of schooling is missing, we average the years of schooling only among grandparents whose years of schooling were reported. In other words, as long as one grandparent's education is available, the case is included in the analysis. Similarly, we average mother's and father's years of schooling to create a variable of parents' years of schooling. By doing so, we do not have any missing case on parents' years of schooling, and we exclude only 49 cases due to missing grandparents' years of schooling, leading to our final analytic sample of 1,745 grandchildren for whom both parents' and grandparents' years of schooling are available.

In estimating the association between grandparents' and grandchildren's years of schooling, we control for a few variables. First, we take into account the gender and age of grandchildren. Considering educational expansion, those born later are likely to have more years of schooling, ceteris paribus. We also control for the number of siblings that grandchildren have, as the number of siblings is one of the robust factors associated with individuals' educational outcomes (Blake 1989). Finally, we include father's occupation as another control. The survey asked respondents to report their "first" occupation, while it also asked respondents to report the occupation that their spouses had at the time of marriage. In other words, depending on whether respondents were female or male, we do not have symmetric information on the occupation of respondents and their spouses. Therefore, although we call it father's first occupation, it actually refers to father's occupation at the time of marriage for children whose mothers reported their husbands' occupation. We could also use father's "current" occupation, as respondents reported their current occupations as well as their spouses' current occupations. However, to reflect father's occupational status as of the period when children grew up, we decided to use father's "first" occupation despite the problem related to the measure. We conducted a supplementary analysis using father's current occupation, and the result was very similar to what we present below with father's first occupation. Moreover, to take into account this asymmetric information, we control for an indicator whether respondents (i.e., parents) of the survey were female or male in the statistical models to be described below.[3] We do not use mother's occupation, as about 40 percent of children have missing information on mother's occupation.

To examine the effects of maternal and paternal grandparents separately, we conduct a supplementary analysis for which we average maternal grandfather's and maternal grandmother's years of schooling to create the measure of maternal grandparents' years of schooling, and separately we average paternal grandfather's and paternal grandmother's years of schooling to create the measure of paternal grandparents' years of schooling. In this analysis that predicts grandchildren's years of schooling by paternal grandparents' and maternal grandparents' years of schooling separately, we distinguish father's and mother's years of schoolings as well. Note that separation of maternal and paternal grandparents results in a smaller number of cases to be analyzed compared to the sample size for the analysis of grandparents without separation by lineage. As in the analysis that does not separate mothers and fathers and maternal and paternal grandparents, we control for grandchildren's number of siblings in addition to their gender and age. However, we do not consider father's first occupation because controlling for father's first occupation may affect the effect of father's years of schooling more than the effect of mother's years of schooling. Note that across all models to be estimated, we do not include mother's first occupation at all. Since we do not control for father's first occupation, we also exclude the indicator of whether respondents were female and male, as the issue of asymmetric information on occupation is irrelevant.

Methods

We use ordinary least squares (OLS) regression to predict grandchildren's years of schooling by parents' and grandparents' years of schooling and other control variables. Specifically, we estimate three OLS regression models. Model 1 includes only parents' years of schooling in addition to controlling variables (age, gender, and number of siblings of grandchildren, father's first occupation, and an indicator whether respondents [parents] were female or male) to predict grandchildren's years of schooling. This is the typical two-generation model that focuses on the relationship between parents and children. Model 2 includes only grandparents' years of schooling without parents' years of schooling in addition to controlling variables (age, gender, and number of siblings of grandchildren and an indicator whether respondents [parents] were female or male). This model shows the overall relationship between grandparents' and grandchildren's years of schooling when parents' years of schooling are not taken into account. Finally, Model 3 adds parents' years of schooling to Model 2 to see how the effect of grandparents' education changes when parents' education is included.

Results

Descriptive Statistics

Looking at the mean years of schooling and their standard deviations across grandchildren, parents, and grandparents in table 6.1, evident is a considerable rise of the mean years of schooling across generations. Grandchildren show almost 15 years of schooling on average, which is substantially higher than 10 years of schooling among parents. Parents, in turn, have a much higher level of education than grandparents, who had only 4 years of schooling on average. Along with the increased level of education over generations, differences in education within each generation have declined over generations. Standard deviations, which indicate variability of years of schooling, have decreased from 3.5 among grandparents to 2.1 among grandchildren.

In addition to means and standard deviations of years of schooling, table 6.1 also presents correlation coefficients between a pair of two schooling variables. Correlation between grandparents and parents is 0.57, which is substantially higher than correlation between parents and (grand)children (0.36). In other words, the association in years of schooling between two generations seems to have weakened over time. However, caution is needed to compare correlation between grandparents' and parents' years of schooling and correlation between parents' and (grand)children's years of schooling. We defined grandparents' years of schooling as the average years of schooling among four grandparents (or among all grandparents whose years of schooling are available) and parents' years of schooling as the average years of schooling between father's and mother's years of schooling. But, a grandchild's years of schooling refer to her or his own years of schooling. Turning to correlation between grandparents and grandchildren, it is relatively small but still not negligible (0.20). It remains to be empirically examined whether this bivariate association between grandparents and grandchildren remains significant even after parents' years of schooling are taken into account. To address this issue, we now move to the results of the regression analysis. Table 6.1 shows descriptive statistics for other control variables as well.

OLS Regression

Table 6.2 presents the results of three OLS regression models predicting grandchildren's years of schooling. Model 1 includes only parents' years of schooling in addition to other control variables, showing a significant association between parents' and (grand)children's years of schooling. Note that the association of parents' years of schooling with (grand)children's years of schooling is net of father's occupation and other control variables. One additional year of parents' years of schooling is related to the increase of (grand)children's schooling by 0.18 years of schooling. Instead of paren-

TABLE 6.1. Descriptive Statistics of Years of Schooling across Three Generations and Other Control Variables

	Mean	Std. dev.	Correlation of years of schooling		
			Grandchildren	Parents	Grandparents
Grandchildren's years of schooling	14.55	2.05	1		
Parents' years of schooling	9.76	3.21	0.36	1	
Grandparents' years of schooling	3.55	3.51	0.20	0.57	1
Gender of grandchildren[a] (1 = female)	0.48				
Age of grandchildren	31.65	5.03			
Number of grandchildren's siblings	1.53	0.93			
Father's first occupation[a]					
Managerial/professional	0.09				
Clerical	0.17				
Sales/service	0.12				
Farmer	0.18				
Manual worker	0.36				
Missing	0.08				

[a] The values for this categorical variable indicate the proportions. $N = 1{,}745$.

tal education, Model 2 assesses the relationship between grandparents' and grandchildren's education without controlling for parents' education. As already seen in the correlation presented in table 6.1, it is not surprising to see a significant relationship between grandparents' and grandchildren's years of schooling when parents' years of schooling are not included in the model. A one-year increase of grandparents' years of schooling is associated with the increase of grandchildren's years of schooling by 0.08 years.

However, when both grandparents' and parents' years of schooling are included simultaneously in Model 3, the significant relationship between grandparents and grandchildren in Model 2 disappears. There is no independent effect of grandparents' years of schooling on grandchildren's years of schooling once parents' years of schooling are taken into account. In other words, the significant effect of grandparents' education on grandchildren's education shown in Model 2 (and also in the correlation analysis) is mainly through grandparents' effect on parents, which in turn affects

TABLE 6.2. OLS Regression of Grandchildren's Years of Schooling ($N = 1,745$)

Independent Variables	Model 1		Model 2		Model 3	
	Coef.	Std. err.	Coef.	Std. err.	Coef.	Std. err.
Parents' years of schooling	0.180	(0.018)***			0.186	(0.020)***
Grandparents' years of schooling			0.084	(0.014)***	−0.011	(0.016)
Age of grandchild	−0.007	(0.011)	−0.037	(0.011)**	−0.008	(0.011)
Gender of grandchild (1 = female)	0.009	(0.094)	0.030	(0.098)	0.011	(0.094)
Number of grandchild's siblings	−0.232	(0.058)***	−0.299	(0.060)***	−0.234	(0.058)***
Father's first occupation (ref. managerial/professional)						
Clerical	−0.078	(0.186)			−0.086	(0.187)
Sales/service	0.038	(0.208)			0.033	(0.208)
Farmer	−0.514	(0.208)*			−0.521	(0.208)*
Manual worker	−0.349	(0.179)			−0.353	(0.179)*
Missing	−0.510	(0.227)*			−0.517	(0.227)*
Intercept	13.667	(0.476)***	15.906	(0.342)***	13.658	(0.476)***
R^2	0.151		0.076		0.152	

Note: Although the coefficient is not reported, an indicator was included in all the models to distinguish whether a survey respondent (i.e., one of the parents) was female or male.

*** $p < .001$; ** $p < .01$; * $p < .05$

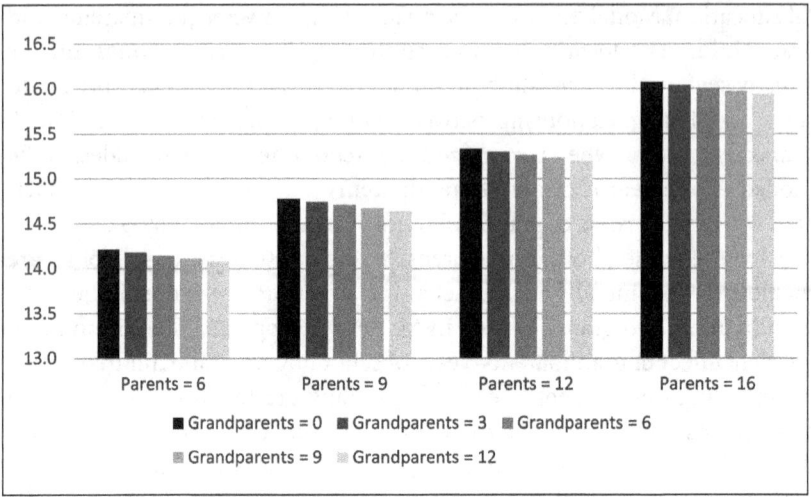

Fig. 6.1. Grandchildren's predicted years of schooling for different combinations of parents' and grandparents' years of schooling

grandchildren (i.e., indirect effects). No significantly direct effect of grandparents' education on grandchildren's education is consistent with the findings in the United States (Warren and Hauser 1997) and Taiwan (Chiang and Park 2015). Including grandparents' education in Model 3 hardly affects the relations of other control variables with grandchildren's years of schooling. Compared to Model 1, coefficients of other control variables in Model 3 do not change much. (Grand)children who grew up in a larger family tend to have fewer years of schooling, while (grand)children whose fathers were farmers and manual workers have less education than their counterparts whose fathers were managers or professionals.

Based on the estimates of Model 3, in figure 6.1 we illustrate the relative effects of grandparents' and parents' years of schooling on grandchildren's years of schooling. Using the coefficients for Model 3 in table 6.1, we calculated the predicted years of schooling for grandchildren who have different combinations of parents' and grandparents' education. Specifically we first present the predicted years of schooling for grandchildren whose parents have 6 years of schooling (i.e., completed primary school) and whose grandparents have one of 0, 3, 6, 9, and 12 years of schooling, respectively. Then we show the predicted years of schooling for grandchildren whose parents have 9 years of schooling and whose grandparents have one of 0, 3, 6, 9, and 12 years of schooling. We repeat for grandchildren whose parents have 12 and 16 years of schooling, respectively.[4]

Figure 6.1 clearly shows that grandchildren's predicted years of schooling increase as parental education increases. Regardless of grandparents' education, (grand)children of parents with more years of schooling are expected to have more years of schooling than grandchildren of parents with fewer years of schooling. At the same time, however, it is clear that within each parental education, grandparents' years of schooling hardly make a difference for grandchildren's years of schooling. The four bars for different years of schooling of grandparents within a given level of parental education are almost identical at every level of parental education. For instance, among (grand)children whose parents have 12 years of schooling, those whose grandparents did not have any formal education are predicted to have 15.3 years of education, whereas their counterparts whose grandparents had 12 years of schooling are also expected to have 15.2 years of schooling.

Maternal versus Paternal Grandparents

Our analysis so far has not distinguished maternal and paternal grandparents by using average years of schooling among all four grandparents. Now, we present the result of a supplementary analysis that separates maternal and paternal grandparents as well as mother's and father's years of schooling. As introduced above, a previous study of grandparent effects in rural China highlighted co-residence with grandchildren as a pathway through which grandparents influenced grandchildren's schooling (Zeng and Xie 2014). Importantly, Chinese children in their study were more likely to live with their paternal grandparents than maternal grandparents, which implies that paternal grandparents may have a stronger impact on grandchildren's schooling than maternal grandparents.

However, it is an open question whether it is co-residence per se or the degree of interactions or closeness that shapes the way in which grandparents affect grandchildren. Even if grandparents do not live together with grandchildren, they can still closely interact with grandchildren. In particular, in contemporary Korea, where the prevalence of co-residence of children with grandparents is fairly low (Park, Choi, and Jo 2016), co-residence seems less relevant to explain the effect of grandparents, if any. Instead, if frequent interactions and close relationships matter for the way in which grandparents influence grandchildren, we may expect that in Korea maternal grandparents rather than paternal grandparents may have a stronger impact on grandchildren. Some evidence suggests that in contemporary Korea grandchildren tend to have a higher level of emotional closeness with maternal parents than paternal parents (Ch'oe and Ch'oe

2012). Unfortunately, our data did not collect co-residence or the degree of interactions with grandparents, and therefore we are not able to examine the specific ways through which maternal and paternal grandparents influence grandchildren's schooling. However, as the first step, it will be useful to see how the relationship of maternal grandparents with grandchildren's years of schooling may or may not differ from the relationship of paternal grandparents with grandchildren's years of schooling.

For the supplementary analysis, we average maternal grandfather's and maternal grandmother's years of schooling to create a variable of maternal grandparents' years of schooling. When only either maternal grandfather's or maternal grandmother's education is available, we use it for maternal grandparents' years of schooling. Similarly, we average paternal grandfather's and paternal grandmother's years of schooling to create a variable of paternal grandparents' schooling. Since we distinguish maternal and paternal grandparents, we also separately examine the effects of mother's and father's years of schooling. Because the analysis requires at least one maternal grandparent and one paternal grandparent, the final sample size was reduced to 1,436 grandchildren. As noted above, we exclude father's first occupation and the indicator of gender of the respondent (parent) to prevent the influence of father's first occupation more on the effect of father's years of schooling than on the effect of mother's years of schooling.

Table 6.3 presents the results of three OLS regression models predicting grandchildren's years of schooling. Model 1 shows that both mother's and father's years of schooling are significantly related to (grand)children's years of schooling in a similar strength (standardized coefficients are similar in the size). Model 2 includes maternal and paternal grandparents' years of schooling separately without mother's and father's years of schooling. Although paternal grandparents' years of schooling are not significantly related to grandchildren's years of schooling, maternal grandparents' education is significantly related. However, when mother's and father's years of schooling are taken into account in Model 3, the relationship between maternal grandparents' and grandchildren's years of schooling becomes tenuous. In other words, the results in table 6.3 are consistent in table 6.2, showing little evidence of independent effects of grandparents' years of schooling, either maternal or paternal, on grandchildren's years of schooling.

TABLE 6.3. OLS Regression of Grandchildren's Years of Schooling ($N = 1,436$)

Independent Variables	Model 1		Model 2		Model 3	
	Coef.	Std. err.	Coef.	Std. err.	Coef.	Std. err.
Mother's years of schooling	0.106	(0.022)***			0.108	(0.023)***
Father's years of schooling	0.108	(0.020)***			0.112	(0.020)***
Maternal grandparents' years of schooling			0.081	(0.018)***	0.015	(0.018)
Paternal grandparents' years of schooling			0.010	(0.017)	−0.028	(0.017)
Age of grandchild	−0.009	(0.012)	−0.040	(0.012)**	−0.009	(0.012)
Gender of grandchild (1 = female)	0.022	(0.102)	0.026	(0.107)	0.026	(0.102)
Number of grandchild's siblings	−0.262	(0.063)***	−0.329	(0.066)***	−0.269	(0.063)***
Intercept	13.167	(0.451)***	16.017	(0.377)***	13.170	(0.452)***
R^2	0.162		0.094		0.164	

*** $p < .001$; ** $p < .01$; * $p < .05$

Conclusions

Korea is often considered a country with strong family ties, which makes it an interesting case in which to study multigenerational effects in educational stratification (Park et al. 2016; Reher 1998). Strong family ties may facilitate grandparent effects on grandchildren's educational and occupational attainment through continued and close relationships across generations. However, our study has not found evidence supporting multigenerational effects on grandchildren's education in Korea. Grandparent effects on grandchildren's schooling are mostly indirect through parents. The significant relationship between grandparents' and grandchildren's years of schooling disappears as soon as parents' years of schooling are introduced into the model. No significant direct effect of grandparents is confirmed even when maternal and paternal grandparents are separately considered. When father's and mother's years of schooling are controlled, none of the maternal and paternal grandparent effects remain significant.

During the last few decades, Korea has experienced a remarkably large expansion of education, leading to drastic changes in the educational levels across generations. In other words, compared to their grandparents, whose average years of schooling were less than four years, three out of four grandchildren have at least some postsecondary education. Under this rapid expansion of education, grandparents might not have a lingering effect on their grandchildren. Previous findings of declining effects of parental characteristics on children's access to higher education among countries with a rapid expansion of higher education may suggest the weak direct effect of grandparents in the context of the rapid expansion of education (Arum, Gamoran, and Shavit 2007). This potential impact of rapid educational expansion on the grandparent effect is worth more careful research. Compared to studies showing a significant association of grandparents' socioeconomic characteristics with grandchildren's socioeconomic characteristics, net of parents' characteristics (e.g., Hällsten 2014; Lindahl et al. 2015; Zeng and Xie 2014), studies in Finland (for social mobility) (Erola and Moisio 2007), Taiwan (Chiang and Park 2015), and the United States (Warren and Hauser 1997) show no evidence of a significant grandparent effect, net of the parent effect. These three countries indeed have experienced a relatively rapid expansion of education, albeit in different time points and in varying degrees. Using data from a more diverse range of countries, future research should assess whether there is any systematic relationship between the degree or speed of educational expansion and the grandparent effect on grandchildren's education.

The null finding of the grandparent effect in the current study does not necessarily mean a generally weak influence of grandparents on grandchildren's educational outcomes. It is notable that we looked at grandchildren's years of schooling as a key outcome. However, the rapid expansion of higher education for the generation of grandchildren may have made quantitative aspects of schooling less relevant for educational competition than qualitative aspects (Gerber and Cheung 2008). As college education is increasingly common, class competition for children's educational success may shift from mere attendance to the type and prestige of higher education attended (Kim and Choi 2015). In other words, in the context of the large expansion of higher education, influences of grandparents as well as parents may be more substantial in affecting the type and prestige of the colleges grandchildren attend rather than the mere years of schooling. Due to the data limitation, we are not able to address this important issue. Another reason for the null effect of grandparents in our study may be related to the time period covered. Note that our study includes grandchildren who already finished education as of 2008 or 2009 and who therefore were less affected by the rising trend of economic inequality and intensified educational competition during the 2000s. The rising concern for inequality and the awareness of the growing relevance of grandparents' wealth for grandchildren's education in Korea are more relevant for school-age children in current years. Moreover, the rapid expansion of education in Korea has relatively leveled off in recent years. Therefore, compared to the previous period considered in our study, in coming years grandparents may become increasingly important for grandchildren's education, as current school-age children, who have lived a different era of rising economic inequality along with a standstill of educational expansion, enter college. Continued research on multigenerational effects will shed a light onto the changing relevance of grandparents for grandchildren's education in different social contexts.

Finally, we recognize that the grandparent effect may not be homogenous but rather may vary according to characteristics of grandchildren and/or parents. For instance, some scholars argued for a compensating effect of grandparent's education: grandparents' education should be more beneficial for grandchildren whose parents have a lower level of education, compensating for the lack of resources that parents have (Jæger 2012). However, using the Taiwanese case, Chiang and Park (2015) demonstrated a contrasting pattern: grandparents' education is more effective for grandchildren whose parents also have a higher level of education, augmenting the already existing inequality in educational opportunity associated with parents' different levels of education. In a supplementary analysis, we tested interactions between grandparents' and parents' years of schooling in affecting grandchildren's years of schooling in Korea. We did not find any evidence for significant interaction effects, supporting neither a compensating nor an augmenting hypothesis. However, potential heterogeneity of the grandparent effect should be explored more carefully in future research, as those studies will help us understand specific conditions under which grandparents' characteristics matter for grandchildren's socioeconomic outcomes.

NOTES

This chapter was presented at Korean Families in Economic and Demographic Transitions: Parenting, Children's Education, and Social Mobility, a conference held on November 11–12, 2016, in the Nam Center for Korean Studies at the University of Michigan, Ann Arbor. Please direct all correspondence to Hyunjoon Park (hypark@sas.upenn.edu), Department of Sociology, University of Pennsylvania, 3718 Locust Walk, Philadelphia, PA 19104.

1. The original surveys were also conducted in 2010 for those born between 1966 and 1975 and in 2011 for those born between 1976 and 1986. However, those born be-

tween 1966 and 1986 are too young to have children who are 25 years old or over. Therefore, we did not use the two later surveys.

2. Additionally, we excluded four respondents whose first children were 25 years old or over but did not report their educational attainment.

3. We do not present the coefficients of the indicator in our result. In all the models, the coefficient of the indicator was not statistically significant.

4. To calculate the predicted years of schooling for specific combinations of parents' and grandparents' years of schooling, we fixed all control variables at their mean values except for father's first occupation (fixed with sales/service) and the indicator whether respondents were female or male (fixed as being male).

REFERENCES

Arum, Richard, Adam Gamoran, and Yossi Shavit. 2007. "More Inclusion Than Aversion: Expansion, Differentiation, and Market Structure in Higher Education." In Yossi Shavit, Richard Arum, and Adam Gamoran, eds., *Stratification in Higher Education: A Comparative Study*, 1–35. Stanford, CA: Stanford University Press.

Blake, Judith. 1989. *Family Size and Achievement*. Berkeley: University of California Press.

Celhay, Pablo, and Sebastián Gallegos. 2015. "Persistence in the Transmission of Education: Evidence across Three Generations for Chile." *Journal of Human Development and Capabilities* 16: 420–51.

Chan, Tak Wing, and Vikki Boliver. 2013. "The Grandparents Effect in Social Mobility: Evidence from British Cohort Studies." *American Sociological Review* 78: 662–78.

Chiang, Yi-Lin, and Hyunjoon Park. 2015. "Do Grandparents Matter? A Multigenerational Perspective on Educational Attainment in Taiwan." *Social Science Research* 51: 163–73.

Ch'oe Sŭl-gi and Ch'oe Sae-ŭn. 2012. "Sedaegan aejŏngjŏk kyŏlsok e issŏsŏ pugye wa mogye ŭi pigyo yŏn'gu" (A Study on Intergenerational Affective Solidarity in Korean Families). *Chosa yŏn'gu* (*Survey Research*) 13: 89–112 (in Korean).

Erola, Jani, and Pasi Moisio. 2007. "Social Mobility over Three Generations in Finland, 1950–2000." *European Sociological Review* 23: 169–83.

Gerber, Theodore P., and Sin Yi Cheung. 2008. "Horizontal Stratification in Postsecondary Education: Forms, Explanations, and Implications." *Annual Review of Sociology* 34: 299–318.

Hällsten, Martin. 2014. "Inequality across Three and Four Generations in Egalitarian Sweden: 1st and 2nd Cousin Correlations in Socio-economic Outcomes." *Research in Social Stratification and Mobility* 35: 19–33.

Hällsten, Martin, and Fabian T. Pfeffer. 2017. "Grand Advantage." *American Sociological Review* 82 (2): 328–60.

Jæger, Mads Meier. 2012. "The Extended Family and Children's Education Successes." *American Sociological Review* 77: 903–22.

Jain-Chandra, Sonali, Tidiane Kinda, Kalpana Kochhar, Shi Piao, and Johanna Schauer. 2016. "Sharing the Growth Dividend: Analysis of Inequality in Asia." IMF Working Paper 16/48, International Monetary Fund, Washington, DC.

Kim, Doo Hwan, and Yool Choi. 2015. "The Irony of the Unchecked Growth of Higher

Education in South Korea: Crystallization of Class Cleavages and Intensifying Status Competition." *Development and Society* 44: 435–63.
Kim, Nak Nyeon, and Jongil Kim. 2015. "Top Incomes in Korea, 1993-2010: Evidence from Income Tax Statistics." *Hitotsubashi Journal of Economics* 56 (1): 1–19.
Knigge, Antonie. 2016. "Beyond the Parental Generation: The Influence of Grandfathers and Great-grandfathers on Status Attainment." *Demography* 53: 1219–44.
Kroeger, Sarah, and Owen Thompson. 2016. "Educational Mobility across Three Generations of American Women." *Economics of Education Review* 53: 72–86.
Lindahl, Mikael, Mårten Palme, Sofia S. Massih, and Anna Sjögren. 2015. "Long-Term Intergenerational Persistence of Human Capital: An Empirical Analysis of Four Generations." *Journal of Human Resources* 50: 1–33.
Mare, Robert D. 2011. "A Multigenerational View of Inequality." *Demography* 48: 1–23.
Organisation for Economic Co-operation and Development (OECD). 2012. *Education at a Glance 2012: OECD Indictors*. Paris: OECD.
Pak Pyŏng-yŏng, Kim Mi-ran, Han Jun, Kim Ki-hŏn, Yu Ki-rak, and Yi Min-ju. 2008. *Kyoyuk kwa sahoe kyech'ŭng idong chosa yŏn'gu: 1943–1955-yŏn ch'ulsaeng chiptan punsŏk (Education and Social Mobility: The Case of 1943–1955 Birth Cohort)*. Seoul: Han'guk Kyoyuk Kaebarwŏn (Korean Educational Development Institute) (in Korean).
Park, Hyunjoon. 2007a. "South Korea: Educational Expansion and Inequality of Opportunity for Higher Education." In Y. Shavit, R. Arum, and A. Gamoran, eds., *Stratification in Higher Education: A Comparative Study*, 87–112. Stanford, CA: Stanford University Press.
Park, Hyunjoon. 2007b. "Inequality of Educational Opportunity in Korea: Gender, Socioeconomic Background, and Family Structure." *International Journal of Human Rights* 11: 179–97.
Park, Hyunjoon. 2013. *Re-Evaluating Education in Japan and Korea: De-mystifying Stereotypes*. New York: Routledge.
Park, Hyunjoon, Claudia Buchmann, Jaesung Choi, and Joseph J. Merry. 2016. "Learning Beyond the School Walls: Trends and Implications." *Annual Review of Sociology* 42: 231–52.
Park, Hyunjoon, Soo-yong Byun, and Kyung-keun Kim. 2011. "Parental Involvement and Students' Cognitive Outcomes in Korea: Focusing on Private Tutoring." *Sociology of Education* 84: 3–22.
Park, Hyunjoon, Jaesung Choi, and Hyejeong Jo. 2016. "Living Arrangements of Single Parents and Their Children in South Korea." *Marriage and Family Review* 52: 89–105.
Park, So Jin, and Nancy Abelmann. 2004. "Class and Cosmopolitan Striving: Mothers' Management of English Education in South Korea." *Anthropological Quarterly* 77 (4): 645–72.
Pfeffer, Fabian T. 2014. "Multigenerational Approaches to Social Mobility: A Multifaceted Research Agenda." *Research in Social Stratification and Mobility* 35: 1–12.
Piketty, Thomas, and Emmanuel Saez. 2014. "Inequality in the Long Run." *Science* 344: 838–43.
Raymo, James R., Hyunjoon Park, Yu Xie, and Wei-jun Jean Yeung. 2015. "Marriage and Family in East Asia: Continuity and Change." *Annual Review of Sociology* 41: 471–92.
Reher, David Sven. 1998. "Family Ties in Western Europe: Persistent Contrasts." *Population and Development Review* 24: 203–34.

Seth, Michael J. 2002. *Education Fever: Society, Politics, and the Pursuit of Schooling in South Korea*. Honolulu: University of Hawai'i Press.

Sorensen, Clark W. 1994. "Success and Education in South Korea." *Comparative Education Review* 38: 10–35.

Warren, John Robert, and Robert M. Hauser. 1997. "Social Stratification across Three Generations: New Evidence from the Wisconsin Study." *American Sociological Review* 62: 561–72.

Zeng, Zen, and Yu Xie. 2014. "The Effects of Grandparents on Children's Schooling: Evidence from Rural China." *Demography* 51: 599–617.

7

Living Arrangements and Obesity among Korean College Students

Living away from One's Family Home as a Factor Affecting Weight Gain

Haram Jeon

For first-year college students who must leave their family homes to attend college, the choice of living arrangements is a new issue. For scholars of adolescent development, living on or off campus without one's parents is considered an important opportunity for young adults to develop their independence (Arnett 1994; Lewis et al. 2015). College students living without parents for the first time may feel a sense of responsibility for their everyday choices, and thus they construct their own lifestyles (Arnett 1994). However, at the same time, young adults are still in the period of adolescence known as "late adolescence," during which they often need their parents' support while establishing their own independent lives (Arnett 2000; Fingerman et al. 2012). In the United States, therefore, dormitory residency is strongly recommended for first-year college students to facilitate their transition to independence from their parents. Such efforts have been proven to relieve the difficulties associated with the absence of one's parents as managers or supervisors (Astin 1973; Schudde 2011). In Korea, however, college students face different circumstances with respect to their living arrangements, specifically a high level of dependency on parental financial and emotional support and a lack of dormitory space.

In Korea, a large number of young adults still depend on their parents financially and emotionally in their everyday lives (O 2015). In particular, parental support plays a significant role in academic and nonacademic development among college students (Kim 2013). The metaphor of baby kangaroos in their mothers' pouches may well represent the strong association between the quality of Korean college students' lives and their parental support. Indeed, the social trend of the "Kangaroo tribe," seen in Korea since early 2000, refers to the young generation not forming independent households, even after college graduation and employment (O 2015). This trend of a lagging transition to adulthood from adolescence reflects unemployment crises and the financial burden of setting up an independent life for young adults. Given this social trend, living with one's parents has become the most common type of living arrangement among college students in Korea (Kim 2013).

In addition, a lack of dormitory room availability on campus forces most college students to find off-campus housing in Korea. Indeed, only about 20 percent of Korean college students reside in dorm rooms (Kim 2013). This is because of land values, particularly for colleges in Seoul and nearby, and because of no legal mandate for colleges and universities to provide on-campus housing facilities (Kim 2013). Therefore, students who are not admitted to dormitories struggle to find comfortable residences with "home-like" housing conditions due to the high cost of rent in areas near campus (Kim 2013; Ch'oe 2014).

In such an environment, living away from home often means poor living conditions and additional financial burdens for college students. In addition, concerns about the difficulty of regulating health-risky behaviors, such as unhealthy diets and heavy drinking, have emerged for Korean college students, much like in the United States (Anderson, Shapiro, and Jundgren 2003; Brevard and Ricketts 1996; Brunt and Rhee 2008; Greaney et al. 2009; Chŏn, Ch'oe, and Pae 2015). Despite these potential concerns regarding students living away from home, little is known about whether and how Korean students living away from home are disadvantaged.

In this study, I examine the relationship between living arrangements and the risk of obesity among Korean college students, using data from the Korean Education and Employment Panel (KEEP). As a key well-being outcome, obesity status is considered an important indicator of an unhealthy diet and a sedentary lifestyle (Brewis 2011; Feinstein 2002; Rigby et al. 2009; Mirowsky and Ross 2003). Additionally, the consideration of college students' socioeconomic status and dormitory residence status in this analysis will help us to understand variations in the relationship between living arrangements and the risk of obesity. Ultimately, the results of this study will shed light on the importance of housing welfare issues among the younger generation, the group that seems most vulnerable in terms of housing.

Background

Living Arrangements for College Students

Deciding where to live is one of the first tasks for prospective college students after being admitted to their chosen higher education institutions. For those whose homes are too far away to permit them to commute to school, living away from home serves as a positive life change. On the one hand, leaving home to attend college can be a meaningful experience, helping a student to develop a sense of independence and to learn how to live as an adult, with adult responsibilities (Arnett 1994; Goldscheider and Goldscheider 1993). Arnett (1994) argued that college students who live apart from their parents must take responsibility for most of their life choices and construct their own lifestyles. Indeed, they must deal with all matters related to establishing an independent household, such as budgeting daily expenses, doing housework, and preparing meals for themselves. In addition, living on or near campus may affect college retention and graduation (Astin 1984; Pascarella and Chapman 1983; Schudde 2011). College students who live on or just off campus are more likely to have opportunities to interact with other students and professors, which leads to increased levels of commitment to and satisfaction with their college education. On the other hand, living away from home may also be disadvantageous for some students because it can be challenging to adjust to a new independent life without readily accessible parental support. Indeed, many college students struggle to become independent (Chŏng and Yi 2011) due to behaviors that can ruin previous positive lifestyle habits; these poor behaviors often include binge drinking and inadequate nutritional intake (Brevard and Ricketts 1996; Chŏn, Ch'oe, and Pae 2015; Yi et al. 2012). With this in mind, many higher education institutions have attempted to support students' departures from their parents' homes, encouraging them to become devoted to academic life on campus without worrying about everyday life (Ch'oe 2014; Im 2009).

In addition, living away from home may also create another concern regarding students' lack (or lower levels) of independence compared to the past. Although living away from home has been acknowledged as a way to help students develop financial and emotional independence and

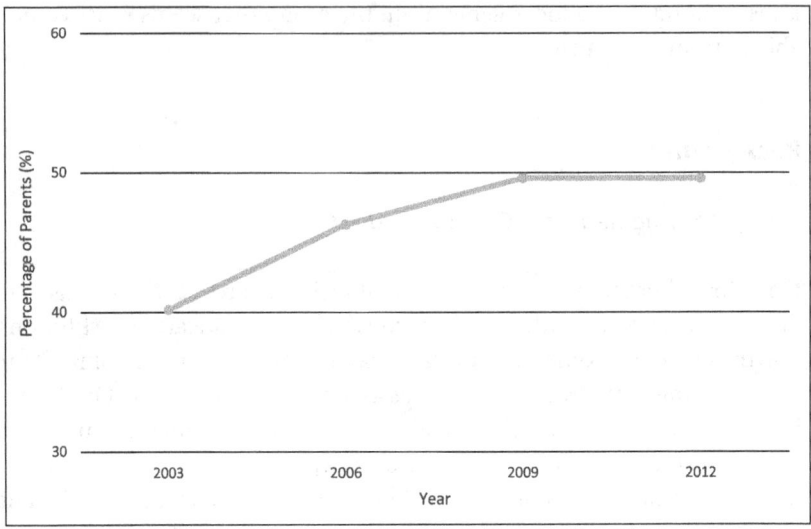

Fig. 7.1. The percentage of Korean parents who think they have to fully support their children until college graduation

take responsibility for their actions, Korean college students have tended to be dependent on their parents in recent decades, even after graduation and entering the workforce (Kim 2015; O 2015). As shown in figure 7.1, more Korean parents have come to believe that they must fully support their children until at least college graduation (Kim et al. 2015), indicating that perceptions of the role of parents have changed and that, in turn, the level of dependency of young adult children in Korea has increased. This recent social trend may accentuate students' difficulties in establishing an independent household. College students living away from home may not only be incapable of budgeting but also have a difficult time preparing meals, getting up in the morning, setting a schedule, and exercising self-control to avoid unhealthy behaviors (e.g., heavy drinking or smoking) on a daily basis. Given that these behavioral concerns, developed during young adulthood, may have long-term health consequences and that these concerns may be more salient among young adults today, I argue that young adults' independent living arrangements should be examined more critically rather than being viewed as a chance to achieve independence.

College-Oriented Policy Interventions to Support an Independent Life and Housing Status among Korean College Students

In an effort to help students in the United States adjust to their new lives away from home, school-level policies have been crafted to promote on-campus living over off-campus arrangements (Astin 1984; Feldman 2005; Kuh et al. 2008; US Department of Housing and Urban Development 2015). Dormitories may be one of the most direct and effective options in terms of housing that is favored by students adjusting to a new life setting. Dormitory residency reduces the pressure to establish a fully independent household. For example, living in a dorm room frees students from concerns about food preparation, housing maintenance, and monthly payments such as utility bills and rent (Arnett 1994). In addition, as a dorm resident, there are regulations for students to follow and guidelines to help them respect other residents (Schudde 2011). In the United States, most previous studies have shown the positive impact of living away from the family home and one's parents on independence among college students, likely because the campus environment is well equipped with on-campus residences, especially for first-year students. In 2014, only 19 percent of first-year students attending a sample of 247 universities in the United States selected off-campus housing or commuted from their parents' homes (Friedman 2016). It is important to determine the current student housing options, including dormitory availability, in Korea in order to investigate the meaning of living away from parents' home among Korean college students. If campuses in Korea are not well equipped with on-campus residences, living away from home will not be a good option for college students.

To describe the housing options for Korean college students, it is necessary to understand the regional imbalance in college distribution between the capital area and other regions. According to the 2016 Statistics in Education, 34.7 percent of higher education institutions in Korea, including two-year junior colleges and four-year universities, are located in the capital area (Seoul, Kyŏnggi, and Inchŏn), and 44.9 percent of all college students are enrolled in these institutions (Ministry of Education 2016). Because the area of the capital has taken the lead in Korean politics, economy, and culture, most colleges have converged upon it (Pan 2016). The extreme concentration of higher education institutions in the capital area leads to large-scale mobility among the young population between their home areas and school areas. The high population density in the capital area has raised concerns related to housing and welfare and has had an impact on housing conditions among college students. The population density, measured as the number of people per square mile (pop/mi^2), was 5,576.5 in the Korean capital area in 2015; this figure is much higher than any state in the United States during the same year (Korean National Index System 2016; United States Census Bureau 2016). The state showing the highest population density in the United States in 2015 was New Jersey, at 1,218.11. The high population density in Korea has given rise to increased land values, a lack of housing supply for the entire population in the capital area, and the relatively poor housing conditions prevalent among Korean college students as compared to their US counterparts. However, the noncapital areas have other concerns related to student housing options. The relatively poorer economy and resources in local governments have limited support for school financing and student recruitment among colleges in outlying areas (Pan 2016). In addition, while the policy goal of boosting higher education away from the capital area prioritizes the establishment of master plans designed to strengthen institutional specialties, student housing policies related to dormitory supply have not been a priority (Im 2009), and there is no legal sanction against the colleges that are reluctant to increase on-campus housing facilities (Kim 2013).

Only about 20 percent of all college students in Korea were accepted into an on-campus dormitory in the 2010s (Kim 2013; Higher Education in Korea 2017). As shown in figure 7.2, the share of students who reside in an on-campus dormitory among total college students has not significantly changed in either public or private colleges in Korea in the 2010s. Because the campus setting is likely favorable to adjusting to a new and independent lifestyle (i.e., via a dormitory) and only limited numbers of students have a chance to live in a dorm, the impact of living arrangements on college students should be examined in a Korean context.

The shortage of on-campus dormitories has forced many students to choose off-campus housing, imposing additional responsibilities on them, such as preparing meals and managing utility bills. Moreover, off-campus housing may raise issues regarding students' right to safe and comfortable living arrangements. The "right to housing" refers to the right to live in acceptable living conditions that protect human dignity (Hong et al. 2011). Considering this right, college students have recently been considered a socially disadvantaged group and thus vulnerable to the infringement of this right (Kim 2013). This is mainly because the percentage of income devoted to housing costs is much higher among college students than among other groups. Schwabe's Law explains the relationship between in-

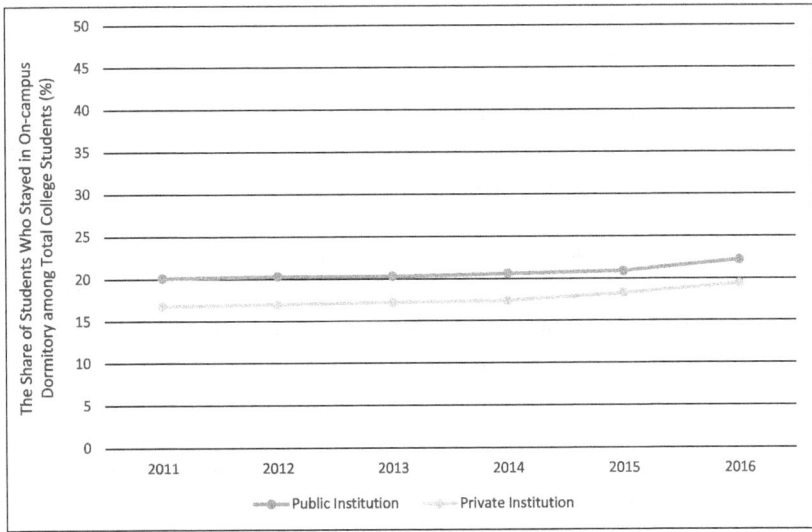

Fig. 7.2. The share of students who stayed in an on-campus dormitory among total college students in Korea in the 2010s

come and housing costs: The higher one's income, the smaller the percentage of housing costs relative to total family expenditures (Singer 1937). Singer (1937) showed that low-income families spent more than 25 percent of their monthly income on rental fees. In other words, if the rent-to-income ratio (RIR) of a family exceeds 25, the family is classified as a low-income family. According to Singer's classification system, Korean college students who live apart from their families exist on the similar level as low-income families because their RIRs were higher than 35 on average in 2013 (Kim 2013). These high RIR values lead to increased pressure to reduce other expenses, such as food, clothing, school-related items, utility bills, and leisure activities. Korean college students who live away from the family home, particularly those living off campus, are more likely to experience higher levels of financial burden, which will lead to lower levels of well-being as compared to students who commute to school from the family home.

Living Arrangements and Obesity among College Students

In the era of the Kangaroo tribe, a lack of affordable off-campus housing options, caused by the shortage of dormitories and the high cost of off-campus rental housing, may be detrimental to the health and well-being of college students who leave home to attend college. However, the impact of living arrangements on Korean college students has not been well addressed. In this chapter, obesity was selected as an outcome related to living arrangements. The risk of obesity has been acknowledged as a primary health concern during young adulthood (Huang et al. 2003; Nelson et al. 2007; Desai et al. 2008); furthermore, obesity is closely associated with unhealthy lifestyles and leads to chronic diseases, such as hypertension and type-2 diabetes (Rigby et al. 2009). Chronic diseases are often referred to as "lifestyle diseases" because they are commonly associated with the way people live their daily lives (Gilmore 2008; Kang 2004; Nishimura, Chikamoto, and Arima 2005; World Health Organization 2003). In particular, lifestyles rife with health-risky behaviors, including binge eating, overeating, a lack of physical activity, heavy alcohol consumption, and smoking, have become a threat to the population in recent decades (Feinstein 2002; Omran 1971). Obesity can serve as a predictor of the incidence of lifestyle diseases, because it reflects weight gain caused by overeating, imbalanced food intake, and sedentary lifestyle (Brewis 2011; Feinstein 2002; Rigby et al. 2009; Mirowsky and Ross 2003). Although obesity is not as serious in Korea as it is in other developed countries, the proportion of those who are obese has been on the rise, and this trend is particularly salient among young adults. The Organisation for Economic Co-operation and Development warned that the pace of increase in obesity rates in Korea has gotten much faster particularly among the young population in recent decades than in the past decades and that the obesity rates will be double in two decades (OECD 2017). Therefore, it is critical to address the question of whether or not living away from home is beneficial for Korean college students by examining the association between living arrangements and the risk of obesity.

In a typical US campus setting, various factors can lead to unintended weight gain. In general, it is challenging to stick to a healthy diet when processed foods and fast food are easily accessible for reasonable prices (Greaney et al. 2009). College students who live away from home are often exposed to such an environment, and they are more likely to eat out, snack, and skip meals than those who commute from home (Nicklas et al. 2001). As a result, college students who live away from home often suffer from inadequate nutrition and have increased intakes of sugar, alcohol, and fast food as compared to students who commute to school (Brevard and Ricketts 1996; Brunt and Rhee 2008; Papadaki et al. 2007; Videon and Manning 2003). In contrast, living with one's parents is associated with a higher consumption of fruits, vegetables, and dairy foods (Papadaki et al.

2007; Videon and Manning 2003). In terms of variation among those who live away from home, students who live on campus tend to be a normal weight (probably due to better dietary choices), while off-campus students are more likely to be overweight or obese (Brevard and Ricketts 1996; Brunt and Rhee 2008; Nicklas et al. 2001).

In Korea, although some studies have focused on the frequency of health-risky behaviors, such as an unhealthy diet, smoking, and binge drinking, among students who live away from home, the research samples were limited to a specific region or a single university (Kim 2013; Yi et al. 2012; O et al. 2011). For example, Yi et al. (2012) collected their sample of 364 students from only one university located in a metropolitan city, which limits the generalizability of their research findings. O et al. (2011) used a larger sample of 2,287 students, but their sample also represented only a specific region, Kyŏngsang-bukto, in the southeast region of Korea. Thus, it is necessary to consider a larger sample related to weight change among students living away from home, taking into account their families' socioeconomic status and other demographic characteristics. Many studies conducted in the United States and elsewhere have documented that overweight and obesity rates are generally higher among students from poor families in developed countries (McLaren 2007; Popkin 2001; Jeon, Salinas, and Baker 2015). Specifically, mothers' educational attainment is considered an influential factor in determining children's health outcomes (Carneiro, Meghir, and Parey 2013) because mothers often play a more critical role than fathers in building healthy diet patterns for their children. A higher family income also has been reported to decrease the risk of obesity via an ability to afford healthy foods (Nelson et al. 2007). Given the overall increases in the intake of animal fat and sugar and the easy access to processed and fast food options in recent years in Korea, we would expect family socioeconomic status to play an important role in adult children's diets and weight gain when they live away from home.

Data and Methods

Data and Sample

To examine the impact of living arrangements on being obese among college students, data from the Korean Education and Employment Panel were used. As a longitudinal study, KEEP was first conducted based on nationally representative samples of 9th graders and 12th graders in 2004 and continued to annually collect information on their educational experiences, as well as their transitions from the adolescent period to early adulthood, until 2015. The current study focuses on respondents who were 9th graders in 2004 (baseline) and enrolled in college in 2008 (sixth wave) to investigate how their experiences of living away from home during their first year in college are associated with weight changes. The total number of cases was 2,000 at the base year, but 918 students either did not enroll in any type of higher education institution or dropped out during their upper-secondary education. Therefore, the number of cases in the final analytic sample is 1,082 in this study.

Variables

Body Mass Index (BMI)

As an outcome variable, body mass index (BMI), measured by an individual's weight over his or her height squared (i.e., BMI = weight(kg)/height^2(m^2)), is used.

Living Arrangements

The respondent's living arrangement was used as a primary independent variable with which to predict BMI, and it was categorized into two groups based on information about whether a student lived at his or her parents' home or away from home in 2008 as a first-year student in college. This was a dichotomous indicator (students living away from their parents' home coded as 1, otherwise 0).

Dormitory Residence

Living in dorm rooms on campus may lead to a different result regarding weight gain than living in off-campus housing. As an additional test, we examined this difference between on- and off-campus residence. It was coded as a dichotomous dummy variable (dormitory residence coded as 1, otherwise 0).

Family Socioeconomic Status

Two indicators of family socioeconomic status were considered in the analysis. The first was maternal education, measured as a continuous variable showing a mother's years of schooling completed. Another indicator was a respondent's family's total household income, measured as average monthly income. The value of family income was transformed using a natural log due to its skewed distribution.

Control Variables

To more accurately estimate the association between living arrangement and BMI score among college students, five control variables were included in the analysis: gender, family structure, area of family residence, four-year university, and BMI before college. Gender is a dichotomous variable, with female students being coded as 1. Family structure indicates whether a student's parents have an intact marital relationship. If their parents experienced divorce or bereavement, this was coded as 1, and otherwise 0. Area of family residence was also measured as a dichotomous variable. If a student's family lived in a rural area, they were coded as 1, and otherwise 0. Four-year university indicates whether a student enrolled in a four-year university or a two- or three-year junior college. Finally, BMI during 12th grade was included as a baseline BMI. Table 7.1 shows the descriptive statistics for all variables mentioned above.

TABLE 7.1. Weighted Descriptive Statistics for Sampled College Students

Variable	Description	Mean	S.D.
BMI	weight (kg)/height^2 (m^2)	20.88	2.91
Living away	Living away from home = 1; living at home = 0	0.33	0.47
Dormitory[a]	Living in a dorm room = 1; living off campus = 0	0.58	0.49
Maternal education	Years of schooling completed by mother	11.73	2.88
Family income	Logged value of monthly income	5.46	1.19
Family structure	Nonintact structure = 1	0.12	0.32
Gender	Female = 1; male = 0	0.74	0.44
Area of family residence	Rural = 1; urban = 0	0.19	0.39
College type	Four-year university = 1	0.63	0.48
Former BMI	BMI at 12th grade	21.10	3.00

$N = 1,082$

[a] Descriptive statistics for dormitory were calculated only among students who lived away from home ($N = 361$).

Analytical Strategies

To investigate the association between living arrangement and weight change among college students, ordinary least squares (OLS) regression modeling was employed. In the regression modeling, two models were designed. In the first model, the effects of living away from one's parents' home and family background on BMI score changes among college students were examined, with BMI during 12th grade being used as a baseline. The second model additionally estimated whether dormitory residence was associated with lower levels of weight gain than off-campus living arrangements among the students who lived away from their parents' homes.

To deal with missing cases in the data set, a multiple imputation technique was employed using the ice command in the STATA software package (Royston 2004). To achieve accurate results for the imputed data sets, five data sets were generated and the coefficients and standard errors were averaged (von Hippel 2007).

Findings

To determine whether living away from one's parents' home is associated with weight gain among college students, the OLS regression models were estimated. Table 7.2 presents the regression coefficients for the living away from home and family socioeconomic status variables in predicting BMI among college students, with other control variables being adjusted for. Model I found a statistically significant result indicating that living away from home increased BMI among college students during their first year. In other words, students who lived in on- or off-campus housing showed BMI increases that were 0.44 points higher than students who lived at their parents' homes during the same period, holding other conditions constant at the average. This result supports the notion that living away from home may be associated with weight gain among college students. Among indicators of family socioeconomic status, only a mother's educational attainment had a significant impact on decreasing BMI. For each additional year of schooling a student's mother completed, his or her BMI decreased by about 0.09 points. The family income status indicator did not have a statistically significant impact on BMI changes among college students. As control variables, gender and previous BMI were statistically significant, but the area of family residence and university type did not play significant roles in BMI change.

Model II additionally examined whether there are buffering effects on the part of dormitory residence on BMI increases. As shown in table 7.2, the residential type of on-campus housing had no significant effect on BMI among college students. As opposed to previous studies, which suggested the advantages of dormitory residence, there was little difference in BMI changes between on- and off-campus residencies during the follow-up period.

As mentioned above, the first model of the OLS regression showed that living arrangements and maternal education have significant impacts on BMI change among college students. Figure 7.3 illustrates the increased amount of weight associated with students' living arrangements and maternal education, assuming the heights of the sampled students to be at the average value for Korean young adults in 2008. Based on the Korea Human Scale administered by the Korean Agency for Technology and Standards, the average heights of Korean male and female young adults ages 20–25 in 2008 were 172.5 centimeters and 159.3 centimeters, respectively. According to these standards, one additional BMI point is equivalent to an increase of 2.98 kilograms (= 1.725^2) for male students and 2.54 kilograms (= 1.593^2) for female students. Compared to the reference group

TABLE 7.2. Regression Analysis of BMI by Living Arrangement and Family Background

Variable	Model I		Model II[a]	
	Coef.	S.E.	Coef.	S.E.
Living arrangement				
Living away	0.441*	0.210		
Dormitory residence			0.415	0.405
Family background				
Maternal education	−0.090*	0.043		
Family income	0.023	0.066		
Control variables				
Gender (Female = 1)	−0.938***	0.195		
Area of family residence (Rural = 1)	−0.443	0.294		
College type (four-year university = 1)	0.085	0.178		
Former BMI	0.779***	0.048		
Intercept	5.934***	1.358		
N	1,082		361	
Adjusted R^2	0.729		0.667	

[a] Model II examines the difference in BMI between dormitory residence and off-campus residence only among students who live away from their family home. Other coefficients are omitted.

* $p < .05$; ** $p < .01$; *** $p < .001$

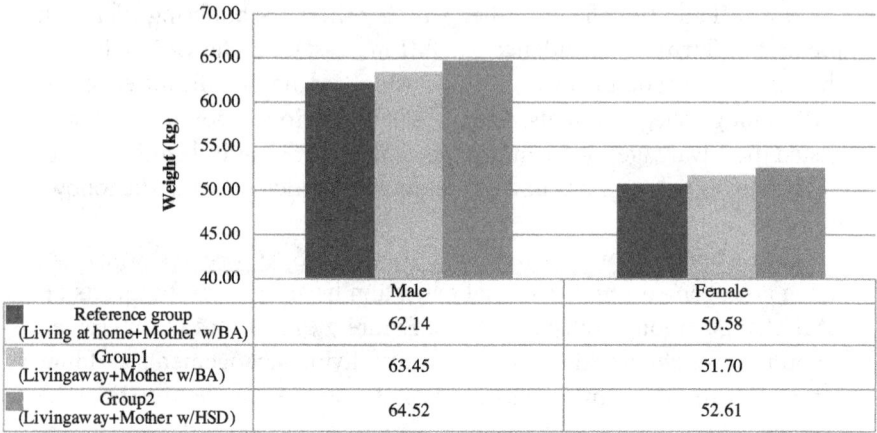

Fig. 7.3. Comparison of increased weight by living arrangement and maternal education

(i.e., students who lived at their parents' homes and whose mothers held at least a bachelor's degree), students who lived away from home and whose mothers held a bachelor's degree showed a BMI increase of 0.44 points, holding other variables constant. For males, a BMI increase of 0.44 equates to 1.31 kilograms, and for females, it equates to an additional 1.12 kilograms. In addition, students who lived away from home and whose mothers held a high school diploma or less were likely to experience an increase in weight of 2.38 kilograms for males and 2.03 kilograms for females, as compared to the reference group. In short, living arrangements and maternal education, ceteris paribus, significantly affect weight gain among college students.

Discussion

This chapter examined the association between living arrangements and students' BMI changes to estimate the effects of living in an independent household, without parents, among college students in Korea. To summarize the findings, after holding other conditions constant, living away from one's family home had a significant impact on increased BMI among college students during their freshman year. This significant association may indicate that college students were more likely to struggle to maintain healthy diets and lifestyles when they lived away from home. While living away seems detrimental overall in this regard, dormitory residence did not seem differ from off-campus living. Living in a dormitory did not ameliorate the negative impact of living away from one's family home. Last, an increase in a mother's education was significantly associated with decreased BMI among all college students.

Living away from one's family home was significantly related to well-being status among Korean college students, but it was more likely to harm rather than benefit students. The weight gain among those who lived away from one's family home has confirmed concerns about students' difficulty in adjusting to a new life setting in an independent household. As previous nutritional studies noted regarding food intake patterns among college students living on and off campus, students are vulnerable to obesity in this environment because they are more likely to eat out, snack, and skip meals. In addition, their weight management may be influenced by health-risky behaviors, including heavy alcohol consumption and a sedentary lifestyle. These mediating mechanisms in the association between living arrangements and weight gain should be further examined.

Whether individual students manage their lifestyle is directly related to the well-being status of college students who leave their family homes. Although living without parents has been reported to be a chance to achieve feelings of independence and responsibility as an adult, living without parental support and supervision presents some challenges while adjusting to a new lifestyle in the face of the potential stress of college as a first-year student (Borawski et al. 2003). Creating and maintaining a healthy lifestyle may thus be related to parental involvement beyond financial support. Because living in an independent household means that college students must deal with various practical issues related to everyday life, a lack of parental support is likely to negatively affect the development of healthy lifestyles among college students. Thus, the significant association between living arrangements and the risk of obesity among college students emphasizes the need for affordable housing options to ensure the well-being of young adults. Because the health concerns of young adults may lead to enduring health issues, the impact of living arrangements on other health outcomes must also be examined in future research.

Additionally, my result regarding the influence of educated mothers on BMI change among college students supports the idea that parenting or parental resources can still help college students maintain a healthy weight, even when they live away from home. This finding underscores the potential health disparity between young adults based on socioeconomic resources. While obesity during childhood and adolescence is significantly influenced by family background (as documented in numerous studies), the results of the current study show that even college students in Korea are clearly affected by their families' socioeconomic status. Among family resources, however, a mother's educational attainment seems to be the only noteworthy factor in terms of affecting weight changes. Family income—an indicator of financial support from one's family—did not significantly impact on- or off-campus residents or commuters. That is, weight gain among college students may be the result of parental involvement in students' lifestyles, not necessarily financial support per se. The significance of maternal education on weight change indicates that parental support in managing everyday life influenced college students' well-being. Conversely, this result also implies that a lack of parental support may exacerbate the negative impact on well-being felt by students who live away from home. While the advantage of an educated mother may offset the disadvantages of living away from one's family home, other students may suffer not only from living away from home but also from a lack of support from their parents.

Last, why did dormitory residence, as compared to off-campus residence, fail to affect BMI? As a straightforward policy intervention, the Korean government and higher education institutions have discussed creating more dormitory housing. However, the above-mentioned results imply that increasing housing facilities on campus may not be enough to protect college students against the negative effects of living away from home. Ideally, living in a dorm room with available meal plans and imposed behavioral expectations and regulations can help college students establish an independent life. However, given a lack of meaningful difference in BMI change between students in dormitory residence and those in off-campus residence, perhaps the behavioral policies and food options available in dormitories should be improved to enhance the well-being of college students.

This research has limitations. First, the analysis used nationally representative data collected in 2008 and 2009. Although they are the most recent nationally representative data sets available that include information about living arrangements and BMI among college students in Korea, it has been almost 10 years since these data were collected, and they may not fully capture the current conditions. For example, the Korean government tried to introduce intervention programs at the higher education level for reducing the pace of increase in obesity rates among young adults (Ryu et al. 2016). Therefore, future research should reexamine this association using more recent data sets. Second, in future research, other health outcomes of living without parents should be examined. For example, self-rated health, depression, and various health-risky behaviors, such as alcohol consumption and smoking, would be helpful to examine in determining how living away from home while in college influences an individual's health and well-being.

REFERENCES

Anderson, Drew A., Jennifer R. Shapiro, and Jennifer D. Jundgren. 2003. "The Freshman Year of College as a Critical Period for Weight Gain: An Initial Evaluation." *Eating Behaviors* 4 (4): 363–67.
Arnett, Jeffrey Jensen. 1994. "Are College Students Adults? Their Conceptions of the Transition to Adulthood." *Journal of Adult Development* 1 (4): 213–24.
Arnett, Jeffrey Jensen. 2000. "Emerging Adulthood: A Theory of Development from the Late Teens through the Twenties." *American Psychologist* 55 (5): 469–80.
Astin, Alexander. 1973. "The Impact of Dormitory Living on Students." *Educational Record* 54 (9): 204–10.
Astin, Alexander. 1984. "Student Involvement: A Development Theory for Higher Education." *Journal of College Student Personnel* 25 (4): 297–308.
Borawski, Elaine A., Carolyn E. Ievers-Landis, Loren D. Lovegreen, and Erika S. Trapl. 2003. "Parental Monitoring, Negotiated Unsupervised Time, and Parental Trust: The Role of Perceived Parenting Practices in Adolescent Health Risk Behaviors." *Journal of Adolescent Health* 33 (2): 60–70.
Brevard, Patricia B., and Crystal D. Ricketts. 1996. "Residence of College Students Affects Dietary Intake, Physical Activity, and Serum Lipid Levels." *Journal of the American Dietetic Association* 96 (1): 35–38.
Brewis, Alexandra A. 2011. *Obesity: Cultural and Biocultural Perspectives*. New Brunswick, NJ: Rutgers University Press.
Brunt, Ardith R., and Yeong S. Rhee. 2008. "Obesity and Lifestyle in US College Students Related to Living Arrangements." *Appetite* 51 (3): 615–21.
Carneiro, Pedro, Costas Meghir, and Matthias Parey. 2013. "Maternal Education, Home Environments, and the Development of Children and Adolescents." *Journal of the European Economic Association* 11 (S1): 123–60.
Ch'oe Ŭn-yŏng. 2014. *Sŏul-si ch'ŏngnyŏn kagu ŭi chugŏ silt'ae wa chŏngch'aek yŏn'gu* (The Policy Study on Living Conditions of Young Adults in Seoul). Seoul: Minju Chŏngch'aek Yŏn'guwŏn (Institute for Democracy and Policies) (in Korean).
Chŏn Ye-suk, Ch'oe Mi-gyŏng, and Pae Yun-jŏng. 2015. "Ilbu taehaksaeng ŭi kŏju hyŏngt'ae e ttarŭn yasik moet ssŭbyangso sŏpch'wi sangt'ae" (Night Eating and Nutrient Intake Status according to Residence Type in University Students). *Han'guk sikp'um ssŭbyang kwahak hoeji* (Journal of the Korean Society of Food Science and Nutrition) 44 (2): 216–25 (in Korean).
Chŏng Min-u, Yi Na-yŏng. 2011. "'Kajok' ŭi kyŏnggye e sŏn chŏngnyŏn sedae: sŏngbyŏrhwa toen tongnip kwa kyubŏmjŏk sigonggansŏng" (Youths on the Boundary of the 'Family'—Gendered Experiences of In/dependence and Normative Spatio-temporality). *Kyŏngje wa sahoe* (Economy and Society) 89: 105–45 (in Korean).

Desai, Melissa N., William C. Miller, Betty Staples, and Terrill Bravender. 2008. "Risk Factors Associated with Overweight and Obesity in College Students." *Journal of American College Health* 57 (1): 109–14.

Feinstein, Leon. 2002. *Quantitative Estimates of the Social Benefits of Learning 2: Health (Depression and Obesity)*. London: Institute of Education.

Feldman, Robert S. 2005. *Improving the First Year of College: Research and Practice*. Mahwah, NJ: Lawrence Erlbaum.

Fingerman, Karen L., Yen-Pi Cheng, Lauren Tighe, Kira S. Birditt, and Steven Zarit. 2012. "Relationships between Young Adults and Their Parents." In *Early Adulthood in a Family Context*, edited by A. Booth, S. L. Brown, N. S. Landale, W. D. Manning, and S. M. McHale, 59–85. New York: Springer.

Friedman, Jordan. 2016. "10 Universities Where the Most Freshmen Commute to Campus." *U.S. News: Higher Education*, July 12. Retrieved January 3, 2017, from http://www.usnews.com/education/best-colleges/the-short-list-college/articles/2016-07-12/10-universities-where-the-most-freshmen-commute-to-campus

Gilmore, Ian. 2008. "Excessive Drinking in Young Women: Not Just a 'Lifestyle Disease.'" *BMJ* 336: 952–53.

Goldscheider, Frances K., and Calvin Goldscheider. 1993. *Leaving Home Before Marriage: Ethnicity, Familism, and Generational Relationships*. Madison: University of Wisconsin Press.

Greaney, Mary L., Faith D. Less, Adrienne A. White, Sarah F. Dayton, Deborah Riebe, Bryan Blissmer, Suzanne Shoff, Jennifer R. Walsh, and Geoffrey W. Greene. 2009. "College Students' Barriers and Enablers for Healthful Weight Management: A Qualitative Study." *Journal of Nutrition Education and Behavior* 41 (4): 281–86.

Higher Education in Korea. 2017. "Share of Students Who Stayed in On-Campus Dormitory among Total College Students." Retrieved October 31, 2017, from http://www.academyinfo.go.kr/ (in Korean).

Hong In-ok, Nam Ki-chŏl, Nam Wŏn-sŏk, Sŏ Chong-gyun, Nam Hye-Sŭng, Kim Su-hyŏn. 2011. *Chugŏ pokchi ŭi saeroun p'aerŏdaim* (*New Paradigm in Housing Welfare*). Seoul: Sahoe P'yŏngnon (Social Critique) (in Korean).

Huang, Terry T-K., Kari Jo Harris, Rebecca E. Lee, Niaman Nazir, Wendi Born, and Harsohena Kaur. 2003. "Assessing Overweight, Obesity, Diet, and Physical Activity in College Students." *Journal of American College Health* 52 (2): 83–86.

Im Yŏn-gi. 2009. "Chibang taehak yusŏng ŭl wihan chŏngch'aek kwaje ŭi usŏn sunwi t'amsaek mit palchŏnjŏk nonŭi" (The Search and Discussion for the Priority of Local University Development Policy Task). *Kyoyuk haengjŏng hagyŏn* (*Journal of Educational Administration*) 27 (4): 411–35 (in Korean).

Jeon, Haram, Daniel Salinas, and David P. Baker. 2015. "Non-linear Education Gradient across the Nutrition Transition: Mothers' Overweight and the Population Education Transition." *Public Health Nutrition* 18 (17): 3172–82.

Kang, Jin Kyung. 2004. "Saenghwal sŭpkwanbyŏng ŭi kaenyŏm" (Lifestyle Disease). *Taehan ŭisa hyŏphoeji* (*Journal of the Korean Medical Association*) 47: 188–94 (in Korean).

Kim Chi-gyŏng. 2013. "Pumo pidonggŏ taehak chaehaksaeng ŭi chugŏ yuhyŏng mit chugŏbi pudam hyŏnhwang" (The Current Status of Residential Types and Cost of Living among College Students Who Live without Parents). *NYPI chŏngsonyŏn chŏngch'aek rip'ot'ŭ* (*NYPI Policy Report*) 42: 1–16 (in Korean).

Kim, Min-kyung. 2015. "More and More Young Koreans Stuck in the 'Kangaroo Tribe.'"

Hankyoreh, August 14. Retrieved October 31, 2017, from http://english.hani.co.kr/arti/PRINT/704476.html (in Korean).

Kim Yu-gyŏng, Yi Yŏ-bong, Ch'oe Sae-ŭn, Kim Ka-hŭi, and Im Sŏng-ŭn. 2015. *Kajok hyŏngt'ae tabyŏnhwa e ttarŭn puyang ch'egye pyŏnhwa chŏnmang kwa kongsa kan puyang pundam pangan* (*The Diversification of Family Structure and the Role of Families and Governments in Family Support*). Sejong: Han'guk pogŏn sahoe yŏn'gu wŏnjang (Korea Institute for Health and Social Affairs) (in Korean).

Korean National Index System. 2016. "Korean National Index." Retrieved January 3, 2017, from http://www.index.go.kr/potal/main/PotalMain.do (in Korean).

Kuh, George D., Ty M. Cruce, Rick Shoup, and Jillian Kinzie. 2008. "Unmasking the Effects of Student Engagement on First-Year College Grades and Persistence." *Journal of Higher Education* 79 (5): 540–63.

Lewis, Jane, Anne West, Philip Noden, and Jonathan Roberts. 2015. "Family Transitions in Early Adulthood: Parental Support of University Students." *LSE Research Brief*. Retrieved October 25, 2016, from www.lse.ac.uk/socialpolicy/pdf/Leverhulmeresearchbrief1students.pdf

McLaren, Lindsay. 2007. "Socioeconomic Status and Obesity." *Epidemiologic Reviews* 29 (1): 29–48.

Ministry of Education. 2016. "2016 Education Statistics." Retrieved October 25, 2016, from http://www.moe.go.kr/web/100026/ko/board/view.do?bbsId=294&encodeYn=&pageSize=10&currentPage=0&boardSeq=64173&mode=view (in Korean).

Mirowsky, John, and Catherine E. Ross. 2003. *Education, Social Status, and Health*. New York: Routledge.

Nelson, Toben F., Steven L. Gortmaker, S. V. Subramanian, Lilian Cheung, and Henry Wechsler. 2007. "Disparities in Overweight and Obesity among US College Students." *American Journal of Health Behavior* 31 (4): 363–73.

Nicklas, Theresa A., Tom Baranowski, Karen W. Cullen, and Gerald Berenson. 2001. "Eating Patterns, Dietary Quality and Obesity." *Journal of the American College of Nutrition* 20 (6): 599–608.

Nishimura, Yumiko, Yosuke Chikamoto, and Hideaki Arima. 2005. "Association between Lifestyle-Disease Diagnosis or Risk Status and Medical Care Costs in a Japanese Corporation." *American Journal of Health Promotion* 19 (S3): 249–54.

OECD. 2017. *Obesity Update 2017*. Paris: OECD.

O Ho-yŏng. 2015. "K'aenggŏrujok ŭi silt'ae wa kwaje" (Status and Problems in Kangaroo Tribe). *KRIVET Issue Brief* 81: 1–4 (in Korean).

O Nan-suk, Pak Chae-yong, Han Ch'ang-hyŏn. 2011. "Taehaksaeng ŭi kisuksa saenghwal yŏbu e ttarŭn kŏn'gang chŭngjin haengwi wa kwallyŏn yoin" (Health-Promoting Behaviors and Related Factors for College Students by Type of Residence). *Pogŏn kyoyuk kŏn'gang chŭngjin hakhoeji* (*Korean Journal of Health Education and Promotion*) 28 (2): 27–40 (in Korean).

Omran, Abdel R. 1971. "The Epidemiologic Transition: A Theory of the Epidemiology of Population Change." *Milbank Memorial Fund Quarterly* 49 (4): 509–38.

Pan Sang-jin. 2016. "Hangnyŏng in'gu kamso taehak chaejŏng chiwŏn saŏp kwa chiyŏkkan taehak kyŏkch'a" (The Decline of School Age Population, Government Sponsored Work Expenditure for Universities, and the Regional Disparity of Higher Education). *Kyoyuk chonghap yŏn'gu* (*Journal of Educational Research*) 14 (2): 213–42 (in Korean).

Papadaki, Angeliki, George Hondros, Jane A. Scott, and Maria Kapsokefalou. 2007. "Eating Habits of University Students Living at, or Away from Home in Greece." *Appetite* 49 (1): 169–76.

Pascarella, Ernest T., and David W. Chapman. 1983. "A Multi-institutional, Path Analytic Validation of Tinto's Model of College Withdrawal." *American Educational Research Journal* 20 (1):87–102.

Popkin, Barry M. 2001. "The Nutrition Transition and Obesity in the Developing World." *Journal of Nutrition* 131 (3): S871–S873.

Rigby, N., R. Leach, T. Lobstein, R. Huxley, and S. Kumanyika. 2009. "Epidemiology and Social Impact of Obesity." In *Obesity: Science to Practice*, edited by G. Williams and G. Fruhbeck, 21–41. Hoboken: John Wiley.

Royston, Patrick. 2004. "Multiple Imputation of Missing Values." *Stata Journal* 4 (3): 227–41.

Ryu, Seung-Hyun, Gwang-Ki Kim, Jung Jegal, Seung-A Choi, Chang-Woo Son, and Nan-Hee Yun. 2016. *Evaluation Framework for Obesity Prevention Policy*. Seoul: Seoul National University and Ministry of Health and Welfare (in Korean).

Schudde, Lauren T. 2011. "The Causal Effect of Campus Residency on College Student Retention." *Review of Higher Education* 34 (4): 581–610.

Singer, H. W. 1937. "Income and Rent: A Study of Family Expenditure." *Review of Economic Studies* 4: 145–54.

United States Census Bureau. 2016. "Population and Housing Unit Estimates." Retrieved January 3, 2017, from http://www.census.gov/programs-surveys/popest.html

US Department of Housing and Urban Development. 2015. "Barriers to Success: Housing Insecurity for U.S. College Students." *Insights into Housing and Community Development Policy*. Retrieved January 3, 2017, from https://www.huduser.gov/portal/periodicals/insight/insight_2.pdf

Videon, Tami M., and Carolyn K. Manning. 2003. "Influences on Adolescent Eating Patterns: The Importance of Family Meals." *Journal of Adolescent Health* 32 (5): 365–73.

von Hippel, Paul T. 2007. "Regression with Missing Ys: An Improved Strategy for Analyzing Multiply Imputed Data." *Sociological Methodology* 37 (1): 83–117.

World Health Organization. 2003. "Diet, Nutrition and the Prevention of Chronic Diseases: Report of a Joint WHO/FAO Expert Consultation." *WHO Technical Report Series* 916. Geneva: World Health Organization.

Yi Pog-im, Kim Yun-mi, Kim Yun-jŏng, Sŏ Ŭn-ok, Yi Tong-gŭn, Yi Sŏk-hŭi, Yi Su-mi, Han Kyŏng-mi, and Han Yu-jin. 2012. "Taehaksaeng ŭi kŏju hyŏngt'ae wa kŏn'gang haengwi kanŭi kwan'gye" (The Relationship of Health Behaviors and Residence Types of University Students). *Han'guk hakkyo pogŏn hakhoeji (Journal of the Korean Society of School Health)* 25 (1): 77–84 (in Korean).

Gender and Family

8

Educational Background, Gender-Role Attitudes, and Parenting Time for Young Children

Yean-Ju Lee, Kitae Park, and Ivan Sanidad

Scholars have noticed that the "gender revolution" stalled in the United States in the mid-1990s. Several measures of gender-role attitudes and behaviors have indicated that the movement toward gender equality has either slowed down or has advanced at an uneven pace (Cotter et al. 2011; England 2010). While female labor force participation has substantially increased without a pause and many women have moved into traditionally male-dominated occupations, men have not participated in traditionally female-dominated activities to a comparable extent. According to England (2010), steadfast gender essentialism ("men and women are innately and fundamentally different in interests and skills") may provide an explanation, and the child-rearing issue may showcase the societal devaluation of female work, with individual mothers and their families being given the sole responsibility for it rather than society seeing it as a collective obligation.

A somewhat contradictory finding to such an argument, however, is that fathers' time with children has increased substantially over the past three decades. When daily tasks are divided into the three categories of paid work, housework, and childcare, fathers' childcare time has increased more rapidly than any other tasks done by either mothers or fathers (Bianchi and Milkie 2010; Sayer, Bianchi, and Robinson 2004; Wang and Bianchi 2009). The disproportionate expansion is partly because fathers' childcare time in earlier periods had been minimal, and therefore an increase of any magnitude will be noticeable. However, even when compared to men's housework time, childcare time has increased to a larger extent (Bianchi et al. 2012). This rather unexpected trend has created a great deal of interest in cross-cultural research on fathering, raising the question of whether men are moving toward egalitarian gender-role performances (Seward and Ritcher 2008).

Mothers' childcare time has also increased, whereas their time devoted to housework has declined substantially due to the continued increase in their paid work time (Bianchi et al. 2012). It seems that investing time in children has taken an increasingly higher priority among both mothers and fathers, which probably reflects an intensifying class strategy of promoting children's success. High-quality human capital becomes essential in achieving socioeconomic success in the globalizing economy as the labor markets are polarized between high-skilled workers who are incorporated into global businesses and workers with limited skills whose labor is targeted at local labor markets that consist largely of person-to-person service jobs. Middle-class parents may intend to transmit their class status to their children, whereas working-class or poor parents may desire to enhance the prospect of their children's upward mobility.

The family environment provides a crucial context that affects children's acquisition of cognitive and noncognitive skills. Most noticeably, evidence in the United States shows that by the time children start attending school, the levels of children's cognitive and noncognitive abilities are already differentiated along the quartile positions of parental socioeconomic status (SES) (Carneiro and Heckman 2003). As important as cognitive skills are noncognitive (or soft) skills that children acquire in the early years of their lives, including motivation, perseverance, and attention capacity, which will facilitate developing cognitive skills in later years (Heckman 2006). Data show that the gaps in children's academic achievements by parental SES widen during the years of schooling and are the cumulative outcomes of parental/familial effects: Gaps in children's academic achievements remain more or less constant during the months of attending schools but widen again during the summer or winter months while schools are in recess (Alexander, Entwisle, and Olson 2001, 2007; Downey, von Hippel, and Broh 2004). These studies suggest two things: First, cognitive stimulation and noncognitive stimulation given to young children during the early years from birth to the start of school play a crucial role in their lifetime achievements via their cumulative effects, and second, parents of lower SES are not as effective as their counterparts with higher SES in facilitating children's development.

Studies suggest that the exact patterns of the association between parental SES and children's academic achievements and the mechanisms behind them vary rather widely by the contexts of education systems and other social institutions including welfare. Under the Korean educational system, which is characterized by government policies emphasizing egalitarian access to educational resources and by the universal school curriculum focusing on preparations for high-stake college entrance exams, parental involvement in the education of school-age children generally has a positive effect on their academic outcomes regardless of their class backgrounds (Park, Byun, and Kim 2011). However, more educated and wealthier parents provide their 15-year-old children with a greater amount of "objectified cultural capital" (including books, arts, and other cultural materials at home) and "children's embodied cultural capital" (visiting museums, concerts, plays, etc.), suggesting that parents of higher SES invest a greater amount of time and money in their children than do lower SES parents (Byun, Schofer, and Kim 2012). Although the latter type of cultural capital actually deteriorates children's academic achievements (reading skills) in the study, it may help enhance children's skills of artistic performances, enabling an alternative passage to a prestigious higher education institution. Furthermore, receiving "shadow education" (i.e., extracurricular education, which requires monetary expenditure on the part of the parents) yields greater gains in math skills among children from lower SES families than among children from higher SES families; in other words, children in more adverse educational environments benefit more from any extra exposure to learning (Choi and Park 2016). These findings indicate that in Korea, parents' investment of time and money will benefit children from families of any socioeconomic positions.

This study examines the time that fathers and mothers spend caring for their young children in Korea. The purpose of this research is twofold: whether parenting time has increased over recent decades and whether and how mothers' and fathers' childcare activities vary by the parents' class status and their gender-role attitudes. After the literature is reviewed below, the research questions will be stated.

Literature Review and Research Questions

Temporal Trend in Parenting Time: Fathers versus Mothers

Studies examining long-term changes in parents' time use in the United States find that both fathers' and mothers' childcare hours have increased despite the substantial increase in the hours of paid work by mothers (Bianchi et al. 2012; Sandberg and Hofferth 2005; Sayer, Bianchi, and Robinson 2004). Fathers' childcare time increased by a greater proportion, which resulted in the reduction in the ratio of mothers' to fathers' childcare time. The ratio was approximately 4:1 (10.5 versus 2.6 hours per week) in 1965 but decreased to 2:1 (13.7 versus 7.2 hours) by 2010 (Bianchi et al. 2012). These findings may be the outcome of diverse social trends: intensifying class strategies and movement toward gender egalitarian division of labor. When comparing how mothers and fathers share childcare in four European countries, Craig and Mullan (2011) find that two lines of theoretical perspectives provide explanations. One perspective views parenting styles as class strategies, and the other perspective views the gender division of labor as the basis of childcare. In the former view, childcare time would show a distinctive trend from time spent for housework, but the two time trends would be similar in the latter.

Furthermore, the social contexts related to women's labor force participation rate and public programs supporting family mediate the effects of these social forces on parenting time (Craig and Mullan 2011). Due to relatively generous family-friendly policies in Europe, the number of childcare hours tends to be much longer in Europe compared to the United States, with mothers spending on average more than 30 hours per week and fathers spending 7 to 19 hours per week. The ratios of mothers' to fathers' childcare time varied across the countries in the late 1990s, from less than 2:1 in northern Europe to between 4:1 and 5:1 in southern Europe, central Europe, and countries located in between (Garcia-Mainar, Molina, and Montuenga 2011; Sandberg and Hofferth 2005). Thus, while the trend in the absolute and relative childcare time spent by fathers and mothers is affected by a complex set of factors, we generally predict that both parents will spend longer hours on childcare over time and that the ratio of fathers' to mothers' childcare time will increase.

Class Differences in Parenting Time

Variability in childcare time by parents' class status or educational attainment is an important issue for its implications for the stratification system. Longer childcare time among parents of higher SES than among parents of lower SES will reproduce and expand the socioeconomic inequality in the next generation; this will be particularly the case in societies where public programs socializing and educating children are limited. In her qualitative research in the United States, Lareau (2002, 2003) finds differences in parenting strategies by parents' class status between the approaches of "concerted cultivation" among middle-class parents and "accomplishment of natural growth" among working-class and poor parents. Referring to these contrasting parenting styles as invisible inequality, she argues that they serve as a mechanism of reproducing class inequality. Middle- and upper-class parents invest time and money to organize and coordinate their 10-year-old children's afterschool activities by engaging their children in several extracurricular activities to "cultivate" their children's talents. Except for providing physical safety and protection for children, poor and working-class parents do not put a great deal of effort into cultivating children's skills or managing schedules but rather allow children to "naturally" grow on their own.

Using data from the Early Childhood Longitudinal Study, Kindergarten Class of 1998–1999, based on a large nationally representative sample in the United States, Cheadle and Amato (2011) confirmed the practice of concerted cultivation among middle-class parents. Parents' SES largely explains the variation in the levels of parental involvement in scholastic activities, children's activities, and academic resources (i.e., how many books children had in their home). When parental SES was disaggregated, occupational prestige accounted for a negligible amount of variance, income accounted for a moderate amount of variance, and education explained a large portion of the variance in the practice of concerted cultivation.

However, not all empirical data support this hypothesis of distinctive parenting strategies by class. Irwin and Elley (2011) used a mixed-method design with a large survey and a small number of interviews to study British parents and found that while there was some evidence of class differences, there were also distinct intra-class differences. Most parents, regardless of class, tend to see education positively and encourage academic excellence. Some middle-class parents took a strategic view in preparing their children, while others took it for granted that their children would succeed in education and later life. On the other hand, some working-class parents emphasized education as a necessary tool for their children's success and engaged in cultivation, while others doubted their ability to be involved with their children's education and future success.

A cross-cultural comparison among Norway, Germany, Italy, and Canada shows that highly educated mothers spend more time with their children than their less educated counterparts in these countries, but among fathers the positive relationship holds true only for Italy and Canada. Education has no effect in Norway and only a weak effect in Germany on fathers' childcare time. Relatively generous parental leave and income-support programs for families in Norway and Germany allow fathers of all levels of SES to spend comparable amounts of time on childcare, whereas fathers in countries with less generous family-supporting policies tend to devote their time to income earning (Sayer, Gauthier, and Furstenberg 2004). This finding indicates that fathers' childcare time is more strongly affected by the social and institutional contexts than is mothers' childcare time.

Parents' educational backgrounds affect not only the total amount of hours spent on childcare but also the time allocated to different types of childcare activities. An earlier study by Kohn (1977) suggests that parents' occupational characteristics determine their parenting styles; middle-class parents with white-collar occupations emphasize autonomy, whereas working-class parents tend to instill conformity to authority. Lareau (2002, 2003) also finds different parenting emphasis by class backgrounds. Middle-class parents encourage their children to use reasoning and verbal expressions in interpersonal relations as a way of achieving everyday needs. Through these practices children of middle-class parents develop a sense of entitlement and confidence with which they would interact with professionals from nonfamily institutions to their own benefit. Poor and working-class parents tend to use directives and physical discipline rather than encourage verbal reasoning; in the process, these parents transmit the attitudes of distrust and fear toward outside institutions and as a result instill into their children a sense of constraint.

Kalil, Ryan, and Corey (2012) translate the concept of concerted cultivation into the detailed types of activities that mothers engage in with young children aged 0 to 12. They hypothesize that mothers would tailor their parenting activities according to the developmental gradients of children by their ages and that the more educated mothers would do so to a greater extent. For example, infants and toddlers (children aged 0 to 2) would benefit most by basic physical care, while preschoolers (children aged 3 to 5) would benefit more by parents engaging them in playing, reading, and teaching activities to prepare them for entry into school. When children are in primary school (aged 6 to 12), they would benefit from management care that cultivates children's social and learning networks. Using data from the American Time Use Survey, they confirm that more educated mothers spend more time overall and allocate more time to specific activities according to the differing needs of children by age than do less-educated mothers. Sanidad and Lee (2014) found a similar pattern in American fathers' time use with young children aged 0 to 12, with more educated fathers tailoring the types of activities to their children's needs to a greater extent.

Gender-Role Attitudes and Other Factors Affecting Parenting Time

Gender-Role Attitudes

A general assumption of gender-role perspectives is that liberalizing norms toward egalitarian gender roles would propel fathers' engagement in childcare (Hochschild and Machung 1997). The literature above also shows that the different gender systems or institutional arrangements across societies result in variations in overall parenting time and educational patterns of parenting time, especially among fathers (Garcia-Mainar, Molina, and Montuenga 2011; Sayer, Gauthier, and Furstenberg 2004). Thus, among fathers, more egalitarian gender-role attitudes (i.e., disagreeing with the strict division of labor between the father as the breadwinner and the mother as the homemaker) will increase the hours of caring for their children. From the perspectives of gender-role attitudes, however, the same liberal view disagreeing with gendered division of labor predicts a different outcome for mothers: more liberal women may be less likely to engage in domestic work and hence may spend less time on childcare than do more traditional women. On the other hand, if childcare time is part of the parenting strategies to promote children's full growth, the effect of gender-role attitudes may not differ by the gender of the parent. If so, for both parents, liberal gender-role attitudes may be associated with closer or more involved relationships with their children and hence with longer hours of childcare, as compared to traditional gender-role attitudes that are associated with more distant relationships with children and hence shorter hours of childcare.

Other Factors Affecting Fathering

Several characteristics related to family interactions and structures are known to affect fathers' childcare time. For example, fathers will spend more time in childcare when mothers spend more time in childcare (Aldous, Mulligan, and Bjarnason 1998), when mothers work longer hours (Jacobs and Kelley 2006; Wang and Bianchi 2009), and when mothers have more nonlabor income (such as property and transfer incomes) than fathers (Garcia-Mainar, Molina, and Montuenga 2011). The more hours fathers work, the less time they are likely to spend in childcare (Aldous, Mulligan, Bjarnason 1998; Jacobs and Kelley 2006). Fathers are more likely to engage with sons rather than daughters (Laflamme, Pomerleau, and Malcuit 2002) and spend more time caring for younger rather than older children (Garcia-Mainar, Molina, and Montuenga 2011). The greater number of children in a household will demand more time of fathers. It will be important to control for the variables that represent either competing demands on time or the availability of substitute childcare, such as the presence of a grandparent in the household, in assessing the effects of the parents' education and gender-role attitudes.

The Literature on Parenting Time in Korea and Research Questions of This Study

Fathers' childcare time has been increasing in Korea, and several studies find that fathers and mothers with college education or professional occupations are more actively engaged in their young children's lives than are their less-educated counterparts (Chŏng and Pak 2013; Hwang, Chŏng, U 2005; Kim and Kim 2013; Yi and Cho 2005; Yi and Min 2007). Fathers with professional occupations (presumably with college education) are more likely to engage in interactive activities with their young children (Yi and Cho 2005). However, these studies focus on the consequences of parental involvement for children's cognitive and social development, and their data are often from small-scale surveys with rather crude measures of childcare involvement, for example, whether or not fathers employ particular types of parenting behaviors.

On the other hand, among all fathers who have high school–age children or younger, Song (2005) finds no difference in the likelihood of participating in childcare activities by the father's educational attainment. Using data from the 2014 Korea Time Use Survey (KTUS), Ko and Kim (2016) classify four types of parenting styles and examine the effects of parental SES on the types by children's age. They find that when children are aged 0 to 2, college-educated fathers are more likely than their less-educated counterparts to adopt "time-intensive parenting (i.e., spending more time both on overall care activities and for interactive activities)," but for children aged 3 to 5, college-educated parents are more likely to adopt "out-sourcing parenting (i.e., spending shorter time both for overall care activities and for interactive activities)." Ko and Kim explain this change of educational patterns by children's ages with the increasing availability of paid caretakers as children get older and the limited time availability of more educated fathers. In summary, previous studies show inconclusive findings on the effects of parents' education, due to the use of different measures of childcare (dichotomous indicators for diverse types of activities or some typology), the use of child samples of different age groups, and the use of different control variables (employment status or their working hours, family income, or family wealth).

Using 1999 and 2014 KTUS data, this study will examine the length of time that fathers and mothers expend on caring for their children. The study is concerned with two research questions: (1) whether mothers' and fathers' total childcare time for children under age 18 increased over time; and (2) how parental time spent caring for young children under age 10 differs by their educational attainment and gender-role attitudes. The latter consists of three subquestions: first, whether college-educated parents spend more time caring for children than do parents with less education; second, whether parents with college education to a greater extent tailor the types of childcare activities to reflect the children's developmental gradients than do their less-educated counterparts (as in Kalil, Ryan, and Corey 2012); and third, whether gender-role attitudes affect childcare time differently among fathers and mothers.

Data and Methods

Data

The data are from the Korea Time Use Survey, which has been conducted every five years since 1999, and are based on nationally representative samples. To answer the first research question, we use the first and most recent waves of KTUS conducted in 1999 and 2014, respectively. The analysis for the second question is restricted to the 2014 data due to limited available information in the earlier survey. Each survey randomly selected households, and all household members aged 10 or older were the subjects for the time use survey. The 1999 sample consists of 42,953 individuals from 16,389 households, and the 2014 sample includes 26,988 individuals from 11,986 households. Each individual reported her or his time use for two consecutive days in 10- minute intervals, contributing two entries in the data that resulted in 85,906 and 53,976 cases in 1999 and 2014 data, respectively.

The sample for the first research question is restricted to married parents who are either the head of the household or his or her spouse and have at least one child under school age (*mich'wihak adong*). Childcare time examined in this analysis is time spent for all children aged 0 to 17. As the two surveys use different age categories when asking about parents' childcare time (and the 1999 data did not contain the information on the number of school-age children under age 10), this was the best way to select samples that can provide comparable data for the two surveys. For the analysis of the second research question, we use data on childcare time for children under age 10 using the sample of parents who have at least one child under age 10 (instead of under school age). We further restrict the analysis to the parents whose spouse is present in the household so that the spouse's information could be attached.

Analysis

To examine the trend between 1999 and 2014, the analysis focuses on childcare time for all ages of children; childcare time was measured separately for younger and older children in both surveys, but the age categories did not match. The sample of each year was further divided into two groups, weekdays and Sunday. Work demand greatly affects the childcare time of working parents, and a weekday-weekend distinction is intended to control for work demand. Yet, the control is only partial, as many parents (mostly mothers) do not work on weekdays while other parents work on Sundays. Saturday data was excluded from the analysis to avoid confusion, as it was not yet considered to be a part of the weekend at the national level in 1999. The results in table 8.1 present weighted means, based on the weight variables provided by the survey to make the sample statistics nationally representative. To calculate weekly childcare minutes in the population, we first multiplied the time spent on a weekday by five and the time spent on Sunday by two and then summed the two values (i.e., estimated total weekly childcare time = time during a weekday × 5 + time during Sunday × 2). This estimation may slightly overestimate the childcare time and underestimate the paid work time in 1999, as Saturday was not yet a part of the weekend for many workers then.

As each individual contributes two entries in the data, we used multilevel modeling for the multivariate analysis of childcare time, with each entry as level 1 and each individual as level 2. Multilevel models take into account intra-individual correlations (i.e., unobserved heterogeneity among individuals). Approximately two dozen entries were excluded from the mother sample, as their spouse did not make an entry into the time diary for the day. The results from the multivariate analysis for fathers and mothers are presented in tables 8.3 and 8.4, respectively.

TABLE 8.1. Time Allocation among Married Parents with at Least One Child under School Age: 1999–2014

	1999		2014		1999–2014	
	Mean	S.D.	Mean	S.D.	Min	Max
Fathers: Weekday						
(*sample size*)	(3,476)		(1,534)			
Personal time (in minutes)	602	96	635	85	130	2,280
Leisure time	212	145	151	94	0	1,080
Work-related time	468	195	463	151	0	1,200
Housework time	11	33	17	40	0	610
Social participation time	4	34	2	22	0	950
Childcare time	19	39	37	47	0	500
Fathers: Sunday						
(*sample size*)	(1,111)		(493)			
Personal time (in minutes)	671	134	758	121	260	1,150
Leisure time	364	194	314	148	0	980
Work-related time	204	258	99	188	0	1,020
Housework time	29	55	63	77	0	700
Social participation time	5	25	5	29	0	400
Childcare time	42	72	89	90	0	570
Estimated weekly childcare time	180 [3.0 hours]		361 [6.0 hours]			
Mothers: Weekday						
(*sample size*)	(3,538)		(1,571)			
Personal time	595	92	641	91	120	1,290
Leisure time	229	134	165	101	0	810
Work-related time	133	204	130	189	0	930
Housework time	230	114	194	101	0	690
Social participation time	10	30	7	31	0	690
Childcare time	163	120	216	132	0	810
Mothers: Sunday						
(*sample size*)	(1,133)		(525)			
Personal time	647	112	728	103	290	1,300
Leisure time	272	145	232	114	0	760
Work-related time	66	160	20	85	0	740
Housework time	227	115	205	113	0	800
Social participation time	10	37	6	28	0	540
Childcare time	131	118	154	116	0	720
Estimated weekly childcare time	1,078 [18.0 hours]		1,388 [23.1 hours]			

Note: Time is measured in minutes. The weekly estimated time is presented also in hours in the brackets.

Variables

Dependent Variables (Childcare Time)

In the 2014 data, time spent on childcare is grouped into five different types of activities, with our analysis focusing on four activities. Nursing, which refers to the caring of sick children and which takes on average a minimal amount of time, is excluded. Thus, the five dependent variables in the multivariate analysis include time spent in (1) basic physical care, (2) reading and playing, (3) teaching, (4) other activities, and (5) the total time aggregating all the categories including nursing. The classification of activity types available in Korean data is similar, though not identical, to the categories used by Kalil, Ryan, and Corey (2012) and Wang and Bianchi (2009) in their US studies. The 2014 KTUS differentiates childcare time between two groups of children, children under age 10 and those over age 10, and this study focuses on the former. Basic care refers to providing physical care and meeting routine needs for survival, such as feeding. Playing and reading were combined in the 2014 KTUS and refer to activities involving reading to and playing with children. Teaching time deals with activities related to educating children. The survey does not clarify the activities included in the "other" category, but it may refer to what American Time Use Survey classifies as management time (organizing or planning for children, including transporting the children). It is noteworthy that this coding scheme was applied by the surveyors after the respondents described their activities without any prior knowledge of the categories. The distributions of these time variables are highly skewed with a small number of fathers spending a great amount of time on childcare, and the values are logged before the multivariate analysis.

Independent Variables

For this study, the age of the youngest child is grouped into three groups: 0–2, 3–5, and 6–9. Another key independent variable is parent education, which is categorized into four categories: high school or less, junior college, four-year university, and postcollege education. To explore the parents' behavioral responses to children's developmental gradients, we include interaction terms between education and age of the youngest child. For the interaction terms, the latter three educational categories are combined into one (junior college or more), as a preliminary analysis showed only minimal differences in the interaction effects among the three groups of college-level education. In other words, we assume that the magnitude of interaction coefficients is the same for the three categories of college education. Also considered in the analysis are liberal gender-role attitudes, measured by the question, "What do you think about the statement defining work is for men and family is for women?" Here, "work" refers to paid work and "family" refers to domestic work. The two categories of "1. Strongly agree" and "2. Agree" are combined and coded as 0, and the remaining two categories, "3. Disagree" and "4. Strongly disagree," are combined and coded as 1.

Control Variables

The model controls for the parent's age, number of children under age 10, number of children aged 10–17, the presence of a grandparent in the household, whether any relatives visited the home for more than an hour on the day of the time diary, whether the spouse (the child's other parent) worked that day, and amount of time the respondent spent at work on the day of the time diary. The inclusion of work time in the analysis is based on the assumption that the parental decision on work time precedes their decision on childcare time. These control variables represent the competing demands for parental time and the availability of substitute childcare. The data show that visiting relatives are mostly the parents or parents-in-law of the respondents. Visiting grandparents may either contribute to caring for grandchildren or consume the respondents' time for other purposes, but in either case, their visiting may decrease the respondents' time for childcare. The preliminary analyses show that the effects of the hypothesized independent variables are fairly stable whether or not we control for these variables.

Findings

Trend between 1999 and 2014

Time allocation among parents with at least one child under school age in 1999 and 2014 is presented separately for fathers and mothers and for weekdays and Sundays (see table 8.1). Childcare time includes the time spent caring for all ages of children, as explained above. A temporal trend in time allocation presented in table 8.1 is generally similar to the pattern observed in the United States, except that mothers' paid work time has not increased in Korea. Related to the research questions, childcare time increased for both mothers and fathers. Fathers on average spent only 3 hours per week for childcare in 1999, but the time doubled to 6 hours by 2014 (where weekly childcare time = weekday time × 5 + weekend time × 2, as discussed in the method section). Even though mothers' childcare time (18 hours) was 6 times as long as fathers' in 1999, it still increased by a greater amount (by 5 hours) to 23 hours. Yet the rate of increase is smaller among mothers, and the ratio of mothers' childcare time to fathers' time decreased from approximately 6 to 4 over the 15-year period. The difference in childcare time spent during a weekday and on Sunday shows the opposite pattern between fathers and mothers: while fathers spend a substantially longer amount of time on Sunday than during a weekday (52 minutes more), mothers spend fewer minutes on Sunday than during a weekday by the comparable margin (62 minutes less).

In parallel with the substantial gap in childcare time between mothers and fathers, the paid work time shows a large gap throughout the 15-year period. On average, mothers spend less than one-third of the paid work time spent by fathers: 130–133 hours versus 463–468 hours per week. In addition, fathers work three to five times as long as mothers do on Sundays, although the average number of hours is much shorter than during the weekdays. Among fathers, housework time also increased between 1999 and 2014, and more substantially on Sundays than on weekdays. Compared to weekdays, both mothers and fathers spend longer personal and leisure time on Sundays, which may be used for activities with other family members.

Differentials by Education and Gender-Role Attitudes

Sample

Table 8.2 presents the sample characteristics of the independent and control variables. The characteristics of the 2014 sample for the multivariate analysis (i.e., married parents with at least one child under age 10) are similar between mothers and fathers, except for their employment status. Both parents are relatively highly educated, with the percentage of parents with college or more education being slightly greater among fathers than among mothers (48 percent versus 37 percent). More than three-quarters of mothers hold liberal gender-role attitudes, whereas only about one-half of fathers do. Across the weekdays and weekends, on average, fathers spend 5.6 hours daily for paid work, whereas the statistic for mothers is 1.7 hours. This gender gap in average working hours is largely due to their employment status: husbands worked 72 percent of the days in the time diary data, while wives worked 27 percent of the days.

Influences of Parent Education and Age of the Youngest Child

The results from the multivariate analysis of care time for children under age 10—total childcare time and time for four categories of childcare activities—are presented in tables 8.3 and 8.4 for fathers and mothers, respectively. To be more concise, the tables present only one regression model for each dependent variable, which includes interaction terms between parent education and the age of the youngest child. There are a few

TABLE 8.2. Characteristics of the Sample for Multivariate Analysis: 2014

	Fathers		Mothers		Both parents	
	Mean	S.D.	Mean	S.D.	Min	Max
Explanatory variables						
Age of the youngest child						
Age 0–2	.43		.43		0	1
Age 3–5	.31		.31		0	1
Age 6–9	.27		.27		0	1
Education						
High school or less	.27		.30		0	1
Junior college	.25		.33		0	1
Four-year college/university	.41		.31		0	1
Graduate school	.07		.06		0	1
Years of schooling	14.5	2.1	14.1	2.1	5	19
Liberal gender-role attitude	.51		.77		0	1
Control variables						
Age 25	13.4	5.0	10.8	4.6	−5	35
Number of children, ages 0–9	1.52	.60	1.52	.60	1	4
Number of children, ages 10–17	.28	.56	.28	.56	0	3
Living with a parent or parent-in-law	.07		.07		0	1
Presence of a visiting relative	.06		.06		0	1
Day of the week						
Monday–Friday	.61		.60		0	1
Saturday	.20		.20		0	1
Sunday	.19		.20		0	1
Hours worked on the day	5.6	3.9	1.7	3.0	0	18.2
Spouse worked on the day	.27		.72		0	1
Number of cases (Level 1)	3,416		3,524			

Note: The sample includes married parents with at least one child aged 9 or younger.

TABLE 8.3. Factors Associated with Father's Childcare Time: Logged Minutes

	Total	Physical care	Reading/ playing	Teaching	Other
	b	b	b	b	b
Independent variables					
Age of youngest child & education					
Age of youngest child (6–9)					
Age 0–2	1.34 **	1.04 **	1.15 **	−.27 **	.13 ^
Age 3–5	.39 *	.29 ^	.39 *	−.08	.08
Education (high school or less)					
Junior college	−.04	.01	−.11	.00	−.03
Four-year college/ university	−.15	−.04	−.17	.03	.02
Graduate school	−.07	.06	−.19	.03	.06
Youngest child * Junior college or more					
Age 0–2 * Junior college or more	.34 ^	.51 **	.12	.00	−.08
Age 3–5 * Junior college or more	.44 *	.27	.35 ^	−.07	.08
Liberal gender-role attitude	.17 *	.11 ^	.07	.06 ^	.07 *
Control variables					
Age 25	.00	−.01	.01	.00	.00
Number of children aged 0–9	−.01	.13 *	−.09	.07 **	.06 *
Number of children aged 10–17	−.35 **	−.12 ^	−.35 **	−.04	−.04
Living with a parent or parent-in-law	−.25 ^	−.16	−.20	−.01	−.18 **
Presence of a visiting relative	−.27 *	.00	−.40 **	−.07	−.09
Day of the week (Monday–Friday)					
Saturday	.13	.00	.23 **	−.07 ^	−.16 **
Sunday	.20 *	.04	.27 **	−.01	−.16 **
Hours worked on the day	−.19 **	−.13 **	−.12 **	−.02 **	−.04 **
Spouse worked on the day	.39 **	.47 **	.02	.11 **	.26 **
Constant	2.43 **	.89 **	1.55 **	.25 *	.24 *
Chi square (df)	1,068 (17)	832 (17)	642 (17)	119 (17)	172 (17)
Between R^2	.29	.27	.20	.06	.06
Mean of childcare time in minutes	44	16	24	2	2
Mean of logged minutes	2.3	1.1	1.5	.2	.2
Number of cases: Level 1 (Level 2)			3,416 (1,708)		

Note: ^ $p < .10$; * $p < .05$; ** $p < .01$

TABLE 8.4. Factors Associated with Mother's Childcare Time: Logged Minutes

	Total	Physical care	Reading/ playing	Teaching	Other
	b	b	b	b	b
Type of childcare activity					
Independent variables					
Age of youngest child & education					
Age of youngest child (6–9)					
Age 0–2	1.23 **	1.78 **	1.87 **	−1.15 **	.07
Age 3–5	.68 **	1.04 **	.81 **	−.39 **	.35 **
Education (high school or less)					
Junior college	.35 **	.15	.26 *	.47 **	.23 *
Four-year college/university	.32 **	.07	.24 ^	.44 **	.15
Graduate school	.30 *	.13	.25	.50 **	.09
Youngest child * Junior college or more					
Age 0–2 * Junior college or more	−.24 *	.10	−.15	−.50 **	−.42 **
Age 3–5 * Junior college or more	−.20 *	.00	.19	−.51 **	−.08
Liberal gender-role attitude	.10 *	.12 **	−.08	.05	−.01
Control variables					
Age 25	−.01	−.01 *	−.02 *	.04 *	.02 *
Number of children aged 0–9	.14 **	.15 **	−.16 **	.52 **	.53 **
Number of children aged 10–17	−.47 **	−.37 **	−.37 **	−.46 **	−.16 **
Living with a parent or parent-in-law	−.14 *	−.15 ^	−.27 *	.10	−.20 *
Presence of a visiting relative	.08	.15	−.20	.01	−.28 *
Day of the week (Monday-Friday)					
Saturday	−.44 **	−.38 **	−.19 *	−.58 **	−1.27 **
Sunday	−.53 **	−.48 **	−.21 *	−.44 **	−1.46 **
Hours worked on the day	−.15 **	−.15 **	−.17 **	−.05 **	−.11 **
Spouse worked on the day	.49 **	.36 **	.48 **	.40 **	.45 **
Constant	3.71 **	2.54 **	1.68 **	.58 **	.71 **
Chi square (df)	2,525 (17)	2,580 (17)	1,277 (17)	823 (17)	1,321 (17)
Between R^2	.43	.43	.28	.19	.24
Mean of childcare time in minutes	161	86	42	14	16
Mean of logged minutes	4.6	3.6	2.3	1.1	1.3
Number of cases: Level 1 (Level 2)			3,524 (1,888)		

Note: ^ $p < .10$; * $p < .05$; ** $p < .01$

interesting results. First, related to the research question on educational differentials in overall childcare time by parents' educational background, when controlling for all the aforementioned independent and control variables, college-educated fathers spend slightly more time in overall childcare time than do high school or less-educated fathers, but the difference is statistically significant only for junior college level. (When not controlling for any other variables in the model, the extra time spent on childcare among college-educated parents compared to less-educated counterparts is even greater for both fathers and mothers.) The coefficients for the main and interaction effects are combined to estimate the gross effects of parent education (note that the non-interaction models are not presented in tables to avoid repetition, but the results are available upon request). These educational differentials in fathers' overall childcare time are mainly due to the differentials in physical care activities, where all three groups of college-educated fathers spend significantly longer amounts of time than do high school or less-educated fathers (test results are not shown but are available upon request). Second, the interaction effects show that compared to their less-educated counterparts, college-educated fathers spend more time in physical care of infants and toddlers (ages 0–2) and in reading and play activities with preschoolers (ages 3–5). In short, as expected, college-educated fathers are more responsive to the developmental gradients of children by their age.

Among mothers, the sum of the main and interaction effects shows the amount of educational differentials in overall childcare time. Again, the non-interaction models that are not presented in the tables show that, while controlling for all the aforementioned independent and control variables, college-educated mothers spend slightly but significantly more time on overall childcare than do high school or less-educated mothers. However, the interaction models in table 8.4 show fairly different findings from those for fathers. The main effects of education show that, among mothers, educational differentials are greatest when the youngest child is in school (ages 6–9). In other words, college-educated mothers spend more time than their less-educated counterparts doing such activities as teaching, reading/playing, and other activities with their children aged 6–9. The negative coefficients for the interaction terms between education and ages 0–2 and 3–5 suggest that there is no educational difference in mothers' care time for children aged 0–5 after all.

Furthermore, the two tables show that for both fathers and mothers, overall childcare time is strongly negatively associated with the age of the youngest child, with the amount of time being much greater when the youngest child is aged 0 to 2 than when the youngest child is older than 2. When looking into the types of activities, this negative effect of the youngest child's age holds true for physical care and reading/playing activities, the two categories of activities that make up the vast majority of the total childcare time. This pattern by child's age is still true even after taking into account the interaction effects with parent education, meaning that the strong negative association between age of the youngest child and time for physical care and reading/playing activities is true for parents with all educational levels. On the other hand, for teaching activities, parents (i.e., both fathers and mothers) spend more time when they have a school-age child, regardless of their educational background.

Putting together the results from tables 8.1 through 8.4, a coherent picture emerges regarding the effects of parent education and age of the youngest child by parent gender. Among fathers, whose childcare time is limited, educated fathers invest more time in their younger children by doing physical care or reading/playing over the weekends, thereby giving the mothers a break. Among mothers, who spend much more time caring for children than do fathers, all educational groups spend equally sufficient time on such basic care activities as physical care and reading/playing. The major educational differential among mothers is evident in the extra amount of time that college-educated mothers spend on teaching their school-age children (ages 6–9) (seemingly more on weekdays). College-educated mothers also spend slightly more time on reading/playing and other activities with their school-age children than do high-school or less-educated counterparts, but these latter differences are relatively minor. In other words, compared to high school or less-educated counterparts, college-educated mothers make extra time investments in school-age children, primarily for teaching but also for reading/playing and other activities.

In summary, it seems that the parenting activities that Lareau (2002) characterizes as "concerted cultivation" start at the early stages of childhood in Korea. Although the differences in the amount of care time are not large, class differences in childcare activities emerge. College-educated fathers of infants and toddlers spend more time on basic physical care and reading/playing than do their counterparts with high school or less education, whereas college-educated mothers with school-age children devote more time to teaching (such as helping with homework) and managing their schedules than do their counterparts with high school or less education. However, it is noteworthy that parents with high school or less education also tailor their care activities substantially by children's developmental gradients.

Influence of Gender-Role Attitudes

Fathers with more egalitarian attitudes tend to spend more time on all four types of care activities than do fathers with more traditional attitudes, although the difference in the amount of time is rather minor; as a result, the difference in overall childcare time is significant (table 8.3). Among mothers, the difference by gender-role attitude is statistically significant for basic care and for the total childcare time, where more liberal mothers spend more time than do mothers with more traditional attitudes (table 8.4). Gender-role perspectives predict that liberal mothers would spend less time on domestic work, but it turns out that childcare time is different. The results do not support the view that childcare is considered to be a domestic task that is usually imposed upon women, the idea that liberal women may resist. Instead, both fathers and mothers with liberal attitudes seem to value childcare activities more highly than do traditional parents, maybe suggesting their emphasis on permissiveness and involvement as opposed to directives and control. The findings are consistent with the literature arguing that childcare time is an outcome from a complex set of social and individual factors (Craig and Mullan 2011; Dermott 2005).

Turning to control variables, those representing competing demands for parental time and availability of substitute childcare show the effects just as expected. Parents' age has no significant effect on overall childcare time for both fathers and mothers (tables 8.3 and 8.4). However, older mothers spent less time on basic care and reading/playing and more time on teaching and managing. Controlling for the age of the youngest child, the greater the number of children under age 10 in the family, the more time parents spent caring for them in three types of activities, except for reading/playing. For the parents who are pressed for time (especially mothers), reducing the time spent on reading/playing may seem the least consequential. Competing time demands for children aged 10 to 17 reduces the care time for all categories of activities for children under age 10, except for father's teaching and other activities where fathers spent trivial amounts of time. The presence of a grandparent in the household helps reduce both mothers' and fathers' childcare time for some categories of activities, but not for others, most notably mothers' teaching time. A non-co-resident grandparent's visit on the day reduces fathers' total childcare time, in particular, time for reading and playing, but does not significantly affect mothers' childcare time except for time of "other" activities. After controlling for the couple's work status, mothers' childcare time is significantly shorter across the categories of activities on weekends, but that is not the case for fathers. The demand on time from work has a strong effect. Respondents' work time reduces the childcare time for both mothers and fathers across virtually all categories of activities, whereas the spouses' work time increases the childcare time.

Conclusion

Parental time (and money) investment in children has been a controversial issue recently in the US media: While some parents are concerned that parental over-involvement may deprive children of the opportunities to grow on their own by trial and error, others believe in the values of parental guidance and support. Sociologists find contrasting parenting strategies by parents' class backgrounds. Most notably, Lareau (2002, 2003) argues that middle-class parents adopt the strategies of "concerted cultivation" and actively coordinate children's afterschool activities in contrast to the parents from working- or lower-class backgrounds who endorse the ideal of "accomplishment of natural growth." While it is well known that many parents in Korea are enthusiastic about children's academic success and educational attainment, empirical studies of the length of parenting time for younger children have been rare. This chapter examines the time mothers and fathers spend caring for their young children, focusing on two research questions: (1) how mothers' and fathers' childcare time changed over time; and (2) whether and how parental childcare time differs by their educational attainment and gender-role attitudes.

For the analysis, we use data from the Korean Time Use Survey. To answer the first research question, we use data from the first and most recent waves of KTUS that were conducted in 1999 and 2014, respectively. However, the classification of time categories was not identical between the two surveys (details in the method section), and we examine the time spent caring for all children aged 0–17 among married parents with at least one child under school age. To answer the second research question, we use data only from the 2014 survey with its rich information on family circumstances, examining the time spent caring for children aged 10 or younger among married parents with at least one child under age 10.

The results show that fathers' childcare time doubled over the 15-year period, from 3 hours to 6 hours per week. Even though mothers' childcare time was 6 times as long as the fathers' in 1999, it still increased by 5 hours, from 18 to 23 hours per week. Thus, the ratio of mothers' to fathers' childcare time reduced from 6:1 to 4:1 over the period. Consistent with the literature in the United States, fathers' housework time increased, particularly on Sundays, while mothers' housework time decreased. These changes in housework time are true even though mothers' time for paid work did not increase over the period in Korea. A reduction in fathers' time for paid work seems to facilitate their increased participation in housework and childcare.

According to the results from the multivariate analysis, among both fathers and mothers, college-educated parents expend a somewhat longer amount of time for childcare than do their less-educated counterparts. All parents modify their time allocation across the four types of childcare activities to best serve the changing needs of children as they get older, but college-educated parents do so to a greater extent than do their high school or less-educated counterparts. College-educated fathers spend more time in physical care of infants and toddlers and in reading/playing for preschoolers than do less-educated fathers. In contrast, mothers with college education spend more time caring for school-age children aged 6–9 by engaging in teaching, reading/playing, and management activities, as compared to mothers with high school or less education. In other words, even though the differences in the amount of care time are not large, class differences in parenting styles emerge early in children's lives in Korea. In short, extra childcare time among college-educated parents compared to less-educated parents, which may be characterized as "concerted cultivation," involves physical care and reading/playing for younger children among fathers and teaching school-age children among mothers.

In addition, liberal gender-role attitudes increase both mothers' and fathers' childcare time, countering a speculation that more liberal women may be more likely to exempt themselves from childcare as they would from housework. These results regarding the effects of gender-role attitudes and parents' educational background suggest that Korean parents may perceive childcare as a class strategy rather than considering it as a part of gendered domestic work. In sum, childcare time is determined by a class strategy adopted by the parents, and it is an area of family practices not governed by the norms of gender division of labor. Still, growing fathering time is concentrated in playing with children and is not spent on as diverse activities as is mothering time. Fathers' involvement in the family's class strategy is constrained by their unfinished decoupling of themselves from gendered roles.

Last, data released by the Korea Time Use Survey report childcare time by age groups of children, not by each child. It will be informative, if we can specify time spent for each child and link the child's characteristics to parental time in future studies. Ultimately, future research needs to show how time allocation among different childcare activities affects children's acquisition of cognitive and noncognitive skills.

REFERENCES

Aldous, Joan, Gail M. Mulligan, and Thoroddur Bjarnason. 1998. "Fathering over Time: What Makes the Difference?" *Journal of Marriage and Family* 60 (4): 809–20.

Alexander, Karl L., Doris R. Entwisle, and Linda S. Olson. 2001. "Schools, Achievement, and Inequality: A Seasonal Perspective." *Educational Evaluation and Policy Analysis* 23 (2): 171–91.

Alexander, Karl L., Doris R. Entwisle, and Linda S. Olson. 2007. "Summer Learning Gap." *American Sociological Review* 72: 167–80.

Bianchi, Suzanne M., and Melissa A. Milkie. 2010. "Work and Family Research in the First Decade of the 21st Century." *Journal of Marriage and Family* 72 (3): 705–25.

Bianchi, Susanne M., Liana C. Sayer, Mellissa A. Milkie, and John P. Robinson. 2012. "Housework: Who Did, Does or Will Do It, and How Much Does It Matter?" *Social Forces* 91 (1): 55–63.

Byun, Soo-yong, Evan Schofer, and Kyung-keun Kim. 2012. "Revisiting the Role of Cultural Capital in East Asian Educational Systems: The Case of South Korea." *Sociology of Education* 85 (3): 219–39.

Carneiro, Pedro, and James J. Heckman. 2003. "Human Capital Policy." In *Inequality in America: What Role for Human Capital Policies?*, edited by J. J. Heckman, A. B. Krueger and B. M. Friedman, 77–237. Cambridge, MA: The MIT Press.

Cheadle, Jacob E., and Paul R. Amato. 2011. "A Quantitative Assessment of Lareau's Qualitative Conclusions about Class, Race, and Parenting." *Journal of Family Issues* 32 (5): 679–706.

Choi, Yool, and Hyunjoon Park. 2016. "Shadow Education and Educational Inequality in South Korea: Examining Effect Heterogeneity of Shadow Education on Middle School Seniors' Achievement Test Scores." *Research in Social Stratification and Mobility* 44: 22–32.

Chŏng Kŭm-ja and Pak Mi-ra. 2013. "Abŏji ŭi yangyuk ch'amyŏdo wa yua ŭi sahoe todŏk sŏnggwa ŭi kwan'gye" (The Relation between Fathers' Participation in Nurturing and Children's Social Morality). *Han'guk yŏngyua poyukhak* (*Korea Association of Child Care and Education*) 80: 43–64 (in Korean).

Cotter, David, Joan M. Hermsen, and Reeve Vanneman. 2011. "The End of the Gender Revolution? Gender Role Attitudes from 1977 to 2008." *American Journal of Sociology* 117 (1): 259–89.

Craig, Lyn, and Killian Mullan. 2011. "How Mothers and Fathers Share Childcare: A Cross-National Time-Use Comparison." *American Sociological Review* 76 (6): 834–61.

Dermott, Esther. 2005. "Time and Labour: Fathers' Perceptions of Employment and Childcare." *Sociological Review* 53: 89–103.

Downey, Douglas B., Paul T. von Hippel, and Beckett A. Broh. 2004. "Are Schools the Great Equalizer? Cognitive Inequality During the Summer Months and the School Year." *American Sociological Review* 69: 613–35.

England, Paula. 2010. "The Gender Revolution: Uneven and Stalled." *Gender and Society* 24: 149–66.
Garcia-Mainar, Inmaculada, Jose A. Molina, and Victor M. Montuenga. 2011. "Gender Differences in Childcare: Time Allocation in Five European Countries." *Feminist Economics* 17 (1): 119–50.
Guryan, Jonathan, Erik Hurst, and Melissa Kearney. 2008. "Parental Education and Parental Time with Children." *Journal of Economic Perspectives* 22 (3): 23–46.
Heckman, James J. 2006. "Skill Formation and the Economics of Investing in Disadvantaged Children." *Science* 312 (30 June): 1900–1902.
Hochschild, Arlie R., and Anne Machung. 1997. *The Second Shift*. New York: Penguin.
Hwang Sun-yŏng, Chŏng Yŏng-suk, and U Su-gyŏng. 2005. "Sahoe in'guhakchŏk pyŏnin e ttarŭn abŏji ŭi yangyuk ch'amyŏdo wa yŏkhal manjokto mit yua ŭi sahoejŏk nŭngnyŏk" (Fathers' Involvement in Parenting, Role Satisfaction, and Young Children's Social Competence as a Function of Socio-demographic Variables). *Han'guk saenghwal kwahak hoeji* (*Korean Journal of Human Ecology*) 14 (4): 521–29 (in Korean).
Irwin, Sarah, and Sharon Elley. 2011. "Concerted Cultivation? Parenting Values, Education and Class Diversity." *Sociology* 45 (3): 480–95.
Jacobs, Julie N., and Michelle L. Kelley. 2006. "Predictors of Paternal Involvement in Childcare in Dual-Earner Families with Young Children." *Fathering: A Journal of Theory, Research, and Practice about Men as Fathers* 4 (1): 23–47.
Kalil, Ariel, Rebecca Ryan, and Michael Corey. 2012. "Diverging Destinies: Maternal Education and the Developmental Gradient in Time with Children." *Demography* 49 (4): 1361–83.
Kim Kŭn-hye and Kim Hye-sun. 2013. "Man 5 se chanyŏ rŭl tun pumo ŭi sahoe, in'guhakchŏk paegyŏng kwa abŏji ŭi yangyuk ch'amyŏ to mit ŏmŏni ŭi yangyuk sŭt'ŭresŭ kan ŭi kwan'gye" (The Relationships between 5-Year-Old Preschooler Parent's Socioeconomic Status and Father's Parenting Involvement and Mother's Parenting Stress). *Adong kyoyuk* (*Journal of Child Education*) 22 (4): 111–29 (in Korean).
Ko Ŭn-ju and Kim Chin-uk. 2016. "Chanyŏ yŏllyŏng kwa kyech'ŭngjŏk yoin i yŏngyua chanyŏ chikchŏp tolbom sigan yuhyŏng e mich'inŭn yŏnghyang: pŏjiset inyŏmhyŏng punsŏk ŭi hwalyong" (The Effects of Social Class on Caring Types for Preschool Children: Adopting Fuzzy-Set Ideal Type Analysis). *Pogŏn sahoe yon'gu* (*Health and Social Welfare Review*) 36 (4): 35–62 (in Korean).
Kohn, Melvin 1977. *Class and Conformity: A Study in Values*. Homewood, IL: Dorsey Press.
Laflamme, Darquise, Andree Pomerleau, and Gerard Malcuit. 2002. "A Comparison of Fathers' and Mothers' Involvement in Childcare and Stimulation Behaviors during Free-Play with Their Infants at 9 and 15 Months." *Sex Roles: A Journal of Research* 47 (11–12): 507–18.
Lareau, Annette. 2002. "Invisible Inequality: Social Class and Childrearing in Black Families and White Families." *American Sociological Review* 67: 747–76.
Lareau, Annette. 2003. *Unequal Childhoods: Class, Race, and Family Life*. Berkeley: University of California Press.
Maume, David J. 2008. "Gender Differences in Providing Urgent Childcare among Dual-Earner Parents." *Social Forces* 87 (1): 273–97.
Park, Hyunjoon, Soo-yong Byun, and Kyung-keun Kim. 2011. "Parental Involvement

and Students' Cognitive Outcomes in Korea: Focusing on Private Tutoring." *Sociology of Education* 84 (1): 3–22.

Sanidad, Ivan, and Yean-Ju Lee. 2014. "Fathers' Childcare Time: Concerted Cultivation?" Paper presented at the Annual Meeting of the Population Association of America, May 1–3, Boston, MA.

Sandberg, John F., and Sandra L. Hofferth. 2005. "Changes in Children's Time with Parents: A Correction." *Demography* 42 (2): 391–95.

Sayer, Liana C., Suzanne M. Bianchi, and John P. Robinson. 2004. "Are Parents Investing Less in Children? Trends in Mothers' and Fathers' Time with Children." *American Journal of Sociology* 110 (1): 1–43.

Sayer, L., A. Gauthier, and F. Furstenberg. 2004. "Educational Differences in Parents' Time with Children: Cross-national Variation." *Journal of Marriage and Family* 66: 1152–69.

Seward, Rudy Ray, and Rudolf Richter. 2008. "International Research on Fathering: An Expanding Horizon." *Fathering: A Journal of Theory, Research, and Practice about Men as Fathers* 6 (2): 87–91.

Song Yu-jin. 2005. "Han'guk kwa Chungguk tosi kajok esŏŭi sŏngyŏkhal pudam pigyo yŏn'gu" (Gender Roles and Childcare—A Comparative Analysis of Chinese and Korean Families). *Han'guk sahoehak (Korean Journal of Sociology)* 39 (1): 111–36 (in Korean).

Wang, Rong, and Suzanne Bianchi. 2009. "ATUS Fathers' Involvement in Childcare." *Social Indicators Research* 93 (1): 141–45.

Yi Chŏng-sun and Cho Hŭi-suk. 2005. "Chigŏp chongnyu e ttarŭn abŏji yangyuk ch'amyŏ wa chigŏp yŏkhal, kajok yŏkhal kwaŭi kwallyŏnsŏng pigyo" (The Relationship of Preschool-children Fathers' Childrearing Involvement to Family and Work Roles: Focusing on the Occupational Class). *Yŏllin yua kyoyuk yŏn'gu (Journal of Korea Open Association for Early Childhood Education)* 10 (3): 339–60 (in Korean).

Yi Yŏng-mi and Min Ha-yŏng. 2007. "Abŏji ŭi yua yangyuk ch'amyŏ e taehan kajok sahoe in'guhakchŏk pyŏnin kwa yua kijil ŭi yŏnghyang" (The Influence of Family Socio-Demographic Variables and Preschoolers' Temperaments on Fathers' Involvement in Child-Rearing). *Han'guk kajŏng kwalli hakhoeji (Journal of Korean Home Management Association)* 24 (4): 93–101 (in Korean).

9

Gender Roles of Married Women in Korean Immigrant Families in the United States

Byung Soo Lee

The number of first-generation Korean immigrants in the United States started to increase rapidly right after the abolition of the national original quota system in 1965 (Kim et al. 2006). While the first wave of Korean immigrants in the 1960s–70s were mainly farmers and laborers, the US Census taken in 1980 indicated that "many new Korean immigrants arrived in the United States with urban, educated, middle class backgrounds" (Kim 1981; Kim and Hurh 1988; Kim and Kim 1998, cited in Kim et al. 2006: 43). Nevertheless, various studies of migration indicate that many first-generation Korean immigrants, as well as other racial and ethnic immigrant groups, are likely to experience downward mobility right after immigrating to the United States. Korean immigrants often experience language barriers, and their educational credentials and job skills acquired in Korea are not acknowledged in the labor market in the United States in the same way as in Korea (Foner 1998; Min 2001; Moon 2003; Kim et al. 2006; Park 2008; Oh 2011; Sun 2013).

Given these circumstances, many Korean immigrant women are required implicitly and explicitly to earn a living to secure the well-being of their families (Kim and Hurh 1988; Kim and Kim 1998; Min 2001). Min (2001) points out that one of the major changes associated with immigration is the increased participation of married women in the labor force. According to Min (2001), approximately 75 percent of Korean immigrant married women living in the United States participated in the labor force in the 1990s (cited in Kim et al. 2006). Meanwhile, relevant studies have shown ambivalent aspects of immigrant women's empowerment after migration. On the one hand, the increase in women's employment outside the home is, to some extent, concomitant with a decrease in women's traditional gender role as caretakers, which might require a more egalitarian division of household tasks (Kim and Hurh 1988; Min 2001). On the other hand, some studies suggest that Korean immigrant women's employment, unless they have a professional career, is not likely to challenge male dominance (Lim 1997; Kim and Kim 1998; Park and Liao 2000; Kim 2006). A substantial portion of Korean immigrants is engaged in small family businesses, which are often run by a wife and husband without employees (Lim 1997; Min 2001). Thus, Korean immigrant women in family businesses may not accumulate their own individual resources because they are often unpaid or underpaid workers regardless of their significant contribution to the family income. Korean immigrant women's engagement in relatively small family-run business can hinder achievement of gender equality within Korean immigrant families despite women's participation in the labor market.

Moreover, because of gender inequality that has long persisted in Korea (Lim 1997), the traditional Korean familial value system among the immigrants has not changed considerably after migration (Kim and Hurh 1987, 1988; Kim 2006; Kim and Kim 1998; Kim, Kim, and Hurh 1991; Lim 1997; Min 2001; Moon 2003). However, other studies implied that while Korean immigrant husbands have not much changed, still preferring traditional gender roles and wife-husband relations, Korean immigrant wives may have a more egalitarian gendered attitude. The discrepancy in gendered attitudes within a couple often leads to higher levels of marital conflict (Lim 1997; Min 1984, 1998, 2001; Rhee 1997). These studies imply that despite some changes, especially among wives, the patriarchal or male-centered family relationship and gender role distinctions are still prevalent among Korean immigrant families. In this situation, the primary role of married Korean immigrant women is often imposed as housewife, and their financial contribution to the family income, regardless of their actual amount of income, is viewed as subsidiary (Lim 1997; Min 1984, 1998; Moon 2003).

However, although previous studies have looked at the relationship between gender-role attitudes and Korean immigrant women's labor force participation, they focused on the wife-husband relationship (Kim and Hurh 1987, 1988; Kim and Kim 1998; Lee 2006; Lim 1997; Min 2001) or the mother-child/intergenerational relationship (Lee and Keith 1999; Moon 2003; Kim et al. 2006). As a result, few studies have paid attention to the lived experiences of Korean immigrant women in the United States and gender ideology in terms of kinship networks and attitudes toward supporting parents, especially parents-in-law who are living in Korea. Previous studies of kin relationships among Korean immigrant families have mostly focused on kin relationships as resources for immigrant families. The immigration experiences of Korean families help strengthen family relationships because of the need for financial, informative, and emotional or caring assistance in the process of preparing for immigration, acculturation, and business ownership (Bankston 2014; Min 1984; Yoo and Kim 2014). These studies deal with kin networks as alternative or subsidiary social capital among adult siblings who begin and maintain self-employed business in the United States and as human resources for emotional and supportive caring work for their elderly parents.

However, these studies did not explore the meaning of maintaining kin networks among immigrant families in relation to gender ideology of immigrant women. The attitude toward kin relationships and the maintenance of the kin tie are also related to unequal gender relations among Korean families. This is because the kin relationship in Korean families is mainly based on Confucian family values. Because of this, so much is centered on the relationship of the husband's kin members, which can facilitate gender inequality and reinforce male-centered family relations (Hurh 1998). The relationship between gender and the responsibility of kinship activities is not just confined to Confucian culture but is also prevalent in the Western world. Several scholars have pointed out that gender ideologies are deeply embedded in kinship activities, and women are normatively expected to play a leading role in maintaining kin ties (Challinor 2017; Di Leonardo 1987; Gerstel 1988; Rosenthal 1985).

This chapter examines how female Korean immigrants' lived experiences in the United States affect practices of and attitudes toward gender roles, including broader family relationships such as kinship and filial piety, by using data collected from group interviews. Fifty-six Korean immigrant women were recruited from a Korean enclave located in a metropolitan area in the United States. Using the interview data, three research questions will be explored: (1) How do gender roles in the household change after respondents settle down in the United States? (2) How have family relationships, such as the frequency of contact with parents-in laws and kin members, changed since immigrating to the United States? and (3) Why or why not have they maintained kin relationships? By analyzing the narratives of the interviewees, I will examine how the respondents rationalize the changes in gender roles of filial piety and intra- and interfamilial relations within kin networks and how they interpret the meaning of kin networks after migration.

Background

Gender Relations among Korean Immigrant Families

In his study of American marriage, Cherlin (2004) argues that although women would remain as primary caregivers, in the 20th century "the roles of wives and husbands became more flexible and open to negotiation" in the marriage where "both the husband and the wife work outside the home" (852). According to Cherlin, during the past century US society has witnessed a process of the "deinstitutionalization of marriage." This means a "weakening of the social norms that define people's behavior in a social institution such as marriage" (848) and the growth of individual autonomy in the choice of the types of marital relationship and cohabitation. Based on Cherlin's (2004) analysis of the weakening of social norms and the increase in personal choice in gender relations, family researchers, including Ferree (2010) and Qian and Sayer (2016), argue that the acculturation of Western ideals of egalitarian gender relations has affected the attitudes toward marital relations in East Asian societies.

Following this idea that the gender norms in Asian societies have become more egalitarian, existing studies have focused on how the lived experiences of Korean immigrant families have had an effect on changes of gender ideology within households. In particular, scholars have explored women's paid employment and its effects on gender relations in immigrant households and communities in the United States. Theoretically, women's increased income is expected to contribute to their empowerment within the household. With their employment, Asian immigrant women in the United States experience more decision-making power, autonomy, and assistance with domestic chores from their husbands (Kibria 1993; Park 1997; Moon 2003; Kim 2014). According to Moon (2003), the more immigrant women financially contribute to household income through paid employment, the more they can demand a more equitable share in decision-making and housework from their husbands. In her study of female Korean entrepreneurs in the United States, Kim (2014) argues that Korean immigrant women's participation in small businesses has significantly contributed to their household income, empowered them to gain autonomy within their families, and improved the welfare of their families and children. "When women make a relatively substantial financial contribution to the family, this leads them to define their husband's share of housework as too low and to articulate a desire for change" (Ferree 1987, cited in Lim 1997: 34).

However, previous research has also found that Korean immigrant husbands rarely participate in household work and are controlling over their wives, suggesting that even dual-earning Korean immigrant families are not gender egalitarian (Lim 1997; Min 2001). In other words, although Korean immigrant women's participation in economic activities has likely contributed to the empowerment of women within the household, women's gain seems limited to the attainment of "psychological resources" (Lim 1997). In other words, they do not obtain a substantial gain of power by subverting unequal gender relations within the household but rather acquire an awareness of their contribution to the family, such as "pride and honor." As Lim (1997) also argues, "However, it is important to recognize that Korean immigrant wives limit their attempts to change unequal marital relations" (40). Similarly, Park (2008) pays attention to the "seeming contradiction between empowering and disempowering forces" (28). On the one hand, paid work gives immigrant women better bargaining power in decision-making and housework sharing. On the other hand, they are still caught in traditional gender ideologies, gender roles, and subordinate domestic responsibilities.

For the differences in the gender-role attitudes between husbands and wives, Bittman and his colleagues (2003) explain why the increase in women's economic contribution to household income does not necessarily lead to a more equal share of household work. In their view, men and women do not follow their internalized gender norms but rather follow others' expectations "to present themselves as cognitively 'making sense' in terms of these norms" (191). This explanation of "doing gender" can be applied to the analysis of Korean immigrant women's ambivalent empowerment. In fact, as emphasized by Min (2001), the role of the Korean community in perpetuating traditional gender norms in Korean immigrants' households may be substantial, given the high levels of cultural homogeneity and economic segregation from the mainstream society among the Korean immigrant community. According to Min, "Korean immigrants' cultural homogeneity, their economic segregation from the main society, and their high affiliation with Korean ethnic churches prevent Korean immigrants from learning the more egalitarian gender-role attitudes prevalent in American society" (309).

Filial Piety and Kin Networks

The notion of filial piety is used to "remember" and "represent" one's ancestors within the household (Lew, Choi, and Wang 2011). However, it has now become one of the most fundamental norms of Confucianism to emphasize the unquestioned obedience to, unconditional respect for, and selfless support for parents by children, particularly by sons and daughters-in-law (Kim 2012; Sung 2003). Traditionally, married women in Korea are expected to serve their husbands' family, particularly their parents-in-law. However, this concept of filial piety can be modified and abandoned, especially in the households where a more egalitarian division of household labor is accepted. Nonetheless, previous studies have shown that many Korean immigrant families and Korean American families still tend to stick to the traditional notion of filial piety and the responsibility for supporting the elderly, especially the husband's parents by the daughter-in-law, whether they live in the same household or not (Kim and Hurh 1988; Kim, Kim, and Hurh 1991; Min 1998, 2001; Yoo and Kim 2014).

Along with the notion of filial piety, scholars of immigrant families have also paid attention to kinship networks among immigrant ethnic groups. Thanks to the development of information communication technologies and internet accessibility, immigrant families can communicate more easily and regularly with other family members left behind in the origin societies (Min 1998; Park and Waldinger 2017). Researchers often see the kin networks as alternative resources for immigrant families who lack social capital and who experience downward mobility in the host societies (Bankston 2014; Lansford, Deater-Deckard, and Bornstein 2007; Min 1984, 2001; Sun 2013). According to Sun (2013), transnational Asian immigrants maintain cross-border kin ties between sending countries and host societies, which Kibria (2011) calls "family-centered transnationalism" (447). Maintaining cross-border kin ties gives Asian immigrant families "the emotional fortitude by which to cope with the experience of downward class mobility as well as the adjustments that had been made necessary by migration" (Kibria 2011, cited in Sun 2013: 448). Research on transnational families has documented that for Asian immigrants, kin members in their origin country can be a resource to tolerate adversities—such as racial discrimination and class, religion, and cultural differentiation—that the migrants might encounter in a host society (Baldassar 2007; Clark, Glick, and Bures 2009; Sun 2013).

Similarly, previous studies of Korean immigrant families have shown that the experiences of immigration enhance kin ties (Kim, Kim, and Hurh 1991; Min 1984). This is because many Korean immigrant families suffer from downward mobility and need to compensate for lack of human and social capital, such as language proficiency, job skills, and informants, that is needed in the process of preparing for and settling down after immigration (Bankston 2014; Kim, Kim, and Hurh 1991; Min 1984).

Thus, maintaining and facilitating kin ties as a compensatory resource varies depending on several factors, including the physical or geographical proximity, the level of intimacy between kin members, the development of information communication technologies, and the stage of immigration (Kim, Kim, and Hurh 1991; Min 1984).

However, maintaining kin networks also reveals the unequal gender relations that immigrant families experience in the United States (Kim and Hurh 1988; Kim and Kim 1998; Yanagisako 1977; Yoo and Kim 2014). This is because the kin relationship is centered more on the husband's side of families, which can facilitate gender inequality and enforce male-centered family relations. In her research on an Italian American community in northern California, Di Leonardo (1987) was able to see that women were involved in three types of work: housework and childcare, work in the labor market, and the "work of kinship." According to Di Leonardo, kinship work refers to the maintenance of, ritual celebrations in, and communication across different households. In her discussion of the "work of kinship," Di Leonardo found that the kin work basically represents unequal gender relations, centered on the husband's side of the kin network. Her female informants remembered details of their husbands' family history and relations that their husbands did not remember and had the responsibility of organizing family gatherings. In her study of Canadian adults aged 40 or over, Rosenthal (1985) also concluded that "kinkeeping" is persistently organized and performed by female "kinkeepers" over time and that the position of kinkeeper is passed from mother to daughter. Even if male family members are involved in kinkeeping activities, the degree of participation is much less than that of female counterparts.

Nonetheless, few of the existing studies of Korean immigrant families deal with the relationship between gender ideology and the maintenance of kin networks. This means that previous studies missed one possible explanation as to why married Korean immigrant women keep performing kinkeeping activities, although their lived experiences of immigration may give them opportunities to ignore or be free from the traditional responsibility for their husbands' kin members. Because the maintaining of the kin tie, "kinkeeping" (Rosenthal 1985) or "work of kinship" (Di Leonardo 1987), is involved in the traditional male-centered familial value system, looking into the changes of the kin relations may tell us whether immigrant women's gender ideology has changed or stayed the same. If Korean immigrant women have experienced a change of gender relations from a traditional gender ideology to a more egalitarian one after migration, they are more likely to deny the role of "kinkeeper."

We can also think about the work of kinship in terms of child-rearing among immigrant families. To borrow from Wolf (2003), the notion of "emotional transnationalism" is also useful for reflecting on children's upbringing among immigrant families. Several scholars point out that children in immigrant families may experience greater changes compared to their nonimmigrant peers and that there are both positive and negative effects of the migratory process on children's outcomes in their lives (Baldassar 2007; Clark, Glick, and Bures 2009; Moon 2003). They argue that although transnational familial arrangements might cause or exacerbate serious intergenerational conflicts, immigrant children who are able to take advantage of resources from both the destination and the origin society are most successful. In addition to material resources, researchers have emphasized the importance of the emotional support from cross-border kin ties.

As Baldassar (2007) argues, "staying in touch" with family members in the country of origin can infuse children of immigrant families with the perceptions of belonging. It is a "work of kinship" to build a reliable relationship, which includes the maintenance of mutually beneficial reciprocal exchange relations as well as a "sense of family" across distance (Di Leonardo 1987: 443). At the same time, the notion of reciprocal exchange means an investment in future obligations in the security of knowing that you can call on help if you need it and be certain to receive it. From this perspective, cross-border kinships can become resources that immigrant children might rely on in their current or later life stage (Sun 2013).

While previous studies mention that Korean immigrant families tend to maintain traditional family values, they do not take a close look at why the kin network has persisted and why Korean immigrant women have accepted the position of kinkeeper in the United States in relation to gender ideology and child-rearing. For this reason, this explorative chapter intends to bridge this gap in the study of married Korean immigrant women in the United States.

Data and Methods

Sampling

This study was conducted in one of the large counties with approximately mid-sized population, located in a northeastern and mid-Atlantic state in the United States. This county was known as one of the Korean "enclaves" in the United States, which refers to a spatial or residential concentration of a specific ethnic group (Logan, Zhang, and Alba 2002). According to the 2010 US Census, over 50 percent of the population in one of the boroughs of this county reported being of Korean ancestry, the highest Korean American density in the United States.

The sampling techniques used in this study were convenience sampling and snowball sampling. At first, some participants were recruited at stores run by Korean immigrant women or at churches whose pastors and main members are of Korean ethnicity. Then by being referred to other respondents, I was able to interview 56 participants. To facilitate group interviews in a more time-efficient manner, I created 16 groups based on the geographical proximity and age of the participants, and each group consisted of between 2 and 6 interviewees.

The size of each group varied depending on the size of the region, which facilitated group meeting. In addition, I considered some other demographic variables in selecting interviewees, such as education, occupation, family income, years of marriage, the length of residency in the United States, and the number and age of children. It is possible that group interviews create potential bias, often caused by "socially desirable" responses among participants and/or influenced by the small number of respondents with more active attitudes. Nonetheless, group interviews facilitate the involvement of group participants and observations of various nonverbal behaviors, which, in turn, encourage interviewees to engage in the discussion actively and interactively. Moreover, through the interactions among participants, unexpected but possibly relevant topics often came out, which made the interviews rich in discussion and interaction. These unexpected but relevant topics and stories reminded other interviewees of related experiences and brought up interesting points of conversations.

Demographic Characteristics of Samples

As shown in table 9.1, all participants were Korean immigrant women from a Korean enclave. Before the interviews, I asked participants to fill out a questionnaire to collect demographic information of the interviewees. Table 9.2 shows the demographic characteristics of participants, including age, number of children, educational background, length of US residence, type of occupation, and income levels of both the respondents themselves and the households as a whole. Forty-three percent of 56 interviewees are aged 41 to 45. Overall, the educational level was high (half of

TABLE 9.1. Description of Each Group Member

Name [*]	Age group	Educational level	Occupation	Years of residency in the U.S.	Children (N)	Income/ month ($)
Group 1						
Kyala	41–45	High school	Office manager	15	2	3,000
Kayle	41–45	Post-BA	Private tutor	3	2	500
Grace	46–50	High school	Service sector	7	1	1,400
Hyon	46–50	High school	Receptionist	27	2	4,000
Group 2						
Jeong	46–50	Junior college	no response	24	2	no response
Eun	41–45	College	Office	6	2	1,200
Julie	41–45	Post-BA	no response	14	2	2,000
Group 3						
Youn	41–45	Post-BA	Graphic design	15	1	3,000
Jin	36–40	College	Part-time job	11	1	1,500
Yun	46–50	College	Kindergarten teacher	16	2	4,000
Jung	51–55	Post-BA	no response	23	2	1,500
Hyun	41–45	College	no response	3	2	no response
Yeon	41–45	Junior college	Salesperson	5	2	2,500
Group 4						
Hwa	41–45	College	Part-time job	9	2	700
Sarah	41–45	Junior college	Part-time job	5	2	1,200
Hye	41–45	College	Salesperson	13	2	1,000
Jiwon	36–40	Post-BA	Part-time job	no response	2	1,700
Group 5						
Sunny	41–45	High school	Manicurist	20	2	3,000
Chahee	41–45	College	Part-time job	27	3	no response
Yerang	41–45	College	School assistant	14	1	2,000
Group 6						
Jinhee	51–55	College	Salesperson	13	2	2,500
Minkyung	51–55	College	Salesperson	25	2	6,000
Gowoon	41–45	College	Manicurist	17	2	4,000
Kelly	41–45	Less than high school	no response	18	3	2,000
Group 7						
Junghwa	51–55	College	no response	20	2	no response
Songyee	51–55	College	no response	32	2	no response
Sanghee	46–50	College	Accountant	23	2	4,000
Group 8						
Miok	41–45	Junior college	Part-time job	12	2	5,000
Hanna	46–50	Post-BA	Pianist	22	2	2,000

TABLE 9.1.—Continued

Name [*]	Age group	Educational level	Occupation	Years of residency in the U.S.	Children (N)	Income/month ($)
Junhee	41–45	College	Part-time job	27	3	2,000
Bangsil	41–45	Post-BA	Part-time job	14	3	300
Group 9						
Kyungmi	41–45	College	*no response*	15	2	*no response*
Namsoo	41–45	College	Manicurist	16	1	2,000
Minhee	36–40	Junior college	Beauty treatment	25	2	1,000
Group 10						
Jihye	36–40	Junior college	Company worker	10	2	2,200
Domi	36–40	Junior college	Company worker	11	2	2,500
Group 11						
Misoo	36–40	Post-BA	Part-time job	9	2	300
Seongok	36–40	College	*no response*	9	2	*no response*
Hwasul	41–45	College	*no response*	2	2	*no response*
Group 12						
Eunsul	46–50	College	Cashier	20	2	3,000
Hungil	46–50	College	*no response*	8	2	3,000
Halee	51–55	High school	*no response*	15	2	*no response*
Jungmi	46–50	College	Laundromat owner	12	1	5,000
Jiyoun	31–35	Post-BA	Children's pastor	7	2	*no response*
Group 13						
Nakyung	41–45	College	Nurse	31	2	9,000
Jungsun	41–45	College	*no response*	34	2	4,300
Rohui	46–50	College	*no response*	14	3	1,870
Group 14						
Lahee	36–40	High school	Receptionist	15	2	2,400
Youngmi	36–40	High school	Bakery manager	6	2	2,000
Group 15						
Sunmi	36–40	Post-BA	Private tutor	14	2	4,000
Haijung	41–45	Post-BA	Missionary	13	2	*no response*
Sumi	46–50	Junior college	Baby sitter	17	3	1,200
Group 16						
Eunhee	46–50	College	*no response*	20	2	*no response*
Hwa	51–55	College	Marketing	26	2	4,000
Ara	51–55	College	*no response*	29	2	*no response*
Mihee	51–55	College	*no response*	12	2	*no response*

* All names are pseudonyms.

TABLE 9.2. Demographics of Respondents

	N	%
Age Group		
31–35	1	1.8
36–40	10	17.9
41–45	24	42.9
46–50	12	21.4
51–55	9	16.0
Total	56	100
Education level		
Less than high school	1	1.8
High school	8	14.3
Junior college	8	14.3
College	28	50
Graduate school	11	19.6
Total	56	100
Employment status		
Full time	30	53.6
Part time	9	16.0
Non-response	17	30.4
Total	56	100
Years of residency in the US		
Less than 5	3	5.4
5–10	9	16.1
11–15	20	35.7
16–20	9	16.1
21–25	4	7.1
26–30	7	12.5
Over 30	3	5.4
Non-response	1	1.8
Total	56	100
Number of children		
1	7	12.5
2	43	76.8
3 or more	6	10.7
Total	56	100

respondents had a four-year college education). Among the interviewees, 11–15 years of residency in the United States was most frequent. The majority of participants had two children (77 percent).

Data Collection

Each interview with a group lasted between one and two hours, depending on the number of group members. All interviews were conducted in the Korean language. All the content of the interviews was recorded using a digital recording device, and then later it was transcribed from the recordings. I conducted semi-structured interviews with each group, whose members were given the same questions in turn (see table 9.3). Before the interview, each participant was given a number, by which they were addressed during the interview. This assigned number was an impromptu suggestion to appease a participant who was reluctant to call herself or to be called by her real name or to be known as the mother of a child whose real name was used while the group interview was recorded, despite that they were allowed to use any nickname or pseudo-name. All the other respondents agreed to use numbers to protect the participants' identity among group members (but not for the researcher), which eventually induced more candid and active responses from the participants.

For semi-structured interviews, a researcher develops general themes to explore but remains open to the participants' preferred topics (Rossman and Rallis 2003). In this study, the same set of common questions was asked to encourage every participant to talk and to prevent a dominant small number of respondents from influencing the rest of the group members. Once the common questions were asked, the rest of the interview session was up to participants' discretion within an overall research theme. For example, I asked if there was any trouble in balancing the different roles at work and at home after migration; if and how those problems are solved; and for more information about the sharing of household tasks with their husbands (e.g., disposal of garbage, grocery shopping, housekeeping, laundry, dishwashing, and management of the family budget, kinship relations, and social networks). These questions also included the time spent on housework by the wife, the husband, and/or a paid worker. Hook (2010) points out the problems of previous measures of housework, which mainly focus on gauging total time spent on housework and "female-typed" tasks, and thus, she argues, the existing studies overlook the "*kinds* of work that men and women do in the home" (1482). That is, researchers should divide "time-flexible" and "male-typed" tasks, such as

TABLE 9.3. Sample Questions for Every Participant

Personal Background
1. How old are you?
2. Why did you/your parents decide to settle down in the United States?
3. How long have you lived in the United States?
4. Are you married? And how long have you been married?
5. Do you have a child? If yes, how many children do you have?
6. What is the highest level of education you have completed?

Economic Activities
1. Could you tell me what is your family income? And what is your income?
2. What kind of job do you have?
3. How much do you think your income contributes to your family finances?

Gender Roles: The Time and Types of Household Work
1. How much time (minutes per day) is spent on the housework by you and your spouse/partner?
2. What kind of housework you and your spouse/partner usually do? (For example, who is mainly responsible for preparing meal, for cleaning, for childcare, etc.?)
3. Do you think that the division of household work has changed after immigration to the United States?
   3-a. If yes, what causes the changes to occur?
   3-b. If no, what hinders the changes from occurring?

Traditional Notion of Family and Family Relationship: The Kin Network and the Filial Piety
1. After immigration, how frequently you keep in contact with kin members including in-laws?
2. What is your opinion about the kinship network and the filial piety?
3. How important do you think the relationship with kin network is?
4. Do you support or have intention to physically or financially support parents-in-law?
5. Has your opinion changed after immigration to the United States?
   5-a. If yes, what makes you have different thoughts on the traditional family relationship?
   5-b. If no, what makes you stick to traditional notion of family relationship?
6. Overall, do you think that the immigration to the United States has a positive or negative effect on the gender equality in the household?
   6-a. If yes or no, why do you think so?

vehicle maintenance and yard work, and "time-inflexible" or "female-typed" tasks, such as cooking and cleaning. Therefore, I asked respondents about which types of housework they share with their spouses, in addition to the amount of time spent on them. Then, I examined whether or not a married female Korean immigrant follows traditional Korean familial norms after migration by asking the following questions: how frequently each female Korean immigrant is in contact with kin members, especially parents-in-law; how important she thinks the relationship with parents-in-law is; and whether and how much she supports or has an intention to support physically or financially her parents-in-law.

Data Analysis

Data analysis was conducted based upon Strauss and Corbin's (1998) grounded theory approach, using three steps of analysis of "open, axial, and selective coding" (Kim et al. 2006). This means that all interview transcripts are repeatedly read, compared, and reanalyzed to capture new and emerging concepts from the previous transcripts, as well as to grasp a main theme across all the transcripts. At the beginning of the analysis, I repeatedly read transcripts to figure out common meanings throughout the entire series of interview transcripts, written in Korean, the language used to collect the data. In addition, during the open coding, possibly relevant concepts concerning the division of household tasks, work, immigration, and relationships among family members were named, labeled, and continually compared.

Next, in the second step, I used axial coding to see how these concepts can be grouped into certain categories and subcategories. Categories included acculturation time, the length of residency in the United States, motivation to start working, strategies employed to balance housework and paid work outside the home, and perceptions of gender ideologies, gender equality, and so forth. According to Strauss and Corbin (1998), as we keep grouping data together under categories by using diagrams and consulting the social construction framework, distinctive and diverse patterns will emerge among the groups. For example, the length of residency in the United States will probably make different trajectories among immigrant women in terms of acculturation, application of strategies for balancing housework and paid work, negotiation with their husband or family members, and so on.

Last, this led to selective coding, integrating categories into a central explanatory concept or category. Once I established a relationship between a concept and the general categories, I continually reassessed the relationships among concepts and categories to verify and modify the relationships as more cases were analyzed. This became the foundation for the emerging narrative of gender role negotiation among respondents in my sample. For example, although a participant had the traditional gender role of caregiver, she did not want to go back to Korea to support her or her husband's parents (filial piety). In this case, the traditional gender norm might not be the only explanatory factor, so I had to go back to the original data to figure out other possible reasons.

Findings

Family Upbringing and Personal Characteristics

With regard to gender roles within the household, the study participants often pointed out that when a husband had a Confucian and/or patriarchal mindset or was brought up in such a familial atmosphere, household work was rarely shared even after migration to the United States. Many participants highlighted upbringing and family background as an important factor affecting their husbands' share of household work. In particular, several respondents complained about patriarchal attitudes toward gender norms, which were "told," "learned," and "taught" by parents-in-law. Sunmi is relatively young (age group 36–40), is highly educated (post-BA graduate), and works as a private tutor. Sunmi and her husband have lived in the United States for 14 years and have two children. Sunmi strongly criticized her husband's male-centered views:

> [My husband] has a [Korean] way of thinking in the 1960s–70s. In his mind, there is a thought like this; man is a sky (which figuratively means "God" in Korea) and woman is an earth. It was taught and learned by his parents. After marriage, we had fought so much over this.

Similarly, Hwa (age group 51–55, with a college education) has the same complaint about her husband. Although she and her husband have lived in the United States for 26 years, she said nothing has changed:

> He was educated in Korea and was nurtured as a first son in a patriarchal family. His attitude toward household work has hardly changed. Getting rid of trash bin is all he does.

Both interviewees thought their husbands' attitudes toward gender norms had been learned and fostered by their familial background. They especially think that the way of thinking and the attitudes of their parents-in-law have been transmitted to their husbands. For example, Sunmi's mother-in-law often says, "Man never enters the kitchen," a phrase used to express the binary division of household labor in Korea. In this way, the meddling of parents-in-law or husbands' kin members makes it difficult to share household labor, even if the husband has an egalitarian mind. Yeon, a salesperson (age group 41–45, with a junior college education), has been in the United States for five years with her husband and two kids. She told me how different her husband's attitude toward household work was in front of his parents:

> Here, my husband does everything that I ask him to do, or at least tries to do something similar. We had visited Korea for about three months in the past, then we stayed at my parents-in-law's. My husband was being super cautious about his mother, and refused to do the dishes, which he usually did here in the United States. At that time, I realized if we lived in Korea with my parents-in-law, my husband wouldn't do much of . . . no . . . almost any of the household chores he did.

Yeon's case illustrates how the presence of parents-in-law or husbands' kin members affects the attitudes of Korean women's husbands toward gender norms. Even though a husband may have an egalitarian norm, the existence of other family members who have more traditional gender ideologies makes it hard for the husband to express his own attitude. In particular, if parents-in-law of an interviewee were first-generation immigrants who moved to the United States in mostly the 1970s or early 1980s, when traditional gendered norms were more strongly upheld in Korea, they are more likely to keep their traditional gendered role attitudes even after living in the United States for decades. Eunsul's case demonstrates this aspect. As a college-educated middle-aged woman, Eunsul has lived in the United States for 20 years and has two kids. She remembered her early days of married life in the United States as follows:

> After marriage, my parents-in-law did not allow me to visit my parents living in Korea, and even to call them. They told me that "you married our son, now you're our family member, so you should become attached." They even referred to an old Korean

saying, "The farther the in-laws and restrooms, the better."* It sounded like they're stuck in the 1970s. I was so scared that I couldn't say anything.

In the olden days, people in Korea used to think that a married daughter was no longer a member of her own family. Sometimes, to suppress sad feeling from a woman's marriage and leaving home, such an old saying was repeatedly used by parent-in-laws. Nonetheless, it is definitely an expression of unequal gender ideology in Korea.

However, the same logic underlining the separation of women from their family upon marriage can be reversely applied to husbands in immigrant families. If geographical proximity to parents-in-law or other family members on the husband's side in the United States tended to fortify traditional gender roles, traditional gender roles had been possibly changed or weakened after migration to the United States if a couple's parents (especially, the husband's parents) still lived in Korea. For example, there were cases in which a patriarchal husband's attitude toward the division of household work had shifted after living in the United States and after being away from his parents in Korea. Misoo works as a cashier. She is relatively young (age group 36–40), finished her college education in Korea, and has lived in the United States for nine years with her husband and two kids. Misoo thought migration and geographical separation from her parents-in-law had contributed to her husband's egalitarian attitudes toward household labor,

> I think my relationship with my husband has become more equal after moving to the US. Because now we are in a situation that we don't have parents' interference. And we should manage our family on our own. There is no one we can depend on, so my husband and I have responsibility for our own things. My husband also knows this situation, and I guess this made him change his attitude toward household labor, too.

The difference between Misoo's case and the other cases was that Misoo and her husband had a relatively more egalitarian attitude toward the division of household labor compared to other respondents. Misoo told me

---

*In a traditional Korean house structure, a restroom is located outside the house for sanitary reasons. This expression has been used to figuratively emphasize that the husband's side of the family is prioritized over the wife's side. Thus, like a restroom, the wife's home should be physically and mentally remote.

that due to his previous experience of studying in the United States as a graduate student, her husband would often help her with childcare and some chores. Misoo said her husband could more flexibly spend time on school and home compared to regular workers. In addition, the physical separation from her husband's parents facilitates a more equal relationship in the household. Misoo still thinks that as a wife, she should be responsible for household work, although her husband is willing to pick up some chores. The case of Misoo and her husband can be classified into the "transitional" type (Hochschild 2012), where both traditional and nontraditional gendered attitudes are present. The transitional type can be located in the middle of the spectrum, with "pure" traditional and "pure" egalitarian types at the ends. Although women in the transitional type emphasize both work and family, they believe in the role of male breadwinner; and men in this type prefer the traditional gendered roles over more egalitarian divisions of household work. Likewise, although Misoo had a part-time job as a cashier, she called herself a "housewife." At the same time, however, her narrative revealed how she and her husband strategically chose and adopted different gender ideologies, depending on their situations. She told me, "When my husband was a graduate student in the US, we shared more household work evenly. He did many chores including cooking and cleaning. But now he is a businessman and I am a housewife, so I can't ask him to do more housework."

Social and Cultural Influence

The demand for more egalitarian gender roles by the women in my sample was also raised through interactions with their neighbors and colleagues. Most of the participants in this study said they and their husbands noticed a more egalitarian gender relationship among couples in the United States, and they thought those notions led them to change their attitudes from an unequal gender relationship to a more egalitarian wife-husband relationship. Unlike in Korea, husbands in the United States repeatedly heard from local friends and coworkers what other American or Korean immigrant husbands and dads should do—and actually do—at home, and they witnessed more equal participation in household work.

As mentioned above, husbands were now also free from the eye of their parents and other family members, who tend to be against gender equity, saying such things as "How man could do such a woman thing!" and "This is a man's or (woman's) work." Some women reported that their husbands gradually changed their attitudes toward gender roles within the household after receiving encouragement for gender-egalitarian ideology or criticism of traditional gender ideology from people who are a part of their social network. Eun is an office worker (age group 41–45, with a college degree) and a mother of two kids. She told me how environmental change had affected her husband's notion of gender roles within the household.

> Environment is important, isn't it? Everybody [here] knows that other husbands living in your neighborhood are doing well, right? In America, all husbands are good ones . . . you know . . . family men. My husband really changed, I think, compared to the days when we're living in Korea. Once, my husband told me that a priority was given to child, woman, dog, and then man here in the United States.

Many respondents mentioned the cultural effect on the changes in their husbands' way of thinking and attitude toward the division of household chores. Their narratives share common thoughts about the behavior of American people around their families, socially desirable expectations for gender roles, a more egalitarian culture, a family-centered lifestyle, and so on. The interviewees attributed their husbands' change to cultural factors, as well as to the geographical change and separation from family members in Korea. Based on their anecdotal experiences, many interviewees thought or believed that American culture emphasizes individualism, and thus women command more respect in the United States as equal individuals of men. Pyke (2000) also finds a similar perception in her research on the way Korean and Vietnamese immigrant children interpret and compare their family lives with that of "the normal American family." According to Pyke, "respondents repeatedly constructed American families as loving, harmonious, egalitarian, and normal. Using this ideal as their measuring stick, Asian families were constructed as distant, overly strict, uncaring, and not normal" (248).

This "social influence" was reinforced by a family-friendly corporate culture in the United States. Jihye (age group 36–40, with a junior college degree) was an office worker in Korea but has been living in the United States for 10 years with two daughters. She and her husband are office workers in the United States, so she compares the different cultures or atmospheres of organizations in Korea and in the United States. She told me that Korea's enterprise culture featured frequent overtime work, various get-togethers after work, and drinking parties, which were all considered an extension of work. It means a lack of time to spend with family members in Korea.

> I have a long experience with a big company in Korea. As you know, Korean companies have too many get-togethers, most of which are not necessary, I think. More ridiculously, you cannot go home until your supervisor leaves the office. Because of the strict hierarchical organizational culture. How dare subordinates leave the office before senior members or supervisors do!

In contrast, American companies and workplaces tend to be more respectful toward employees' work hours and their time outside of work, and people do not usually have work-related gatherings after work. Therefore, it is easier to spend more time with family, particularly for men, allowing them to be more actively involved in family events and household work. Jihye goes on to say,

> My husband works in an American company, and I have seen him attend get-togethers once or twice a year, usually at the end or beginning of a year. Such an atmosphere [at work] helps to make husband family-friendly.

Many other participants provided similar responses about the family-friendly company culture in the United States. More flexibility in one's work schedule and stricter rules for overtime work in American businesses, compared to Korean companies, were especially regarded as influential factors that facilitate a more egalitarian attitude for husbands.

Filial Piety and "Work of Kinship": For the Children

The relationship with in-law families after marriage, especially with the husband's side, is a strong factor that obligates many Korean immigrant married women to fulfill their duty as daughters-in-law, including supporting old-age parents (filial piety). This is at odds with the more egalitarian attitudes mentioned earlier. If a husband is the eldest or the only son, it is even more likely that his wife feels responsibility for supporting her parents-in-law. The second son's and the younger sons' wives said they feel relatively less pressure. According to Jihye,

I have no desire to [support my parents-in-law]. 'Cause my husband is the second son, and has an older brother. So, I think, they [the brother and his wife] should take care of parents-in-law.

Unlike Jihye, those study participants who were wives of an eldest son or an only son feel pressured and anxious about supporting their parents-in-law. Eun (age group 41–45, with a BA degree) was the wife of an only son, and she found it unfeasible to take care of her parents-in-law living in Korea.

My husband has two sisters. So, if anything happens to my parents-in-law, we can help them financially, but taking care of them physically would not be possible. It doesn't seem feasible for us to come back to Korea, or for his parents to come here, I think.

Most respondents in my study emphasize their "inevitable" situation, whether it is for economic or geographic reasons. This indicates that Korean immigrant women are not free from the traditional value system. Most participants were not free from the traditional gender role in filial piety, or moral obligation, even though immigration (geographical disconnection) was regarded as a kind of exoneration that made a daughter-in-law feel less guilty and exempt from social stigmatization. Immigrant women were the people in charge of maintaining cross-border or domestic family communication ties as well as hosting events to bring the extended family together.

However, despite the development of communication technology such as free internet-based telephone, most respondents answered that they did not keep in touch with relatives or kin, unless they live close by. They also did not think of cutting off the connection with kin network as harmful to them. Hyun (age group 41–45, with a college degree) has lived in the United States for three years. She said her social relations with locals and friends in the United States were more important than her kin network in Korea:

Other family members are in Korea, and here, only my children and I live. Honestly, my neighbors and friends here are more helpful and important than my family and kin members in Korea.

Yeon also said, "Even though I care for my family and kin members, I also try to take care of local friends and acquaintances in a practical sense." However, at the same time, Yeon mentioned something interesting:

As my children grow up, they talk about their [Korean American] friends' visits to Korea hanging around with kin members during the visits. Nowadays, I start to feel it's important for my kids. They want and need it.

Yeon's narrative of the necessity of a kin network can be found in other participants' responses and in different narratives that I would call "for the children." In many narratives of the kin networks among Korean immigrant women, there was no "I" but instead "children."

Interestingly, the responses of the participants who had children indicated that it was important to maintain the kin network in Korea because of their children. Given the current low fertility rate of Korean families, with fewer siblings compared to the past, participants worried that their kids may not have good connections with family in Korea later on in life when their mothers are absent. Therefore, the respondents said that they maintained the kinship network in the hope that the kinship would give protection to their children on behalf of them in the future, functioning as an extended family. Gowoon (age group 41–45, with a BA degree) works in a nail shop and has lived in the United States for 17 years. She is a mother of two kids. Gowoon said, "Cutting relationships with kin members in Korea is not harmful to me," but she thought maintaining kin relationship in Korea might be helpful for her children:

If my children have no such [family] gathering and it's just us . . . if so, it would be bad for the children's [emotional] development. For instance, in the case of the Thanksgiving holiday . . . for this reason, I think it [kin network] is important.

Eun also emphasizes the importance of maintaining kin networks for her children:

We have no relatives in the U.S., and they all live in Korea, so if I discontinue contact with them, there would be no one for my children later in their lives. I am worried about it. For this reason, I am trying to care for kin members in Korea and keep in touch with them. To be honest, for my kids.

A similar narrative of "for the children" was found in the context of filial piety. Some interviewees whose children are in college were considering going back to Korea to take care of old parents. However, participants who have school-age children rarely said that they would return to Korea to support their parents, citing the need to stay in the United States for the education of their children. Gowoon added,

> Under the current situation in which my children are school-aged, I cannot go back to Korea to support my parents-in-law. However, someday when my kids grow up and attend college, then, I think, I could go.

Many interviewees expressed similar thoughts. Jeong (age group 46–50, with a junior college degree) has lived for 24 years in the United States. As a mother of two, she said,

> It depends on the children's age, whether to come back to Korea for supporting parents-in-law or even my own parents. If the kids are in the lower grades, it would be a hard decision, but things are going to change, as my children age.

Relatively young (age group 36–40) and with a college degree, Jin agreed with Jeong's comment. Jin has one child, works part-time, and has lived in the United States for 11 years.

> If you asked the same question in the past, I would have hesitated to answer, but now it would be alright to go back to home country. In order to take care of parents . . . only if my kid has grown up enough to live independently.

After migration, it seems that traditional gender roles, such as the unequal division of housework, filial piety, and the responsibility for kin networks, have changed, if only a little, compared to life in Korea. Nevertheless, most of the respondents seem to stick to the traditional gender role as a mother who should fulfill her role "for the children." Interestingly, their excuses were frequently related to their children, using statements such as "because of the children," "for the kids' education," and "in order to help them adapt to life in the United States." On the one hand, they want to be free from traditional gender roles; some started to acquire an equal relationship with their husbands to some extent in the household. On the other hand, they want to maintain the traditional gender roles in pursuit of child-mother relations.

Traditional Korean culture has been influenced by the different elements of Shamanism, Taoism, Buddhism, and Confucianism. However, the Confucian ideology has been most often cited to explain a strong emphasis on education (Min 2001; Park 2007; Sorensen 1994). In terms of gender roles, this high valuation of education is combined with the ideal of good mothering, since mothers have been implicitly and explicitly considered the "educational manager" (Park 2007) in Korean households. Based on this cultural tradition of good mothering, "the level of women's success is largely determined by the level of their children's success in education" (Min 2001: 305). Even many Korean immigrant parents who suffer from economic hardships tend to underline the education of their children (Pyke 2000). Min (2001) also argues that Korean immigrant husbands prioritize children's education over their wives' contribution to the household economy, such that they do not favor wives' economic activities outside the home and that women themselves have internalized this emphasis on educational support as well. "Even Korean women with a school-attending child have difficulty working outside because support for their child's education is considered their important job (Min 2001: 305). Jihye's comment reveals how women's status is evaluated by these cultural norms, especially children's educational achievement:

> Unlike in Korea, [in the United States] people [around me] do not meddle in every single thing. There is nothing to fight over. Because, in Korea, being meddlesome, kin members used to evaluate my children and interfere with a trifle thing; which school my kids attend, after graduation what they would do, what the school record is, and so on. These things cause quarrel between family members. But, here, something like that does not happen. I didn't realize how annoying that kind of thing was, when in Korea, and thought it was natural and acceptable among kin members, because it was a culture. But, no. After migration, after comparing two different cultures, I think this [American culture] is right.

Therefore, the "child needs" in this study can be said to be a result of a traditional gender ideology that emphasizes the role of parents, especially of women, in managing and facilitating children's education, based on the Confucian value system.

Conclusion and Discussion

By analyzing respondents' narratives and linking them to a sociological framework, this study reaffirms the dynamics of an internalized attitude toward gender norms and socially restructured unequal gender relations. Most Korean immigrant women in this study reveal ambivalent attitudes toward gender relations: On the one hand, they experienced more egalitarian wife-husband relations and changes of husbands' attitudes. But on the other hand, women are still viewed as the parent in charge of housework, caregiving, and kinkeeping activities, especially for the children. In conclusion, this finding shows that although Korean immigrant women feel more egalitarian toward gender relations within the household, unequal gender relations are deeply rooted in family life even after migration to the United States.

Interestingly, many interviewees in this study thought their husbands' attitudes or ways of thinking had changed after migration to the United States. However, as we can see in Misoo's account, there was a gap between respondents' perception of more egalitarian gender relations and "pure egalitarian" relations, the concept suggested as one of the "three types of ideology of marital roles" by Hochschild (2012). Most of the interview cases in which respondents described their wife-husband relations as quite equal, even, or egalitarian actually fell under a "transitional" marital role rather than a "pure egalitarian" one. I found that the majority of respondents in this study described themselves as housewives, regardless of their employment status. Even when they participated full-time in the paid labor force, the respondents tended to think that the primary "housekeeper" in a family was the woman. The gap between what they say and what they do might explain how strongly even women themselves have internalized the traditional gender norms of the male breadwinner and the female caregiver.

In addition, if we look into broader family relationships such as kin networks and filial piety, we can see why these women fall into the "transitional type" of marital role. Most of the respondents who had parents and/or parents-in-law frequently expressed their "inevitable" situation in which they could not afford to support them. Typically, respondents gave reasons of geographical segregation, the existence of other siblings, and birth order. Except for only 2 out of the 56 participants, all interviewees were not free from the traditional norm of filial piety. Their narratives were filled with excuses (in most of the cases) and relief (in the case of not being a first son's wife or of having other siblings). Even though it was from a sense of duty, they fulfilled the minimum role expectations in contacting parents-in-law, such as making a phone call on the parents' birthday and on national holidays. In other words, these women were "doing gender" (Bittman et al. 2003). As Bittman and his colleagues indicate, men and women do not follow their internalized gender norms but follow others' expectations "to present themselves as cognitively 'making sense' in terms of these norms" (191). This can help us understand the disjuncture between egalitarian attitudes and an egalitarian social context, coupled with persistent gender inequality in the division of labor among Korean immigrant families.

The narratives included in this research (especially related to filial piety, kin networks, and work-family balance) reveal how Korean immigrant women adapt to US society as well as adopt a variety of strategies within their daily lives to fulfill their traditional gender role as mothers. Although some participants in this study spoke out about their complaints of their husbands' disobliging manner, most interviewees reported that the changes of their husbands' attitudes were related to a more egalitarian division of household labor. Given the immigrant families' struggles to settle down in American society, women's contribution to the household economy plays a significant role in establishing a more egalitarian relationship between wife and husband.

More importantly, despite the variety of changed gender roles and a seemingly more egalitarian wife-husband relationship, these women's relationships with their children remained intact, strengthened in a traditional way. The experiences of Korean immigrant women in this study converged on their efforts "for the children." Both working-class and middle-class women whom Damaske (2011) interviewed relied on "family needs" excuses to protect themselves from negative cultural judgments. Similarly, many of the Korean immigrant women in this study used phrases like "for the child" or "because of my child" as an excuse for the negligence of filial piety and kin networks. However, at the same time, many of the Korean immigrant women in this study continue to be kinkeepers, trying to maintain kin relationships with family members in both Korea and the United States "for the children."

While existing research has largely focused on the relationship between wife and husband, between family and work, and between generations within a household among Korean immigrants, this study has extended this line of the literature by looking at gender relations from a child-centered perspective. Nevertheless, this study has several limitations that could be addressed in further research. In this chapter, husbands' attitudes toward the division of gender roles is expressed in their wives' narratives of personal (a husband's individual characteristic and his familial upbringing style), social, and cultural (the influence of workplace, community, and religious attendance) factors. The wives' accounts of their husbands' attitudes are valid, as they may be less subject to potential biases caused by "social desirability" concerning masculinity as a head of household.

However, we cannot rule out the possibility that the information collected here through the wives' voices may not accurately reflect the husbands' attitudes toward gendered norms. Moreover, it is still less clear what has caused the changes or constancy of the husbands' attitudes toward gender relations within the household. Thus, husbands' perspectives should be incorporated into future research. Relevant to this, we need to explore the effects of generational differences on the attitudes toward gendered norms among Korean immigrants. As discussed above, many female participants contended that the upbringing and family background of their husbands affected their husbands' attitudes toward the gendered division of household work. Then, it would be necessary to figure out whether married couples are both or either 1st, 1.5, or 2nd generation and whether the generational differentiation has affected the notion of a gendered division of housework and the relationship with kin members.

Finally, despite the importance of church for Korean immigrants, the current study is unable to look at how religion may have played some meaningful roles in the changes and continuity of gendered norms and attitudes among Korean immigrants. The association between religious involvement (i.e., the Korean Christian church) and traditional family values has been documented in previous literature. However, the results are somewhat inconsistent. For example, in their research on Korean Protestants in the United States, Min and Kim (2005) argued that attendance at religious activities among Korean immigrants has weakened traditional gendered ideology. In the same study, however, the authors also noted that pastors' sermons in Korean churches often focus on upholding Korean culture, including patriarchal family roles as husbands and wives. Studying this conflicting role of the Korean church among Korean immigrants would further increase our understanding about the marriage relationships and family lives of Korean immigrants in the United States.

NOTE

This study was approved by SUNY University at Buffalo Social and Behavioral Sciences IRB (SBSIRB). Project Title: [778821-1] Changes of the Gender Roles of Working Women in Korean Immigrant Families Living in the United States. Effective Date: August 11, 2015.

REFERENCES

Baldassar, Loretta. 2007. "Transnational Families and the Provision of Moral and Emotional Support: The Relationship between Truth and Distance." *Identities* 14 (4): 385–409.
Bankston, Carl L. 2014. *Immigrant Networks and Social Capital*. Cambridge, UK: Polity.
Bittman, Michael, Paula England, Liana Sayer, Nancy Folbre, and George Matheson. 2003. "When Does Gender Trump Money? Bargaining and Time in Household Work." *American Journal of Sociology* 109 (1): 186–214.
Challinor, Elizabeth. 2017. "Caught between Changing Tides: Gender and Kinship in Cape Verde." *Ethnos* 82 (1): 113–38.
Cherlin, Andrew. 2004. "The Deinstitutionalization of American Marriage." *Journal of Marriage and Family* 66 (4): 848–61.
Clark, Rebecca L., Jennifer E. Glick, and Regina M. Bures. 2009. "Immigrant Families over the Life Course: Research Directions and Needs." *Journal of Family Issues* 30 (6): 852–72.
Damaske, Sarah. 2011. *For the Family? How Class and Gender Shape Women's Work*. New York: Oxford University Press.
Di Leonardo, Micaela. 1987. "The Female World of Cards and Holidays: Women, Families, and the Work of Kinship." *Signs* 12 (3): 440–53.
Ferree, Myra Marx. 2010. "Filling the Glass: Gender Perspectives on Families." *Journal of Marriage and Family* 72 (3): 420–39.
Foner, Nancy. 1998. "Benefits and Burdens: Immigrant Women and Work in New York City." *Gender Issues* 16 (4): 5–24.
Gerstel, Naomi. 1988. "Divorce and Kin Ties: The Importance of Gender." *Journal of Marriage and Family* 50 (1): 209–19.
Hochschild, Arlie. 2012. *The Second Shift*. New York: Avon Books.
Hook, Jennifer. 2010. "Gender Inequality in the Welfare State: Sex Segregation in Housework, 1965–2003." *American Journal of Sociology* 115 (5): 1480–23.
Hurh, Won Moo. 1998. *The Korean Americans*. Westport, CT: Greenwood Press.
Kibria, Nazli. 1993. *Family Tightrope: The Changing Lives of Vietnamese Americans*. Princeton: Princeton University Press.
Kibria, Nazli. 2011. *Muslim in Motion: Islam and National Identity in the Bangladeshi Diaspora*. New Brunswick, NJ: Rutgers University Press.
Kim, Illsoo. 1981. *New Urban Immigrants: The Korean Community in New York*. Princeton: Princeton University Press.
Kim, Jeehun. 2012. "Remitting 'Filial Co-habitation': 'Actual' and 'Virtual' Co-residence between Korean Professional Migrant Adult Children Couples in Singapore and Their Elderly Parents." *Ageing and Society* 32 (8): 1337–59.
Kim, Kwang Chung, and Woon Moo Hurh. 1987. "Employment of Korean Immigrant Wives and the Division of Household Tasks." In Eui-Young Yu and Earl H. Phillips, eds., *Korean Women in Transitions: At Home and Abroad*, 199–218. Los Angeles: Center for Korean-American and Korean Studies, California State University.

Kim, Kwang Chung, and Woon Moo Hurh. 1988. "The Burden of Double Roles: Korean Immigrant Wives in the U.S.A." *Ethnic and Racial Studies* 11 (2): 151–67.

Kim, Kwang Chung, and Shin Kim. 1998. "Family and Work Roles of Korean Immigrant Wives and Related Experiences." In Young I. Song and Ailee Moon, eds., *Korean American Women: From Tradition to Modern Feminism*, 103–14. Westport, CT: Praeger.

Kim, Kwang Chung, Shin Kim, and Woon Moo Hurh. 1991. "Filial Piety and Intergenerational Relationship in Korean Immigrant Families." *International Journal of Aging and Human Development* 33 (3): 233–45.

Kim, Nadia Y. 2006. "'Patriarchy Is So Third World': Korean Immigrant Women and 'Migrating' White Western Masculinity." *Social Problems* 53 (4): 519–36.

Kim, Seon Mi. 2014. "The Impacts of Gender Differences in Social Capital on Microenterprise Business Start-Up." *Journal of Women and Social Work* 29 (4): 404–17.

Kim, Seongeun, Kate Conway-Turner, Bahira Sherif-Trask, and Tara Woolfolk. 2006. "Reconstructing Mothering among Korean Immigrant Working Class Women in the United States." *Journal of Comparative Family Studies* 37 (1): 43–58.

Lansford, Jennifer E., Kirby D. Deater-Deckard, and Marc H. Bornstein. 2007. *Immigrant Families in Contemporary Society*. New York: Guilford Press.

Lee, Eunju. 2006. *Gendered Processes: Korean Immigrant Small Business Ownership*. New York: LFB Scholarly Pub.

Lee, Sookhyun C., and Pat M. Keith. 1999. "The Transition to Motherhood of Korean Women." *Journal of Comparative Family Studies* 30 (3): 453–70.

Lew, Seok-Choon, Woo-Young Choi, and Hye Suk Wang. 2011. "Confucian Ethics and the Spirit of Capitalism in Korea: The Significance of Filial Piety." *Journal of East Asian Studies* 11 (2): 171–96.

Lim, In-Sook. 1997. "Korean Immigrant Women's Challenge to Gender Inequality at Home: The Interplay of Economic Resources, Gender and Family." *Gender and Society* 11 (1): 31–51.

Logan, John R., Wenquan Zhang, and Richard D. Alba. 2002. "Immigrant Enclaves and Ethnic Communities in New York and Los Angeles." *American Sociological Review* 67 (2): 299–322.

Min, Pyong Gap. 1984. "An Exploratory Study of Kin Ties among Korean Immigrant Families in Atlanta." *Journal of Comparative Family Studies* 15 (1): 59–75.

Min, Pyong Gap. 1998. *Changes and Conflicts: Korean Immigrant Families in New York*. Boston: Allyn and Bacon.

Min, Pyong Gap. 2001. "Changes in Korean Immigrants' Gender Role and Social Status, and Their Marital Conflicts." *Sociological Forum* 16 (2): 301–20.

Min, Pyong Gap, and Dae Young Kim. 2005. "Intergenerational Transmission of Religion and Culture: Korean Protestants in the U.S." *Sociology of Religion* 66 (3): 263–82.

Moon, Seungsook. 2003. "Immigration and Mothering: Case Studies from Two Generations of Korean Immigrant Women." *Gender and Society* 17 (6): 840–60.

Oh, Joong-Hwan. 2011. "Immigration, Cultural Adjustment, and Work Values: The Case of Korean Nail Care Workers in New York." *Development and Society* 40 (2): 261–88.

Park, Juhee, and Tim Futing Liao. 2000. "The Effect of Multiple Roles of South Korean Married Women Professors: Role Changes and the Factors Which Influence Potential Role Gratification and Strain." *Sex Roles* 43 (7–8): 571–91.

Park, Keumjae. 2008. "'I Can Provide for My Children': Korean Immigrant Women's Changing Perspectives on Work outside the Home." *Gender Issues* 25 (1): 26–42.

Park, Kyeyoung. 1997. *The Korean American Dream: Immigrants and Small Business in New York City.* Ithaca: Cornell University Press.

Park, So Jin. 2007. "Educational Manager Mothers: South Korea's Neoliberal Transformation." *Korea Journal* 47 (3): 186–213.

Park, Sung S., and Roger D. Waldinger. 2017. "Bridging the Territorial Divide: Immigrants' Cross-Border Communication and the Spatial Dynamics of Their Kin Networks." *Journal of Ethnic and Migration Studies* 43 (1): 18–40.

Pyke, Karen D. 2000. "'The Normal American Family' as an Interpretive Structure of Family Life among Grown Children of Korean and Vietnamese Immigrants." *Journal of Marriage and Family* 62 (1): 240–55.

Qian, Yue, and Liana C. Sayer. 2016. "Division of Labor, Gender Ideology, and Marital Satisfaction in East Asia." *Journal of Marriage and Family* 78 (2): 383–400.

Rhee, Siyon. 1997. "Domestic Violence in the Korean Immigrant Family." *Journal of Sociology and Social Welfare* 24 (1): 63–77.

Rosenthal, Carolyn J. 1985. "Kinkeeping in the Familial Division of Labor." *Journal of Marriage and Family* 47 (4): 965–74.

Rossman, Gretchen B., and Sharon F. Rallis. 2003. *Learning in the Field: An Introduction to Qualitative Research.* Thousand Oaks, CA: Sage.

Sorensen, Clark W. 1994. "Success and Education in South Korea." *Comparative Education Review* 38 (1): 10–35.

Strauss, Anselm, and Juliet Corbin. 1998. "Grounded Theory Methodology: An Overview." In K. Denzin and Y. S. Lincoln, eds., *Strategies of Qualitative Inquiry*, 158–83. Thousand Oaks, CA: Sage.

Sun, Ken C. 2013. "Rethinking Migrant Families from a Transnational Perspective: Experiences of Parents and Their Children." *Sociology Compass* 7 (6): 445–58.

Sung, Sirin. 2003. "Women Reconciling Paid and Unpaid Work in a Confucian Welfare State: The Case of South Korea." *Social Policy and Administration* 37 (4): 342–60.

Wolf, Diane L. 2003. "There's No Place Like 'Home': Emotional Transnationalism and the Struggles of Second-Generation Filipinos." In Peggy Levitt and Mary Waters, eds., *The Changing Face of Home: The Transnational Lives of the Second Generation*, 255–94. New York: Russell Sage Foundation.

Yanagisako, Sylvia Junko. 1977. "Women-Centered Kin Networks in Urban Bilateral Kinship." *American Ethnologist* 4 (2): 207–26.

Yoo, Grace J., and Barbara W. Kim. 2014. *Caring across Generations: The Linked Lives of Korean American Families.* New York: NYU Press.

Family Formation and Alternative Family Life

10

Who Gets Married?

Parent's Household Income, Individual's Education, and Entry into Marriage in South Korea

Jihye Oh, Jae Kyung Lee, and Hyeyoung Woo

While the world's lowest level of fertility in South Korea (hereafter Korea) has received much attention in recent years, there has been little research on explaining the likelihood of getting married. However, it is critical to examine marriage behaviors to better understand contributing factors for childbearing. Marriage is closely tied to fertility, especially in a society such as Korea, where nonmarital fertility is very low.[1] In fact, in Korea, although marriage is still highly valued and normatively expected for adults when they reach certain ages (i.e., mid-20s through early 30s), marriage rates have dramatically declined during the past decades (e.g., Raymo et al. 2015). According to the 2016 marriage and divorce statistics in Korea, the average age of first marriage is 32.8 for men and 30.1 for women, and the number of registered marriages per 1,000 people is fewer than 6, indicating the lowest level of marriage rate since the records began in 1970.[2] That is, people wait longer for their first marriage until around or after age 30, implying that more people stay unmarried. Perhaps it is also the case that more people think of marriage as a life choice transition rather than a must-do for their life.[3]

Previous research suggests that in the United States, those with a college education and higher economic prospects are more likely to be married compared to their counterparts (Anderson 2016; Cutright 1970; Goldstein and Kenney 2001; Oppenheimer 1988; Sweeney 2002; Torr 2011). This positive association has been historically consistent for men in the past, while the results for women are somewhat mixed (Cookingham 1984; Bloom and Bennett 1990; Blossfeld and Huinik 1991). It suggests that the association between socioeconomic status and marriage may vary by social and cultural context for men and women given the variations in women's social status and gender role expectations in marriage across societies. For example, Park, Lee, and Jo (2013) found a negative association between education and marriage among women in Korea: Those with higher education were the least likely to be married, especially among the older cohorts. However, this negative association was not found among the younger cohorts. In fact, the association was the opposite in that lower educated women were more likely to stay unmarried (Park, Lee, and Jo 2013). These findings imply that perhaps the gender specialization hypothesis, originally proposed by Becker (1981), may be less relevant in current Korea, in consistency with the trend observed in the United States (Anderson 2016; Cutright 1970; Goldstein and Kenney 2001; Oppenheimer 1988; Sweeney 2002; Torr 2011).

Despite the advances in the study of marriage associated with one's own education in Korea, it still remains unclear whether and how parent's socioeconomic status, often measured by parental education and income, influences the likelihood of adult children's marriage. In Korea, marriage is viewed as a family formation not only between two individuals but also between two families, those of the groom and bride. Therefore, it is reasonable to expect that people take into account factors of their potential marriage partner's parents when deciding to marry him or her (Chang 2003). In particular, given growing concerns for economic conditions in Korea (i.e., highly competitive labor market, growing income inequalities, and declining social mobility), parents' financial resources may be even more critical in recent years than they were in the past (Lee et al. 2017). Due to these economic circumstances in Korea, young adults these days, especially those with less affluent parents, are more likely to see marriage as "something special"—a life transition for only those who can afford it rather than anyone who would like it (Hankyoreh Economy and Society Research Institute 2015).[4]

Surprisingly, to our knowledge, there is only one study examining how parent's socioeconomic status is associated with adult children's marriage. Kim, Lee, and Park (2016) explored how unmarried women perceived marriage in their qualitative study and found that women were uncertain about their marriage prospects in the near future partly due to the lack of economic and emotional support from their parents (Kim, Lee, and Park 2016). While insightful, this study, however, relied on interview data from a small sample of women, remaining unclear about the question of whether parental resources influence offspring's entry into marriage for men as well as for women. Moreover, their results based on qualitative data from a small sample are generalizable to a larger population in Korea. In the current study, we investigate various factors influencing entry into marriage, with special attention to parent's socioeconomic status, using data from the Korean Labor and Income Panel Study (KLIPS) conducted from 1998 to 2015. As a longitudinal survey for a nationally representative sample of adults in Korea, the KLIPS provides detailed information about the socioeconomic status of parent's as well as respondent's social attainments and demographic characteristics, allowing us to estimate the influence of parent's socioeconomic status on probabilities of getting married among young adults.

Socioeconomic Status and Entry into Marriage

Previous literature suggests two primary social factors that influence an individual's decision to get married: individual's sociodemographic conditions, such as age, educational attainment, occupation, and income; and parent's socioeconomic status, often measured by their educational attainment and financial resources. Getting married is an important life event sensitive to age, more common among those who are in their 20s and 30s, with women likely to get married two or three years earlier than men. As for the association between marriage and individual socioeconomic conditions, entering a marriage appears to be more common among men with higher socioeconomic status. This overall positive association for men holds true across adult age groups in various countries (Goldscheider and Waite 1986; South 2001; Xie et al. 2003). However, this association is not as straightforward for women as it is for men. For example, on the one hand, several studies reported that women with higher socioeconomic status are less likely to get married in the United States (Lichter, Leclere, and McLaughlin 1991; Thornton, Axinn, and Teachman 1995). On the other hand, more recent studies found that women with higher levels of education and greater economic resources show a higher likelihood of getting married eventually (Anderson 2016; Goldstein and Kenney 2001; Sweeney 2002; Torr 2011). That is, while women with higher socioeconomic status may delay their marriage, they are more likely to get married in the long run compared to women with lower socioeconomic status (Oppenheimer and Lew 1995).

Additionally, there are good reasons to believe that the association between entry into marriage and individual's economic resources may be even more salient in recent years compared to the past in Korea, given the recent economic recession as well as growing income inequalities (Carbone and Cahn 2014; Park and Kim 2012). The increase in income inequality in the labor market might lead upper-class men to be (even) more competitive in the marriage market, while making it (even) more difficult for those in either the middle class or the working class to be attractive as a potential spouse (Carbone and Cahn 2014). With respect to women, while the association between socioeconomic status and the likelihood of getting married may not be as salient as it is for men, it is reasonable to assume that women who are highly educated and thus have greater income potentials are more likely to get married. Due to the adverse economic circumstances since the economic recessions in the last two decades, men, even those who are in higher social classes, may also prefer to marry women in the higher classes (i.e., those who are socioeconomically similar to themselves) to maintain their socioeconomic status. Conversely, the marriageability of men (and women, though to a lesser degree) in the lower class may be even more problematic in current Korean society.

Influences of Parent's Socioeconomic Status on Adult Children's Marriage

Despite its importance for an individual's likelihood of getting married, parents' socioeconomic status tends to be overlooked as a main mechanism in most existing studies. We found only a few studies examining the influence of parents on marriage intension or the timing of marriage for adult children (Axinn and Thornton 1992; South 2001). According to Axinn and Thornton (1992), parent's high levels of economic resources and educational attainment may lead children to be less financially independent, and thus they may take a longer time until they can afford a marriage. As a result, children of more affluent parents get married at later ages compared to those whose parents are less affluent. However, the study also indicated that parent's socioeconomic status may ultimately increase the offspring's probability of getting married. Affluent parents may make their children more "attractive" in the marriage market, and they may also offer material resources to have a marriage ceremony and to establish an independent living arrangement (Axinn and Thornton 1992). Another study (South 2001) shows that there is a positive association between parental resources and the likelihood of an offspring's marriage, especially among young adults, as the association declines as children age. The findings of these studies imply that while parent's socioeconomic status may matter for an offspring's marriage, the influence may be less for older children, probably reflecting the social norm in the United States that adult children live independently from their parents even if they are not married.

While informative, the findings of the previous studies are less clear about whether and how parent's resources are associated with the probability of an offspring's entering into marriage in Korea, where parents still play a critical role in deciding whom their children marry, the wedding preparations, and their subsequent marriage life. A majority of unmarried young adults in Korea tend to live with their parents until marriage, and thus they often have to find their own place to live as a couple upon marriage. Because of the high costs for housing, which is typically considered a man's responsibility to provide for the family, the average cost associated with marriage is much higher in Korea compared to most developed countries (Korea Institute for Health and Social Affair 2012). For example, average marriage-related expenses in Korea are more than $200,000,[5] while in the United States they are $38,000.[6] Thus, it is difficult for young adults to get married without their parents' financial help in contemporary Korean society.

In Korea, the university entrance rate has increased since the 1980s, and currently almost 70 percent of high school graduates enter college. Along with the high levels of overall education attainment, the labor market has been competitive, making it difficult for young adults to be able to purchase a house. As Korea has undergone two major economic recessions in the last two decades, the labor market conditions have become more precarious, and the real estate market also has been unstable, which pushes young couples further away from establishing a family as a married couple on their own. In fact, results of a recent survey show that on average parents of a groom spend $80,000 or more for their son's wedding, while parents of a bride on average spend $60,000 or less for their daughter's wedding. Additionally, 90 percent of all respondents who recently married received some monetary support from their parents for the marriage.[7] Other survey data also revealed that parent's financial resources also seem to be associated with the quality of marriage life. Those whose parents had lower levels of resources see marriage as a burden and feel less confident about their marital relationship.[8]

In addition to parental financial support for the marriage and the wedding ceremony, the socioeconomic status of parents may have a direct impact on their adult children's marriage in Korea. The matching process by marriage consulting companies illustrates this point well. While specific mechanisms are not clearly known, marriage consulting companies make a match based on a wide range of information that they collect from their clients. The information includes not only education, income, and occupation of both the clients and their parents but also the clients' elementary schools in order to gain additional information on the family's socioeconomic status during their childhood. Based on comprehensive information on both the clients' own individual background and their family's background, the clients have exposures to meetings with only a selected group of potential partners in Korea.[9]

This context offers some unique perspectives for why the economic resources of parents are critical (possibly more for men than for women) in Korea when considering a marriage. However, most of the existing research in Korea has focused on the socioeconomic status of single men and women to predict the probability of getting married (Park, Lee, and Jo 2013; Park and Lee 2017; U 2009; Yun 2012). A few studies that considered the influence of parents on marriage decisions either treated parent's economic resources as one of the control variables, failing to examine its influence on entry into marriage properly (Oh and Lim 2016), or estimated the predicted levels of "desire to marry" rather than probabilities of "getting married" (Kim, Lee, and Park 2016). This research addresses this gap in the literature by exploring the association between parent's economic resources and adult children's transition into marriage. More specifically, we test the following hypotheses. Given the importance of educational attainment as the most critical factor predicting the likelihood of getting married (Oh and Lim 2016; Park, Lee, and Jo 2013; Woo 2009) and its crucial links to an individual's overall socioeconomic position (measured by employment status, occupational prestige, and income) over the life course (Blau and Duncan 1967; Swell and Hauser 1975), we first test the following hypothesis:

H1. Both parents' income and individual's education are positively associated with entry into marriage for both men and women.
H1-1. Considering the gendered expectation for cost of housing, we expect this positive association to be more salient for men.

Then, we test our second hypothesis for the possible variations by parent's household income.

H2. We expect to see gendered variations in the association between individual's education and entry into marriage by parent's household income.

H2-1. For men, the positive association between individual's education and the likelihood of getting married may be more salient among those whose parents have lower levels of income.

H2-2. For women, the positive association between individual's education and the likelihood of getting married may not differ by parent's household income.

Methods

Data

We used data from the Korean Labor and Income Panel Study. The KLIPS has been conducted annually by the Center for Labor Statistics Research (CLSR) in Korea and the Korea Labor Institute (KLI) to collect information about labor force activities based on a probability sample in Korea. Since the KLIPS conducted its first wave in 1998, all 18 waves have been publicly available (1998–2015). Because of its detailed information about socioeconomic conditions as well as its demographic characteristics over almost two decades of the follow-up period with a large sample size, the KLIPS is an ideal data source for this study, allowing us to capture the influence of individuals' education and their parents' household income on entry into marriage with other covariates adjusted for. Using data from the KLIPS, we limited our analysis to the respondents aged 19 to 41 who were not married at the baseline (N = 3,800 respondents: 2,063 men and 1,737 women). The age range of 19–41 years old was selected because these ages are often considered the primary ages for a first marriage in Korea, where age norms for marriage are still rather strictly applied in general perception. Thus, those who are still unmarried after 40 may be different from the general adult population in Korea in terms of their marriage intention. Or they may not be "desirable" as a marriage partner in some ways, such as low levels of socioeconomic conditions, poor interpersonal skills, or health issues. To appropriately capture the influence of individual's education and parent's household income on entry into marriage, we reconstructed the data set into a person-year format to easily measure independent variables as well as confounding factors from year $t - 1$, while our outcome variable was observed from year t.

Measures

Our outcome was whether respondents entered into marriage at year t (married = 1; unmarried = 0). Once respondents entered into marriage at year t, they were right censored in the data set, dropped from the person-year formatted data file at year $t + 1$ and onward. Our primary independent variables were respondents' educational attainment and their parents' economic resources. For respondents' educational attainment, we separated the values from "the highest degree of education completed" into four categories: "high school or less," "junior college," "university," and "graduate school." The reference category was "high school or less." We used household income collected at each wave to measure parent's economic resources. While time varying, household income was recoded into four quartiles: 1 is assigned for those whose income is at the top 25 percentile; 2 for the 26–50 percentile; 3 for the 51–75 percentile; and 4 for the 76–100 percentile.[10] For additional information for parent's socioeconomic status, we included father's educational attainment, with the categories of "less than high school" (ref.), "high school," and "some college or higher," and father's employment status (full-time = 1; other = 1). For the respondents who were missing the father's education variable, we used educational attainment of mothers instead.

We also considered a number of control variables as either time varying or time invariant. Specifically, time-varying variables included respondent's employment status (employed versus nonemployed), income (logged), and age (in years, centered on 30 for men and 28 for women) observed at each wave. Time-invariant variables were gender and birth cohort (i.e., whether respondents were born before or after 1970 for men and 1973 for women). We used the years 1973 (for women) and 1970 (for men) for the cutoff points because those who were born after 1973 have faced more unfavorable labor market conditions since the 1997 economic crisis, such as increased unemployment, higher precarious employments, and more commonly forced pay cuts (Woo 2009; Yoon 2012). Given the military service that most men (aged 18 and above) in Korea are expected to serve for two to three years, the year 1970 was used for men. Other time-varying variables are whether respondents were enrolled in school, religious affiliation (1 = have a religion; 0 = no religion), and residential region (1 = urban; 0 = rural). Another time-invariant control was whether respondents grew up in urban areas (1 = yes; 0 = no). Table 10.1 presents all of the measures used in this study.

TABLE 10.1. Measurements of Variables

Variable	Measurement of variable
Dependent variable	
Marital status	Marital status unchanged = 0
	Changes in marital status = 1
Independent variable	
Household income	First quartile: $12,220 or less
	Second quartile: $ 12,221 – $24,000
	Third quartile: $ 24,001 – $36,000
	Fourth quartile: $36,001 or more
Education level	High school or less (reference group)
	Junior college
	University
	Graduate school
Control variable	
Employment status	Unemployed = 0
	Employed = 1
Age	Centering for men 30, and 28 for women
	Age squared
Affiliation with school	Not in school = 0
	In school = 1
Religious affiliation	Not having a religion = 0
	Having a religion = 1
Growth areas	Rural areas = 0
	Urban areas = 1
Live in areas	Rural areas = 0
	Urban areas = 1
Cohort	Birth men before 1970, and birth women before 1973 = 0
	Birth after 1970 and 1973 = 1
Father's education	Middle school or less (reference group)
	High school
	More than junior college
Full-time job	Non-regular worker = 0
	Regular worker = 1
Monthly income	Monthly income after tax measure: $10
	(natural log transformation)

Analytic Approaches

We employed two main analytic approaches: Kaplan-Meier survival analysis and discrete-time survival analysis. First, we used Kaplan-Meier survival analysis to calculate the approximate function of the cumulative probability of getting married (i.e., those who experienced first marriage) within a sample. This analysis is expressed by the following equation:

$$G(t) = \prod_{t:T_t < t} < t\left(1 - \frac{E_t}{R_t}\right)$$

Where E_t refers to the number of occurrences for an event at time T_t, and R_t refers to the number of occurrences for being in a hazard group at time T_t.

Second, we conducted discrete-time survival analysis to estimate the probability of getting married with other controls accounted for. As mentioned earlier, we converted the data set to a format of person with period (i.e., "person-year"), so that the duration until the occurrence of an event (i.e., enter into marriage) was estimated with the age difference from the baseline. We used the complementary log-log baseline hazard function to estimate the probability to more accurately capture the nonlinear function of the marriage occurrence with age. The equation is shown below.

$$\log[-\log(1 - \lambda_i)] = \beta_0 + \beta_1 X_{1i} + \beta_2 X_{2i} + \cdots + \beta_k X_{ki}$$

Given that the age variable was centered on 30 years old for men and 28 years old for women, the intercept coefficient represented a log-log hazard value at age 30 for men and age 28 for women with other covariates adjusted for. Additionally, we also included the age squared variable to better count for the quadratic function of an age variable. All the coefficients of variables could be interpreted as exponentiated coefficients or hazard ratios (Woo 2009). All of the analysis is conducted by STATA 13.0.

Descriptive Statistics

We began by using descriptive statistics of variables to show the sample characteristics. According to the results in table 10.2, 41 percent of unmarried men and 51 percent of unmarried women at the baseline got married during the follow-up period. The average household income (i.e., parent's household income) was slightly higher for women. Given that we limited our sample to those who were aged 19 to 41, the average ages were relatively younger: 35 for men and 33 for women. As expected, the levels of educational attainment were fairly high for both men and women. While 36 percent of men had a high school degree or less, 20 percent, 37 percent, and 7 percent completed junior college, four-year university, and a graduate degree, respectively. Educational attainment was slightly higher for women: 34 percent of women were high school graduates or less; 24 percent were junior college graduates; 39 percent were university graduates; and 7 percent had a graduate degree. Respondents who were in school were around 2 percent for both men and women. For other controls, 37 percent of men and 46 percent of women had a religion, and the majority of men and women grew up in urban areas (60 percent for men and 55 percent for women). Respondents who lived in urban areas at the time of the survey were 57 percent for men and 62 percent for women. In terms of parent's information, 50 percent of the respondents reported that their father's education level was middle school or less, and 16 percent and 45 percent of them reported high school and junior college, respectively. Similarly, 45 percent of women reported that their father's education level was middle school or less, and 36 percent and 19 percent reported high school and junior college, respectively. In our sample, about 80 percent of respondents were born after 1970 for men and 1973 for women, implying that most of the respondents might experience an unstable labor market at some point. Among men, 41 percent of the respondents were employed, while only 29 percent of women were employed. Similarly, the proportion of full-time employees was lower among women compared to men (21.2 percent versus 29.8 percent). Men also had a higher level of monthly income on average than women did.

Individual's Education, Parent's Household Income, and Entry into Marriage

Before multivariate analysis, we first estimated the survival function using Kaplan-Meier survival analysis for the association between education and the probability of staying unmarried by parent's household income. We presented the results in four graphs for the four quartiles of parent's household income. Figure 10.1 depicts the results for men; the results for women are in figure 10.2.

While the calculated survival function was based on individual's education and parent's household income without other controls adjusted for, all of the four graphs consistently showed that those who have higher lev-

TABLE 10.2. Descriptive Statistics

Variable			N	Mean	S.D.	Min	Max
Marital status (1 = first marriage occurred)		Men	2,063	0.411		0	1
		Women	1,737	0.515		0	1
Household income	Men	All	2,063	3444.962	2924.531	0	32,900
		1Quartile	517	913.056	477.612	0	1,610
		2Quartile	517	2163.692	317.731	1620	2,760
		3Quartile	514	3551.486	484.458	2768	4,500
		4Quartile	514	7175.198	3426.881	4525	32,900
	Women	All	1,737	3486.701	3304.334	0	63,800
		1Quartile	446	903.061	461.198	0	1,560
		2Quartile	423	2155.801	310.335	1580	2,750
		3Quartile	436	3568.606	508.67	2760	4,560
		4Quartile	432	7374.579	4427.196	4570	63,800
Education level	High school or less	Men	2,063	0.36		0	1
		Women	1,737	0.30		0	1
	Junior college	Men	2,063	0.20		0	1
		Women	1,737	0.24		0	1
	University	Men	2,063	0.37		0	1
		Women	1,737	0.39		0	1
	Graduate school	Men	2,063	0.08		0	1
		Women	1,737	0.07		0	1
Age		Men	2,063	35.152	4.57	22	40
		Women	1,737	33.165	5.036	20	41
Religious affiliation (1 = having a religion)		Men	2,063	0.37		0	1
		Women	1,737	0.458		0	1
Growth areas (1 = urban areas)		Men	2,063	0.599		0	1

Live in areas (1 = urban areas)		Women	1,737	0.547	0	1
		Men	2,063	0.572	0	1
Father's education level	Middle school or Less	Women	1,737	0.624	0	1
		Men	2,063	0.50	0	1
	High school	Women	1,737	0.45	0	1
		Men	2,063	0.34	0	1
	More than junior college	Women	1,737	0.36	0	1
		Men	2,063	0.16	0	1
Affiliation with school (1 = in school)		Women	1,737	0.19	0	1
		Men	2,063	0.019	0	1
Cohort (1 = birth after '70 ('73))		Women	1,737	0.022	0	1
		Men	2,063	0.800	0	1
Employment status (1 = employed)		Women	1,737	0.777	0	1
		Men	2,063	0.406	0	1
Full-time job (1 = regular worker)		Women	1,737	0.287	0	1
		Men	2,063	0.298	0	1
Monthly income (after Tax)		Women	1,737	0.212	0	1
		Men	2,063	190.1129	94.74293	0	1,115
		Women	1,737	143.4077	75.28524	0	500

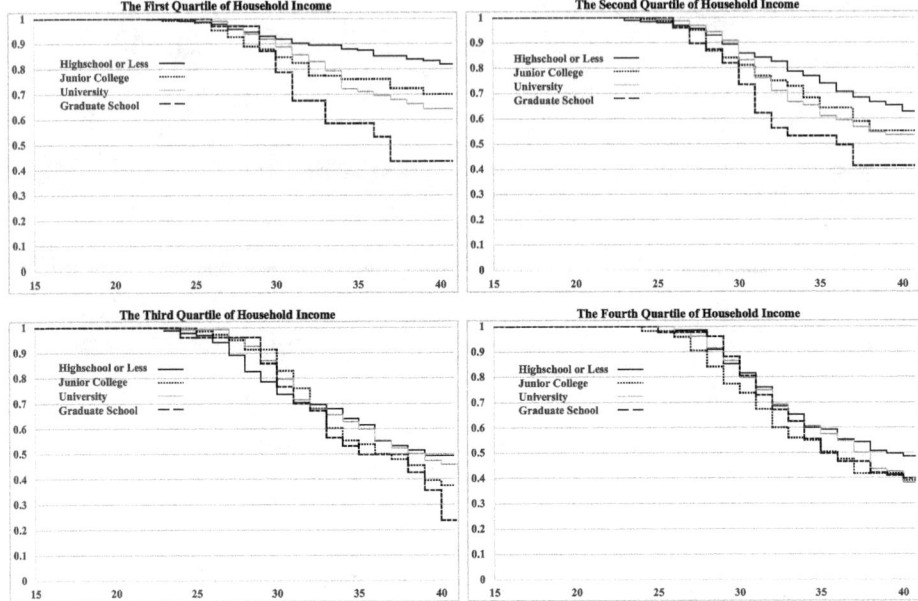

Fig. 10.1. The survival function of men

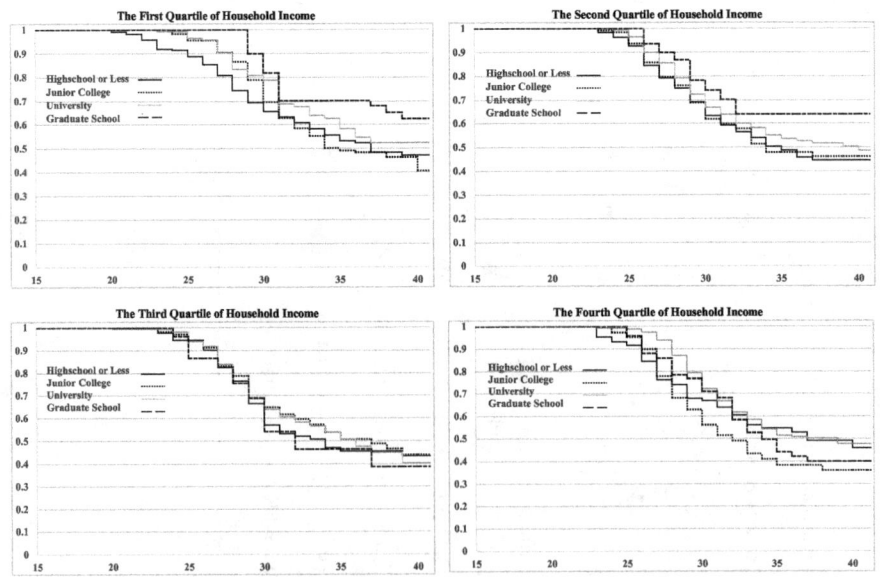

Fig. 10.2. The survival function of women

els of education were more likely to get married during the follow-up period, and the gaps in the probabilities by the education levels were much greater in the lower quartiles of parent's household income. For example, among those in the first quartile of parent's household income, the cumulative probability of getting married by age 41 for men with a graduate school degree was 62 percent. However, this probability was only 20 percent for those with a high school education or less. However, among those in the fourth quartile of parent's household income, the difference in the corresponding probabilities between the high school graduates or lower and the graduate degree holders was less than 10 percentage points.

Unlike men, women revealed higher probabilities of getting married among the lower educated ones compared to those with higher education, especially among the ones in the first and second quartiles of parent's household income. However, this inverse association between women's education and the probability of getting married did not seem to be held among women with affluent parents. For example, while the cumulative probability of getting married by age 41 for women with a graduate degree was only 38 percent when the household income was in the first quartile of parent's household income, the corresponding probability is higher (i.e., more than 60 percent) among women with a graduate degree *and* the highest levels of parent's income (i.e., fourth quartile).

Also different from the results of men, the probability of getting married for women did not seem to greatly change as parent's household income increases. The difference in the cumulative probability of marriage by age 41 between women with household income in the first quartile and their counterparts in the fourth quartile was 54–57 percent for women with a high school degree or less, 60–64 percent for junior college graduate women, and 48–52 percent for university graduate women. These results indicated that parent's household income might not be a critical factor for entry into marriage for women. We describe the result of the discrete-time survival analysis below.

Results of Discrete-Time Survival Analysis

We performed the discrete-time survival analysis separately by gender, and the results are presented in table 10.3 for men and table 10.4 for women.

As shown in table 10.3, we ran five models: Model 1 is for all male respondents; Models 2–5 are for men for each of the four income quartiles, respectively. First, the results of Model 1 indicated that the probability of

TABLE 10.3. Coefficients of Discrete-Time Survival Analysis for Entry into Marriage among Men

		Men	First quartile	Second quartile	Third quartile	Fourth quartile
		Model 1	Model 2	Model 3	Model 4	Model 5
Household income (Ref: first quartile)	Second quartile	0.208+ (0.117)				
	Third quartile	0.404** (0.124)				
	Fourth quartile	0.417** (0.126)				
Education level (Ref: high school or less)	Junior college	0.322** (0.104)	0.563* (0.252)	0.182 (0204)	0.227 (0.208)	0.322 (0.199)
	University	0.354*** (0.094)	0.653** (0.228)	0.371* (0.177)	0.117 (0.189)	0.343+ (0.184)
	Graduate school	0.622*** (0.135)	1.564*** (0.313)	0.67* (0.281)	0.432 (0.264)	0.37 (0.244)
Age		0.111*** (0.010)	0.095*** (0.022)	0.104*** (0.022)	0.105*** (0.021)	0.134*** (0.02)
Age squared		−0.021*** (0.002)	−0.02*** (0.004)	−0.025*** (0.003)	−0.019*** (0.003)	−0.023*** (0.004)
Unemployed (Ref: employed)		−3.363*** (0.761)	−2.402 (1.492)	−6.231** (2.025)	−3.758* (1.876)	−3.627** (1.358)
Enrolled in school		−0.445* (0.206)	−1.01* (0.547)	0.167 (0.34)	−0.961+ (0.513)	−0.532 (0.384)
Religious affiliation		−.171* (0.072)	0.291 (0.194)	0.095 (0.147)	0.25+ (0.146)	0.115 (0.126)
Grew in urban areas		0.049 (0.09)	−0.059 (0.219)	0.133 (0.173)	−0.021 (0.193)	0.099 (0.166)
Living in urban areas		−0.373*** (0.089)	−0.337 (0.215)	−0.475** (0.177)	−0.366* (0.186)	−0.298+ (0.159)
Father's education (Ref: middle school or less)	High school	−0.052 (0.08)	−0.357+ (0.209)	0.081 (0.163)	−0.23 (0.169)	0.058 (0.136)
	More than Junior college	−0.175 (0.111)	−0.325 (0.328)	0.235 (0.226)	0.156 (0.211)	−0.507** (0.185)
Cohort (birth after '70 ('73))		−0.361*** (0.095)	0.2 (0.234)	−0.45** (0.172)	−0.472* (0.19)	−0.705** (0.211)
Full-time job		0.156 (0.131)	0.403 (0.359)	0.078 (0.226)	0.298 (0.286)	0.01 (0.234)
Log(monthly income)		0.547*** (0.106)	0.395+ (0.219)	1.003*** (0.28)	0.566* (0.252)	0.568** (0.182)
Constant		−2.142*** (0.308)	−3.067*** (0.605)	−1.023*** (0.739)	−1.381*** (0.695)	−1.22*** (0.559)
N		2,063	393	550	443	677

+ $p < 0.1$; * $p < 0.05$; ** $p < 0.01$, *** $p < 0.001$; standard errors are in parentheses.

TABLE 10.4. Coefficients of Discrete-Time Survival Analysis for Entry into Marriage among Women

		Women	First quartile	Second quartile	Third quartile	Fourth quartile
		Model 1	Model 2	Model 3	Model 4	Model 5
Household income (Ref: first quartile)	Second quartile	0.054 (0.104)				
	Third quartile	0.105 (0.111)				
	Fourth quartile	0.141 (0.106)				
Education level (Ref: high school or less)	Junior college	0.002 (0.095)	−0.069 (0.199)	−0.054 (0.178)	−0.164 (0.214)	0.366+ (0.208)
	University	−0.071 (0.089)	0.018 (0.195)	−0.118 (0.169)	−0.054 (0.2)	0.07 (0.195)
	Graduate school	0.026 (0.10)	−0.344 (0.465)	−0.305 (0.388)	−0.121 (0.354)	0.274 (0.251)
Age		0.135*** (0.012)	0.071*** (0.023)	0.156*** (0.021)	0.125*** (0.024)	0.193*** (0.028)
Age squared		−0.028*** (0.002)	−0.017*** (0.003)	−0.037 (0.005)***	−0.027*** (0.005)	−0.036*** (0.005)
Unemployed (Ref: employed)		−2.789*** (0.72)	−4.534 (2.461)	−2.535+ (1.386)	−2.44 (1.482)	−3.669* (1.458)
Enrolled in school		−0.279 (0.192)	−1.081 (0.55)	−0.304 (0.416)	−0.462 (0.456)	0.22 (0.265)
Religious affiliation		0.020 (0.069)	0.035 (0.158)	0.057 (0.137)	−0.075 (0.156)	0.052 (0.123)
Grew in urban areas		−0.27** (0.091)	−0.416* (0.192)	−0.204 (0.18)	−0.241 (0.208)	−0.242 (0.18)
Living in urban areas		−0.007 (0.093)	−0.11 (0.188)	−0.037 (0.179)	−0.144 (0.207)	0.168 (0.184)
Father's education (Ref: middle school or less)	High school	−0.283*** (0.077)	−0.557** (0.184)	−0.349* (0.153)	−0.098 (0.174)	−0.15 (0.143)
	More than junior college	−0.467*** (0.107)	−0.848** (0.319)	−0.56* (0.235)	0.044 (0.243)	−0.499** (0.176)
Cohort (birth after '70 ('73))		−0.306*** (0.086)	−0.688*** (0.178)	−0.082 (0.165)	−0.357+ (0.189)	−0.061 (0.196)
Full-time job		0.068 (0.143)	−0.959** (0.32)	0.357 (0.298)	0.219 (0.311)	0.336 (0.264)
Log(monthly income)		0.429*** (0.103)	0.79* (0.374)	0.396+ (0.203)	0.375+ (0.205)	0.485* (0.202)
Constant		−1.245*** 0.294	−0.052*** (0.892)	−1.398*** (0.548)	−1.251*** (0.594)	−1.496*** (0.612)
N		1,737	343	448	340	606

+ $p < 0.1$; * $p < 0.05$; ** $p < 0.01$; *** $p < 0.001$; standard errors are in parentheses.

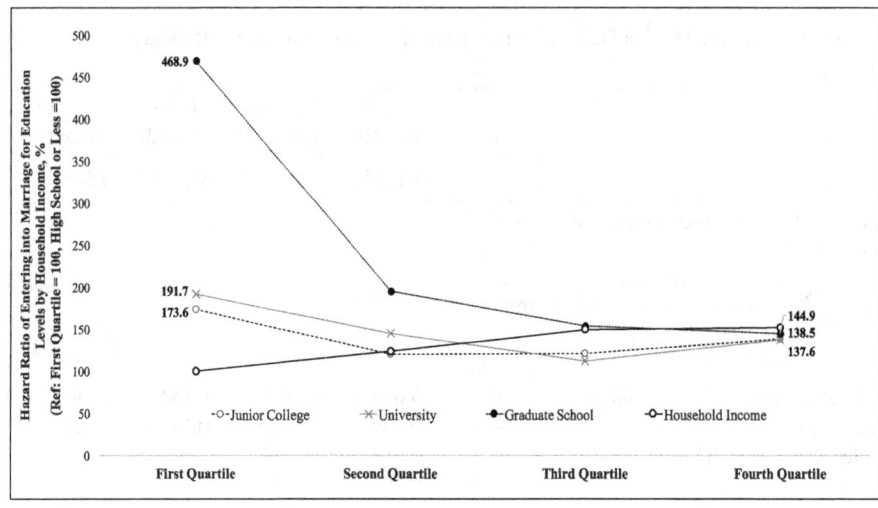

Fig. 10.3. Discrete-time survival analysis (clog-log) of transition to marriage among men stratified by parent's household income

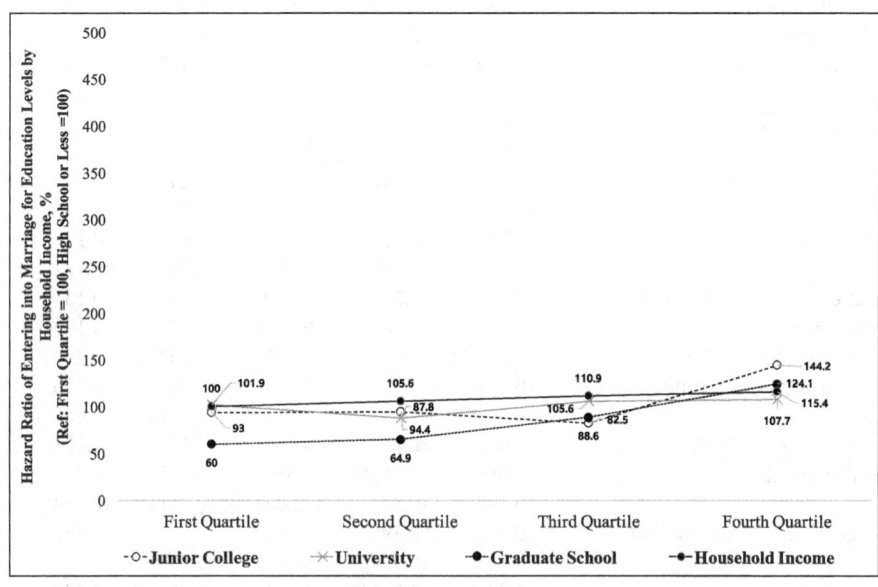

Fig. 10.4. Discrete-time survival analysis (clog-log) of transition to marriage among women stratified by parent's household income

getting married increased as the level of parent's household income and educational attainment increased among men even after controlling for other covariates, such as family background (i.e., father's education), individual's income, as well as sociodemographic characteristics. While these findings were expected, our results of Models 2–5 also showed that the association between education and the chance of getting married varied by parent's household income. For example, among men in the first quartile of parent's household income, those with junior college were 76 percent more likely to get married (i.e., 1.76 relative risk ratio = EXP [.56]) compared to those with high school education or lower, and the relative risk ratios were even higher with higher levels of education (i.e., "college graduate" and "graduate school graduate"). In fact, the probability of getting married among those with a graduate degree was almost five times higher than for those who were high school educated or lower (i.e., 4.78 relative risk ratio = EXP [1.56]).

While this pattern was also found among those in the second quartile of parent's household income, the education gradient in the probability of getting married appeared less. Those with a four-year college education and a graduate degree were 45 percent (i.e., 1.45 relative risk ratio = EXP [.37]) and 95 percent (i.e., 1.95 relative risk ratio = EXP [.67]) more likely to get married compared to those who were high school educated or lower, respectively, and those with junior college did not seem different from those with a high school education or lower in a statistically meaningful way. Coefficients of individual's educational attainment categories were not significant among those in the third and fourth quartiles, indicating that when parent's household income is high, at least in the top 50 percent, individual's education was not associated with entry into marriage.

Interestingly, the results for women were different from those for men. According to table 10.4, none of the coefficients of the parent's household income variable in Model 1 and the education variables in Models 1–5 were statistically significant with other controls accounted for—with an exception of the coefficient of "junior college" in Model 5, which was only marginally significant. These results indicate that unlike for men, for women, education was not significantly associated with entry into marriage, and this association did not vary by parent's household income—the difference in probabilities of getting married among women with a graduate degree across different levels of household income appeared significant in the Kaplan-Meier survival analysis but was no longer statistically significant when the other variables were controlled.

These gendered patterns are also depicted in figures 10.3 and 10.4.

Again, among men, the higher educated ones showed the higher probability of getting married even after controlling for other covariates, and this pattern was more salient in the lower quartiles of parent's household income. Among women, however, education was not associated with entry into marriage when parent's household income as well as other controls were taken into account. These results were consistent with the results of our Kaplan-Meier survival analysis, indicating that the influence of educational attainment on entry into marriage by parent's household income was not much explained by other covariates included in the discrete-time survival analysis models.

Although it is not our primary focus of the current study, there are some interesting gender differences in how other variables are related to marriage. According to the results in table 10.3, father's education did not seem to have a significant influence on the probability of getting married for men, although parent's household income appeared critical—the higher the levels of parent's income, the higher the probabilities of the son's marriage. However, for women, father's education was negatively associated with the daughter's marriage—the higher the levels of father's education, the lower the probabilities of the daughter's entry into marriage. And this negative influence seemed greater for women whose parents had income in the first quartile. Moreover, parent's household income was not associated with entry into marriage, and the (insignificant) association between education and marriage for women did not vary by parent's household income level either.

The finding that women whose fathers had a higher level of education were more likely to marry later or stay unmarried might reflect the father's attitudes toward gender egalitarianism. Fathers (and also mothers) with a higher education might encourage their daughters to be more independent while pursuing education and a career (Oh and Lim 2016). Therefore, women with highly educated fathers were more likely to hold nontraditional attitudes on marriage and the timing of marriage compared to women with lower educated father (Thornton and Freedman 1979; Trent and South 1992).

Conclusions and Discussion

This study examined how an individual's education and parental socioeconomic status were associated with adult children's entry into marriage, using a national sample of adults who were within the prime ages for transition to marriage (i.e., ages 19–41) in Korea. Our key findings include the following: (1) As parent's household income increases, the probability of getting married increases for men but not for women. (2) For men, an individual's educational attainment is also positively associated with the entry into marriage, but this association seems stronger among those whose parent's household income is in the first and second quartiles (i.e., lower levels of income). (3) For women, different from the results of men, neither parent's household income nor individual's educational attainment is associated with the probability of getting married. (4) Also different from men, father's educational attainment is negatively associated with the probability of getting married for women, and this association seems stronger among those whose father's income is in the lower quartiles.

The first finding suggested that parent's economic resources such as household income greatly affect marriage for men. As mentioned earlier, men are generally expected to be responsible for securing a place to live for the newlywed couple upon marriage in Korea. Although renting a place, rather than purchasing one, is an option, it is not very common to rent a place with a monthly payment contract in Korea, partly due to its high cost, requiring a fairly high proportion of income to spend for rent. Instead, people often lease a living place with a good amount of money up front, usually around 40–80 percent of the property value depending on the location and the overall conditions of the place, and this payment in a lump sum typically is returned to the renters when the lease is up. Young men with limited work experience do not usually have enough financial resources (or a good credit score to take out a mortgage loan) to either buy or rent a house without any help from their parents, and thus parent's financial resources could be an important factor to predict the probability of getting married for men in Korea.

Our second finding about the positive association of education with the likelihood of getting married among men also indicated that economic potentials, which are often predicted by educational attainment, are important especially for marriage for men in Korea. Given that educational attainment is probably the strongest aspect of income potential for young adults, it is reasonable to see the significant association of education with the probability of getting married for men, especially when their parents have lower levels of household income. From this perspective, it is also reasonable to see that educational attainment for men is not critical among those with a father who has a higher level of income. That is, even if an individual's education (i.e., income potential) may not be high enough to have promising income potentials, men with affluent parents may still be considered "marriageable" or somewhat "attractive" in the marriage market in Korea.

As for women, however, we did not find the same patterns. For example, parent's household income did not appear to significantly influence the probability of getting married for women. As described above, men are expected to provide housing upon marriage in Korea. While men are responsible for the house, women are expected to fill the house with furniture, appliances, and other necessities to live in the house. Although purchasing a number of items necessary to live in a house can also cost a considerable amount of money, it is not nearly as much as the housing cost. Women may have enough money saved from a few years of employment to cover the expenses without having to rely on their parents' income.

In addition, unlike the findings of the literature based on Western societies, where women with higher levels of education are more likely to get married (Blossfeld and Huinink 1991; Brancher and Santow 1998; Goldstein and Kenney 2001; Sweeney 2002; Thornton, Axinn, and Teachman 1995), it is interesting that educational attainment did not appear to be associated with the probability of entry into marriage for women in Korea. In general, higher levels of education increase the likelihood of getting married, as the highly educated ones tend to be more attractive in the marriage market because of reasons such as greater financial resources, better communication skills, and higher health status. However, this did not seem to be the case in Korea. It may be that women do not gain much return on education in the marriage market partly due to lower levels of gender egalitarianism in Korea. Compared to other industrialized countries, women may be still strongly expected to prioritize family over work responsibilities, and the utilization of family-friendly policies for work-family balance among women with young children and older parents or relatives may also be low in Korea due to a lack of the cultural acceptance of taking advantage of family policies. In fact, in Korea, despite high levels of educational attainment, women's labor force participation is much lower among those in their 30s and 40s, the life stages where the double burden from family and work responsibilities tends to be greater compared to other life stages (Statistics Korea 2014). Partly due to these reasons, education was not a strong predictor for entry into marriage among women.

Considering the gendered role expectations toward marriage and family and the lower levels of gender equity at workplaces in Korea, it is not surprising that women with highly educated fathers tend to delay marriage or stay unmarried. Highly educated fathers (and mothers) may be equally likely to encourage both daughter and son to complete a higher education and pursue a career instead of getting married, given the higher levels of work-family incomparability in Korea compared to lower educated fathers who may prioritize their son's education over their daughter's (Chang 2004; Lee 1998). As a result, women who grew up with highly educated parents are more likely to develop nontraditional ideologies about marriage (Thornton and Freedman 1979; Trent and South 1992) and thus to make career-oriented choices rather than forming a family at younger ages.

It is not clear what may explain the finding that this negative association between father's education and woman's probability of getting married is stronger among those with lower levels of father's income. While speculating, it may be that educated fathers whose income is not high are more likely to be interested in personal growth and career development for their daughters. It is also possible that women with highly educated fathers whose income is not high are somewhat more encouraged to make career-oriented choices instead of getting married. Given that resources from parents to help them balance work and family may be limited, they may feel that combining work and family is not feasible.

There are several limitations in this study. First, we used the term "unmarried" to define those who have not been married at the baseline instead of "never married"—a more common term in the literature when selecting respondents based on marital status. We were unable to distinguish cohabiting individuals from the never married ones because there is no information on cohabiting status in the data set. Thus, we admit there is a possibility that we might have included some respondents who were cohabiting in our sample of unmarried ones and treated them as the same as the never married respondents to estimate the probability of getting married. We are aware that cohabiting individuals who are not getting married are not the same as the never married ones in terms of the transition to marriage. However, we would argue that our findings in this study are not likely to be altered in any significant ways, given that cohabitation, while increasing, is still uncommon in Korea.

Another limitation is that we used household income and father's education to measure parent's socioeconomic status. We were unable to separate children's income from the household income in the KLIPS due to the data limitation. In addition, we did not include information on mother's education because while the KLIPS collected father's information from wave 1 through all 18 waves, mother's information on education has only been collected from wave 4. However, these limitations are not likely to alter our findings in significant ways, and we believe that household income and father's education served as valid proxies for parent's socioeconomic status. The majority of parents were of working age, and unmarried young adults are not expected to substantially support their parents financially in Korea. Also, although mothers are more likely to be the primary care provider for children in Korea and thus their influence on children's marriage would be critical in various ways, mothers also tend to have lower levels of educational attainment compared to fathers in general. Combined with limited opportunities for women in the labor market, especially for the older women of the parental generation in our data set, we decided to use father's information only for the analysis.

Despite the above limitations, this study provides insights for a better understanding about the current marriage pattern in Korea among young adults by offering the findings about the gendered association between parent's resources and marriage probability. Based on our study, future research should look further into the associations between socioeconomic status and family behaviors, such as marital quality, marriage duration, transition to parenthood, divorce and remarriage, and division of labor at home. Results of this line of research would shed light on important issues that Korea has currently faced, including the lowest level of total fertility rate in the world.

NOTES

An earlier version of this chapter was presented at the Korean Families in Economic and Demographic Transitions: Parenting, Children's Education, and Social Mobility conference in Ann Arbor, Michigan, on November 11–12, 2016, and at the Annual Meeting of the American Sociological Association in Philadelphia, Pennsylvania, on August 13, 2018. The authors greatly appreciate Yean-Ju Lee, Hyunjoon Park, and James Raymo, as well as the two anonymous reviewers, for their helpful comments on earlier drafts of this chapter. Direct correspondence to Jihye Oh.

1. The share of births to unmarried mothers has been lower than 2 percent in Korea for the past three decades. In other words, fewer than 2 births out of 100 births were to unmarried women (Statistics Korea 2016a).

2. The number of new marriages has declined by 0.9 percent from the previous year (2015) to 300,280 cases, and the number of new marriages per 1,000 people was 5.9 in 2015. These statistics indicate the lowest level of new marriages in the modern history in Korea (Statistics Korea 2015).

3. In 1998, 73.5 percent of the respondents answered either that people should get married or that it would be better to get married. However, almost two decades later, this percentage has dropped to 52.3 percent, implying that only about half of adults in South Korea see marriage as necessary in 2016 (Statistics Korea 2016b).

4. The lower the economic status of parents, the more respondents feel the economic burden. In the case of those economically disadvantaged, respondents seem more concerned about married life and extramarital affairs, 76.7 percent and 83.9 percent, re-

spectively, compared to those in the middle or upper class (Hankyoreh Economy and Society Research Institute 2015).

5. According to a survey by marriage consulting company Duo Human Life Research Institute, the average cost of getting married in 2014 was $249,960 in Korea. The cost includes expenses for traveling for the honeymoon ($4,410), the wedding ceremony ($65,270), and housing ($180,280), twice that in the United States.

6. Using results from another survey data set by the US marriage consulting company The Knot of over 18,000 brides in the United States who married in 2015, the average cost of getting married in the United States in 2015 was $32,641. This amount is less than half the average amount that people in Korea spend for a wedding ceremony (i.e., $65,270).

7. This is based on results from a survey of 1,200 respondents who were either parents aged 55–69 or recently married men and women aged 25–39 within the last three years (Korean Women's Development Institute 2015).

8. The economic burden that respondents feel is heavier among those whose parents' economic status is lower (Hankyoreh Economy and Society Research Institute 2015).

9. It has been argued that dating companies tend to classify member profiles by their parents' occupations and educational attainments (http://www.hani.co.kr/arti/politics/politics_general/442323.html) (Kim 2010).

10. For the household income variable, we considered the respondent's monthly income, other household members' monthly income, as well as other sources of income, such as interest, real estate, social insurance, and stocks.

REFERENCES

Anderson, Lydia R. 2016. "First Marriage Rate in the U.S., 2014." *Family Profiles*, FP-16-18. Bowling Green, OH: National Center for Family and Marriage Research. https://www.bgsu.edu/content/dam/BGSU/college-of-arts-and-sciences/NCFMR/documents/FP/anderson-first-marriage-rate-2014-fp-16-18.pdf

Axinn, William G., and Arland Thornton. 1992. "The Influence of Parental Resources on the Timing of the Transition to Marriage." *Social Science Research* 21 (3): 261–85.

Becker, Gary. 1981. *A Treatise on the Family*. Cambridge, MA: Harvard University Press.

Blau, Peter M., and Otis D. Duncan. 1967. "The Process of Stratification." In *Social Stratification: Class, Race, and Gender in Sociological Perspective*, 4th ed., edited by David B. Grusky, 506–17. Boulder, CO: Westview Press.

Bloom, David E., and Neil G. Bennett. 1990. "Modeling American Marriage Patterns." *Journal of the American Statistical Association* 85 (412): 1009–17.

Blossfeld, Hans P., and Johannes Huinink. 1991. "Human Capital Investments or Norms of Role Transition? How Women's Schooling Affects the Process of Family Formation." *American Journal of Sociology* 97 (1): 143–68.

Brancher, Michael, and Gigi Santow. 1998. "Economic Independence and Union Formation in Sweden." *Population Studies* 52 (3): 275–94.

Brooks-Gunn, Jeanne, and Greg J. Duncan. 1997. "The Effects of Poverty on Children." *Future of Children* 7 (2): 55–71.

Carbone, June, and Naomi Cahn. 2014. *Marriage Market*. Oxford: Oxford University Press.
Chang Sang-su. 2004. "Hangnyŏk sŏngch'wi ŭi kyegŭppyŏl, sŏngbyŏl ch'ai" (Class and Gender Differentials in Educational Attainment in Korea). *Han'guk sahoehak (Korean Journal of Sociology)* 38 (1): 51–75 (in Korean).
Chang Un-yŏng. 2003. "Kyŏrhon sijang esŏ yŏsŏng ŭi kyohwan chawŏn e kwanhan yŏn'gu" (A Study on Exchange Resource of Women in Marriage Market). PhD diss., Chungang Taehakkyo (Chung-Ang University), Seoul, Korea (in Korean).
Cookingham, Mary E. 1984. "Combining Marriage, Motherhood, and Jobs before World War II: Women College Graduates, Classes of 1905–1935." *Journal of Family History* 9 (2): 178–95.
Cutright, Phillips. 1970. "Income and Family Events: Getting Married." *Journal of Marriage and the Family* 32 (4): 628–37.
Duo Research. 2015. *Kyŏrhon piyong silt'ae pogosŏ (Survey on Wedding Expenses)*. Seoul, Korea: Duo Human Life. https://www.duo.co.kr/html/meetguide/research_list_view.asp?idx=1414&page=4&ct=research_all (in Korean).
Goldscheider, Frances K., and Linda J. Waite. 1986. "Sex Differences in the Entry into Marriage." *American Journal of Sociology* 92 (1): 91–109.
Goldstein, Joshua R., and Catherine T. Kenney. 2001. "Marriage Delayed or Marriage Forgone? New Cohort Forecasts of First Marriage for US Women." *American Sociological Review* 66 (4): 506–19.
Hankyoreh Economy and Society Research Institute. 2015. *I ttang esŏ chŏngnyŏn ŭro sandanŭn kŏt (Living as Young Adults in Korea)*. Seoul, Korea: Hankyoreh Economy and Society Research Institute. http://heri.kr/149099 (in Korean).
Kim, Bo-Hwa, Jae Kyung Lee, and Hyunjoon Park. 2016. "Marriage, Independence and Adulthood among Unmarried Women in South Korea." *Asian Journal of Social Science* 44 (3): 338–62.
Kim So-yŏn. 2010. "Pumo tŭnggŭphwa pogŏn pokchibu hwangdang kyŏrhon sait'ŭ" (Grading System for Parents of Users at Government Supported Marriage Consulting Companies). *Han'gyŏre (Hankyoreh)*, October 5. http://www.hani.co.kr/arti/politics/politics_general/442323.html
The Knot. 2016. "Wedding Spend Reaches All-Time High as Couples Look to Make the Ultimate Personal Statement." http://ir.xogroupinc.com/investor-relations/press-releases/press-release-details/2016/Wedding-Spend-Reaches-All-Time-High-As-Couples-Look-To-Make-The-Ultimate-Personal-Statement-According-To-The-Knot-2015-Real-Weddings-Study/default.aspx
Korea Institute for Health and Social Affairs. 2012. "2012-yŏn chŏn'guk kyŏrhon mit ch'ulsan tonghyang chosa" (2012 National Marriage and Childbirth Trend Survey). https://www.kihasa.re.kr/common/filedown.do?seq=16531 (in Korean).
Korean Women's Development Institute. 2015. "A Study on Policy Measures for Improvement of High Cost Marriage Culture" https://www.google.co.kr/url?sa=t&rct=j&q=&esrc=s&source=web&cd=1&ved=2ahUKEwiX9e2ClZziAhVF5awKHY-uCTUQFjAAegQIAhAC&url=http%3A%2F%2Fwww.prism.go.kr%2Fhomepage%2FresearchCommon%2FdownloadResearchAttachFile.do%3Bjsessionid%3DC83794C264B6D61A7A51CC482CFD0411.node02%3Fwork_key%3D001%26file_type%3DCPR%26seq_no%3D001%26pdf_conv_yn%3DY%26research_id%3D1382000-201500026&usg=AOvVaw3cAwWVHaRWcVORXIxSzWUG (in Korean).

Lee, Mi-jeong. 1998. *Women's Education, Work, and Marriage in Korea: Women's Lives Under Institutional Conflicts*. Seoul, Korea: Seoul National University Press.

Lichter, Daniel T., Felicia B. LeClere, and Diane K. McLaughlin. 1991. "Local Marriage Markets and the Marital Behavior of Black and White Women." *American Journal of Sociology* 96: 843–67.

Oh, Jihye, and Jeong-jae Lim. 2016. "Han'guk mihon namnyŏ ŭi kyŏrhon sigi wa kyŏrhon kanŭngsŏng e kwanhan yŏn'gu" (The Timing and Possibility of Marriage among Single Men and Women in Korea). *Han'guk sahoehak* (*Korean Journal of Sociology*) 50 (5): 203–45 (in Korean).

Oppenheimer, Valerie K. 1988. "A Theory of Marriage Timing." *American Journal of Sociology* 94 (3): 563–91.

Oppenheimer, Valerie K. 1997. "Women's Employment and the Gain to Marriage: The Specialization and Trading Model." *Annual Review of Sociology* 23: 431–53.

Oppenheimer, Valerie K., and Vivian Lew. 1995. "American Marriage Formation in the 1980s: How Important Was Women's Economic Independence?" In *Gender and Family Change in Industrialized Countries*, edited by Karen Oppenheimer Mason and An-Magritt Jensen, 105–37. Oxford: Clarendon Press.

Park, Hyunjoon, and Kyung-Keun Kim. 2012. "Education Homogamy in Korea: 1966–2010." *Korean Journal of Sociology of Education* 22 (4): 113–39 (in Korean).

Park, Hyunjoon, and Jae Kyung Lee. 2017. "Growing Education Differentials in the Retreat from Marriage among Korean Men." *Social Science Research* 66: 187–200.

Park, Hyunjoon, Jae Kyung Lee, and Inkyung Jo. 2013. "Changing Relationships between Education and Marriage among Korean Women." *Korean Journal of Sociology* 47 (3): 51–76.

Raymo, James M., Hyunjoon Park, Yu Xie, and Wei Jun J. Yeung. 2015. "Marriage and Family in East Asia: Continuity and Change." *Annual Review of Sociology* 41: 471–92.

Sewell, William H., and Robert M. Hauser. 1975. *Education, Occupation and Earnings*. New York: Academic Press.

South, Scott J. 2001. "The Variable Effects of Family Background on the Timing of First Marriage: United States, 1969–1993." *Social Science Research* 30 (44): 606–26.

Statistics Korea. 2014. "2014 Economically Active Population Survey." http://kosis.kr/statisticsList/statisticsListIndex.do?menuId=M_01_01&vwcd=MT_ZTITLE&parmTabId=M_01_01&statId=1962002&themaId=B#

Statistics Korea. 2015. "2015 Population and Housing Census." http://kosis.kr/statHtml/statHtml.do?orgId=101&tblId=DT_1B8000F&vw_cd=MT_ZTITLE&list_id=A2_6&seqNo=&lang_mode=ko&language=kor&obj_var_id=&itm_id=&conn_path=MT_ZTITLE

Statistics Korea. 2016a. "Population Trends Survey." http://kosis.kr/statisticsList/statisticsListIndex.do?menuId=M_01_01&vwcd=MT_ZTITLE&parmTabId=M_01_01&statId=1962004&themaId=A#

Statistics Korea. 2016b. "Social Survey." http://kosis.kr/statisticsList/statisticsListIndex.do?menuId=M_01_01&vwcd=MT_ZTITLE&parmTabId=M_01_01&statId=1962004&themaId=A#SelectStatsBoxDiv

Sweeney, Megan M. 2002. "Two Decades of Family Change: The Shifting Economic Foundations of Marriage." *American Sociological Review* 67 (1): 132–47.

Thornton, Arland, William G. Axinn, and Jay D. Teachman. 1995. "The Influence of School Enrollment and Accumulation on Cohabitation and Marriage in Early Adulthood." *American Sociological Review* 60: 762–74.

Thornton, Arland, and Deborah Freedman. 1979. "Changes in the Sex Role Attitudes of Women, 1962–1977: Evidence from a Panel Study." *American Sociological Review* 44 (5): 831–42.

Torr, Berna. 2011. "The Changing Relationship between Education and Marriage in the United States, 1940–2000." *Journal of Family History* 36 (4): 483–503.

Trent, Katherine, and Scott J. South. 1992. "Sociodemographic Status, Parental Background, Childhood Family Structure, and Attitudes toward Family Formation." *Journal of Marriage and the Family* 54 (2): 427–39.

Woo, Haebong. 2009. "Kyoyuk i ch'ohon hyŏngsŏng e mich'inŭn yŏnghyang: kyŏrhon yŏn'gi hogŭn toksin?" (The Impact of Educational Attainment on First Marriage Formation: Marriage Delayed or Marriage Forgone?) *Han'guk in'guhak* (*Korean Journal of Population Studies*) 32 (1): 25–50 (in Korean).

Xie, Yu, James M. Raymo, Kimberly Goyette, and Arland Thornton. 2003. "Economic Potential and Entry into Marriage and Cohabitation." *Demography* 40 (2): 351–67.

Yeung, Jean W., Miriam R. Linver, and Jeanne Brooks-Gunn. 2002. "How Money Matters for Young Children's Development: Parental Investment and Family Processes." *Child Development* 73 (6): 1861–79.

Yi Sŭng-yun, Paek Sŭng-ho, Kim Mi-gyŏng, Kim Yun-yŏng. 2017. "Han'guk chŏngnyŏn nodong sijang ŭi puranjŏngsŏng punsŏk" (Analysis of Precariousness in Korean Youth Labor Market). *Pip'an sahoe chŏngch'aek* (*Journal of Critical Social Policy*) 54: 487–521 (in Korean).

Yoon, Jayoung. 2012. "Nodong sijang t'onghap kwa kyŏrhon ihaeng" (Labor Market Integration and Transition to Marriage). *Han'guk in'guhak* (*Korean Journal of Population Studies*) 35 (2): 159–84 (in Korean).

11

Integrating Men's Gender Roles and Fertility Attitudes into the Study of Low Fertility in South Korea

Soo-Yeon Yoon

Gender-role attitudes have changed over time. The proportion of Koreans who support an equal share of housework between couples increased from 30 percent in 2002 to 45 percent in 2012 (Han 2015). Moreover, the majority of young single men want to form a dual-earner family rather than a traditional male-breadwinner family. In 2015, the Ministry of Women and Family honored "Dads over Flowers," which comprised 20 fathers who actively participated in childcare in order to promote greater use of fathers' parental leave and greater involvement of fathers in childcare.[1] Despite the continued efforts of the media and the government to promote work-family balance and increase the use of fathers' parental leave, most working fathers do not take parental leave. According to the Ministry of Employment and Labor, the proportion of male workers taking childcare leave was approximately 8 percent of all workers on childcare leave in 2016.[2] In contrast, a substantial proportion of female workers, especially women aged 30 to 39, leave the labor force either voluntarily or involuntarily due to marriage, pregnancy, childbirth, and/or childcare needs. Over 40 percent of women leave the labor market within the six months around marriage. Moreover, nearly 45 percent of women leave the labor market within the six months around their first childbirth (Park 2016). As a consequence, Korea has displayed low fertility and relatively low female labor force participation despite increased levels of educational attainment since the early 2000s.

Existing literature offers two perspectives to explain low fertility regarding the role of gender equity. On the one hand, higher levels of gender equity have been a driving force to lower fertility in less-developed countries (McDonald 2000). Evidently, South Korea experienced rapid fertility decline across the 1926–70 birth cohorts because of educational expansion, especially among women (Yoo 2014), and the implementation of strong family-planning programs. This, in turn, increased gender equality in the labor market. On the other hand, in advanced countries in which women have already experienced the transition to low fertility, the inconsistency in the levels of gender equity in different social institutions leads to very low fertility (McDonald 2000). To be specific, persistent traditional gender-role expectations, especially regarding women's roles in the private sphere, are one of the main contributing factors to very low fertility in Korea (McDonald 2008; Park 2008). In this chapter, I focus on the relationship between attitudes toward the gender-specific roles within the family and fertility ideals in Korea, an advanced country with low fertility. Because of increasing economic insecurity since the 1997 Asian economic crisis, the need to form dual-earner families has increased. At the same time, women still take on the bulk of family responsibilities, and tension has been arising from the inconsistency in levels of egalitarianism in the public and private spheres (Goldscheider, Bernhardt, and Lappegård 2015; Raymo et al. 2015).

Recent theoretical discussion has highlighted the importance of egalitarian gender relations, especially providing support for women to combine family and work roles, in fertility reversals (Esping-Andersen and Billari 2015; Goldscheider, Bernhardt, and Lappegård 2015; McDonald 2000). With regard to egalitarian gender relations, previous studies on Korean low fertility have shed light on the ways in which women postpone and forego their childbearing desires in connection with their increasing educational attainment and labor force participation (Eun 2007; Suzuki 2008). In contrast, men's gender-role attitudes and childbearing ideals have not been thoroughly studied, although men too are making fertility decisions. As men's roles in the family have gained importance in both theory and policy, it is worth examining both men's and women's gender roles and their link to fertility to assess the issues of low fertility in Korea.

To fill in this gap, I examine gender-role attitudes and the relationship between those attitudes and fertility ideals,[3] further investigating whether they differ by gender. In this chapter, I focus on attitudes concerning gender roles within the family, including the male-breadwinner family model, the mother-child relationship, and childcare arrangements. Using data from the 2012 International Social Survey Programme (ISSP) on Family and Changing Gender Roles IV Module, as part of the 2012 Korean General Social Survey, findings of this chapter will contribute to extending existing literature by integrating men's perspectives into research on the relationship between gender-role attitudes and fertility. Understanding men's attitudes regarding gender roles should help scholars and policy makers understand Korean families.

Theoretical Background and Previous Findings

Gender Relations and Their Link to Fertility

Recent theories of family demography postulate that increasing egalitarianism in gender roles ultimately leads to strengthened families by increasing union formation, increasing fertility, and decreasing marital dissolution (Esping-Andersen and Billari 2015; Goldscheider, Bernhardt, and Lappegård 2015; McDonald 2000, 2013). Among the demographic changes that have been taking place, the trend toward increased fertility is most noticeable for its close relationship with egalitarian gender relations, starting in Western and Northern Europe.

Although egalitarian gender roles serve as a key component in explaining the recent fertility reversal in gender-equal societies, theoretical stances differ regarding mechanisms that link changing gender roles to low fertility. On the one hand, McDonald (2000) and Esping-Andersen and Billari (2015) emphasize the role of the state and institutional support in reducing the conflict between work and family for women. On the other hand, Goldscheider, Bernhardt, and Lappegård (2015) state that fertility reversals (recovering fertility close to a replacement level of a total fertility rate of 2) are more closely associated with the ongoing gender revolution, which has two stages: During the first stage, family-related outcomes are weakened because of considerable strain from work-family conflict as women increasingly participate in the labor force; in the second stage, however, families are strengthened by men's increased involvement in the family. Put another way, the second part of the gender revolution, with its increase in male roles in the family, is necessary to produce relatively high fertility (i.e., fertility reversals).

Studies concerning the levels of gender equity at the macro level tie continued very low fertility to a lack of national-level support for families with effective policy programs to reduce work-family conflict (e.g., Thévenon 2011). Limited state support for gender equality also corresponds to low levels of public awareness and policy enforcement addressing issues of gender equality, such as fathers' use of parental leave (Yoon 2017). In addition to providing limited state support, Korea creates a unique context for linking gender relations to fertility, because of its cultural emphasis on high educational aspirations and traditional notions of gender roles in the family (Yoon 2016). This cultural and institutional intersection may reflect the current status of the gender revolution in Korea.

The gender revolution framework helps understand the relationship between gender-role attitudes and fertility as people's attitudes generally reflect the structural constraints and opportunities (Goldscheider, Bernhardt, and Lappegård 2015). Previous comparative research investigating attitudes toward men's participation within the family suggests that a country's family policy influences and shapes couples' preferences about the distribution of paid work and unpaid work and parental leave arrangements (Edlund and Öun 2016). Despite the increasing theoretical and policy importance of egalitarian gender relations on family outcomes, we know little about the link between gender-role attitudes and fertility ideals among Koreans, especially concerning men's perspectives. Yoon (2016) suggests that married women holding egalitarian attitudes concerning the equal distribution of household labor were more likely to realize their fertility intentions than their traditional counterparts. However, we still know little about the relationship between men's gender-role attitudes and fertility. The gender revolution framework would be useful to investigate whether gender-role attitudes exert different association with fertility by gender, as they would reflect the current structural conditions for having children.

Measuring Gender-Role Attitudes

Scholars have conceptualized and operationalized gender-role attitudes in a variety of terms, including gender-role attitudes, gender-related attitudes, gender ideology, and attitudes toward gender equality (Davis and Greenstein 2009). These varying terms are operationalized to represent "individuals' levels of support for a division of paid work and family responsibilities" (Davis and Greenstein 2009: 88). Previous demographic studies of gender-role attitudes have focused mainly on attitudes regarding women's roles in the public spheres and their link to family outcomes (Philipov 2008; Westoff and Higgins 2009). However, studies of gender-role attitudes regarding men's involvement in the private sphere have been relatively rare.

Recent studies have added additional dimensions of gender-role attitudes, including attitudes toward men's participation in the family, and several of these studies document the positive effect of men's involvement in housework and childcare on fertility (Cooke 2004, 2009; Goldscheider, Bernhardt, and Brandén 2013; Hook 2006; Puur et al. 2008). Another recent study examining the relationship between gender-role attitudes and family transitions includes attitudes toward childcare arrangements as part of gender-role attitudes (Kaufman, Bernhardt, and Goldscheider 2017). It is important to differentiate gender-role attitudes focusing on women's roles in the public sphere from attitudes concerning men's roles in the private sphere, because these lead to different family outcomes, either positive or negative, with regard to fertility.

Research suggests that people in Korea have ambivalent attitudes toward women's roles in the public and private spheres. Whereas nearly 90 percent of adults in Korea show positive attitudes toward female labor-force participation, only half of them think that it is all right for women to work regardless of family transitions, including childbirth or having a young child (Han 2015). This finding suggests that Koreans might hold varying degrees of egalitarianism about women's roles in the public and private spheres. Guided by the previous literature on the link between gender-role attitudes and fertility, the current study pays special attention to gender-role attitudes concerning the intersection of work and family, including the family model, the mother-child relationship, and parental-leave arrangements.

Social and Demographic Correlates of Gender-Role Attitudes

Historically, both men and women have developed increasingly egalitarian gender attitudes over time. However, although attitudes about gender roles in different spheres have moved in the same direction, the pace of change toward gender egalitarianism differs by dimensions of gender equality and gender. Previous studies have suggested that gender-role attitudes are associated with sociodemographic characteristics.[4] Marriage is associated with less-egalitarian attitudes (Bolzendahl and Myers 2004). Similarly, parenthood is linked to support for more traditional attitudes (Davis 2007; Davis and Greenstein 2009; Fan and Marini 2000). Americans living in bigger cities report more egalitarian attitudes than those living in small cities or rural areas (Powers et al. 2003).

Several other studies have documented that men are less likely than women to hold egalitarian gender-role attitudes (Bolzendahl and Myers

2004; Cunningham 2005; Fan and Marini 2000; Thornton and Young-DeMarco 2001).[5] In addition, prior studies also suggest that the direction of the relationship between certain sociodemographic characteristics and gender-role attitudes varies by gender. Several studies have found that higher educational attainment is associated with more egalitarian attitudes among both men and women (Bolzendahl and Myers 2004; Brewster and Padavic 2000; Brooks and Bolzendahl 2004; Ciabattari 2001; Corrigall and Konrad 2007; Fan and Marini 2000). Employment status is associated with more egalitarian attitudes among women (Bolzendahl and Myers 2004; Corrigall and Konrad 2007; Cunningham 2005; Fan and Marini 2000). In contrast, only men who have experienced employment difficulties (e.g., blocked opportunities) displayed egalitarian attitudes (Coltrane 1997).

Prior studies examining the Korean case also suggest that several sociodemographic characteristics are associated with gender-role attitudes. Using data from the Korean Social Surveys, Han (2015) found that gender, age, educational attainment, and household income are associated with gender-role attitudes. Young people are more likely to agree with the statement that men and women should share housework equally. In general, men and the less educated are more likely to support the traditional gendered division of labor than their counterparts. Household income showed a U-shaped relationship: people with low and high household income are more likely to hold traditional gender attitudes.

Scholarly Debate on Fertility Ideals

Scholars have studied fertility from several viewpoints, with debates in the literature concerning issues of measurement. When it comes to measuring attitudes toward fertility, previous studies have used many concepts, such as fertility ideals and desired, intended, or expected fertility (Hin et al. 2011; Testa and Grilli 2006). Scholarly debates about the issues of measuring fertility ideals originate mostly from two phenomena: The ideal number hovers with little variation around two children; and changes in fertility ideals bear little relation to changes in actual fertility levels (Testa and Grilli 2006: 101). However, fertility ideals have gained fresh attention in recent literature, given that there is a persistent gap between fertility attitudes and actual fertility across low-fertility countries (Bongaarts 2001; Harknett and Hartnett 2014; Testa and Grilli 2006). Thus, fertility ideals can shed light on ideas about family formation as well as future fertility levels in post-transitional fertility (Bongaarts 2001; Hin et al. 2011; Testa and Grilli 2006). In addition, fertility ideals are a useful measurement for understanding reproductive cultures in societies as well as for identifying variations across different subgroups within a society (Hin et al. 2011). For instance, European countries that have indicated very low fertility since the 1970s, such as Germany and Austria, now indicate the ideal number of children to be fewer than two (Goldstein, Lutz, and Testa 2003; Harknett and Hartnett 2014; Testa and Grilli 2006).

The gap between fertility ideals and actual fertility has also been documented in Korea. Although Korea has shown one of the world's lowest fertility rates since the early 2000s, the average ideal number of children consistently remains two or more children. About 68 percent of Koreans aged 20–29 and 67 percent of those aged 30–39 reported in 2015 that their ideal number of children was two (Chang et al. 2015). Given that fertility ideals can also change depending on the current context of childbearing, examination of fertility ideals and their correlates can contribute to our understanding of within-country heterogeneity in fertility ideals.

Research Questions

Drawing on the reviewed theoretical and empirical literature so far, this chapter addresses three specific research questions: (1) What proportion of respondents hold egalitarian gender-role attitudes, and do the proportions vary by gender? (2) What is the relationship between gender-role attitudes and fertility ideals? (3) Do the relationships between gender-role attitudes and fertility ideals differ by gender? The answers to these questions can provide insight on attitudes toward fertility and gender roles and their variations by gender.

Data and Methods

The 2012 International Social Survey Programme Survey

Data for this study come from the 2012 International Social Survey Programme on Family and Changing Gender Roles IV, a topical module survey included in the 2012 Korean General Social Survey (KGSS). The KGSS is a repeated cross-sectional nationally representative survey, drawn by probability sampling procedures. Data were collected by the Survey Research Center at Sungkyunkwan University via face-to-face interviews from June to August 2012. The target population of the KGSS is the adult population aged 18 or over who live in households. The response rate of this survey was approximately 60 percent, resulting in a total of 1,396 respondents. Questionnaires asking about gender-role attitudes and the ideal number of children come from the topical module of the ISSP, and the background information is from the KGSS.

Because this study concentrates on young adults and middle-aged people who are still in their reproductive years, the analytic sample is restricted to respondents aged 18 to 49 ($N = 672$). The sample for the current study consists of all respondents aged 18 to 49 who answered all questions about gender-role attitudes, the ideal number of children, and other control variables. Due to missing values, 28 males and 16 females were eliminated from the analysis. The final sample size includes 288 males and 340 females. By including both male and female respondents in the analysis, I could examine gender differences in gender-role attitudes and their link to fertility ideals. The data used throughout the analyses were weighted to adjust sampling probability.

Measure of Fertility Ideals

The dependent variable was the ideal number of children. I used the following question: "All in all, what do you think is the ideal number of children for a family to have?" The original responses were as high as 12 children, but with a very low frequency of responses above 4 children. The distribution of fertility ideals is presented in table 11.1. In general, respondents reported relatively high fertility ideals. Approximately half of the respondents reported that their ideal number of children was 2, followed by 3, children. The proportion of people who reported no children as their ideal number was minimal for both genders. The average ideal number of

TABLE 11.1. Frequency and Weighted Percent of Ideal Number of Children for Koreans Aged 15–49, 2012 KGSS

Ideal number of children (fertility ideals)	All		Men		Women	
No children	8	(1.25)	3	(0.97)	5	(1.54)
One child	33	(4.8)	14	(4.35)	19	(5.25)
Two children	356	(53.52)	161	(51.39)	195	(55.72)
Three children	207	(30.57)	109	(34.08)	98	(26.94)
Four or more children	68	(9.86)	29	(9.2)	39	(10.54)
Total	672	(100)	316	(100)	356	(100)

Source: 2012 ISSP, KGSS.

children, as determined by the respondents in the sample, was 2.48 children (S.E. = .04). Although men reported a slightly higher ideal number of children (mean = 2.54), their responses were not statistically different from those of women (mean = 2.44). Ideals of 3 or more children indicate a preference for large families, so distinguishing between the higher would not have significant meaning. Therefore, I combined the ideals of 3 or more children into a single category in the regression analysis below.

Measures of Gender-Role Attitudes

In measuring respondents' gender-role attitudes, first I looked at the items that were designed to capture both men's and women's gender-role expectations. Of the six categories of gender-role attitudes that Davis and Greenstein (2009) classified, the 2012 ISSP included three: primacy of the breadwinner role, working women and relationship quality, and motherhood and the feminine self. One item is available to measure each category in the data set. Many previous studies constructed a composite measure by combining a set of items measuring different aspects of gender roles (Greenstein 2009; Kim and Ryu 2016; Miettinen, Basten, and Rotkirch 2011). However, I chose to use different measures for differently related dimensions instead of creating a single composite measure, because people may be more supportive of gender egalitarianism in the specific realms of family roles than in other dimensions (Kaufman, Bernhardt, and Goldscheider 2017).[6] For instance, people in Korea may show different levels of support for gender equality concerning women's labor force participation than for men's use of childcare leave. The statements I used to measure gender-role attitudes were as follows: (1) "A man's job is to earn money; a woman's job is to look after the home and family" (primacy of breadwinner role). (2) "A preschool child is likely to suffer if his or her mother works" (working women and relationship quality). (3) "Being a housewife is just as fulfilling as working for pay" (wife/motherhood and the feminine self). The responses were collected on a 5-point Likert scale, ranging from 1 (strongly agree) to 5 (strongly disagree). The response categories were entered so that higher responses indicated more egalitarian (i.e., less separation of spheres) gender-role attitudes.

I also measured attitudes toward parental leave arrangements since my theoretical focus is the integration of male perspectives, including men's attitudes toward their involvement in the private sphere. The ISSP module includes one question about a couple's parental leave arrangement: "Consider a couple who both work full-time and now have a newborn child. If both are in a similar work situation and are eligible for paid leave, how should this paid leave period be divided between the mother and the father?" Response choices were "Mother entire, father none"; "Mother most, father some"; "Mother and father each receive half"; "Father most, mother some"; and "Father all, mother none." No response chose the last response option, and only one chose the fourth option. Because of the limited number of responses, these last two response options were eliminated from the analysis. The finalized variable was a categorical variable with three options; and I used "Mother most, father some" as a reference category.

Control Variables

Taking into account the findings from previous studies, I controlled for ideational factors potentially associated with childbearing. As family-related attitudes are associated with family outcomes such as childbearing (Kim and Cheung 2015), I also controlled for an ideational factor measuring attitude toward children. I used the following item—"Having children interferes too much with the freedom of parents"—with response categories of "strongly agree," "agree," "neither agree nor disagree," "disagree," and "strongly disagree." For analytic purposes the responses were coded as 1 = strongly agree through 5 = strongly disagree; that is, higher scores indicated more positive attitudes toward children.

I included several sociodemographic control variables in the analysis. Respondents' age, employment status (not working versus working), paid work hours, educational attainment (high school degree or below, some college, bachelor's degree or above), parental status (parent versus nonparent), residence in metropolitan areas (yes or no), income (logged), and squared income were controlled in the full models.

Methods

By operationalizing the dependent variable as an ordered categorical variable, I estimated the generalized ordered logit regression models, separately by gender. The estimated model is interested in examining how one's gender-role attitudes are associated with his or her ideal number of children, controlling for family-related ideational factors and some sociodemographic variables. The generalized ordered logit model is similar to the ordered logit model in that both of them are used for ordered categorical outcome variables. However, as shown in table 11.1, the original item of the ideal number of children shows a highly skewed distribution, which violates the assumptions of the ordered logit model. The generalized ordered logit model does not assume normal distribution, and thus estimates in this study using the generalized ordered logit model are not expected to be biased.[7] Since the effect of gender-role attitudes differs greatly across the cumulative logits, the coefficients of explanatory variables must be interpreted separately at each comparison (Williams 2016). The model reports how each predictor (an aspect of gender-role attitudes) influences the odds of being in one category (i.e., $Y > 1$) compared to the other category ($Y \leq 1$) and being in the category of $Y > 2$ compared to being in the category of $Y \leq 2$.

Results

Gender-Role Attitudes among Koreans: Traditional or Egalitarian?

Table 11.2 presents the means of three measures of gender-role attitudes for men and women aged 18–49 years. A higher score indicates more egalitarian gender-role attitudes. The data reveal noticeable differences between measures of gender-role attitudes included in the analysis. Korean men and women both hold egalitarian views in terms of the breadwinner family model, with averages of 3.32 and 3.62, respectively. Not surprisingly, women hold more egalitarian attitudes than do men ($p < .01$). However, the other two measures of gender-role attitudes appear to be more traditional than egalitarian. With regard to the dimension of working women and relationship quality, results show that Korean adults hold traditional attitudes, with means of 2.42 for men and 2.31 for women. On the dimen-

TABLE 11.2. Means of Gender Role Attitudes by Gender, Korean Men and Women Aged 49 or Younger, 2012 KGSS

	Men		Women	
	Mean	SD	Mean	SD
A man's job is to earn money; a woman's job is to look after the home and family	3.32	.07	3.62	.06**
A preschool child is likely to suffer if his or her mother works	2.42	.06	2.31	.06
Being a housewife is just as fulfilling as working for pay	1.90	.05	1.80	.05

** Significant at .01 level according to a *t*-test.

sion of wife/motherhood and the feminine self, both men and women show solid traditional attitudes.

To effectively present the varying patterns of gender-role attitudes for three dimensions, I categorized gender-role attitudes into three categories: traditional, intermediate, and egalitarian.[8] Table 11.2 presents the distribution of men and women according to their gender-role attitudes for each respective measure. Results reveal that Korean adults hold varying opinions regarding gender-role attitudes. While slightly more than half of the women and men disagreed with the primacy of breadwinner role in the family, the majority of women and men held traditional gender-role attitudes toward mothers' work with preschool children. Approximately 61 percent of men and 67 percent of women agreed or strongly agreed that a preschool child is likely to suffer if his or her mother works. Regarding ideas about being a housewife and motherhood, 77 percent of men and 80 percent of women agreed that being a housewife was just as fulfilling as working for pay.

These descriptive results indicate that both Korean men and women hold ambivalent attitudes toward gender roles. The pattern is not straightforward. What is interesting is that the majority of men and women, with an even higher proportion of women than men, still hold traditional gender-role attitudes toward working mothers and their potential negative influence on their children. Likewise, nearly 80 percent of men and women held traditional gender-role attitudes regarding being a housewife. This percentage is exceptionally high when compared to responses from other countries included in the 2012 ISSP.

TABLE 11.3. Distribution (%) of Gender Role Attitudes by Gender, Korean Men and Women Aged 49 or Younger, 2012 KGSS

	A man's job is to earn money; a woman's job is to look after the home and family	A preschool child is likely to suffer if his or her mother works	Being a housewife is just as fulfilling as working for pay
Men			
Traditional	26.45	60.97	77.07
Intermediate	23	20.19	16.7
Egalitarian	50.55	18.84	6.23
Women			
Traditional	20.54	67.5	80
Intermediate	20.38	16.49	13.78
Egalitarian	59.08	16.01	6.22

Note: Weighted percent.

For comparative purposes, I investigated five other countries included in the 2012 ISSP survey. I included two Northern European welfare state countries (Finland and Sweden), the United States, and two East Asian countries (China and Japan). A social welfare system that includes family policies is well established in both Finland and Sweden, countries that have relatively high fertility. The United States is unique among advanced countries in having relatively higher fertility with limited institutional support. Although a substantial proportion of US women underachieve their fertility intentions, the United States still has higher fertility than other advanced countries. Studies suggest that it is because of an overachievement of fertility intentions of a substantial proportion of individuals, the relatively younger age at first birth, and higher unwanted fertility (Morgan and Rackin 2010). Japan has displayed very low fertility since the mid-1970s and the so-called marriage package, which expects women to fulfill numerous caregiving roles within the institution of marriage (Bumpass et al. 2009). Although East Asian countries share a Confucian culture, China is different from other East Asian countries with respect to its stage of economic development and politico-institutional contexts, which provides higher gender equality in paid work (Qian and Sayer 2016). I examined how patterns of egalitarian gender-role attitudes appear in these five countries by comparing the percentage of disagreement or strong disagreement with each measure of gender-role attitudes. I confined the sample to people aged 49 or younger, just as I did in my sample from Korea. Figure 11.1 consists of three graphs for each respective measure of gender-role attitudes.

The figure on the left side shows that people in five out of the six countries (with China being the exception) hold egalitarian attitudes toward gendered division of labor. However, there are considerable differences across countries. Finnish and Swedish respondents show the most egalitarian attitudes, followed by their US counterparts. Slightly more than half of the Korean respondents show egalitarian attitudes toward gendered division of labor. The middle figure shows a greater difference in gender-role attitudes regarding working mothers and their potential negative influence on their children. As in the first figure, Finnish and Swedish respondents show strongly egalitarian gender-role attitudes, indicating that more than 70 percent of their respondents do not think working mothers have a negative influence on their preschool children. Even among the three East Asian countries, there are substantial differences. It appears that Koreans hold more traditional attitudes than Japanese or Chinese respondents in this area. Less than 20 percent of Korean respondents hold egali-

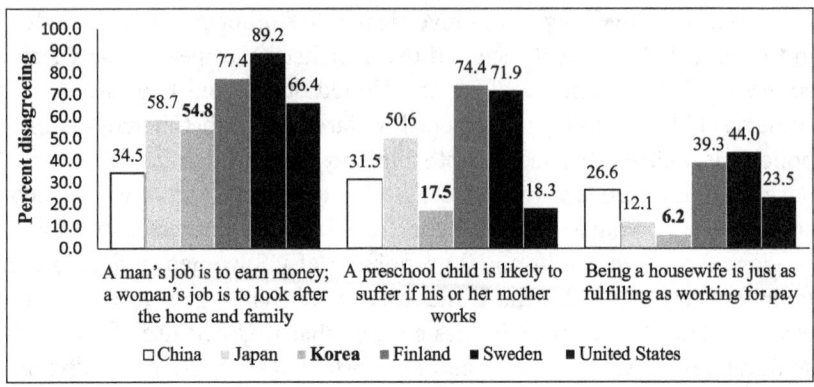

Fig. 11.1. Percent disagreeing or strongly disagreeing with each measure of gender-role attitudes, men and women aged 49 or younger, selected countries, 2012 ISSP

tarian attitudes regarding working mothers and their potential negative influence on their children. Put differently, the majority of Koreans support mothers taking intensive roles in caring for their young children. The last figure demonstrates that in each country, the percentage of respondents holding egalitarian attitudes about feminine gender roles is substantially lower than the percentage of egalitarian views for the previous two dimensions. Most respondents in all six countries show more traditional attitudes than egalitarian attitudes. Among these, Koreans show the most traditional attitudes, with only 6 percent showing egalitarian attitudes.

These findings suggest that people hold varying attitudes by dimension of family roles. While more than half of adults in Korea disagree with the traditional notion of gendered division of labor, an even greater percentage of Koreans support the idea that mothers should take an intensive role in the care of their young children or that women should take care of their families. However, these ambivalent gender-role attitudes are observed in varying degrees in all six countries studied.

The last dimension of gender-role attitudes that I examined in this chapter is work-family balance. Table 11.4 demonstrates that attitudes toward parental leave arrangement differ by gender ($p < .10$). As expected, the majority of women and men think that the ideal parental leave arrangement is "Mother most, father some." However, a larger proportion of women than men responded that "Mother and father each receive half" is the ideal option. Nearly 40 percent of female respondents chose "Mother and father each receive half" as the best arrangement, while 32 percent of male counterparts chose it as the best. Still, approximately 10 percent of women and men think that "Mother all, father none" is the best parental leave arrangement for dual-earner couples.

Gender-Role Attitudes and Fertility Ideals

I estimated the generalized ordered logit regression models of fertility ideals to examine whether gender-role attitudes had an effect on fertility ideals when controlling for social and demographic characteristics. Separate models were run for each of the four measures of gender-role attitudes. The results of the regression analysis for men and women are presented in table 11.5 and table 11.6, respectively. A positive coefficient from the regression tables means that the increase in the independent variable is associated with higher levels of fertility ideals (or a higher ideal number of children). Likewise, a negative coefficient indicates that higher values on the independent variable are associated with a lower category of the dependent variable (Williams 2016).

Overall, the relationship between gender-role attitudes and fertility ideals differs by gender-role attitudes and by gender. Moreover, four aspects of gender-role attitudes show inconsistent findings among male respondents. Table 11.5 presents the coefficients for the generalized ordered logit models for men. Model 1 shows that the attitudes toward the primacy of the breadwinner family model are not significantly associated with fertility ideals. Model 2 indicates that men with more egalitarian attitudes toward working mothers' influence on their children are more likely to have fertility ideals of *less than* two children. Model 3 also presents the negative link between egalitarian gender-role attitudes and fertility ideals. Men with more egalitarian attitudes toward the value of being a housewife are more likely to have lower fertility ideals. Results from Model 4 are in line with these findings. Men who think that mothers should take the en-

TABLE 11.4. Distribution (%) of Attitudes Toward Parental Leave Arrangement by Gender, Korean Men and Women Aged 49 or Younger, 2012 KGSS

	Men	Women
Mother all, father none	12.34	8.28
Mother most, father some	55.45	52.12
Mother and father each receive half	32.21	39.6
Total	100	100

Note: Chi-square = 11.417 ($p < .10$)

tire portion of parental leave are more likely to express higher levels of fertility ideals ($p < .10$).

The effect of gender-role attitudes on ideal fertility for women is even less marked. Table 11.6 shows that gender-role attitudes are not significantly associated with women's fertility ideals, controlling for other factors. Results reveal that the ideational factors regarding attitudes toward children are significantly associated with both men's and women's fertility ideals. Men and women who held positive attitudes toward having children are more likely to report a higher ideal number of children. Of the control variables, parenthood is significantly associated with men's fertility ideals. Fathers are more likely than non-fathers to express their ideal number of children as being greater than two.

Instead of gender-role attitudes, some sociodemographic control variables have significant effects on women's fertility ideals even though most of these variables are not significantly associated with men's fertility ideals. Educational attainment shows an interesting finding. Highly educated women (i.e., college graduates or higher) are more likely than less educated women to express fertility ideals of greater than two children ($p < .10$). Not surprisingly, working women are more likely than unemployed women to express fertility ideals of fewer than two children. Women residing in metropolitan areas are likely to have fertility ideals of fewer than three children. Income (logged) and its squared term have a significant inverted-U pattern association with women's fertility ideals. Increases in income are initially associated with higher fertility ideals, but beyond a certain level, subsequent increases in income are associated with declines in women's fertility ideals.

Discussion

The ongoing discussion on the link between gender equality and fertility includes various aspects and approaches. Although each theory differs in the extent of its respective focus, scholars have agreed that gender equality or egalitarian gender relations should lead to higher fertility in low-fertility settings, including in East Asia (e.g., Raymo et al. 2015). Drawing on a body of theoretical frameworks emphasizing egalitarian gender relations in family demography (Esping-Andersen and Billari 2015; Goldscheider, Bernhardt, and Lappegård 2015; McDonald 2000), this study incorporated men's views into fertility ideals by investigating the patterns of gender-role attitudes associated with fertility ideals for both men and

TABLE 11.5. Coefficients from the Generalized Ordered Logit Regression Models of Fertility Ideals among Korean Men Aged 49 or Younger, 2012 KGSS

	Model 1		Model 2		Model 3		Model 4	
	Y > 1 vs. Y ≤ 1	Y > 2 vs. Y ≤ 2	Y > 1 vs. Y ≤ 1	Y > 2 vs. Y ≤ 2	Y > 1 vs. Y ≤ 1	Y > 2 vs. Y ≤ 2	Y > 1 vs. Y ≤ 1	Y > 2 vs. Y ≤ 2
Gender role attitudes								
Primacy of breadwinner model (division of labor)	.020	−.130						
Working mother and relationship quality			−.779**	−.108				
Wife/motherhood and feminine self					−.957***	−.261+		
Parental leave arrangement (ref. mother most, father some)								
Mother all, father none							.811	.671+
Mother and father each receive half							−.094	.407
Attitudes toward children	.472*	.296*	.385+	.282*	.531+	.274*	.497*	.334*
Age	−.086	−.025	−.067	−.024	−.102	−.027	−.085	−.045*
Education (ref. less than high school diploma)								
Some college	.780	.333	.691	.235	1.053	.317	.808	.275
Bachelor's degree or higher	1.829	.111	2.570+	.045	1.681	.081	1.883+	.168
Employment status (employed)	.559	.100	.337	.038	.236	.033	.608	.138
Paid work hours	.011	.002	.000	.002	.019	.002	.009	.004
Parenthood (being a parent)	.505	.974**	.138	.964**	.973	1.041**	.333	1.106**
Metropolitan residence (yes)	−.213	.128	−.102	.093	−.495	.069	−.124	.170
Income (logged)	11.517+	−1.034	13.867+	−1.848	9.247	−1.342	14.557*	1.215
Squared income	−.417+	.040	−.493+	.068	−.336	.049	−.515*	−.034
Constant	−75.340	5.890	−91.242	11.819	−56.987	8.765	−98.849	−11.288
Model fit	Chi²₍₂₂₎ = 37.46*		Chi²₍₂₂₎ = 44.24*		Chi²₍₂₂₎ = 50.68***		Chi²₍₂₄₎ = 42.05*	

+ $p < .10$; * $p < .05$; ** $p < .01$; *** $p < .001$

TABLE 11.6. Coefficients from the Generalized Ordered Logit Regression Models of Fertility Ideals among Korean Women Aged 49 or Younger, 2012 KGSS

	Model 1		Model 2		Model 3		Model 4	
	Y > 1 vs. Y ≤ 1	Y > 2 vs. Y ≤ 2	Y > 1 vs. Y ≤ 1	Y > 2 vs. Y ≤ 2	Y > 1 vs. Y ≤ 1	Y > 2 vs. Y ≤ 2	Y > 1 vs. Y ≤ 1	Y > 2 vs. Y ≤ 2
Gender role attitudes								
Primacy of breadwinner model (division of labor)	−.124	.028						
Working mother and relationship quality			−.024	−.158				
Wife/motherhood and feminine self					.071	−.145		
Parental leave arrangement (ref. mother most, father some)								
Mother all, father none							.992	−.237
Mother and father each receive half							.140	−.395
Attitudes toward children	.914**	.175	.875*	.208+	.863***	.187	.851*	.164
Age	−.035	.032	−.031	.026	−.033	.030	−.032	.031
Education (ref. less than high school diploma)								
Some college	.012	−.478	.001	−.500	−.030	−.498	.283	−.380
Bachelor's degree or higher	1.284+	−.411	1.247+	−.383	1.256+	.410	1.315+	−.375
Employment status (employed)	−2.224**	−.462	−2.201**	−.385	−2.273**	−.426	−2.108*	−.245
Paid work hours	.033+	.010	.032+	.009	.033	.010	.033	.009
Parenthood (being a parent)	.680	−.266	.719	−.276	.754	−.288	.834	−.323
Metropolitan residence (yes)	.175	−.412+	.178	−.397+	.205	−.440+	.098	−.475*
Income (logged)	−10.444	18.660*	−9.570	20.090*	−10.744	19.350*	−10.007	19.464*
Squared income	.359	−.600*	.328	−.647*	.366	−.622*	.342	−.628*
Constant	77.840	−146.270	71.340	−156.480	80.131	−151.258	74.319	−151.692
Model fit	Chi²$_{(22)}$ = 48.07**		Chi²$_{(22)}$ = 49.35*		Chi²$_{(22)}$ = 49.26***		Chi²$_{(24)}$ = 50.44**	

+ $p < .10$; * $p < .05$; ** $p < .01$; *** $p < .001$

women in Korea. Guided by the recent debate and mixed findings about the relationship between gender-role attitudes and fertility (Kaufman, Bernhardt, and Goldscheider 2017; Miettinen, Basten, and Rotkirch 2011), I operationalized gender-role attitudes with four different aspects instead of one single composite construct.

I found that the majority of Koreans hold ambivalent attitudes toward different aspects of gender roles. Both men and women show less support for a traditional gendered division of labor based on the male-breadwinner model, although women showed significantly less support than men. However, the majority of both men and women hold more traditional attitudes toward the belief that mothers should stay home when their children are young, as well as on the value of being a housewife. These findings are in line with my arguments that gender-role attitudes are a multidimensional concept, in which people show different levels of support for egalitarianism. The majority of adults in Korea no longer view the male-breadwinner family model as ideal. At the same time, however, changes in attitudes regarding family expectations and obligations for women are limited.

The findings indicated that the link between gender-role attitudes and fertility ideals differs by gender. The results also suggest that, for men, the association of gender-role attitudes with fertility ideals differs according to the dimension of the gender role in question. While men's egalitarian attitudes toward the primacy of the male-breadwinner family model are not significantly associated with fertility ideals, the other aspects of gender-role attitudes showed significant associations with fertility ideals. Men holding egalitarian attitudes toward a working mother's relationship quality with her young child and the value of being a housewife are more likely to wish for no more than two children. By contrast, men who think women should take full responsibility for parental leave under the dual-earner couples' arrangement are more likely to express a higher ideal number of children. Thus, the evidence from Korea presented here provides some support for the gender-revolution framework, given that egalitarian gender relations in the public sphere are negatively associated with fertility until the society reaches the second half of the gender revolution (Goldscheider, Oláh, and Puur 2010; Goldscheider, Bernhardt, and Lappegård 2015). The second half of the gender revolution requires both men and women to integrate their work and family responsibilities, especially through men's greater involvement in family lives (Goldscheider, Bernhardt, and Lappegård 2015). However, women's gender-role attitudes are not significantly associated with their fertility ideals. Instead, women's employment status shows a strong negative association with high fertility ideals. This would reflect the high levels of incompatibility between work and family responsibilities for women.

As indicated by weak institutional support for families, Korea has not achieved the second half of the gender revolution; thus the current state of the gender revolution in Korea is "stalled" or "incomplete" (England 2010; Esping-Andersen 2009). Furthermore, the findings regarding the negative link between women's employment and fertility ideals signal work-family conflict, especially for women. Despite the considerable ongoing progress toward gender equality with new family policies implemented by the Korean government, several existing structural and cultural factors make progress to the second half of the gender revolution difficult. Due to the experience of the 1997 Asian financial crisis and increasing economic insecurity, people in Korea have realized that the male-breadwinner family model is not the optimal choice to maintain their standard of living (Eun 2007; Park, Lee, and Jo 2013).

Concurrently, however, strong cultural expectations regarding children's education and mothers' dedication to child-rearing (i.e., intensive mothering) still play a part in shaping gender-role attitudes in Korea (Yoon 2016). Although people recognize the demand for gender equality in both the public and private spheres, the robust patriarchal gender relations embedded in family life prevent women from having stable long-term careers in the labor market. Because women are expected to provide extensive caregiving work within the family compared with men, many women choose part-time or temporary jobs that allow them to contribute to the family income to some extent while taking care of their family as needed. The growth in this one-and-a-half-earner family model reflects existing traditional gender-role expectations. In this model, women almost exclusively adjust their time allocation (Craig and Powell 2012), which is also shaped by institutional arrangements and public discourse.

Structural constraints in the labor market and cultural gender expectations contribute to "incomplete" gender equality in both the public and private spheres, as evidenced by stagnant female labor force participation and limited male involvement in the family. I argue that these structural conditions influence the ambivalence in gender-role attitudes, which might reflect the transitional "stage" between the first and the second half of the gender revolution with unclear gender roles and expectations (Goldscheider, Oláh, and Puur 2010: 193). The evidence presented here shows that expectations for mothers to take primary care of their children are still strong, but these expectations conflict with more egalitarian views of the traditional breadwinner family model. These ambivalent gender-role attitudes delay widespread shifts toward the second stage of the gender revolution. The institutional arrangements, including changes in family policy and organizational practice in the labor market, are necessary to lead progress to egalitarian gender relations, including both egalitarian attitudes and actual practices in the public and private spheres. This, in turn, ultimately will influence fertility attitudes and actual fertility.

It is important to note a few limitations. As documented, the link between gender-role attitudes and fertility varies depending on what measures of fertility are examined. As such, future studies examining different fertility variables, such as fertility intentions or actual fertility, may provide different findings regarding the association between gender-role attitudes and fertility. Additionally, in the current study, I relied on cross-sectional survey data to examine the association between gender-role attitudes and fertility ideals. However, previous studies have shown that gender-role attitudes change over time as people experience different family-related transitions (e.g., marriage formation and first births) (Kaufman, Bernhardt, and Goldscheider 2017). To estimate the role of gender-role attitudes in fertility ideals over the life course, future studies using longitudinal data would be able to document changes in gender-role attitudes with a series of family transitions taken into account.

NOTES

1. Kwŏn Hye-jin, "Yŏgabu, appa ŭi yuga ch'amyŏ tongnyŏ wihae 'kkot poda appa' wich'ok." *Yŏnhap nyusŭ*, July 26, 2015, http://www.yonhapnews.co.kr/bulletin/2015/07/26/0200000000AKR20150726001200005.HTML?input=1195m

2. http://www.index.go.kr/potal/main/EachDtlPageDetail.do?idx_cd=1504

3. In this chapter, I use "fertility ideals" and "the ideal number of children" interchangeably.

4. The effects on gender-role attitudes of social and demographic characteristics are based on two main explanations: interest based and exposure based (see Bolzendahl and Myers 2004 for details).

5. See Ridgeway and Correll (2004) for a theoretical explanation of gender difference.

6. In the analysis process, moreover, I tried to construct a composite measure for gender-role attitudes based on several items in the ISSP questionnaire. Although exploratory factor analysis confirmed that items are unidimensional, the alpha coefficient was not high enough for constructing a composite measure.

7. A detailed explanation about the assumption of the ordered logit model (also known as the proportional odds assumption) is beyond the scope of this chapter. Readers can find a nice explanation from Williams (2016).

8. Respondents were classified as having traditional attitudes if their responses were either "strongly agree" or "agree." Intermediate attitudes were represented by responses of "neither agree nor disagree." Respondents were classified as having egalitarian attitudes if their responses were either "strongly disagree" or "disagree."

REFERENCES

Bolzendahl, Catherine I., and Daniel J. Myers. 2004. "Feminist Attitudes and Support for Gender Equality: Opinion Change in Women and Men, 1974–1998." *Social Forces* 83 (2): 759–89.

Bongaarts, John. 2001. "Fertility and Reproductive Preferences in Post-Transitional Societies." *Population and Development Review* 27: 260–81.

Brewster, Karin L., and Irene Padavic. 2000. "Change in Gender-Ideology, 1977–1996: The Contributions of Intracohort Change and Population Turnover." *Journal of Marriage and Family* 62 (2): 477–87.

Brooks, Clem, and Catherine Bolzendahl. 2004. "The Transformation of US Gender Role Attitudes: Cohort Replacement, Social-Structural Change, and Ideological Learning." *Social Science Research* 33 (1): 106–33.

Bumpass, Larry L., Ronald R. Rindfuss, Minja Kim Choe, and Noriko O. Tsuya. 2009. "The Institutional Context of Low Fertility: The Case of Japan." *Asian Population Studies* 5 (3): 215–35.

Chang, Hye Kyung, Jeong-Im Hwang, In-Hui Choi, Young-Ran Kim, Jae-Sun Ju, and So-Young Kim. 2015. *The 2015 Current Family Survey Analysis Research Report.* 2015-65. Seoul: Korean Women's Development Institute (in Korean).

Ciabattari, Teresa. 2001. "Changes in Men's Conservative Gender Ideologies: Cohort and Period Influences." *Gender & Society* 15 (4): 574–91.

Coltrane, Scott. 1997. *Family Man: Fatherhood, Housework, and Gender Equity.* New York: Oxford University Press.

Cooke, Lynn P. 2004. "The Gendered Division of Labor and Family Outcomes in Germany." *Journal of Marriage and Family* 66 (5): 1246–59.

Cooke, Lynn P. 2009. "Gender Equity and Fertility in Italy and Spain." *Journal of Social Policy* 38 (1): 123–40.

Corrigall, Elizabeth A., and Alison M. Konrad. 2007. "Gender Role Attitudes and Careers: A Longitudinal Study." *Sex Roles* 56 (11): 847–55.

Craig, Lyn, and Abigail Powell. 2012. "Dual-Earner Parents' Work-Family Time: The Effects of Atypical Work Patterns and Non-Parental Childcare." *Journal of Population Research* 29 (3): 229–47.

Cunningham, Mick. 2005. "Gender in Cohabitation and Marriage: The Influence of Gender Ideology on Housework Allocation Over the Life Course." *Journal of Family Issues* 26 (8): 1037–61.

Davis, Shannon N. 2007. "Gender Ideology Construction from Adolescence to Young Adulthood." *Social Science Research* 36 (3): 1021–41.

Davis, Shannon N., and Theodore N. Greenstein. 2009. "Gender Ideology: Components, Predictors, and Consequences." *Annual Review of Sociology* 35 (1): 87–105.

Edlund, Jonas, and Ida Öun. 2016. "Who Should Work and Who Should Care? Attitudes towards the Desirable Division of Labour between Mothers and Fathers in Five European Countries." *Acta Sociologica* 59 (2): 151–69.

England, Paula. 2010. "The Gender Revolution: Uneven and Stalled." *Gender and Society* 24 (2): 149–66.
Esping-Andersen, Gøsta. 2009. *The Incomplete Revolution: Adapting Welfare States to Women's New Roles*. Cambridge: Polity Press.
Esping-Andersen, Gøsta, and Francesco C. Billari. 2015. "Re-Theorizing Family Demographics." *Population and Development Review* 41 (1): 1–31.
Eun, Ki-Soo. 2007. "Lowest-Low Fertility in the Republic of Korea: Causes, Consequences and Policy Responses." *Asia-Pacific Population Journal* 22: 51–72.
Fan, Pi-Ling, and Margaret Mooney Marini. 2000. "Influences on Gender-Role Attitudes during the Transition to Adulthood." *Social Science Research* 29 (2): 258–83.
Goldscheider, Frances, Eva Bernhardt, and Trude Lappegård. 2015. "The Gender Revolution: A Framework for Understanding Changing Family and Demographic Behavior." *Population and Development Review* 41 (2): 207–39.
Goldscheider, Frances, Eva Bernhardt, and Maria Brandén. 2013. "Domestic Gender Equality and Childbearing in Sweden." *Demographic Research* 29: 1097–1126.
Goldscheider, Frances, Livia Sz. Oláh, and Allan Puur. 2010. "Reconciling Studies of Men's Gender Attitudes and Fertility: Response to Westoff and Higgins." *Demographic Research* 22 (8): 189–98.
Goldstein, Joshua, Wolfgang Lutz, and Maria Rita Testa. 2003. "The Emergence of Sub-Replacement Family Size Ideals in Europe." *Population Research and Policy Review* 22 (5): 479–96.
Greenstein, Theodore N. 2009. "National Context, Family Satisfaction, and Fairness in the Division of Household Labor." *Journal of Marriage and Family* 71 (4): 1039–51.
Han, Kyeng-Hye. 2015. "Women's Experience of Work-Family Balance and Social Support." *Korean Social Trends 2014*. Daejeon: Statistical Research Institute.
Harknett, Kristen, and Caroline Sten Hartnett. 2014. "The Gap between Births Intended and Births Achieved in 22 European Countries, 2004–07." *Population Studies* 68 (3): 265–82.
Hin, Saskia, Anne Gauthier, Joshua Goldstein, and Christoph Bühler. 2011. "Fertility Preferences: What Measuring Second Choices Teaches Us." *Vienna Yearbook of Population Research* 9: 131–56.
Hook, Jennifer L. 2006. "Care in Context: Men's Unpaid Work in 20 Countries, 1965-2003." *American Sociological Review* 71 (4): 639–60.
Kaufman, Gayle, Eva Bernhardt, and Frances Goldscheider. 2017. "Enduring Egalitarianism? Family Transitions and Attitudes Toward Gender Equality in Sweden." *Journal of Family Issues* 38 (13): 1878–98.
Kim, Erin Hye-Won, and Adam Ka Lok Cheung. "Women's Attitudes Toward Family Formation and Life Stage Transitions: A Longitudinal Study in Korea." *Journal of Marriage and Family* 77: 1074–90.
Kim, Young-Mi, and Yunkyu Ryu. 2016. "A Comparative Analysis on the Structural Determinants of Male Gender Role Attitudes Across 26 Countries." *Social Sciences Research Review* 32 (2): 271–99.
McDonald, Peter. 2000. "Gender Equity in Theories of Fertility Transition." *Population and Development Review* 26 (3): 427–39.
McDonald, Peter. 2008. "Very Low Fertility Consequences, Causes and Policy Approaches." *Japanese Journal of Population* 6 (1): 19–23.
McDonald, Peter. 2013. "Societal Foundations for Explaining Fertility: Gender Equity." *Demographic Research* 28: 981–94.

Miettinen, Anneli, Stuart Basten, and Anna Rotkirch. 2011. "Gender Equality and Fertility Intentions Revisited: Evidence from Finland." *Demographic Research* 24: 469–96.
Morgan, S. Philip, and Heather Rackin. 2010. "The Correspondence Between Fertility Intentions and Behavior in the United States." *Population and Development Review* 36 (1): 91–118.
Park, Hyunjoon, Jae Kyung Lee, and Inkyung Jo. 2013. "Changing Relationships between Education and Marriage among Korean Women." *Korean Journal of Sociology* 47 (3): 51–76.
Park, Jongseo. 2016. "Work-Family Balance and in Working Women and Its Policy Implications." *Health and Social Welfare Forum* 236: 18–36.
Park, Soomi. 2008. "A Study on the Relationship of Gender Equity within Family and Second Birth." *Korea Journal of Population Studies* 31 (1): 55–73 (in Korean).
Philipov, Demitri. 2008. "Family-Related Gender Attitudes: The Three Dimensions— 'Gender Role Ideology,' 'Consequences for the Family,' and 'Economic Consequences.'" In Charlotte Höhn, Dragana Avramov, and Irena Kotowka, eds., *People, Population Change and Policies: Lessons from the Population Policy Acceptance Study*, 153–74. Springer.
Powers, Rebecca S., J. Jill Suitor, Susana Guerra, Monisa Shackelford, Dorothy Mecom, and Kim Gusman. 2003. "Regional Differences in Gender—Role Attitudes: Variations by Gender and Race." *Gender Issues* 21 (2): 40–54.
Puur, Allan, Livia Sz. Oláh, Mariam Irene Tazi-Preve, and Jürgen Dorbritz. 2008. "Men's Childbearing Desires and Views of the Male Role in Europe at the Dawn of the 21st Century." *Demographic Research* 19: 1883-1912.
Qian, Yue, and Liana C. Sayer. 2016. "Division of Labor, Gender Ideology, and Marital Satisfaction in East Asia: Division of Labor and Marital Satisfaction in Asia." *Journal of Marriage and Family* 78 (2): 383–400.
Raymo, James M., Hyunjoon Park, Yu Xie, and Wei-jun Jean Yeung. 2015. "Marriage and Family in East Asia: Continuity and Change." *Annual Review of Sociology* 41 (1): 471–92.
Ridgeway, Cecilia L., and Shelley J. Correll. 2004. "Unpacking the Gender System: A Theoretical Perspective on Gender Beliefs and Social Relations." *Gender & Society* 18 (4): 510-31.
Suzuki, Toru. 2008. "Korea's Strong Familism and Lowest-Low Fertility." *International Journal of Japanese Sociology* 17 (1): 30–41.
Testa, Maria Rita, and Leonardo Grilli. 2006. "The Influence of Childbearing Regional Contexts on Ideal Family Size in Europe on JSTOR." *Population* 61: 107–37.
Thévenon, Olivier. 2011. "Family Policies in OECD Countries: A Comparative Analysis." *Population and Development Review* 37 (1): 57–87.
Thornton, Arland, and Linda Young-DeMarco. 2001. "Four Decades of Trends in Attitudes Toward Family Issues in the United States: The 1960s through the 1990s." *Journal of Marriage and Family* 63 (4): 1009-37.
Westoff, Charles F., and Jenny Higgins. 2009. "Relationships between Men's Gender Attitudes and Fertility: Response to Puur et al.'s 'Men's Childbearing Desires and Views of the Male Role in Europe at the Dawn of the 21st Century', *Demographic Research* 19: 1883–1912." *Demographic Research* 21: 65–74.
Williams, Richard. 2016. "Understanding and Interpreting Generalized Ordered Logit Models." *Journal of Mathematical Sociology* 40 (1): 7–20.

Yoo, Sam Hyun. 2014. "Educational Differentials in Cohort Fertility during the Fertility Transition in South Korea." *Demographic Research* 30: 1463–94.

Yoon, Soo-Yeon. 2016. "Is Gender Inequality a Barrier to Realizing Fertility Intentions? Fertility Aspirations and Realizations in South Korea." *Asian Population Studies* 12 (2): 203–19.

Yoon, Soo-Yeon. 2017. "The Influence of a Supportive Environment for Families on Women's Fertility Intentions and Behavior in South Korea." *Demographic Research* 36: 227–54.

12

Kwinong kwich'on kwihyang (Back to the Land) Discourse of Young South Korean Families

Exchanging "Hell Chosŏn" for Breathing Room (*Yŏyu*)

Bonnie Tilland

It is common knowledge that South Korea is an urban society. History books and tourist pamphlets alike detail the nation's rapid industrialization in the 1960s through the 1980s, when young people flooded the capital city of Seoul from countryside villages. Even prior to the rapid industrialization period, Seoul's importance during the Chosŏn dynasty (1392–1910) and its further elevation in status as the highly modern capital during the Japanese colonial period (1910–45) cannot be overestimated; a well-known proverb hints at the pull of Seoul, instructing that one should "send horses to Cheju and send people to Hanyang [Seoul]."[1] Koreans old enough to have lived through these turbulent decades often brag that South Korea industrialized even faster than neighboring Japan, turning up their noses at what they see as the West's misplaced fascination with Japan's modernization success story. Visitors to South Korea would notice the urban density just minutes into the drive from Incheon Airport— massive apartment towers stretch skyward in all directions, bearing names of the nation's powerful conglomerates (*chaebŏl*)—Posco, Hyundai, Daelim—with aspirational, if sometimes nonsensical, English, French, or Korean subheadings (We've, Eccoleur, Humansia). These apartment towers stretch out into the surrounding countryside as well, so that one has to travel to fairly remote areas to guarantee vistas free of boxy buildings.

Although these high-rise apartments only began to be built for the wealthy in the late 1960s and 1970s and became a more general fixture of Korean life in the 1990s, it is easy to forget that in the not-so-distant past expectations for dwellings, as well as the connections of city residents to nonurban areas, were quite different. In her book *Apartment Republic* (*Ap'at'ŭ konghwaguk*), cultural geographer Valerie Gelezeau (2007) disputes South Koreans' frequent claim that high-rise apartment living is the only way to deal with South Korea's population density. She points to Tokyo as a counterexample; despite Tokyo's greater population density, high-rise apartments are not nearly so prevalent. Instead, she argues, South Koreans have come to associate high-rise apartments with high status, comfort, and security. And yet, this positive association shows some signs of shifting. Between 2013 and 2016 reported incidences of conflicts with neighbors over apartment noise pollution escalating to police involvement and sometimes fatal violence rose sharply.[2] The largest South Korean earthquake in modern recorded history (5.4 on the Richter scale) in September 2016 brought shoddy construction of even expensive apartments under national scrutiny.

Changes in public perceptions of apartment living come as more young Koreans starting families embark on the process with rather different ideas of what constitutes a "nice" home than their parents' generation. While single-family houses (*chut'aek*) in Korea still have the reputation of being dirty, poorly insulated, inconvenient, and infested with bugs, a not insignificant number of younger people in Korea are plotting their exit from cramped and competitive city conditions.[3] Although urban-to-rural migration in Korea is a slow trickle compared to the flood that was rural-to-urban migration in the 1960s through 1990s, my analysis of the how-to literature on the back-to-the-land movement, as well as my conversations with parents of young children undertaking or contemplating the move, indicates that this is more than a passing trend. What are the motivations and ideals of young families who move to the countryside, and what is the impact of this kind of urban-to-rural migration on families in South Korea? While both motivations and impacts are varied, urban-to-rural migration indicates not only a response to economic conditions but also a shift in social values and a change in family member roles and identities.

"Back to the Land" in the Korean Context

In this chapter, I examine the shift from economic motivations for going back to the land (*kwinong kwich'on kwihyang*, "back to the farms, back to the land, and back to ancestral hometowns," hereafter abbreviated to the catchall *kwich'on*, unless otherwise stated) of earlier decades to more recent health rationales or even utopian visions. Through analyzing memorials and manuals, blogs, and other media about *kwich'on* I argue that the back-to-the-land movement as practiced by parents of young children, in their 30s and 40s—the fastest-growing *kwich'on* demographic group— simultaneously represents a search for health in an individualistic, neoliberal mode and a desire for an open, nurturing, self-consciously anti-neoliberal yet globally oriented community.[4]

The existing academic literature on recent iterations of the *kwich'on* movement (Song 2014) suggests that most young families' primary motivations for moving to the countryside are not economic. This contrasts starkly with the *kwich'on* movement of the late 1990s and early 2000s, which was primarily a response to the brutal effects of the 1997 Asian financial crisis in South Korea, with young adults in their 20s through 40s going to the countryside to wait out economic catastrophe.[5] The current iteration of the *kwich'on* movement is also not parallel to the first iteration in the 1980s—when *kwinong* was tied in those days with the *minjung* or "folk" movement—since, as analyzed by scholars such as Seungsook Moon (2005) and Jesook Song (2009), South Korean civic participation and public discourse have largely shifted from the *minjung* ("the people") mode of public engagement (confrontational, unified front) to the civil society mode (focused on *simin*, "citizens") of post-democratization.

Rather, I observe that many current *kwich'on* practitioners draw on the fundamentally neoliberal "well-being" discourse that emerged in the early to mid-2000s, framing their decisions in terms of individual physical and mental health and the consumer practices that enable these. This is not to suggest that these decisions are simply selfish but rather that it is impossible to completely escape the overall neoliberal framework of South Korean society, in which all actions should "build value" in one way or another, in the short or long term. Escaping city life becomes a way to psychologically fortify children and families and to effectively "bank" health before the eventual return to competitive life. And yet, beyond individual and family pursuits of consumable *kwich'on*-related products and programs, my analysis of interviews and *kwich'on* books and blogs illuminates real soul searching regarding the national direction of South Korea and the responsibilities of its citizens. If immigration or long-term study abroad represents opting out of the nation for many South Koreans, *kwich'on* represents staying in the nation while opting out of the aspects of South Korean society viewed as most harmful. Interviewees' and blog and memoir writers' discussions of their goal of wanting their children to be comfortable as Koreans and yet global at the same time speak to new imaginings of the countryside as being simultaneously quintessentially Korean and multicultural by virtue of the many *tamunhwa* (multicultural; also, multiculture) families in rural areas.

Moreover, as analyzed in blogs and how-to manuals, whereas farming was undervalued during South Korea's industrialization, now living on the land and working with the land reflects a global focus on environmentalism and sustainability. In the countryside, children—as well as their formerly stressed-to-the-breaking-point parents—are imagined to develop a connection to the land, to grow up strong, *and* to encounter more diversity among their neighbors than they might in an urban environment. The dream is that they can escape the cutthroat competition that characterizes South Korean society—sometimes termed "Hell Chosŏn" in recent years—while staying in a more "pure" Korea, giving up the trappings of social mobility in exchange for living life on their own terms.

While the popular "Hell Chosŏn" internet meme—a retooling of a screenshot of the "Hellfire Peninsula" from the online game World of Warcraft, with the various sad life stages of the South Korean non-elites represented on the map—was created by disillusioned youth in 2015 and has mainly circulated among youth in their 20s, it also holds salience among parents of preschool or school-age children in their 30s and 40s, who are not members of the so-called *sampo* generation (giving up dating, marriage, and children) but who are now facing rising costs and high stakes in educating their children.[6] Faced with finding an outlet from the competitive Korean education system, some of these parents are choosing *kwich'on* over moving abroad.

Several women I interviewed in 2012 and 2013 spoke about early study abroad and *kwich'on* in the same breath, presenting *kwich'on* as an alternative escape from the quotidian that they had considered for their family. As *kwich'on* numbers for this age bracket have steadily risen over the last five years, numbers for early study abroad (*chogi yuhak*) have steadily fallen, though in terms of absolute numbers early study abroad as an educational strategy remains more prevalent.[7] South Korean undergraduates still study abroad in significant numbers, third only to India and China.[8] But the tide of public opinion about early study abroad for the purpose of learning English has shifted, with more parents worried about their children's insufficient socialization in Korea and even their command of English outpacing their Korean. The growing interest in *kwich'on* has been framed as a backlash against intensive study abroad pressures; however, *kwinong* itself also involves some of the "cultural work" (Albelmann and Kang 2014) that "goose families" (*kirŏgi kajok*)[9] abroad go through and requires its own reworkings of subjectivities.

Parents follow certain scripts in planning *kwich'on* and continue to make adjustments to family rhythms as they live out these plans. Just as Abelmann and Kang traced "study abroad mother memoirs/manuals" as a "window to the challenges and anxieties of PSA [precollege study abroad] in South Korea today" (2014: 1), I perform a similar treatment on memoirs and manuals about *kwich'on*, as *chogi yuhak* (precollege study abroad) declines and family *kwich'on* gradually rises. Some manuals and memoirs (including Yun 2014, which I analyze in more detail later) even refer to *kwich'on* as a kind of domestic "study abroad" (*yuhak*), in which children learn about nature as if it is a new language and adjust to the hybrid new culture of the countryside, interacting with natives of that place (many of them elderly), fellow internal migrants from cities, and migrant women from other Asian countries who marry South Korean men and subsequently raise half-Korean children. The countryside becomes invested with hope for local rural community with globalist benefits.

To date few scholars have addressed the most recent iteration of the *kwich'on* movement, even as personal memoirs and how-to manuals proliferate. Song (2014) provides the most comprehensive analysis of the movement's history and practitioners' various motivations. He divides *kwich'on* practitioners into those who choose it for economic motivations, ecological values, and retirement. The young families in his study who migrated for economic or "ecological" motivations or a combination of the two frequently referenced the shift in family dynamics in new lives in the countryside and expressed greater satisfaction with family relationships. Sohn (2015) and Tran (2015) look at *kwich'on* and newcomer-local relationships in the case of Cheju Island. Nemeth (2008) and Park (2016) both discuss *kwich'on* connections to the earlier Saemaŭl Undong (New Village Movement) and agricultural cooperatives, although they do not specifically delve into *kwich'on*. Nemeth discusses the destruction of Korea's natural villages due to the "progress" the New Villages represented; although the movement connected the cities and the countryside, rural values and ecology were rejected in order for this connection to occur. Park analyzes the agricultural cooperative movement and role of coops such as iCOOP and Hansallim (Hansallim) in educating urban consumers about rural life and farming; unlike the *kwinong* and *kwich'on* movement, he argues, the cooperatives do not romanticize the rural. Sŏng (2014) has interviewed women about their adaptation to farming life when they follow their husbands in migration for *kwinong*—though her interviewees were mainly women in their 50s whose children were already grown. There has been much more substantive research on migrant brides and their children and husbands in the South Korean countryside, with Chŏn (2008) writing on school socialization issues, Rhee (2014) on narratives about migrant brides and foreign workers, and Minjeong Kim (2014) on South Korean rural husbands and compensatory masculinity. Finally, examinations of similar processes of youth migration—also encompassing young families—to the countryside in Japan elucidate the trans-Asian nature of urban-to-rural migration, as families seek stability, community, and clean air amid climate change and social anomie (Arai 2016; Love 2013).

The Korean Education System and Its Discontents

The *kwich'on* phenomenon cannot be understood without an understanding of the South Korean education system and common criticisms leveled against it. Like other Asian education systems, the system is competitive and oriented toward a high-stakes university entrance exam (known in South Korea as the *sunŭng*). It achieves tangible results in indicators such as international standardized tests in mathematics and science, but the question of whether these results are worth the pressure on children and families is hardly a new concern. There are also ongoing concerns about the broader efficacy of even the world's highest math and science scores, as stories circulate about South Korean students and graduates being unable to apply this knowledge in creative and flexible ways, particularly when placed in competition with foreign students and graduates.[10] This has led to the addition of "creativity" components to the curriculum across all levels, as well as units focused on "character" (*insŏng*), out of concerns for Korean students' moral and emotional development. Yet to many students and parents, these additions of "creative" and "character-building" elements to the curriculum feel like just more to add to an already long list of skills to master.

Part of the reason for South Korea's competitive educational environment in fact stems from attempts at egalitarianism in the recent past. While educational opportunities expanded for the elite and small middle class under Japanese occupation in the first half of the 20th century, it was not until after the Korean War (1950–53) that the government began systematically to work toward universal literacy and school enrollment. By 1964, some 90 percent of primary school students were enrolled, and 90 percent was achieved at the middle school level by 1979 and high school level in 1993 (Sorensen 1994). Nearly that rate (86 percent) of high school graduates enrolls in higher education programs.[11] This has led to a striking gap in educational attainment between South Koreans currently in their 20s and their grandparents, of whom only 43 percent have a secondary education or above (see Oh, this volume, for more on this gap).[12] With so many South Koreans going to university, competition for slots at the top universities—and, later, for jobs—is fierce, and to manage these desires and expectations educational assessment particularly at the high school level is chiefly done through testing, so that bias will not come into play. In the interest of fairness, the university entrance exam is only offered once a year. But fairness aside, South Korean parents' "education fever" cannot typically be met by the public school system alone, and so parents turn to the *hagwŏn* industry (supplementary private education, sometimes called the "shadow education sector") to help their children keep up and get ahead. There are significant disparities in the cost of the most prestigious *hagwŏn* (such as those in Taech'i-dong or Mok-dong) and ordinary *hagwŏn*.[13] Although *hagwŏn* were banned by the Chun Doo Hwan (Chŏn Tu-hwan) administration in the 1980s on the basis of their promoting socioeconomic inequality, the ban was ruled unconstitutional after the democratic transition in the 1990s. Since then the government routinely drafts laws with the goal of keeping the runaway *hagwŏn* industry in check, with greater or lesser degrees of enforcement. A law passed in 2010 that requires *hagwŏn* to keep a curfew of 10:00 p.m. has been only intermittently enforced, with reports of *hagwŏn* turning off lights in the main room and retreating to a back room to enable high school students to cram for the entrance exam until midnight or later. In my interviews with mothers in 2010–12, *hagwŏn* were described as a blessing and a curse, enabling the outsourcing of "cramming" to the experts but also filling kids' schedules, causing stress and limited time for family activities.

In my research in Chŏnju (the provincial capital of South Korea's southwestern province of North Chŏlla, population 650,000) in 2010–12 (with a follow-up visit in 2013) and in Wŏnju (a city of 350,000 in Kangwŏn province) in 2016–17, I frequently heard the phrase "I don't send my kids to *hagwŏn*" in proud tones. There are profound class implications in this statement—by not sending children to *hagwŏn* in such a high-stakes environment, especially once they are in junior high school or high school, there is a calculation that one possesses the resources to move the child forward through one's own investment of time and knowledge. The phrase "I don't send my kids to *hagwŏn*" is also uttered by mothers of a lower socioeconomic class, but not in the same proud tones. To do well on the university entrance exam, a child from a lower class position would need to be extraordinarily academically inclined and self-motivated or have an exceptional high school teacher assisting with the process.

As discussed throughout this chapter, one way to escape the *hagwŏn* grind is to send kids to study abroad or to accompany them abroad. Then they can focus on learning English—or, more recently in some cases, Chinese—intensively and work with tutors or do workbooks on their own to keep up with their grade level in Korea in math, Korean, and other subjects. In cities with a large Korean population abroad, *hagwŏn* franchises such as Kumon have opened up to address the demand, but the scale is still much less than in any Korean city. Moving to the countryside for *kwich'on* poses similar supplementary education constraints. Without *hagwŏn* nearby, parents must rely on after-school programs, but one of the perks of the *kwich'on* lifestyle is that parent work schedules and children's school schedules are aligned, and families have much more time to spend with each other than they did in the city. One blogger on the popular blog *Rediscovering Chŏnbuk* (Chŏnbuk ŭi chaebalgyŏn)[14] writes about how he and his wife, a fellow SKY (Korean Ivy League) graduate, left big company jobs to raise their kids in the countryside, shifting from *sagyoyuk* (supplementary private education) to *san'gyoyuk* (mountain education). All that their town has is a cultural center, and their kids learn through watching ants and drawing vegetables they directly help to harvest. The town also has a *nongch'on yuhak* (farm study abroad) program for kids from the outside to experience countryside living. Study abroad and countryside study abroad are both ways to opt out of the *hagwŏn* race and all that it symbolizes, and some mothers I interviewed vacillated between these two possibilities.

Multiculturalism: Korea's Salvation or Korea's Ruin?

In tracing motivations for *kwich'on*, it is also important to understand the changed meaning of "the rural" for South Koreans in the 21st century. Agriculture has had a fraught relationship to nation-building projects in modern South Korean history, with Korea's colonization by Japan and low level of economic development in the postliberation period at times pinned on its rural "backwardness." While rapid urban development was valorized in the 1960s through the 1980s, a key project of the *minjung* movement was recentering the importance of farmers' knowledge and folk traditions linked to agrarian lifestyles (Lee 2009). With the neoliberal economic paradigm of the 1990s and 2000s, farming was relegated to a marginal occupation, with those engaged in farming generally assumed to be elderly—those left behind by Korea's economic development miracle.

Starting in the mid-1990s, however, the increase in rural bachelors emerged as a social issue, and an international matchmaking industry grew rapidly to supply brides to these men. The largest percentage of women consist of both ethnic Koreans from China and Han majority Chinese, with the remainder from Vietnam, the Philippines, Mongolia, and Central Asia (mainly Uzbekistan, which has a significant ethnic Korean population, the *Kŏryo saram*). A relatively low number of marriage immigrants are from Japan—mainly through matches arranged by the Unification Church. Cambodia also supplied brides from the mid- to late 2000s but shut down its market after several high-profile cases of domestic violence against Cambodian brides. The influx of foreign brides led to a widespread discussion about the *tamunhwa* that South Korea was becoming. In addition to "multicultural centers" set up to aid in women's smooth assimilation linguistically and culturally into Korean society, rural schools developed programs to accommodate students who did not necessarily speak much Korean at home, or at least who could not rely on maternal support for academics. With *tamunhwa* policies in their second decade now, many Koreans accept that South Korea is no longer a "single-ethnic group society" (*tanil minjok*), but still many urban South Koreans have not had personal experiences with *tamunhwa kajok* (families).[15] While "multicultural families" receive certain financial benefits from the government, these benefits are a double-edged sword, as then they are viewed simply as "welfare recipients" who take from rather than give to Korean society. Ku (2016: 177) quotes from interviews from (among others) a Mongolian wife of a Korean in Ansan city, who succinctly summarizes Korean society's evaluation of her: "lower class, partnered with a rural bachelor, incapable . . . tight purse strings with none left over . . . a target of gossip, welfare recipient, and vulnerable member of society." The "other Asian" women who make up the majority of "migrant brides" (*iju yŏsŏng*) are widely viewed as beneficiaries of South Korea's rising economic star rather than as contributors toward a more global Korea. This has led to a significant backlash against multiculturalism in Korea.

Due to *tamunhwa*'s embedded meaning of "less than," Korean parents are not lining up to expose their children to these multicultural elements. Yet there are small signs of change: community centers sponsor workshops on "understanding *tamunhwa*," and in some cities (such as the Seoul suburb of Ansan) and rural or semirural districts the numbers of "multicultural" children are impossible to ignore now that they are reaching middle school and high school. Korean women I interviewed in Chŏnju in 2011 referenced a hierarchy of migrant women: the *Chosŏnjok* (ethnic Koreans from China) were in particular demand as nannies and Chinese tutors due to their bilingual ability, and Chinese were also seen as potentially useful; Filipinas in Korea tended to have superior English language ability and could therefore impart that marketable knowledge to their children. Vietnamese, Mongolians, or Central Asians, on the other hand, were seen as contributing less to Korean society, as their native languages were not strategically useful.

Parents who are taking their children to the countryside for *kwich'on* are abandoning obsessions with speed, academics, and social norms. Encountering *tamunhwa kajok* is part of this overall package, in which children learn to be more tolerant of others and more aware of Korea's place in the world. For these urban-to-rural families, multiculturalism is neither Korea's salvation nor its ruin but rather a changed social landscape to learn anew in a rural site of possibility, along with planting and harvesting.

Data and Methods

In the second half of this chapter I turn to my analysis of *kwich'on* memoirs and manuals, even as I continue to reference Song's 2014 work on the nationwide *kwich'on* project, to date the only comprehensive research on the topic. As the bulk of ethnographic interviews and participant observations for this project are ongoing, what I am primarily analyzing for this chapter are the memoirs, manuals, and online publications (mainly blogs) of *kwich'on* practitioners themselves. After providing an overview of what kinds of materials on *kwich'on* are available—both for purchase as books or e-books or online—I analyze a few key texts, following Abelmann and Kang's (2014) example with "study abroad mother memoirs/manuals" of dividing them into stories of success and cautionary tales. I also reference some interviews with mothers, specifying whether these interviews were in Chŏnju (2010–12) or Wŏnju (2016–17). Most interviews were with married, university-educated, middle-class (broadly defined) mothers (typically of one or two children) in Chŏnju, and their answers are drawn from interviews over a period of two years about Korean family issues and parenting concerns. The core interviewees for the project were 12 women, and they and other more marginal participants (20 more women were interviewed just once or a handful of times) were all selected by snowball sampling. Interviews with 5 women in Wŏnju specifically on *kwich'on* motivations began in late 2016, but this part of the project is still in the early stages and is still recruiting new participants. The women in Chŏnju were interviewed as part of a broader project on changes to family life in South Korean provincial cities, and I carried forward the *kwich'on* aspect of the project after moving to Wŏnju in 2015. Both Chŏnju and Wŏnju have a different relationship to the rural as provincial cities when compared to the Seoul area, with both the greater North Chŏlla province and Kangwŏn province attracting a moderate number of *kwich'on* migrants.[16]

"Studying Abroad" in the Countryside?

The genre of study abroad mother memoirs/manuals in South Korea was a highly popular one in the mid- to late 2000s. But the number of mothers and children going overseas for early study abroad, particularly to the United States, was already declining by the late 2000s. Indeed, in the 2010s, early study abroad in countries that had overall strong English proficiency but that are closer to Korea geographically has been on the rise; when I was doing fieldwork in 2010–12 all the mothers I interviewed knew someone who had migrated to the Philippines, Singapore, or Malaysia with their children. The addition of the Chinese language as *p'ilsu* (mandatory) is also relatively new; when I returned to Chŏnju for a short trip in 2013, one of the women I had interviewed had moved to China with her two middle school boys in order for them to learn Chinese.

Along with an overflow of books about learning Chinese, doing business with China, and living in China, I began noticing quite an opposite kind of bestseller in places like the Kyobo bookstore, one of the largest bookstores in Korea: books on *kwich'on* and related topics. In late 2015 one of the featured books, while not on *kwich'on* specifically, was titled *Chibang ŏmma ŭi yuk'waehan kyoyuk hyŏngmyŏng* (A provincial mother's pleasurable education revolution) (Kim Hang-sim 2015), with the subtitle *Not "In Seoul" but "In Soul."* In this manual the "provincial mother" in question gives out rather standard advice (at least to a Western audience) about raising children with love as the foundation, not pushing them too hard, and guiding them as a supportive rather than panicky mother; but what interested me was the header for her introductory remarks section: "If I see the province/region [*chibang*] I live in as the center, then Taech'i-dong and Mok-dong [famous areas of "education fever" in Seoul] are just regions [*chibang*] too." In other words, she advises readers not to disparage their own not-in-Seoul locations and obsess over how the privileged mothers of Taech'i-dong and Mok-dong are getting ahead; instead, she urges a shift in the mental geography of "region" and "center," decentering Seoul and being satisfied with a home in the provinces as the center of one's own universe. While she does not speak much about rural excursions or nature, she encourages outings with children that relax them and get them invested in their community: trips to the bathhouse, to the traditional market, and to provincial civil society organization meetings. By emphasizing holistic maternal guidance and investment in local community, she decenters Seoul as the education mecca. While many provincial (non-Seoul) residents complain that *chibang* (the provinces) does not equal *sigol* (the countryside) despite Seoul residents' conflation of the two, it is true that in most smaller provincial cities the possibility of *kwich'on* is closer, both physically and psychologically. While this particular memoir/manual-writing mother does not turn to *kwich'on*, her rejection of Seoul as the center is echoed in much of the *kwich'on* literature.

A keyword search in October 2016 for *kwinong* and *kwich'on* on the website Aladin, a major online bookseller, revealed 190 books, with the majority of them broadly in the category of manuals, meaning that they provide organized instructions for the process of moving to the countryside. A few of the books discussed back-to-the-land movements in the West or in Japan, but most were about South Korea. The earliest books that specifically mentioned *kwinong* were from 1998, but the vast majority of titles were published after 2010. The search also reveals that *kwich'on* has become a more popular possibility than *kwinong* specifically in recent years. The highest-rated books in terms of reader reviews were part of a how-to series published between 2014 and 2016, with titles such as *Succeeding with a Back-to-the-Land Minbak* (inn) (Yu Sang-o 2016) and *Succeeding at Back-to-the-Land at Half the Cost* (Jung and Cho 2014). (Books that focus on starting a *minbak* often are addressing a recent trend of moving to Cheju Island and opening these boarding houses as both a new way of life and a second career.) Many of the books are in list form—*88 Things You Need to Know about Back-to-the-Land* (Cho 2013), *114 Questions about Back to-the-Land Answered* (Ch'ae 2015), *7 Rules to Follow to Succeed in Kwinong Kwich'on* (Sawaura 2013)—and others are collections of testimonials by people who did *kwinong* and/or *kwich'on*.

One specific *kwinong* series includes 45 titles, though only a handful showed up in the initial Aladin search because they did not have *kwinong* in the title. Several books in this particular series are about cultivating a plot of land with one's children—one title from 2015 is an encyclopedia of activities to do with children in nature in between planting and cultivating vegetables; activities include looking for four-leaf clovers and building a fire.[17] While some of the books that came up in searches focused on the economic aspects of *kwich'on*, more of them centered in on the inherent humane qualities of farming and living in the countryside, qualities that would positively affect children and whole families. *Kwich'on* practitioners write these books or online accounts for *kwich'on* hopefuls, and the discourse circulates both online and in the public spaces of bookstores, libraries, and community centers, where successful *kwich'on* practitioners and memoir writers might give public talks. *Kwich'on* discourse has been around for long enough that most of the South Korean public are familiar with it—and similar to early study abroad, everyone seems to know someone who has tried it.

Sociologist Song In-ha, mentioned previously, traces motivations for *kwich'on* and finds that "ecological values" are the main reason parents in their 30s or 40s with young children migrate from cities to the countryside (Song 2014). "Ecological values" means not just a general sense of environmentalism but also concerns about how their own family fits into the ecology of a changing, globalized world. Parents whom Song interviewed about their adjustment to educational facilities in the countryside said that even if their children did not achieve as much academically as their peers in the cities, they were learning to be more creative and self-motivated. One mother planning *kwich'on* mentioned that the countryside junior high schools her child might attend have never had a student commit suicide. According to Song's research, however, many parents worried about their children's education once they got to junior high school or high school, with some city transplants deciding to again send their children to *yuhak* (literally, "study away," generally used to mean "study abroad") in nearby cities to keep up academically. While some expressed regret that these older children now had to return to the city, they did not see the return as contradicting an instilling of ecological values, as it was thought that the most crucial time for developing ecological appreciation in children was in early childhood.

For parents who are undecided about family *kwich'on*, or for whom it is simply not feasible, there are *kwich'on yuhak* programs in all provinces. In these sorts of programs, students go to the countryside and live apart from their parents, attending local countryside schools, boarding in communal facilities run by the *kwich'on yuhak* centers, and experiencing life in nature for shorter- or longer-term programs. These types of *yuhak* programs are one way of outsourcing the "cultural work" it takes to guide a child toward self-realization outside of a regimented private education (*sagyoyuk*) system, normally an intense experience for mothers. It also supports the idea of the Korean countryside as an exotic enough place for most South Korean children that they can now "study abroad" there. Although the etymology of the word *yuhak* (留學) does not specifically include "abroad," it is a common enough usage that its use in the *kwich'on* context to refer to children moving domestically, between city and country, speaks volumes about the divide between city and country in South Korea today.[18]

Seoul has been classified as a "megacity" for quite some time, and since the 1960s its population density has steadily increased. However, 2016 was the first time in nearly three decades that the population of Seoul dropped below 10 million residents.[19] As the cost of real estate and the general cost of living have skyrocketed in Seoul, to the extent that economists have warned of a bubble, Seoul residents have been pushed out to nearby suburbs and satellite cities. These suburbs and suburb-like cities are still within commuting distance for those who work or attend school in Seoul, and many (Pundang and Ilsan, among others) have become education centers in their own right, with state-of-the-art *hagwŏn* popping up to rival those in Seoul. Provincial cities—such as Chŏnju, where Song (2014) conducted his research on *kwinong*, and Wŏnju, where I currently conduct mine—are too far away from Seoul to be a comfortable regular commute, but they offer urban *hagwŏn* resources and a handful of competitive public and private schools. Mothers I interviewed for a previous research project in Chŏnju (Tilland 2015, 2016) said that "education fever" (*kyoyugyŏl*) was more intense in Chŏnju than many other provincial cities, as education and the "culture industries" were the only "industries" in town, due to the Honam (Chŏlla) region's long-term exclusion from industrialization.[20] Wŏnju residents complain that the city's educational facilities are lacking vis-à-vis Seoul, but as with Chŏnju and certain other provincial cities, its central government-supported development of a *hyŏksin tosi* (innovation city) neighborhood—which brings in civil servants and their families from the capital—is contributing to the growth of local elite primary and secondary education. But burgeoning elite options aside, mothers in provincial cities speak of feeling stuck in between ultracompetitive Seoul and the idyllic countryside. In Seoul their children might have more resources to compete for admission to top universities, but in provincial cities many mothers felt that their children were engaged in never-ending, brutal competition with no prize at the end. Even if their children gained admission to a university in Seoul—almost always more prestigious than any provincial university—they recognized that admission to an elite SKY university (Seoul National University, Korea University, or Yonsei University) would be a reach. As Seoulites relocate to suburbs from the crowded, expensive capital, it is these mothers in provincial cities who are more likely to view *kwich'on* as a possibility. If their children are competing for nothing, is it not better to move to the slower-paced countryside, where competition is not really part of the equation? The idea that a relatively stress-free, noncompetitive childhood may actually lead to children finding a productive niche in society—in agriculture or in other ecological pursuits—is highly appealing.

As previously mentioned, Song (2014) is careful in his study of *kwinong* practitioners in the Chŏnju area to differentiate between those who migrate for *kwich'on* with their families for economic reasons and those who do so for "ecological" reasons. Because "ecological" does not simply refer here to an interest in nature but also to sensitivity to the place of the individual or family in an interconnected world, migration for the purposes of escaping a school system that parents perceive as unjust and counterproductive can also be included in the "ecological" category. Parents who view *kwich'on* as a possibility for their children's exit from the school system will be less likely to desire "education as usual" for their children once the move to the countryside is completed. Song found that "ecological" *kwich'on* practitioners tended to send children to local schools or, in some cases, to homeschool. Three of Song's informants referenced *nongch'on* (countryside) schools as promoting the natural environment and as being more "favorable" (*yurihada*) than city schools (2014: 305). One mother said in an interview, "Since we are doing *kwinong*, my kids may not study very well compared to the competitive atmosphere in the cities, but with the mindset that it's good for them to find their own place creatively [*ch'angŭijŏk ŭro chagi yŏkhal*], I think that the *nongch'on* is a better educational environment" (307). Song found that while those who moved to the countryside for "ecological" reasons—which I also take to mean reasons of family balance and child physical and psychological health—tend to want to pass down values of respect for nature, communitarianism, and harmony to children, those who move for primarily economic reasons do not integrate as well into local communities and also are more inclined to send children back to *yuhak* in cities, particularly once they have reached junior high or high school.

As suggested at the beginning of this chapter, the slow but perceptible diversification in ideals from urban high-rise to countryside home points to a shift in broader social ideals. High-rise apartments have eliminated annoyances from the rural past such as bugs and other pests, as well as the necessity of engaging with community members, but have also led to alienation and a level of standardization of living space that many younger Koreans find unappealing. Although apartments became desirable in the 1980s and 1990s largely due to associations with advanced capitalist modernity, ironically some Koreans are inclined toward countryside homes now for similar reasons. Rather than buying or renting a cookie-cutter apartment unit, having a house with a garden that has been built or renovated in the countryside illustrates class distinction. Even as parents in their 30s and 40s may to some degree associate the countryside with poor hygiene and poor quality of life due to the stories of their parents and grandparents, they may also associate the countryside with cleaner air and water and luxurious new countryside homes (*chŏngwŏn chut'aek*) with a Westernized lifestyle. As the countryside comes to represent physical and mental health, *kwich'on* risks becoming an individualistic, neoliberal search for health for one's children and the family as a whole. Yet the deeper community ties of the countryside can trigger a shift from the individualistic neoliberal mode to the global community mode.

Kwinong Kwich'on Memoir as a New Genre

In Abelmann and Kang's (2014) analysis of the "study abroad mother memoirs/manuals" as a genre, they divide the works they found into three categories: narratives of failure, narratives of success, and more ambivalent narratives of maternal sacrifice through feminine labor. Compared to this earlier genre, there are not nearly as many books specifically written by mothers reflecting on their *kwich'on* experience with their families. Many of the books on *kwinong* specifically are aimed at the men who are assumed to be the primary farmers, and books on financing *kwinong*, *kwich'on*, or *kwihyang* are typically aimed at both men and women (as women are often the ones managing household finances in Korea). One male *kwinong* practitioner wrote a comedic "novel-like" account of his experience, including persuading his reluctant wife to move to the countryside (Kim T'ae-hwan 2015); and two female best friends in their 30s and 40s (unmarried and without children) decided to do *kwich'on* together and wrote a graphic novel detailing the experience, *Tu yŏja wa tu nyangi ŭi kwich'on ilgi* (The back-to-the-land diary of two women and two cats, 2011). A few books that highlight women's experience in their families stand out and are often in the form of short essays collected by several people.

One true example of the *kwinong kwich'on* memoir genre is by Yun Insuk, titled *Settling the Heart: One Mother's Back-to-the-Land Story in Five Provinces and Two Villages* (*Maŭm ŭl chŏnghada: 5 do 2 ch'on ŏmma ŭi kwich'on iyagi*, 2014). Yun's *kwich'on* follows a similar trajectory as many found on blogs and community sites: she had a large age gap between her children and was shocked when she found out how much competition and pressure in even preschool and early elementary school had intensified since her eldest was young. Although her eldest got through the education system in the Seoul suburb of Pundang without incident, her youngest was already suffering. First she sent him to a *kwich'on yuhak* program in Kangwŏn-do for two years, and then he attended an alternative school in Kyŏngsang-namdo for two years. At the time when she wrote the memoir, her son was attending a "Gandhi" middle school also in Kyŏngsang-namdo, after having attended another branch of the experiential education-focused alternative school closer to the central city of Taejŏn for a short while. (The Gandhi schools are Korea's earliest alternative education model in Korea, and with both stronger competition for admission and higher tuition than most other alternative schools in Korea, they are widely views as "elite" alternative schools).

In her book she describes her entry into the village, her developing relationship to her community, her experiences making and selling strawberry jam, and the positive effects of village life on her child. In the epilogue to her book she describes finally quitting her research institute job—she has been renting a small house in the country while her son boards at the countryside alternative school, only spending weekends in the village and living in the Seoul suburb of Pundang during the week—and taking her youngest son along with her and her husband to walk the Camino de Santiago in Spain. (This is a path to the shrine of the apostle of St. James the Great, which traditionally is undertaken as a spiritual quest but which many Korean cycling and hiking enthusiasts have become interested in after the popularization of the path on Korean travel programs.) Then Yun finally moves to the village she has come to consider home and sends her youngest son, now in high school, back to the Philippines, where he is attending the newly established international branch campus of the Gandhi School. (Until this point the book has followed quite a common trajectory, but the shift from *nongch'on yuhak* to actual international *yuhak* is surprising. Yet when one examines the curriculum of the "Gandhi School" as outlined in the book this makes somewhat more sense, as the alternative school program encourages experimentation, discussion, and collaboration, things mainstream education in South Korea is not known for.) In

Yun's case, the *kwich'on* experience leads directly to global experience and global citizenship for her children.

Contrasting with Yun's narrative is a blog post from June 2016, titled "*Kwinong* Is Ultimately a Kind of Lifestyle," published by the *Kwinong t'ongmun* newsletter. The author, Yu Sŭng-yŏn, is an after-school program teacher and describes her process of becoming more and more frustrated by researching *kwich'on* options. She writes,

> Many people have done *kwinong* or plan to do *kwinong*. Among these, some succeed and some fail and return to their old lives. Those who hate the competitive lives of the city surrounded by concrete and pollution, and so yearn to enjoy life while relaxing in nature and joining some kind of communal family have close to a 100 percent chance of failure. Nature itself is straightforward, but there are too many variables otherwise that are hard to predict. People cannot live alone. Whether you live in an apartment tower or countryside village, without information about your environment or concern about the people around you, you'll never be happy.

The author goes on to describe the short-term fermented food workshop she attended in Sunch'ang (the town in North Chŏlla province famous for bean paste and soy sauce), which after years of agonizing over how and where to do *kwinong* finally set her mind at ease that what she was seeking was a shift in lifestyle and frame of mind rather than *kwinong* itself and that leaving the city when it was not what she really desired would be taking things too far. Her decision reminded me of several of my interviewees in North Chŏlla's provincial capital of Chŏnju in 2010–12, who debated embarking on *kwinong* but ultimately decided to forge the necessary connections for frequent weekend trips while staying in the city.

Whether parents—and most often mothers, as they are the parent most often tasked with planning a child's education trajectory—decide to embark on *kwich'on* or to stay in the city, what is interesting here is the common acceptance that extended exposure to nature and countryside values is good for children. The flip side of Korea's "convenience culture," which encompasses the ubiquity of food delivery and *hagwŏn* study until late into the evening, is a lack of green space and crowding. Awareness of the dangers of air pollution—both produced by China and homegrown—is also growing. The age of children is commonly taken into consideration in *kwich'on* planning, as while countryside living may be extremely beneficial for preschool and elementary school children, it may be regarded as unrealistic for middle school and high school children, who should be positioned to take advantage of urban or suburban private education resources. Parents who envision extended nonurban lifestyles for their families may be more inclined to immigrate to countries with much less urban density, given the resources. However, some like Yun intend *kwich'on* as a temporary experiment to deal with unexpected elementary school stress, only to recognize its ongoing benefits for children and families and commit to it for the long haul, letting go of the focus on "academic achievement."

Among those practicing *kwich'on* or intending to make the move, some speak of a single moment that motivated them to leave the city: a child's manifestations of acute stress or reactions to falling behind in school or a local or national news report of school bullying or youth suicide. Others point to a long-term desire to go back to the land, finally possible now due to changes in their husband's or their own employment. Yun (2014: 6–7) describes this moment in the prologue to her book:

> The *hagwŏn* increased one by one, until suddenly there were six. My child came back late in the evening, so there was no time to play. I had given birth to this child with difficulty at the age of thirty-six, and watched him grow in an incubator for the first week of his life. My weak child got frequent nosebleeds, and would collapse in exhaustion when he got home. We quit the other *hagwŏn*, but the emphasis on English in school implemented under the [former president] Lee Myung-bak [Yi Myŏng-bak] regime was a problem. There was no time for what was learned to sink in, and kids constantly took vocabulary tests and were ranked. I wondered if it was really necessary to go to school and never catch your breath, so I started looking into alternative schools, and finally at the end of my son's second year of elementary school I went to a parents' meeting [about countryside *yuhak*].

Yun (2014: 10) details the positive transformation of both her son and herself in the rest of the *kwich'on* memoir, foreshadowing some of the happy results in the prologue:

> There is no more trace of that weak child in my son now, due to the countryside life he has experienced since the age of ten [six years ago]. Even if he plays soccer until sunset he is energetic the next day, and he goes around even in the winter in shorts. After years of eating clean and hearty countryside food his skin rashes have dis-

appeared. After six years of communal living he has deep relationships with friends. He takes responsibility for his belongings and has no great interest in nice things or nice clothes. When neither parents nor child are obsessed with studying, there is not much reason for conflict between them. Even my mother, who once accused me of being a "senseless mom" who would "make my son an idiot by shutting him off in the countryside" now says that he is the happiest kid.

In contrast to the cautionary tales of *kwich'on* that proliferate online, Yun's published memoir is an unqualified success story. In the final section of this chapter I examine a final element of *kwich'on* discourse, still largely implicit—that of the countryside's shifting relationship to globalism and multiculturalism and the perceived benefits in this arena.

The *Nongch'on* as Multicultural, Globalized Land of Opportunity

In *kwich'on* memoirs and manuals, blogs, and online forums, the concepts of globalization (*segyehwa*) and multiculturalism (*tamunhwajuŭi*) come up much less frequently than do ideas of going back to Korean "roots" or finding balance or "breathing room" (*yŏyu*) in the countryside. However, given that parents in their 30s and 40s embarking on family *kwich'on* came of age during the 1990s—when then president Kim Young-sam (Kim Yŏng-sam) made "globalization" a household word—it would follow that their personal ideals are colored by *segyehwa* and related concepts. While families who relocate overseas for the purposes of study abroad and English acquisition for their children explicitly reference globalization and the importance of making children "global citizens," globalization and "globalist" values tend to arise more implicitly in *kwich'on* discourse. Parents who move to the countryside with school-age children must let go of attachments to *hagwŏn*-assisted English language acquisition, and indeed the disconnection from the entire *sagyoyuk* (private education) system that a move to the countryside typically brings means that the real-time nature of long-term test preparation quickly falls out of sync. Yet as found in Yun's memoir, this severing from the temporality of the Korean education system is part of the appeal of *kwich'on*. Yun laments that under the pressures of nearly constant English vocabulary tests and subsequent class rankings, her son had no mental space or energy to absorb what he was supposed to learn. Advocates of *kwich'on* argue that the countryside allows space, or breathing room (*yŏyu*) in both a spatial and a temporal sense, for children to process information and experience deeper learning. This more relaxed and deeper learning is implicitly a "global" quality, as it has more in common with Western education systems as opposed to the rote-learning test preparation priorities of East Asian education. The more relaxed pace of countryside schools—or, for those parents who choose, homeschool—together with the absence of *sagyoyuk* options, allows for the more flexible study of all subjects, including global issues. It also allows for short international trips abroad during breaks—for those with the resources—as there is no pressure to send children to summer and winter break *hagwŏn* programs to keep up with peers.

If *segyehwa* was the buzzword of the 1990s in South Korea, *tamunhwa* was the buzzword of the 2000s. Although school textbooks proudly pointed out that South Korea was a "single ethnic origin society" (*tanil minjok sahoe*) until the mid-2000s, policies rapidly shifted to reflect changes in immigration patterns, namely, the influx of foreign wives from other Asian countries. As policy makers and the public recognized the low birthrate problem (*chŏch'ulsan munje*), these women were meant to solve this problem through reproduction with South Korean men who had not been able to marry through ordinary routes. These less than desirable bachelors became a source of national consternation, as most remained in the countryside assisting with family farms or other rural businesses. Documentary television programs about these men's sacrifice for their elderly parents and for the nation itself, as guardians of the land, tugged at the heartstrings of urban Koreans. The demographic characteristics of the migrant women (*iju yŏsŏng*) who married these men have changed continuously throughout the 2000s and 2010s. As the concept of *tamunhwajuŭi* matured throughout the 2000s, concern arose over the product of these marriages, multiethnic children in the countryside. The South Korean government and NGOs mobilized to develop resources for these *tamunhwa kajok* in terms of linguistic and cultural adjustment. Although public opinion is still divided in South Korea over the advantages of multiculturalism, many countryside schools are experiments in multicultural living, with sizeable portions of the student population made up of the children of *tamunhwa kajok*.

Kwich'on practitioners are moving to the same rural areas where such experiments in multiculturalism have been going on for over a decade. Although mothers with whom I discussed *kwich'on* plans did not often refer to these families and still seemed to imagine interpersonal challenges in their new communities as largely involving adapting to a slower pace of life with older local villagers, in discussions about schooling most articulated a general awareness of multicultural students. While not necessarily clearly articulated, the growing diversity of countryside schools was seen as a part of the overall *yŏyu* that was a primary goal of family *kwich'on*. Moreover, parents embarking on *kwich'on* often see themselves as another kind of migrant (*ijumin*) and thus as sharing a responsibility for empathy and cooperation in the contact zone of the countryside. An OhmyNews article from November 24, 2016, urges *kwich'on* practitioners to think of themselves as migrants (*ijumin*), not people who have simply completed a move (*isa*): "Leaving the city to move to the countryside is not a simple 'move.' It is moving one's residence to an entirely new culture. When doing *kwinong kwich'on*, one should use the word 'migration' just as if one is moving to a foreign country. In the countryside *kwinong kwich'on* practitioners are called 'migrants.'"[21] In the spaces between long-standing local villagers, multicultural families, and migrants for *kwich'on*, a new etiquette and ethics emerges.

Conclusion

In this chapter I have traced emergent different types of public discourse about *kwich'on* as they circulate for parents (and particularly mothers) of preschool and school-age children. While there is not a specific literature on "*kwich'on* failures" as there is for study abroad mother memoirs/manuals, there are plenty of cautionary tales online about jumping into family *kwich'on* blindly, including blog posts such as Yu's, mentioned above. *Kwich'on* hopefuls such as Yu invest time and money into finding the perfect *kwich'on* location and setup, only to come to the realization that their family's needs are better satisfied by weekend trips to the countryside or participation in short-term programs. Many of the mothers with young children I interviewed in Chŏnju participated in such programs even as they contemplated future full-time *kwich'on* or *kwinong*, and many had parents or extended family in the countryside around Chŏnju, where they could spend weekends. In contrast, the parents I talked to in Wŏnju (Kangwŏn-do) do not tend to have family in countryside areas of the province, as not many Wŏnju residents are natives of the area. These parents are more likely to take advantage of formal programs or to relocate for *kwich'on* in another area altogether.

Yun's story, also detailed above, is an example of "*kwich'on* success" literature, although "success" here is separate from the straightforward academic success that will get a child through the Korean formal education system and into a top university. Success here is thought of as something bigger—as it is in the study abroad mother manuals/memoirs that Abelmann and Kang (2014) analyzed—including physical and psychological health, resilience, and self-motivation. In Yun's memoir, the *kwich'on* journey may begin as an individual search for health in the neoliberal mode, but it evolves into a process of community making with like-minded globally oriented, ecologically motivated neighbors, one that surprises the newbie *kwich'on* practitioner herself. Yun notes several times in her book that she did not consider herself someone suited for communal living but found herself in unanticipated ways by working, chatting with, and caring for villagers. However, despite the truly hopeful aspects of the *kwich'on* trend, it is on the whole too decentralized and too individualized to constitute a widespread social movement at this time. *Kwich'on* as a practice with socially transformative possibilities is structurally bound by the general inflexibility of the South Korean education system (rules about entering and exiting the system, lack of accreditation for most alternative schools), even as it is transformative for individual families in the short or long term. Moreover, as Albert Park (2016) briefly notes in a related article, and as Yu's blog post illustrates, the idealism and the romanticism associated with *kwinong* or *kwich'on* too often lead to failure once would-be practitioners cannot find the idyllic countryside of their dreams.

A final piece of my consideration of *kwinong kwich'on kwihyang* has to do with the multicultural families who have lived in the countryside in significant numbers since the mid-2000s. The existence of ethnic and cultural diversity in the countryside was something that frequently came up in interviews, even as interviewees were not always sure what a more diverse school for their children and village for their family would mean in practice. Whereas at first the cultural and linguistic background of migrant brides from the Philippines, Vietnam, China, and other countries was not appreciated as an asset to the nation, in recent years Koreans have become more aware of Southeast Asian countries (and of course China) as potential business partners, and more South Korean universities have begun to offer courses in these countries' languages. While discrimination against the children of *tamunhwa kajok* is still a serious concern, shifting demographics, especially in the countryside, are changing the field. Although South Korea's model of "multiculturalism" remains assimilationist, there are more and more news reports that mention the cultural diversity of the countryside and the potential benefit of this diversity to *kwinong kwich'on* newcomers from the city. The most Korean thing (the Korean countryside) now has the potential to be the most global thing, and all in a place of less stress and competition and with a connection to nature.

NOTES

1. Mal ŭn Chejudo ro, saram ŭn Sŏul ro ponaera (말은 제주도로 사람은 서울로 보내라).
2. This *Korea Herald* article claims that noise complaints (to police, not merely to apartment management offices) increased from 7,020 cases in 2012 to 15,450 cases in 2013. http://www.koreaherald.com/view.php?ud=20140305001110&mod=skb
3. Diana Tomale, "18,000 South Koreans Leave Cities to Settle in Rural Areas in 2014, Young Koreans in Their 30s Account for 27.2 Percent of Resettlers." *Korea Portal*, November 9, 2015. http://en.koreaportal.com/articles/1583/20151109/south-koreans-cities-rural-areas.htm
4. Parents in their 30s and 40s with children were a rapidly increasing *kwinong kwich'on* demographic. This article from 2015 is just one of many that report that those in their 30s were the largest group, followed by those in their 40s. http://www.jutek.kr/user/selectBbsColumn.do?BBS_NUM=7098&COD03_CODE=c0318
5. See Youngmin Choe's analysis of director Hong Sang-su's 2002 film *Turning Gate*, in which she examines the *kwinong* motivations of one character during the 1997 Asian financial crisis. "Farming was seen simultaneously as a viable measure to absorb the shock of massive unemployment while reversing the rural-to-urban drain that had depleted the countryside of young people over decades, thereby reinvigorating it with more youthful segments of the population.... The nature of *kwinong* as a countermeasure against unemployment in the late 1990s is a major departure from its ideological origins of *kwinong* as a 'social democratization movement' (*sahoe minjuhwa undong*)" (2009: 23). Song In-ha (2014) also details the history of the movement.
6. The *sampo* generation has now begun to call themselves the *N-po* generation, meaning that the list of things that youth outside of the 1 percent (the so-called golden spoons) have to give up in Korea (not just dating and marriage, but also a house, car, etc.) is ever-lengthening.
7. This article is one of many that describe the slow but steady increase in the *kwich'on* demographic: http://www.hani.co.kr/arti/economy/economy_general/800762.html. See this article for a breakdown of the decrease in early study abroad numbers in the 2000s versus the 2010s: https://news.joins.com/article/21733971
8. See this Institute for International Education report on international student numbers in US higher education: https://www.iie.org/en/Research-and-Insights/Open-Doors/Data/International-Students/Places-of-Origin. Another article from 2015 notes falling overseas university study numbers in the face of a stagnant South Korean economy but also observes that Korean students are shifting from expensive higher education destination such as the United States to countries such as China and the Philippines: http://monitor.icef.com/2015/02/number-korean-students-abroad-declines-third-straight-year/
9. "Goose families" refer to families in which the children and mother go abroad

and the "goose father" stays in South Korea to earn money. He is called a "goose father" because he only flies to see his family periodically. See Abelmann and Kang (2013) for more on this phenomenon.

10. Popular articles such as this one frequently come out lamenting the creativity-suppressing nature of South Korean education and the test-prep focus in particular: https://news.joins.com/article/22296598

11. http://asiasociety.org/global-cities-education-network/south-korean-education-reforms

12. Randall S. Jones, "Educational Reform in South Korea," OECD Economics Department Working Papers No. 1067, 2013.

13. See Michael Seth, *Education Fever* (Honolulu: University of Hawaii Press, 2002), for an overview of the supplementary education industry in South Korea and its origins. For a more updated treatment, see Adrienne Lo, Nancy Abelmman, Soo Ah Kwon, and Sumie Okazaki, eds., *South Korea's Education Exodus: The Life and Times of Early Study Abroad* (Seattle: University of Washington Press, 2015).

14. http://m.blog.naver.com/jbgokr/220190235214

15. This 2015 interview transcript discusses the shift from *tanil minjok* to *tamunhwa* in South Korean schools (http://news.sbs.co.kr/news/endPage.do?news_id=N1002869781), and an article from 2007 laments the excessive focus on *tanil minjok* in South Korean elementary school textbooks: http://news.khan.co.kr/kh_news/khan_art_view.html?art_id=200708212359521. When I conducted interviews in Chŏnju during a pilot study in summer 2008, I heard from parents of an elementary school student that references to *tanil minjok* had been removed just that year. Later, in interviews with mothers in Chŏnju in 2010, I frequently heard that these middle-class Korean mothers saw *tamunhwa* families in their midst but had little experience with them personally.

16. See this KOSIS chart for a breakdown of *kwich'on* statistics in 2018: http://kosis.kr/statHtml/statHtml.do?orgId=101&tblId=DT_1A02015. It is telling that regions such as Kangwŏn and the Chŏlla provinces (North and South) are still less popular as destinations than the Kyŏngsang provinces or the Kyŏnggi area immediately surrounding Seoul, both of which have higher population density due to larger cities. This suggests that some families see *kwich'on* closer to a sizeable city as a safer bet.

17. The name of the series is *Nongbu ka sesang ul pakkunda kwinong ch'ongsŏ* (Farmers change the world, back-to-the-land series).

18. For a recent article on such *kwich'on yuhak* centers and programs, see http://www.hankookilbo.com/News/Read/201807121125077213

19. Won Nak-yeon, "Seoul's Population Falls below 10 Million for the First Time in 28 Years," *Hankyoreh*, June 2, 2016. http://english.hani.co.kr/arti/english_edition/e_national/746525.html

20. Sallie Yea (2009) details social and cultural factors in this regional alienation.

21. Chŏng Myŏngjin, "Five Aspects of Back-to-the-land that Are Easy for City People to Mindunderstand," *OhmyNews*, November 24, 2016 (in Korean). http://www.ohmynews.com/nws_web/view/at_pg.aspx?cntn_cd=a0002264016

REFERENCES

Abelmann, Nancy, and Jiyeon Kang. 2014. "Memoir/Manuals of South Korean Pre-College Study Abroad: Defending Mothers and Humanizing Children." *Global Networks* 14 (1): 1–22.

Arai, Andrea Gevurtz. 2016. *The Strange Child: Education and the Psychology of Patriotism in Recessionary Japan.* Stanford, CA: Stanford University Press.

Ch'ae Sang-hŏn. 2015. *Kwinong kwich'on 114 mundap p'uri* (*114 Questions about Back to-the-Land Answered*). Seoul: Koryŏ Ak'ademi K'ŏnsŏlt'ing Ch'ulp'anbu (in Korean).

Cho Tong-jin. 2013. *Kwinong kwich'on araya hal 88 kaji* (*88 Things You Need to Know about Back-to-the-Land*). Kyŏngju: Simp'oni (in Korean).

Choe, Youngmin. 2009. "Transitional Emotions: Boredom and Distraction in Hong Sang-soo's Travel Films." *Korean Studies* 43: 1–28.

Chŏn Kyŏng-su. 2008. "Ch'abyŏl ŭi sahoehwa wa sisŏn ŭi chŏngch'i kwajŏngnon: tamunhwa kajŏng chanyŏ e kwanhan yebijŏk yŏn'gu" (Socialization of Discrimination and Political Processes of Stigmatized Staring: A Preparatory Research on Children from Multicultural Families in Rural Korea). *Han'guk munhwa illyuhak* (*Korean Cultural Anthropology*) 41 (1): 5–50 (in Korean).

Chŏng Ku-hyŏn and Cho Kŭm-sŏn. 2014. *Kwinong kwich'on pangap e sŏnggong hagi* (*Succeeding at Back-to-the-Land at Half the Cost*). Seoul: Raon Book (e-book) (in Korean).

Gelezeau, Valerie. 2007. *Apartment Republic* (*Ap'at'ŭ konghwaguk*). Seoul: Humanit'asŭ (in Korean).

Kim Hang-sim. 2015. *Chibang ŏmma ŭi yuk'waehan kyoyuk hyŏngmyŏng* (*A Provincial Mother's Pleasurable Education Revolution*). Changsu: Naeil ŭl Yŏnŭn Ch'aek (in Korean).

Kim, Minjeong. 2014. "South Korean Rural Husbands, Compensatory Masculinity, and International Marriage." *Journal of Korean Studies* 19 (2): 291–325.

Kim T'ae-hwan. 2015. *Kwich'on* (*Back-to-the-Land*). Seoul: Pap Puk (in Korean).

Ku Pon-gyu. 2016. "'Tamunhwa' nŭn ŏttok'e ijumin kajok ŭl piha hanŭn mal i toeŏnna?" (How Did "Multicultural" Become a Word to Disparage Migrant Families?). In *Han'guk tamunhwajuŭi pip'an* (*Critique of Korean Multiculturalism*), edited by Yi Chin-hyŏng, 177–233. Diaspora Humanities Series 002, Konkuk University, Center for Asia and Diaspora. Seoul: LP (in Korean).

Kwon, Kyŏnghŭi. 2011. *The Back-to-the-Land Diary of Two Women and Two Cats.* Seoul: Midia Ilda (in Korean).

Lee, Namhee. 2009. *The Making of Minjung: Democracy and the Politics of Representation in South Korea.* Ithaca: Cornell University Press.

Love, Bridget. 2013. "Treasure Hunts in Rural Japan: Place Making at the Limits of Sustainability." *American Anthropologist* 115 (1): 112–24.

Moon, Seungsook. 2005. *Militarized Modernity and Gendered Citizenship in South Korea.* Durham, NC: Duke University Press.

Nemeth, David. 2008. "Blame Walt Rostow: The Sacrifice of South Korea's Natural Villages." In *Sitings: Critical Approaches to Korean Geography*, edited by Timothy R. Tangherlini and Sallie Yea, 83–97. Honolulu: University of Hawai'i Press.

Park, Albert L. 2016. "Social Renewal through the Rural: Agricultural Cooperatives in South Korea as a Form of Critiquing Capitalism." *Global Environment* 9: 82–107.

Rhee, Jooyeon. 2014. "Migrant Workers and Foreign Brides in 'Multicultural Korea.'" *Perspectives Internationales*, November 11. http://perspectivesinternationales.com/?p=1257

Sawaura Syoji. 2013. *Kwinong kwich'on 7 kaji sŏnggong pŏpch'ik (7 Rules to Follow to Succeed in Kwinong Kwich'on)*. Translated by Pak Hyŏng-gu. Seoul: Maeil Kyŏngje Sinmunsa (in Korean).

Sohn, Agnes. 2015. "Urban Exodus: The Back-to-the-Land Movement." *Korea File*, July 1. http://koreabridge.net/post/urban-exodus-back-land-movement-korea-file

Sŏng Chi-hye. 2014. "Kwinongji chŏgŭng e taehan yŏsŏngjuŭijŏk yŏn'gu: 'namp'yŏn yŏn'gohyang' yŏsŏng ŭl chungsim ŭro" (Feminist Research on Adaptation of the Return-to-the-Soil: With a Woman, Who Has a Husband Who Returns Hometown, as the Central Figure). *Korean Women Studies* 30 (2): 161–202 (in Korean).

Song In-ha. 2014. *Kwinong haengbok: kwinong silch'ŏn esŏ hyŏnmyŏnghan chanyŏ kyoyuk kkaji (The Happiness of Kwinong: From Practice to Revolutionary Education for Children)*. P'aju: Idam (in Korean).

Song, Jesook. 2009. *South Koreans in the Debt Crisis: The Creation of a Neoliberal Welfare Society*. Durham, NC: Duke University Press.

Sorensen, Clark. 1994. "Success and Education in South Korea." *Comparative Education* 38 (1): 10–35.

Tilland, Bonnie. 2015. "Hateful and Heartwarming Bonds: The Senses as Strategy in the South Korean Family." PhD diss., University of Washington.

Tilland, Bonnie. 2016. "Family Is Beautiful: The Affective Weight of Mothers-in-Law in Family Talk in South Korea." *Journal of Korean Studies* 21 (1): 213–44.

Tran, Tommy. 2015. "Imagining Urban Community: Contested Geographies and Parallax Urban Dreams on Cheju Island, South Korea." *Cross-Currents: East Asian History and Culture Review*, December (e-journal), 17: 86–113.

Yea, Sallie. 2000. "Maps of Resistance and Geographies of Dissent in the Chŏlla Region of South Korea." *Korean Studies* 24: 69–93.

Yu Sang-o, ed. 2016. *Kwich'on kwinong minbak ŭro sŏnggong hagi (Succeeding with a Back-to-the-Land Minbak)*. Seoul: Hans Media (in Korean).

Yu Sŭng-yŏn. 2016. "Kwinong to kyŏlguk hana ŭi saenghwal pangsik" (*Kwinong* Is Ultimately a Kind of Lifestyle). *Pressian (Kwinong t'ongmun)*, June 24. Accessed October 15, 2016. http://www.pressian.com/news/article.html?no=138249&ref=nav_search (in Korean).

Yun In-suk. 2014. *Maŭm ŭl chŏnghada: 5 do 2 ch'on ŏmma ŭi kwich'on iyagi (Settling the Heart: One Mother's Back-to-the-Land Story in Five Provinces and Two Villages)*. P'aju: Hanul (in Korean).

Contributors

Hyunjoon Park is Korea Foundation Professor of Sociology at the University of Pennsylvania. His research interest includes social stratification, education, and family in comparative perspective, focusing on East Asian societies. He is the director of Korean Millennials Lab, which investigates diverse pathways to adulthood in the context of rising inequality in Korea. He is also engaged in a project on multigenerational effects. Park published a single-authored book, *Re-Evaluating Education in Japan and Korea: De-mystifying Stereotypes*.

Hyeyoung Woo is Associate Professor of Sociology at Portland State University. Her research centers on family behaviors and their associations to health and well-being over the life course, and her recent work has appeared in journals, including *Journal of Gerontology, Series B: Psychological Sciences and Social Sciences* and *Research on Aging*. She also published a coauthored book, titled *Social Foundations of Behavior for the Health Sciences* (Springer, 2017). Currently, she is the coeditor of *Sociological Perspectives*.

Paul Y. Chang is Associate Professor of Sociology at Harvard University. He is the author of *Protest Dialectics: State Repression and South Korea's Democracy Movement, 1970–1979* (Stanford University Press, 2015) and the coeditor of *South Korean Social Movements: From Democracy to Civil Society* (Routledge, 2011). His research on social and political change in South Korea has appeared in several disciplinary and area studies journals.

Eunsil Oh is Assistant Professor of Sociology at the University of Wisconsin at Madison. She received a PhD in sociology from Harvard University. Her research focuses on women's lives, with a focus on education, employment, and gender in East Asia. Additionally, Eunsil has collaborative projects that use a comparative lens to explore how labor markets, welfare systems, and gender norms shape individual- and couple-level understandings of work and family.

Hyejeong Jo is Adjunct Professor of Sociology at Hanyang University. She received her PhD in sociology at the University of Pennsylvania in 2017. Her research interests are in education, family, social stratification, and qualitative method. She is currently conducting a qualitative study about how social inequalities shape people's demographic behaviors in the context of South Korea. Her research explores the ways that people make a decision regarding family formation—including marriage and fertility—differently for their social positions.

Soo-yong Byun is Associate Professor of Education and Demography at Pennsylvania State University. His research investigates variation in mechanisms and processes of social stratification across different countries and geographic contexts using large-scale national and international data. His work has appeared in journals, including *American Educational Research Journal*, *American Journal of Education*, *Comparative Education Review*, and *Sociology of Education*.

Yifan Bai is a researcher at the American Institutes for Research. Her scholarly interests focus on understanding factors related to children's achievement in the United States and other countries by analyzing national and international large-scale data sets.

Hee Jin Chung is a lecturer at Hongik University. Her research interests lie in the areas of sociology of education and international education. She is particularly interested in the long-term consequences of educational inequality across different social contexts.

Sojung Lim is Assistant Professor of Sociology at Utah State University. She received her PhD from the University of Wisconsin at Madison. Her research interests center on social inequality with a particular focus on the consequences of family and labor market changes in both the United States and East Asia. Her research has been published in various journals, such as the *Journal of Marriage and Family*, *Population Studies*, *Demographic Research*, and *Social Science Research*.

Sun Young Jeon is a senior statistician in the Department of Medicine at the University of California, San Francisco. Working with investigators and fellows, she conducts research on prediction of mortality and life expectancies among senior populations. She also provides support for study design and proposal development and consults on appropriate statistical approaches. She has expertise in data analysis from national health interview surveys, Medicare claims data, and Veterans Affairs data.

Wonjeong Jeong received a BA and an MA in sociology from Yonsei University in Korea. Currently, she is a PhD student in the Department of Sociology and a student affiliate at the Center for the Study of Inequality at Cornell University. She is interested in looking at the intersections of demographic processes and intergenerational stratification, along with changes in social institutions.

Heewon Jang is a PhD candidate in Educational Policy at the Stanford Graduate School of Education. Her research focuses on the patterns and consequences of residential and school segregation regarding racial and socioeconomic achievement gaps as well as the effects of educational policy on educational opportunities and social mobility.

Haram Jeon is Assistant Professor of Education at Chonnam National University, South Korea. His research interest lies in education policy analysis, sociology of education, and comparative and international education. He is currently working on research about cross-national differences in the associations between educational attainment and health outcomes.

Yean-Ju Lee is Associate Professor of Sociology at the University of Hawai'i at Mānoa. Her research concerns family changes in South Korea and other East Asian societies and has explored how gender and generational relations are shaped by dynamic social environments, including rapid economic growth and rising inequality. Her book *Divorce in South Korea: Doing Gender and the Dynamics of Relationship Breakdown* is forthcoming by the University of Hawai'i Press.

Kitae Park is Associate Research Fellow at the National Assembly Futures Institute in South Korea. He was a postdoctorate researcher at the Center for SSK Multicultural Research at Hanyang University in South Korea. His current research interests include the sociology of the family, social demography, and medical sociology.

Ivan Sanidad earned an MA in sociology at the University of Hawaiʻi at Mānoa, specializing in medical sociology and population studies (demography), and an MA in humanities at Tiffin University, focusing on cultural and fandom studies. He worked as a research assistant and technical writer for *The Feasibility of a Long-Term Services and Supports Social Insurance Program for Hawaii*. He currently works for the Hawaii Department of Education.

Byung Soo Lee is a PhD candidate in the Department of Sociology at the University at Buffalo, SUNY. His research focuses on how Asian immigrant families in the United States experience the changes of family relations and the narratives of the families that reveal the gap between the subjective perception of family relations and the structural changes in a given society. His current research examines how Asian immigrant family members interpret the meaning of parenthood.

Jihye Oh is a PhD candidate in the Department of Sociology at Yonsei University. She received a BA in urban sociology from the University of Seoul and an MA in sociology from Yonsei University in Seoul, South Korea. Her research interests focus on family demography, specifically differences in life course such as marriage and divorce. She was awarded the young sociologist grand prize in South Korea and has received several fellowships. She is the author of "The Timing and Possibility of Marriage of Single Men and Women in Korea" (*Korean Journal of Sociology*, 2016) and several chapters for edited volumes on issues related to families.

Jae Kyung Lee is Professor Emerita of Women's Studies at Ewha Womans University in Seoul. Trained as a sociologist, she has specialized in family issues and gender policies in South Korea. She has published numerous articles and book chapters and has authored and edited several books, including *Modern Korean Family and Feminism*, *The State and Gender in South Korea*, *Feminist Oral History: Deconstructing Institutional Knowledge*, and *National Development and Gender Politics*. She is currently writing a book tentatively titled *The South Korean Family at the Crossroads*.

Soo-Yeon Yoon is Assistant Professor in the Department of Sociology at Sonoma State University. She holds a PhD in sociology from the University of Illinois at Urbana-Champaign. Her primary research interests lie in the areas of family, gender equality, and population changes. Much of her work focuses on the theoretical importance of the intersection of work and family. Her current research involves a comparative and critical understanding of families in East Asia.

Bonnie Tilland is Assistant Professor of Anthropology in the East Asia International College at Yonsei University, Wŏnju campus, in Korea. Her research thus far has focused on South Korean women's negotiations of care labor in the family, the senses, and the affective afterlives of television dramas. She received her PhD in sociocultural anthropology from the University of Washington, where she also completed a graduate certificate in feminist studies and an MA in Korea studies.

Index

Note: Page numbers in *italics* refer to tables and figures.

abortion, 23
affairs, 266n4
after-school programs, 138
age (adults): in assortative mating study, 102, *105*, *109*; in childcare time study, 197, 204; in fertility and gender roles study, 280; and gender role attitudes, 276; in gender roles in immigrants to US study, 218, *219–21*; in information gathering study, 53; at marriage, 1, 25, 37, 243, 249; in marriage probability study, 245, 246, 247, 249, 250, *251*, 252, 253, *254–55*
age (children): and back to the land movement, 313–14; in educational attainment of grandparents study, 149, 150, 151, *152*, *153*, *157*; as factor in childcare time, 191, 192, 199, 202–3; in marital status and children's health study, 127, 128, 129, *130*, *132–34*, 135, *136*
aggression in marital status and children's health study, 124, 125, *125*, 126, *130*, *134*, 134–35, *136*, 137
agricultural cooperatives, 300
alcohol use: by children of divorce, 122, 123; by college students, 164, 165, 170, 177, 179
American Time Use Survey, 190, 196
anxiety in information gathering study, 64–66, 67
apartments, 25–26, 296–97, 310–11
arranged marriages, 31

Asia: Central Asian immigrants, 78, 304, 305; Confucianism as pan-Asian, 283; second demographic transition, 20
assortative mating study, 95–118; background, 96–98; data and methods, 99–104, *100*; discussion, 114–15; findings, 104–14, *105–9*; overview, 7, 9, 33, 95–96, 98–99

back to the land movement, 296–322; as alternative to Korean life, 298–99, 318; background, 297–301; conclusions, 317–19; data and methods, 305–6; and education, 301–3, 308, 309–10; as form of study abroad, 300, 308–9; literature, 306–15, 317–18; motivations, 37, 298–99, 300, 308, 310; overview, 3, 13, 36, 296–97; youth programs, 308–9
Bai, Yifan, 7, 33, 95–118
banking, 32–33
Behavior Problems Index, 126
Body Mass Index (BMI), 172–78, *173*, *175*. *See also* obesity and living arrangements of college students study
Bourdieu, Pierre, 73–74
breadwinner family model: and father's parenting time, 191; and father's role in education, 76, 145; and fertility, 271, 272, 279, *281*, 281–84, *282*, *284*, 285, *287*, *288*, 289; and Korean immigrants in US, 228, 235
breathing room concept, 315–17. *See also* back to the land movement

329

Index

Britain, concerted cultivation in, 189
Byun, Soo-yong, 7, 33, 95–118

Cambodian immigrants to Korea, 304
Canada: childcare time in, 189–90; kinship relations, 216
censorship laws, 28, 29
Center for Epidemiologic Studies Depression Scale (CES-D), 126
Central Asian immigrants, 78, 304, 305
Chang, Paul Y., 5, 19–40
character in Korean education, 301
childcare: availability of, 137, 138; conflicts over, 97; factors affecting time spent, 191–93; in fertility and gender roles study, 272, 275, 279–80; in information gathering study, 56, 56; ratio of father's to mother's time, 10, 188, 198, 205; in US, 10, 185–86, 187–90, 205. *See also* childcare time study; marriage probability study; parental leave
childcare time study, 185–209; background, 187–93; conclusions, 205–7; data and methods, 192–97, *195*; differences in activities, 193, 202–3; factors affecting time spent, 191–93; findings, 197–205, *199–201*; general increase in time with child, 10, 185–86; increase in Korean fathers', 10, 192, 198, 205–6; increase in Korean mothers', 10, 198, 205; literature review, 187–90, 192–93; overview, 10–11, 33–34, 185–87; sample characteristics, 198–99, *199*
children: and back to the land movement, 298–99, 307–8, 313–15; child characteristics in assortative mating study, 98–99, 103–10, *105–9*, 113–14; custody laws, 30; increase in single parents, 2, 120; and kinship networks, 11, 217, 232–34, 236; rates of foreign-born parents, 2, 71. *See also* age (children); assortative mating study; childcare; childcare time study; educational attainment of children; educational attainment of grandparents study; family size; fertility and gender roles study; habitus transformation study; information gathering

study; intensive parenting; living arrangements of college students study; marital status and children's health study
China: Chinese immigrants to Korea, 78, 80, 304, 305, 318; gender role attitudes, 283–84, *284*; grandparents' role and effects, 146, 155; study abroad in, 303, 306
Chinese language achievement, 303, 306, 318
Chung, Hee Jin, 7, 33, 95–118
class: in childcare time study, 186–87, 188–90, 204, 206; and early childhood education, 45–47; and extracurricular activities, 45–46, 47, 187, 189; farming as low class, 304; and gender role attitudes, 275–76; and habitus transformation, 74; and homogamy, 97, 98; and housing, 311; and intensive parenting/concerted cultivation, 6, 45, 189, 203, 205; and natural growth parenting, 45, 189; and shadow education, 48, 187, 302–3. *See also* assortative mating study; educational attainment of grandparents study; educational attainment of parents; marriage probability study; men's educational attainment; middle class; socioeconomic resources and status; upper class; women's educational attainment; working class
cohabitation, 5, 20
cohort. *See* age (adults); age (children)
competitiveness: and back to the land movement, 299, 301–3, 309–10; in educational attainment of grandparents study, 146, 158; in habitus transformation study, 75, 82; historical context, 33, 37; and homogamy, 97; in information gathering study, 55, 57; of Korean education, 75, 146, 187, 301–3, 309–10
compressed modernity, 19, 48
concerted cultivation: activities, 190; in childcare time study, 189, 190, 203, 206; and class, 6, 45, 189, 203, 205; pressure for, 34, 54–55. *See also* intensive parenting

Confucianism: and focus on education, 234; and focus on husband's family, 212, 214–15; in husband's upbringing, 225–26; as pan-Asian, 283
consumerism, 27, 29
contraception, 23
cooperatives, agricultural, 300
costs: housing costs, 12, 164, 168–69, 177, 247, 263, 309; of marrying, 12, 247, 263; shadow education, 44, 86, 87, 89n4, 145, 302
creativity in education, 301, 308, 310
cultural activities: cultural capital activities, 187; as extracurricular activities, 48; popular culture, 29
cultural mentors, 72, 75, 76–78, 83–87

dating companies, 248
debt, household, 33
debt-to-income ratio, 33
democratization, 21, 27–29, 37
demographic transitions, 20
depression: college students, 179; in marital status and children's health study, 124, 125, *125*, 126, 128, *130*, 131, *133*, 133–34, 135–36, *136*
diet: and children of divorce, 123; of college students, 9, 164, 165, 170, 176, 177; and grandparents, 131
divorce: health effects on child, 122–23; increase in, 1, 7–8, 25, 120, 138; laws, 30; in obesity and living arrangements of college students study, 173, *173*; socioeconomic factors for, 123–24, 138; stigma of, 120, 123–24, 137
domestic migration, 24, 25. *See also* urbanization
domestic spending, 27–28
dormitories: lack of in Korea, 164, 168, *169*; in obesity and living arrangements of college students study, 164, 172, *173*, 175, *175*, 177, 178; as transition to independent living, 163, 167, 178; in US, 163, 167
dropout rates, 73, 88, 89n2
duration of residence in immigrant gender roles in US study, 218, *219–21*, 222

Early Childhood Longitudinal Study, Kindergarten Class of 1998–1999, 189
ecological values in back to the land movement study, 300, 308, 310
economy: development plans, 5, 23, 24; financial crisis of 1997, 5, 25–26, 32, 37, 97, 298; historical context, 23–33, 37; and industrialization, 5, 19, 21, 23–26; neoliberal, 32–33, 37; service economy, 25, 27
education: after-school programs, 138; and back to the land movement, 301–3, 308, 309–10; competitiveness of, 75, 146, 187, 301–3, 309–10; and Confucianism, 234; cultural field, 75–78; early childhood education and class, 45–47; and employment opportunities, 75–76, 82, 302; equalization policies, 147, 187; Gandhi schools, 312; generation gap in educational attainment, 43, 146–47, 151, 152, 157–58, 302; historical context, 2, 5, 23, 26–27, 37, 48–49. *See also* assortative mating study; childcare time study; educational attainment of children; educational attainment of grandparents study; educational attainment of parents; educational expectations; habitus transformation study; information gathering study; living arrangements of college students study; marriage probability study; men's educational attainment; shadow education; tertiary education; women's educational attainment
educational attainment of children: in assortative mating study, 7, 102, 103–4, *105–7*, 110–14, *111*, *112*; in childcare time study, 188, 190; and health, 119; and immigrant mothers, 72, 88; in marriage probability study, 12, 243–44, 248–49, 250, *251*, 253, *254*, 256, 257, *258–60*, 261–62, 263. *See also* educational attainment of grandparents study; educational expectations; habitus transformation study; information gathering study; living arrangements of college students study

educational attainment of grandparents study, 144–62; conclusions, 157–59; context, 146–48; data and methods, 148–51; differences between maternal and paternal grandparents, 148–49, 150, 155–56, *157*; findings, 151–56, *152*, *153*, *154*; overview, 8–9, 34, 144–46

educational attainment of parents: in childcare time study, 189, 190, 192–93, 196, 198, *199–201*, 199–203; and concerted cultivation, 189; and divorce rates, 123; in fertility and gender roles study, 280; in marital status and children's health study, 127, 129, *130*, 132–34, 135, *136*; in marriage probability study, 12, 244, 246–50, 251, 253, 255, 258–60, 261–66. *See also* assortative mating study; men's educational attainment; women's educational attainment

educational expectations: of child in assortative mating study, 103, 104, *105*, *107–9*, 110; of parent in assortative mating study, 102, *105*, *108*, *109*, 115

Education and Social Mobility Survey, 148–50

education fever, 146, 302, 309–10. *See also* competitiveness; information gathering study; shadow education

embodied cultural capital, 187

employment: in childcare time study, 191–92, *195*, *197*, 198, *199–201*, 205; and educational attainment gap, 43; in educational attainment of grandparents study, 148, 149–50, 152, *152*, *153*, *154*; as factor in father's childcare time, 191–92; family-work conflicts/support, 120, 273–74, 284–85, *285*; in fertility and gender roles study, 273–74, 280, 284–85, *285*; and gender gap in working hours, 198–99; and gender role attitudes, 276; gender wage gap, 10; and housing costs, 247; in immigrant gender roles in US study, 211, 213, 218, *219–21*, 222; in marital status and children's health study, 127, 129, *130*, 132–34, 135, *136*; in marriage probability study, 250, 251, 253, 255, 258–59; opportunities and childhood health, 119; opportunities and educational stratification, 75–76, 82, 302; rigidity of labor market, 120; and service economy, 25, 27; underemployment of young people, 164; US corporate culture as family-friendly, 229–30; work time in childcare time study, *195*, *197*, 198, *199–201*, 205. *See also* women in workforce

English language achievement: in assortative mating study, 7, 102, 103–4, *105–7*, 110–14, *111*, *112*; and immigrant mothers, 305; in information gathering study, 57, 63; in KELS, 99, 102; as mark of class, 48; pressure for, 57, 63; and study abroad, 303

enjoyment, pursuit of, 30, *31*

entrance exams, 48, 301, 302

Europe: childcare time in, 188, 189–90; fertility ideals, 277; first demographic transition, 20; gender role attitudes, 283–84, *284*

exams, entrance, 48, 301, 302

extracurricular activities: attitudes on, 48; and class, 45–46, 47, 187, 189; cultural capital, 187; in information gathering study, 57, 61, 63, 64

extramarital affairs, 266n4

family: family law reforms, 30–31; historical context, 1–2, 19, 21–33; primacy of, 157; as term, 19. *See also* assortative mating study; back to the land movement; childcare time study; children; educational attainment of grandparents study; family size; fertility and gender roles study; gender; grandparents; habitus transformation study; immigrant gender roles in US study; information gathering study; living arrangements of college students study; marital status and children's health study; marriage probability study; siblings

Family Planning Counseling Centers, 22–23

family planning programs, 21–23, *22*, 25, 272

family registration system, 21
family size: in assortative mating study, 102, *105*, *109*, 110; in childcare time study, *199–201*; in educational attainment of grandparents study, 149, 150, *152*, *153*, *157*; as factor in father's childcare time, 192; fertility ideals, 12–13, 272, 276–77, *278*, 278–79, 280–81, 285–86, *287*, *288*; and housing, 25–26; in immigrant gender roles in US study, 218, *219–21*; and state family planning programs, 21–23, *22*, 25, 272; and urbanization, 25–26, *26*, 37
farming, 300, 304
fertility: actual fertility *vs.* fertility ideals, 276, 291; and demographic transitions, 20; ideals, 12–13, 272, 276–77, *278*, 278–79, 280–81, 285–86, *287*, *288*; in Japan, 20; men's attitudes, 272, 275, 279; nonmarital, 5, 8, 20, 243; rates, 3, 5, 22, 25, 243, 266, 271, 277; reversals and gender equality, 272, 273, 286; state efforts to lower, 21–23, *22*; and women in workforce, 25, 271–72, 279, *281*, 281–84, *282*, *284*, 285, 286, *287*, *288*; women's attitudes, 272, 275, 279. *See also* fertility and gender roles study
fertility and gender roles study, 271–95; background, 273–77; data and methods, 277–81, *279*; discussion, 286–91; findings, *281*, 281–86, *282*, *284*, *285*, *287–88*; limitations, 291; overview, 12–13, 35–36, 271–73
field concept, 73–74
filial piety: and economic precarity, 37; and focus on husband's family, 214–15; in immigrant gender roles in US study, 11, 212, 214–15, 230–31, 232–33, 235–36
financial crisis of 1997, 5, 25–26, 32, 37, 97, 298
Finland: gender role attitudes, 283–84, *284*; grandparents' role and effect, 158
first demographic transition, 20
Five-Year Economic Development Plans, 5, 23, 24
foreigners, marriage to. *See* international marriage

Gandhi schools, 312
gender: of child as factor in father's childcare time, 191; of child in assortative mating study, 103, *105–6*, *108–9*; of child in educational attainment of grandparents study, 149, 150, 151, *152*, *153*, *157*; family law reforms, 30–31; gap in working hours, 198–99; gender revolution, 185, 190; in marital status and children's health study, 127, 129, *130*, *132–34*, *136*; in marriage probability study, 250; in obesity and living arrangements of college students study, 173, *173*, 174, *175–76*, *176*; ratios in international marriage, 1–2, 71; revolution, 273, 274, 289–91; wage gap, 10. *See also* childcare time study; fertility and gender roles study; gender role attitudes; immigrant gender roles in US study
gender role attitudes: ambivalence about women's role, 13, 289; and church, 237; egalitarian attitudes, 13, 228, 235, *282*, 282–84; and expanded education, 2; liberal attitudes, 11, 191, *199–201*, 204, 206; in marital status and children's health study, 127, 129, *130*, *132–34*, *136*; and presence of relatives, 225–27, 228, 229; questions on in childcare time study, 197; reinforcement by kinship relationships, 216; and surrounding culture, 228, 229; traditional attitudes, 2, 13, 191, 204, 228, *282*, 282–84; transitional attitudes, 228, 235. *See also* childcare time study; fertility and gender roles study; immigrant gender roles in US study
generational differences: gap in educational attainment, 43, 146–47, 151, *152*, 157–58, 302; immigrant gender roles in US, 237
Germany, childcare time in, 189–90
globalization and back to the land movement, 315–17
goose families, 300
graduation rates, 165

grandparents: in childcare time study, 197, *199–201*, 204; in China, 146, 155; and diet, 131; in Finland, 158; in information gathering study, 59; and life expectancy, 144–45; in marital status and children's health study, 127, 129, *130*, 131, *132–34*, *136*, 137; qualitative effects of, 158; role in Korea, 146; and social mobility, 144–45; socioeconomic resources and status, 145, 146, 147–48, 158–59; in Taiwan, 147, 154, 158, 159; in US, 154, 158. *See also* educational attainment of grandparents study; filial piety

habitus hysteresis, 72, 74–75, 76, 81–83
habitus transformation study, 71–92; background, 73–78; conceptual framework, 73–75; conclusions, 87–89; cultural mentor stage, 72, 75, 76–78, 83–87; data and methods, 78–80, *79*, *80*; findings, 81–87; habitus hysteresis stage, 72, 74–75, 76, 81–83; overview, 3, 6–7, 34, 71–72; success/failure of strategies, 88
hagwŏn (cram schools): and back to the land movement, 302–3; costs, 86, 87, 89n4, 302; defined, 89n3; in habitus transformation study, 84, 86–87
haksŭpchi (workbook delivery service), 89n3
health: and back to the land movement, 13, 298, 313, 318; and educational attainment, 119, 171; effects of divorce, 122–23; obesity as health indicator, 164, 170. *See also* living arrangements of college students study; marital status and children's health study
Hell Chosŏn, 299. *See also* back to the land movement
higher education. *See* tertiary education
homework: in assortative mating study, 103, *104*, *106–9*, 110; parental help with, 64
homogamy: advantages of, 113; decrease in, 97; and highly educated mothers, 101; high rate of in Korea, 7, 96; literature on, 96–98; in US, 98. *See also* assortative mating study

horizontal diversification, 6, 54, 60–64, *61*, 67
housework: changes in gender role attitudes, 2, 271, 275; and Korean immigrants to US, 11, 214, 225–28, 229, 236, 237; time in childcare time study, *195*, 198, 206
housing: in apartments, 296–97, 310–11; and back to the land movement, 309; and class, 311; costs, 12, 164, 168–69, 177, 247, 263, 309; costs in US, 247; and family size, 25–26; options for college students, 9, 167–69; and probability of marriage, 12, 247, 263; renting, 263; right to, 168. *See also* living arrangements of college students study
hypergamy in assortative mating study, 98–99, 101, *106*, *108*
hypogamy in assortative mating study, 98–99, 101, *107–8*, 114

immigrant gender roles in US study, 210–40; background, 213–17; conclusions, 235–37; and cultural homogeneity, 214; data and methods, 217–25, *219–21*, *223*; empowerment of women, 210–11, 213–14; filial piety, 11, 212, 214–15, 230–31, 232–33, 235–36; findings, 223–34; kinship networks, 11, 212, 215–17, 230–34, 235–36; limitations, 236–37; overview, 11, 36, 210–13; sample characteristics, 217–22
immigrants and immigration: disadvantages to children's education, 6, 71–72, 88; educational attainment, 78, *80*, 218–19, *219–21*; hierarchy of, 305; immigration as alternative to Korean life, 298; and multiculturalism, 6, 71, 304, 318; scholarly interest in, 301; state programs, 77, 84–85, 304, 316. *See also* habitus transformation study; immigrant gender roles in US study
income: in assortative mating study, 102, *104*, *105–7*, *109*, 110, 113; and concerted cultivation, 189; debt-to-income ratio, 33; in educational attainment of grandparents study, 148; and educational

stratification, 75–76; in fertility and gender roles study, 280, 286, *287*, *288*; and gender role attitudes, 276; and housing spending, 168–69; in immigrant gender roles in US study, 213, 218, *219–20*, 236; of immigrant women to Korea, *79*; in information gathering study, 53, *61*, 62, 64, 66; in marital status and children's health study, 127, 129, *130*, *132*, *133*, 135, *136*, 137, 248–49; in marriage probability study, 12, 244–46, 250, *251*, *252*, 253, *254–55*, *258–59*, 263; mother's income as factor in father's childcare time, 191; need for dual-incomes, 271, 272; in obesity and living arrangements of college students study, 171, 173, *173*, 174, *175*, 178; one-and-a-half earner model, 290–91; rent-to-income ratio, 169; and risk of obesity, 171; shadow education spending, 44, 89n4
independence, transition by college students, 163–64, 165–67, 177–78
individualism, 30
industrialization: and back to the land movement, 296; Five-Year Economic Development Plans, 5, 23, 24; and modernization, 4–5, 19, 21, 23–26
information gathering study, 43–70; and academic success, 145; background, 43, 45–49; data and methods, 49–54, *51*; discussion, 66–68; emotional effects, 64–66, *67*; findings, 54–66; horizontal diversification, 6, 54, 60–64, *61*, *67*; mobilizing and sorting of information, 58–60, *59*, *67*; overview, 6, 33, 44–45; and social ties, 47–48, 58–60, *59*, 66, *67*; and socioeconomic status, 46, *67*; use of information, 60–64, *67*; vertical cultivation, 6, 54, 60–64, *61*, *67*
inheritance rights, 30
institutional gatekeepers as cultural mentors, 72, 77, 83–85
institutional habitus, 73
intensive parenting: centrality of, 3, 5–6, 34; and class, 6, 45, 189, 205; and homework help, 64; and mother's status, 49,
68, 234; pressure on women, 46, 49, 54–55, 57, 68
international marriage: gender ratios, 1–2, 71; rates of, 1, 71; state programs for, 77, 84–85. *See also* habitus transformation study
International Monetary Fund (IMF), 32
International Social Survey Programme (ISSP), 123, 273, 277–78
Italian-American kinship relations, 216
Italy, childcare time in, 189–90
Item Response Theory (IRT) scores, 99, 102, 103–4

Jang, Heewon, 8–9, 34, 144–62
Japan: back to the land movement, 301; fertility rates, 20; gender role attitudes, 283–84, *284*; Japanese immigrants to Korea, 78, *80*, 81, 82, 86–87, 304
Jeon, Haram, 9–10, 34–35, 163–82
Jeon, Sun Young, 7–8, 34, 119–43
Jeong, Wonjeong, 7–8, 34, 119–43
Jo, Hyejeong, 6–7, 34, 71–92

Kangaroo tribe, 164, 169–70
kinship networks: focus on husband's family, 212, 215, 216, 230; Italian Americans, 216; Korean immigrants to the US, 11, 212, 215–17, 230–34, 235–36; literature on, 212; preserving for sake of child, 11, 217, 232–34, 236; as resource, 215–16, 217
Korea: domestic spending, 27–28; population density, 168, 309. *See also* economy; modernization; state
Korea Family Planning Association, 23
Korea Human Scale, 175
Korean Children and Youth Panel Survey (KCYPS), 121, 124, 125–28
Korean Educational Development Institute (KEDI), 99, 148–50
Korean Education and Employment Panel (KEEP), 164, 171–72
Korean Education Longitudinal Study of 2005–2007 (KELS), 99–100, 102, 115
Korean Families in Economic and Demographic Transitions conference, 4

Korean General Social Survey, 273, 277–78
Korean Labor and Income Panel Study (KLIPS), 245, 249
Korean language and immigrant mothers, 6, 71, 72
Korean Social Surveys, 273, 276, 277–78
Korea Time Use Survey (KTUS), 192, 193, 196, 205, 206
kwich'on. *See* back to the land movement
"*Kwinong* Is Ultimately a Kind of Lifestyle" (Yu), 313, 317, 318
kwinong kwich'on kwihyang. *See* back to the land movement
Kwinong t'ongmun (newsletter), 313

labor: educational attainment gap, 43; labor immigrants to Korea, 71; labor laws liberalization, 32; and service economy, 25, 27; urbanization of, 23–26. *See also* employment
language development: and immigrant mothers, 71–72; and women's educational attainment, 47. *See also* Chinese language achievement; English language achievement
Lee, Byung Soo, 11, 36, 210–40
Lee, Jae Kyung, 12, 35, 243–71
Lee, Yean-Ju, 10–11, 33–34, 185–209
leisure: in childcare time study, *195*, 198; spending on, 30, *31*
lexical choice, 47
life expectancy, 144–45
Lim, Sojung, 7–8, 34, 119–43
living arrangements of college students study, 163–82; background, 164, 165–70; college polices on, 167, 168; data and methods, 171–74; discussion, 176–79; in dormitories, 164, 167, 168, *169*, 172, *173*, 175, *175*, 177, 178; findings, 174–76, *175–76*; housing costs, 164, 168–69, 177; limitations of, 178–79; in off-campus housing, 9, 168–69; overview, 9–10, 34–35, 163–65; and parental support, 163–64, 166, *166*; with parents, 163, 172, *173*, 174–76, *175–76*

"love marriage," popularization of, 31
lower class. *See* working class

marital status and children's health study, 119–43; background, 121–24; data and methods, 124–28; disadvantages of single-parent households, 8, 121–23, 129, 137, 138; discussion, 135–38; findings, 128–35, *130*, *132*, *133*, *136*; limitations of, 137–38; overview, 7–8, 34, 119–21; sample characteristics, 128–29, *130*
marriage: affairs, 266n4; age at, 1, 25, 37, 243, 249; arranged marriages, 31; attitudes and socioeconomic resources, 244; as choice *vs*. requirement, 243, 244; costs of marrying, 247, 263–64; decline in rates, 243; deinstitutionalization of, 213; delay in, 1, 3, 12, 37; international marriage, 1–2, 71, 77, 84–85; "love marriage," 31; marital status in assortative mating study, 102, *105–7*, 109, 110, 113; marital status in marriage probability study, 250, *251*; and need for two-incomes, 271, 272. *See also* divorce; marital status; marital status and children's health study; marriage probability study
marriage consulting companies, 248
marriage probability study, 243–71; background, 245–49; conclusions, 262–66; data and methods, 249–52, *251*; findings, 252–62, *254–56*, 258–60; limitations of, 265–66; overview, 2, 12, 35, 243–45; parental influence on spousal choice, 248; sample characteristics, 252–53
matriculation rates, 27
media: and habitus transformation, 74; relaxation of censorship laws, 28, 29
men: allocation of time, *195*; childcare time in Europe, 190; childcare time in US, 185–86, 187–88, 190; employment in educational attainment of grandparents study, 149–50, 152, *152*, *153*, 154; fertility attitudes, 272, 275, 279; fertility ideals, 12–13, 279, 285–86, *287*; focus on husband's family, 212, 214–15, 216, 230;

in international marriages, 1–2, 71; parental leave, 274; role in fertility reversals, 273; role in social reproduction, 76; socioeconomic resources and status in marriage probability study, 12, 252–62, *254–56*, *258*, *260*; socioeconomic resources and status in US, 243–44, *245*, *246*. *See also* assortative mating study; childcare time study; educational attainment of grandparents study; fertility and gender roles study; gender; grandparents; immigrant gender roles in US study; marital status and children's health study; marriage probability study; men's educational attainment
men's educational attainment: in childcare time study, 10, 189, 190, 192–93, 196, 198, *199*, 199–203, *200*; and fertility rates, *287*; and gender role attitudes, 2, 276; in marital status and children's health study, 127, 129, *130*, 132–34, *135*, *136*; in marriage probability study, 12, 244, 246, 248–49, *250*, *251*, 253, *255*, *258*, *260*, 261–62, 263–64. *See also* assortative mating study; educational attainment of grandparents study
mental health. *See* anxiety; depression
mentors. *See* cultural mentors
middle class: and early childhood education, 45–46; and habitus transformation, 74; and intensive parenting, 45, 189, 205; rise of, 27–28; shrinking of, 33; and time spent with child, 186; and transition to democracy, 27
minbak, 307
minjung (folk) movement, 298, 303
modernization: compressed modernity, 19, 48; democratization, 21, 27–29, 37; and expansion of education, 5, 23, 26–27, 48–49; Five-Year Economic Development Plans, 5, 23, 24; and industrialization, 5, 19, 21, 23–26
Mongolian immigrants to Korea, 78, *80*, 84, 304, 305
monitoring in assortative mating study, 102, 103, *105–6*, *108–9*
Multicultural Family Support Centers, 77

multiculturalism: in back to the land movement, 13, 299, 300, 303–5, 315–17, 318–19; from international marriages, 6, 71, 304, 318; state programs, 77, 84–85, 304; as term, 88. *See also* habitus transformation study

Nam Center for Korean Studies, 4
National Youth Policy Institute, 124
natural growth parenting, 45, 189
networks, personal. *See* social ties
new generation culture, 27, 29–31
New Village Movement, 300
noise complaints, 297
nonacademic activities. *See* extracurricular activities
Norway, childcare time in, 189–90
N-p'o generation, 319n6
nursing, in childcare time study, 196

obesity and living arrangements of college students study, 163–82; background, 164, 165–70; data and methods, 171–74; discussion, 176–79; findings, 174–76, *175–76*; obesity as health indicator, 164, 170; obesity rates, 170, *171*; overview, 9–10, 34–35, 163–65; in US, 170–71
objectified cultural capital, 187
Oh, Eunsil, 6, 33, 43–70
Oh, Jihye, 12, 35, 243–71
Olympics, 27, 29
one-person households, 25, *26*
out-of-wedlock births, 5, 8, 20, 243
Overy, 49, 68n1

parental leave: in fertility and gender roles study, 279–80, 284–85, *285*, *286*, *287*, *288*; policy, 271, 274
parents: death of, 122, 173, *173*; involvement in education in assortative mating study, 102–3, *105–9*, 110, 113, 114–15; parental involvement in college-age students, 163–64, 177–78; parent-child discussion in assortative mating study, 102, 103, *105–6*, *108–9*, 110. *See also* assortative mating study; back to the

parents (*continued*)
    land movement; childcare time study; educational attainment of parents; fertility and gender roles study; habitus transformation study; immigrant gender roles in US study; information gathering study; marital status and children's health study; marriage probability study
Park, Hyunjoon, 1–15, 8–9, 34, 144–62
Park, Kitae, 10–11, 33–34, 185–209
personal networks. *See* social ties
personal time in childcare time study, *195*, 198
Philippines and immigrants to Korea, 78, 80, 84–86, 304, 305, 318
physical care in childcare time study, 196, 202, 203, 204, 206
playing in childcare time study, 196, 202, 203, 204, 206
popular culture, 29
post-secondary education. *See* tertiary education
prior achievement of child in assortative mating study, 103–4, *105*, *107–9*, 113–14
private education. *See* shadow education

reading and playing in childcare time study, 196, 202, 203, 204, 206
regions: in assortative mating study, 116n2; in fertility and gender roles study, 280, 286, *287*, *288*; in marital status and children's health study, 127, *130*, *132–34*, *136*; in marriage probability study, 250, *251*, 253, *255*, *258–59*; in obesity and living arrangements of college students study, 173, 174, *175*. *See also* back to the land movement
religion: and immigrant women in Korea, 77, 86–87; and Korean immigrants to US, 214, 237; in marriage probability study, 250, *251*, 253, *254*, *258–59*
rent-to-income ratio (RIR), 169
resources. *See* income; information gathering study; socioeconomic resources and status
retention and graduation rates, 165

Revised Family Registration Law, 21
risk aversion, 67
Rosenberg Self-Esteem Scale, 126–27
rural regions. *See* back to the land movement; regions

samp'o generation, 299
Sanidad, Ivan, 10–11, 33–34, 185–209
school contact in assortative mating study, 102–3, *105–6*, *108–9*
school readiness and homogamy, 98
Schwabe's Law, 168–69
second demographic transition, 20
sedentary lifestyle, 170, 177
self-esteem: in information gathering study, 57, 61–62, 68; in marital status and children's health study, 124, *125*, *125*, 126–27, 128, 129, *130*, 135–37, *136*; of mother, 68; Rosenberg Self-Esteem Scale, 126–27
self-rated health in marital status and children's health study, 124, *125*, 125–26, 131, *132*, 135–37, *136*
self-study in assortative mating study, 103, 104, *106–9*, 110
Seoul, living costs, 309
service economy, transition to, 25, 27
Settling the Heart (Yun), 312–13, 314–15, 317–18
shadow education: in assortative mating study, 102, 103, *106–9*, 110; and back to the land movement, 302–3; and class, 48, 187, 302–3; costs, 44, 86, 87, 89n4, 145, 302; defined, 76; dissatisfaction with, 76, 302–3; as dominant practice, 76; in habitus transformation study, 76, 84, 86–87; size of, 44; state policies, 77, 84–85, 302; workbook delivery service, 89n3. *See also hagwŏn* (cram schools); tutoring
siblings: in assortative mating study, 102, *105*, *109*, 110; in educational attainment of grandparents study, 149, 150, *152*, *153*, *157*; as factor in father's childcare time, 192; in immigrant gender roles in US study, 218, *219–21*; and single-parent families, 137

single-parent households: disadvantages of, 8, 121–23, 129, 137, 138; increase in, 2, 120. *See also* marital status and children's health study
smoking: children of divorce, 123; college students, 170, 179
social participation time in childcare time study, *195*
social reproduction, 73, 75–76, 95, 96. *See also* assortative mating study
social skills and children of divorce, 122, 138
social ties: and children of divorce, 122; and cultural mentors for immigrant mothers, 72, 76–78, 83–87; and educational stratification, 75–76; personal networks and information gathering, 47–48, 58–60, *59*, 66, 67; and single-parent families, 137
social workers as cultural mentors, 77
socioeconomic resources and status: and academic achievement, 186–87; in childcare time study, 186, 188–90; and childhood health, 119; and divorce, 123–24, 138; and early childhood education, 45–47; and educational attainment gap, 43, 147; and educational stratification, 75–76; and gender role attitudes, 275–76; of grandparents, 145, 146, 147–48, 158–59; and habitus transformation study, 73, 75–76, 78, *79*, 82, 88; of immigrant women in Korea, 78, *79*; in information gathering study, 46, 67; of Korean immigrants to US, 210–11, 215; in marital status and children's health study, 120, 121–22, 123–24, 129, 133–38, *136*; and marriage attitudes, 244; and marriage in US, 243–44, 245–47; in marriage probability study, 12, 245–46, 250, 251, 252–62, 254–56, 258–60; of men with immigrant wives, 72, 78, *79*; in obesity and living arrangements of college students study, 164, 172–73, *173*, 174, *175*, 178–79; and obesity risk, 171; and parenting styles, 192. *See also* assortative mating study; class; educational attainment of grandparents study; educational attainment of parents; marriage probability study; men's educational attainment; women's educational attainment

state: censorship laws, 28, 29; education equalization policies, 147; family law reforms, 30–31; family planning programs, 21–23, *22*, 25, 272; fertility reversal role, 273; housing policy, 25–26; immigrant programs and policies, 77, 84–85, 304, 316; shadow education policies, 77, 84–85, 302; and single-parent families, 137, 138; travel bans, 28–29; and work-family conflicts, 188, 273–74, 290

study abroad: as alternative to Korean life, 298, 299, 303; areas of, 306; back to the land movement as form of, 300, 308–9; literature on, 306, 307; memoirs, 312–13, 313–14, 317–18; old limitations on, 28–29; rates, 299

supplemental education. *See* shadow education

Sweden, gender role attitudes, 283–84, *284*

Taiwan, grandparents' role and effects, 147, 154, 158, 159

tamunhwa. *See* habitus transformation study; immigrants and immigration; multiculturalism

teachers as cultural mentors, 77, 84–85

teaching in childcare time study, 196, 203, 204, 206

"10-Year Plan for Family Planning Program," 23

tertiary education: distribution of, 167–68; and English acquisition by child, 113–14; expansion of, 5, 23, 26–27, 37; generation gap, 43, 146–47, 151, *152*, 157–58, 302; historical context, 23, 26–27, 37; of immigrant women, 78, *80*; level of and obesity, 173, *173*, 174, *175*; matriculation rates, 27; numbers of students, 26–27; retention and graduation rates, 165; stratification of, 75–76. *See also* assortative mating study;

tertiary education (*continued*)
educational attainment of children; educational attainment of grandparents study; educational attainment of parents; living arrangements of college students study; men's educational attainment; women's educational attainment
textile industry, 23–25
Thai immigrants in habitus transformation study, 78, *80*, 81, 82–83
Tilland, Bonnie, 13, 36, 296–322
time: allocation of parents', *195*, 198, 206; constraints and children of divorce, 122–23; spent in information gathering study, 55, 56, *56*. *See also* childcare time study
travel, 28–29, *30*. *See also* study abroad
Turning Gate, 319n5
tutoring: in assortative mating study, 102, 103, 104, *105–9*, 110, 115; and class, 48; *kwaoe*, 89n3; mother's role in, 115; for multicultural children, 77, 84–85. *See also* shadow education

United States: academic achievement and socioeconomic status, 186–87; childcare time in, 10, 185–86, 187–90, 205; educational homogamy, 98; family-friendly work culture, 229–30; gender revolution in, 185; gender role attitudes, 283–84, *284*; grandparents' role and effects, 154, 158; housing costs, 247; immigration rates, 210; living arrangements of college students, 163, 167; marriage and socioeconomic status, 243–44, 245–47; obesity in college students, 170–71; single-parent households, 8, 120; study abroad in, 306; women in workforce, 185; women's educational attainment, 47–48, 190. *See also* immigrant gender roles in US study
University of Michigan, 4
upper class: approach to early childhood education, 45; and shadow education, 302–3; tendency to intensive parenting, 45, 189

urbanization: and back to the land movement, 303–5; historical context, 5, 23–26, 37; rates, *24*
Uzbek immigrants in habitus transformation study, 78, *80*

vasectomies, 23
vertical cultivation, 6, 54, 60–64, *61*, 67
Vietnam: immigrants to Korea, 78, *80*, 304, 305, 318; immigrants to US, 229
vocabularies, size of, 47

wage gap, 10
women: allocation of time, *195*; fertility attitudes, 272, 275, 279; fertility ideals, 12–13, 279, 285–86, 288; Korean women in international marriages, 1–2, 71; motherhood in fertility and gender roles study, 272, 279, *281*, 282, *282–84*, *284*, *287*, *288*; native mothers as cultural mentors, 72, 84, 85–87; pressure for intensive parenting, 46, 49, 54–55, 57, 68; private *vs.* public roles, 275; responsibility for education, 115, 234; social reproduction role, 76; socioeconomic resources and status in marriage probability study, 12, 252–62, *254–55*, *256*, *259*, *260*; socioeconomic resources and status in US, 244, 245–46; status and intensive parenting, 49, 68, 234. *See also* assortative mating study; childcare time study; fertility and gender roles study; gender; grandparents; habitus transformation study; immigrant gender roles in US study; information gathering study; marital status and children's health study; marriage probability study; women in workforce; women's educational attainment
women in workforce: in assortative mating study, 96, 102, *105*, *109*, 113; in childcare time study, 197; constraints on/dismissal of, 235, 290–91; disruptions in, 10, 271; and fertility, 25, 271–72, 279, *281*, 281–84, 282, *284*, 285, 286, *287*, *288*; gender gap in working hours, 198–99; historical context, 5, 24–25, 37, 49; and

homogamy, 96; in immigrant gender roles in US study, 210–11, 213–14, 218, *219–21*, 222, 234, *235*, 236; immigrant women in Korea, 77, 78, *79, 80*; in information gathering study, 50, *51*, 52, 53, 55; in marital status and children's health study, 120, 127; in marriage probability study, 264; policies and programs, 188, 290; rates of participation, 10, 25, 49, 271; and responsibility for education, 234; service economy, 25, 27; and time spent on childcare, 185, 188; in US, 185; wage gap, 10

women's educational attainment: in childcare time study, 10, 190, 192–93, 196, 198, *199*, 199–203, *201*; and child's language development, 47; and fertility rates, 272, 286, *288*; and gender role attitudes, 2, 276; and homogamy, 96–97, 101; in immigrant gender roles in US study, 218–19, *219–21*; immigrant women in Korea, 78, *80*; in information gathering study, 56, *56*; in marriage probability study, 12, 244, 245–46, 248–49, 259, *260*, 261–62, 263, 264, 265–66; as measure of socioeconomic status, 46–47; in obesity and living arrangements of college students study, 171, 172–73, *173*, 174, *175*, 175–76, 177–78; rates, 48, 49; and social ties, 59–60; in United States, 47–48, 190. *See also* assortative mating study; educational attainment of grandparents study; information gathering study

Woo, Hyeyoung, 1–15, 34, 35, 119–43, 243–71

work. *See* employment; women in workforce

workbook delivery service *(haksŭpchi)*, 89n3

working class: approach to early childhood education, 45; and habitus transformation, 74; and increase in time spent with child, 186; and shadow education, 302–3

Yoon, Soo-Yeon, 12–13, 35–36, 271–95
Yu, Sŭng-yŏn, 313, 317, 318
yuhak. See study abroad
Yun, Insuk, 312–13, 313–14, 317–18